States of Exception in American History

States of Exception in American History

Edited by
Gary Gerstle
Joel Isaac

The University of Chicago Press :: Chicago and London

The University of Chicago Press, Chicago 60637
The University of Chicago Press, Ltd., London
© 2020 by The University of Chicago
All rights reserved. No part of this book may be used or reproduced in any
manner whatsoever without written permission, except in the case of brief
quotations in critical articles and reviews. For more information, contact
the University of Chicago Press, 1427 E. 60th St., Chicago, IL 60637.
Published 2020
Printed in the United States of America

29 28 27 26 25 24 23 22 21 20   1 2 3 4 5

ISBN-13: 978-0-226-71229-1 (cloth)
ISBN-13: 978-0-226-71232-1 (paper)
ISBN-13: 978-0-226-71246-8 (e-book)
DOI: https://doi.org/10.7208/chicago/9780226712468.001.0001

Library of Congress Cataloging-in-Publication Data

Names: Gerstle, Gary, 1954– editor. | Isaac, Joel, 1978– editor.
Title: States of exception in American history / edited by Gary Gerstle
  and Joel Isaac.
Description: Chicago ; London : The University of Chicago Press, 2020. |
  Includes bibliographical references and index.
Identifiers: LCCN 2019057903 | ISBN 9780226712291 (cloth) |
  ISBN 9780226712321 (paperback) | ISBN 9780226712468 (ebook)
Subjects: LCSH: War and emergency powers—United States—History. |
  Crises—Political aspects—United States—History. | United States—
  Politics and government—History. | Schmitt, Carl, 1888–1985.
Classification: LCC KF5060 .S73 2020 | DDC 342.73/062—dc23
LC record available at https://lccn.loc.gov/2019057903

In memory of Ira Berlin and Michael O'Brien

Contents

	Acknowledgments	ix
	Introduction Gary Gerstle and Joel Isaac	1

Part One: The Challenge of Carl Schmitt

1	What Is the State of Exception? Nomi Claire Lazar	17
2	Negotiating the Rule of Law: Dilemmas of Security and Liberty Revisited Ewa Atanassow and Ira Katznelson	39
3	Beyond the Exception David Dyzenhaus	68

Part Two: The American Experience with Emergency Powers

4	The American Law of Overruling Necessity: The Exceptional Origins of State Police Power William J. Novak	95
5	To Save the Country: Reason and Necessity in Constitutional Emergencies John Fabian Witt	123

6	Powers of War in Times of Peace: Emergency Powers in the United States after the End of the Civil War Gregory P. Downs	154
7	Was There an American Concept of Emergency Powers? John Dewey, Carl Schmitt, and the Democratic Politics of Exception Stephen W. Sawyer	178
8	Charles Merriam and the Search for Democratic Power After Sovereignty James T. Sparrow	199
9	Constitutional Dictatorship in Twentieth-Century American Political Thought Joel Isaac	225

Part Three: Broadening the Exception

10	Frederick Douglass and Constitutional Emergency: An Homage to the Political Creativity of Abolitionist Activism Mariah Zeisberg	257
11	Delegated Governance as a Structure of Exceptions Elisabeth S. Clemens	288
12	Spaces of Exception in American History Gary Gerstle and Desmond King	313
	Afterword Gary Gerstle and Joel Isaac	341
	Contributors	349
	Index	353

Acknowledgments

The origins of this work stretch back to discussions the two of us began to have in 2014. We have both learned a great deal about our subject and from each other across the last six years. It has been an immensely rewarding experience.

We thank those who presented at an initial conference, "States of Exception in American History," that we organized at the University of Cambridge in May 2015. We are grateful to the Paul Mellon Fund and the Faculty of History for funding this event. A workshop on draft chapters for the book was held at the University of Chicago in May 2018, with support from the Paul Mellon Fund (again) and the John U. Nef Committee on Social Thought. Special thanks go to the chair of the Committee on Social Thought, Robert Pippin, for his encouragement and support of this project. At the University of Chicago Press, Charles Myers has been an absolute pleasure to work with, as have Michael Koplow, Joe Brown, Alicia Sparrow, Melinda Kennedy, and Holly Smith. Jim O'Brien has once again designed for us a splendid index. Back in Cambridge, Jonathan Goodwin has been with us since we started and has helped us in myriad ways, big and small, along the way. Thanks, finally, to our authors for staying the course and for giving us guide rails for thinking about liberal democracy in troubled times.

Since beginning this project we have had to say good-bye to two individuals who have meant a great deal to us. Ira Berlin and Michael O'Brien were American historians of the first rank. They were also our mentors and friends. We miss their intellectual brilliance, their capacity to inspire, their stimulating and steady companionship, and their playful wit. They will forever remain for us examples of lives well lived.

Introduction

Gary Gerstle and Joel Isaac

On May 27, 1941, as war raged in Europe, the president of the United States of America, Franklin D. Roosevelt, proclaimed an "unlimited national emergency."[1] Explaining his decision to the American people on the radio that evening, Roosevelt stressed that his declaration had been made necessary by the aggressive actions of the Axis powers. "[W]hat started as a European war," he intoned, "has developed, as the Nazis always intended it should, into a world war for world domination."[2] Hitler's war machine, the president informed his listeners, was gearing up to destroy democracies in the Western Hemisphere as well as in Europe; the United States would have to be ready for armed conflict. Since the outbreak of the war, the Roosevelt administration had been ramping up its efforts to defend the homeland and also to aid democracies across the globe. Within the confines of what the political climate would allow, FDR had sought to aid the Allies and to prepare the United States for war. Operating at the brink of his authority, the president led the way in a series of measures: the proclamation of a "limited national emergency" in September 1939; the repeal of the arms embargo provisions in the Neutrality Act; the "destroyer deal" and the Lend-Lease Act allowing for vast military and financial aid to Great Britain.

According to Roosevelt, German attacks on merchant shipping in the Atlantic in the early spring of 1941 signaled the next stage in the Nazi war of conquest. His proclamation of May 27 did not mince words: "[I]ndifference on the part of the United States to the increasing menace would be perilous, and common prudence requires that for the security of this nation and of this hemisphere we should pass from peacetime authorizations of military strength to such a basis as will enable us to cope instantly and decisively with any attempt at hostile encirclement of this hemisphere, or the establishment of any base for aggression against it, as well as to repel the threat of predatory incursion by foreign agents into our territory and society." The "basis" that the president had in mind was preparation for war short of state-enforced mobilization: "loyal" workers, citizens, and state and local leaders were exhorted to place the nation before their own immediate concerns. National defense would henceforth come first.[3]

May 27, 1941, was evidently a day of unprecedented drama. But what, exactly, had happened? What did the declaration of an unlimited national emergency mean in practice? In truth, Roosevelt was making things up as he went along. His earlier proclamation of a limited national emergency was, as one early commentator observed, "completely unrecognized by statute or constitutional practice."[4] Still, it had allowed him to activate statutory executive powers over the armed forces during peacetime. But the implications of his proclamation of a state of unlimited national emergency were murky. His statement did not give him any additional powers, statutory or otherwise. More to the point, the Constitution did not—and to this day does not—contain explicit provisions for states of emergency. Why, then, did Roosevelt bother to issue the proclamation? Was he overstepping the boundaries of the Constitution? Yes. Did the proclamation enhance, as a matter of fact if not of law, his power to control industrial production, civilian organization, and military forces? Almost certainly. But, if it did, on what basis did it do so if emergency declarations were outside the provisions of the Constitution?

At the root of these dilemmas of presidential power lies a fundamental conundrum. It is a conundrum that has bedeviled, enticed, and repelled the American people since the Founding of the Republic. What are constitutional regimes like that of the United States permitted to do in situations in which the survival of the regime appears to be at stake?[5] It seems paradoxical to claim that the best way to preserve the rule of law in situations of extreme danger is to suspend the Constitution or to permit executive action outside the law. If we allow ourselves to violate the rules, then by that token we must undermine their authority. On the other hand, perhaps this seeming paradox is simply something that liberal democracies must allow for since the alternative may be a constitutional rigidity—the rule of law at all costs—that spells the end of the regime itself. Allowance must surely be made—even in a constitutional order—for rulers to display initiative and exercise discretionary power during moments of severe crisis, when quick solutions are needed to pressing problems. As Judge Richard Posner has memorably put it, a constitution is not supposed to be "a suicide pact."[6] To save the rules, it may be necessary to set them aside temporarily.

In the modern United States, these difficult questions about the politics of necessity and the Constitution have usually been framed in terms of the discretionary powers that may be exercised by the executive branch of government, in particular by the president. That was certainly the case during the long crisis of the Second World War. But these dilemmas of constitutional governance have come up repeatedly in the history of the United States and not just in relation to the presidency. From the Founding onward, there have been heated debates about the nature and extent of the "police power," about the war powers granted to federal authorities under the Constitution, about the obligations of the government under the humanitarian laws of war. Controversies have erupted over what government authorities may do with impunity, over when and to what extent the state may withdraw legal rights, and over how individuals are classified as recipients of rights. What are the criteria of a public emergency, and who decides when they obtain? When does, or should, martial law replace ordinary law? Who is a prisoner of war, protected by international conventions, and who is considered outside the protections of the law altogether?

Battles over the correct answers to these questions have never been purely philosophical. American history is strewn with examples of how these tensions in liberal theory have exploded onto the political scene. The Founders fretted about the implications of the politics of necessity for the Constitution they created. In the early Republic, state legislatures gave themselves sweeping police powers as a corollary of their democratic powers of lawmaking. During the War of 1812, the imposition of martial rule in New Orleans by General Andrew Jackson kicked off a debate about proper criteria for the suspension of the rule of law. The Civil War famously triggered a set of debates about laws of war and occupation as democracy and dictatorship seemed to come into direct conflict during the period stretching from the war itself through the end of Reconstruction. The issue of dictatorship then became a recurrent feature of political conflict throughout the twentieth century, from the

Wilson administration in World War I, to the Roosevelt administration during depression and war, and into the Cold War and its new resources of atomic weaponry.

The peoples of the United States and the territories it has controlled were equally immersed in these pressing issues of constitutional order and public power. Consider the citizens denied the writ of habeas corpus and black Union soldiers captured by the Confederacy during the Civil War, or the American citizens of Japanese descent forced into internment camps during the Second World War, or persons placed under American control but denied full access to the rights of legal redress or citizenship, from blacks in the Jim Crow South to the US nationals of Puerto Rico. Questions about rights and the rule of law are in play in these contexts, but so too are even more fundamental matters about, not this or that right or status, but simply the right to have rights, to be recognized by the state as a person with a legal status.

Exceptions to the rule of law—especially in times of public emergency or political crisis—have been a defining feature of American history since the Founding. These exceptions have posed problems at once theoretically acute and practically urgent. They go to the heart of what the United States is as a constitutional regime. Yet, for all the visibility of certain moments of exception, no attempt has been made to assess these moments in a systematic fashion or to think about the theoretical and practical implications of the American experience with crisis government, discretionary executive power, and exceptions to the rule of law.

States of Exception in American History aims to meet this challenge. It offers both theoretical perspectives on and a series of case studies of emergencies and exceptions in American political history. A comprehensive account of this history would require an even larger book than this one. But that simply underscores how urgent the need is for orientation in such a vast and important field of inquiry. Our hope is that our project will provide the outlines of such a road map.

The time seems ripe for a volume such as this one. Our book builds on two important bodies of scholarship that have come to fruition over the last two decades. One comes from the realm of legal and political theory. Ever since the terrorist attacks of 9/11, there has been a growing interest in the tensions between the principles of liberalism—the rule of law, the separation of powers, the defense of individual rights and freedoms—and the increasing centralization of powers within the executive in the face of existential threats to the state. With regard to the United States, these tensions have been explored in terms of the growth of the executive branch of government and its prerogative power under the Constitution. At the level of theory, the new literature has turned for guidance to the German jurist Carl Schmitt and the Italian philosopher Giorgio Agamben, whose works have been extensively translated and republished in English over the last two decades. Their ideas, in turn, have been discussed by political theorists and legal scholars.[7] More will be said below about their ideas and how our book departs from their work.

Overlapping with this theoretical literature is a body of scholarship focused on the US experience with emergencies and enhanced executive powers. Some of these works address matters of constitutional law.[8] Others are more political in orientation.[9] *States of Exception in American History* weaves together these separate strands of scholarship in American history and in applied political theory. The conversation about emergency powers and the strengths and weaknesses of American liberalism when faced with emergencies has been gathering steam for more than a decade now. Yet there is no work that puts the theory and the history into direct contact with one another. That is what this book aims to do.

: : :

Any discussion of the most fundamental of political decisions—the decision whether to suspend the rule of law—has to reckon with the towering figure of the German legal theorist and jurist for the Nazi regime Carl Schmitt. Schmitt is widely thought to have shown that emergencies—decisions on the exception—pose a profound challenge to the principles of liberal constitutionalism.[10] The essence of constitutional government is to restrict the decisions of the sovereign to those powers ascribed to it by the constitution. It gives us the rule of laws instead of the rule of—capricious, fallible, power-hungry—individuals. But what happens when liberal regimes such as that of the United States face emergencies that appear to demand the suspension of legal rules? By definition, there can be no constitutional rule that governs the decision on when to suspend constitutional rules since such a paradoxical rule—one that gives authority to abolish the rules—would likely compromise the very idea of a liberal constitutional order. What, after all, would ground the authority of such a constitutional rule, given that its very purpose would be to suspend the constitution? Schmitt believed that liberals were evasive on this issue: their efforts to avoid the problem of the decision on the exception, he charged, led them either to normalize exceptions to the rule of law, thus undermining constitutional government, or simply to deny, ostrich-like, that there could be such existential dilemmas for the state, thus leaving the liberal state highly vulnerable in moments of crisis.

Many scholars who are sympathetic to the cause of constitutional democracy are nonetheless convinced by Schmitt's critique of the weaknesses of "legal liberalism." For some, Schmitt provides a challenge that either is insurmountable or must be overcome by means of a careful revaluation of the very foundations of liberalism itself. The chapters in part 1 of this volume address Schmitt's thought and its implications for American political and constitutional history. They display considerable skepticism that his challenge is as unavoidable, or as telling for liberal democracy, as much of the earlier commentary has supposed. The claim that the state of exception—and the whole logic of sovereignty that Schmitt believed was involved in the exception—is an insoluble problem for liberal regimes was already being contested in Schmitt's own time. Indeed, not only did liberal jurists of the era issue powerful rejoinders to Schmitt's metaphysics of the exception; Schmitt himself, it turns out, had originally argued that liberal regimes could use the "technical" innovation of "commissarial dictatorship" to protect the constitutional order during times of crisis. In his earliest post–World War I writings, Schmitt viewed Abraham Lincoln as just such a temporary dictator during the American Civil War, even crediting him with preserving the Republic during a time of crisis. Only after he took increasing fright at the possibility of the spread of Bolshevism across Europe in the early 1920s did Schmitt embrace his more drastic perspective on the unbounded nature of sovereignty and what he saw as the constitutive weaknesses of legal liberalism.[11]

If these counterblasts against Schmitt's critique of liberalism suggest that acceptance of his theory of sovereignty is not obligatory, the essays in part 1 of this volume show how the American context loosens Schmitt's grip on our political imaginations yet further. In chapter 1, "What Is the State of Exception?," Nomi Claire Lazar addresses the idea of a state of exception head-on. Putting Schmitt in his proper perspective, she distinguishes between three distinct senses of the state of exception: moral, legal, and political. Schmitt's exception was political, not legal or moral. What is more, Lazar goes on to argue, even in the political sense the United States has never seen a genuine state of exception. To be sure, there have been crises, public emergencies, and exercises of discretionary power, but these, Lazar insists, have never met Schmitt's criteria for a genuine exception since they have typically been subject to *ex post facto* legislative or legal adjudication. The greatest danger posed by the idea of a state of exception, she concludes, is that, by constantly invoking it as a threat to the constitutional order, we run the risk of eroding the legitimacy and downplaying the achievements of republican institutions. In chapter 2, "Negotiating the Rule of Law: Dilemmas of Security and Liberty Revisited," Ewa Atanassow and Ira Katznelson also raise questions about Schmitt's challenge to liberalism. They argue that a distinguished tradition of liberal thinkers and leaders, beginning with Locke and encompassing the Founders, Lincoln, and a number of twentieth-century political theorists, accepted that liberal regimes would inevitably face states of exception. However, unlike antiliberals like Schmitt, these writers believed that liberal democracies had the resources to cope with exceptional conditions. The advent of atomic weapons and the hypersecuritized state of the Cold War and the War on Terror, Atanassow and Katznelson concede, did diminish the ability of American republican institutions to limit the exercise of discretionary executive power. Yet, they conclude, the possibility of squaring strong emergency powers with the rule of law remained within the grasp of those operating within the American political tradition.

In chapter 3, "Beyond the Exception," David Dyzenhaus closes out the first part of the volume with a broader set of reflections on Schmitt's reception in the United States and the limited relevance of his attack on the Weimar constitution in understanding the operation of the American state. Dyzenhaus notes that the appeal to legal norms *can* become vacuous if a regime abandons its commitment to the rule of law. But if that commitment is and remains substantive—as evinced by efforts to uphold a culture of the rule of law—then constitutional polities can be both flexible and forceful in meeting emergencies without undermining their constitutive principles.

The chapters in part 2 take up a series of case studies of the theory and practice of emergency powers in American history. They range from the Founding to the middle of the twentieth century. Each chapter in this section shines light on crucial aspects of the American experience with emergency powers. One strand of that experience concerns how the American Republic's expanding commitment to democratic rule since the nineteenth century has created new configurations of ideas concerning prerogative power, emergencies, and legal order. Chapters by William J. Novak, Stephen W. Sawyer, and James T. Sparrow are especially concerned with the democratic perspective on crises and the politics of necessity. In chapter 4, "The American Law of Overruling Necessity: The Exceptional Origins of State Police Power," Novak examines the development of the police power in the early Republic. He shows us that the radical democratic experimentalism of the state legislatures meant that there was no conceptual problem reconciling strong discretionary power to uphold law and order with democratic values. The power of the people to give themselves laws and ensure that they could be upheld never lost its democratic character. These early Americans were not wedded to the formal ideals of the rule of law; concerns that liberals in the twentieth century would raise about excessive discretionary power did not trouble them much. In chapter 7, "Was There an American Concept of Emergency Powers? John Dewey, Carl Schmitt, and the Democratic Politics of Exception," Sawyer argues that the great theorist of American democracy, John Dewey, was not as stymied by problems of emergency and discretion as were his liberal colleagues. His democratic theory did not accord sovereignty the fundamental importance that Schmitt thought inherent in the very existence of the state. Sparrow, meanwhile, provides a more ambiguous portrait of the greatest American political scientist of his age, Charles Merriam. In chapter 8, "Charles Merriam and the Search for Democratic Power after Sovereignty," Sparrow explains how Merriam was able to describe the operation of the administrative state in ways that highlighted how democratic states had defused the dangers of unitary, unbounded sovereign power. Yet he also shows that Merriam's commitments to this theory of the state blinded him to the ways in which militarism and war could undercut democracy and push sovereign power toward the brink of dictatorship.

The other chapters in part 2, by John Fabian Witt, Gregory P. Downs, and Joel Isaac, examine more immediate questions of emergency powers during wartime and their relationship to the ordinary constitutional order. Each of these case studies reveals that the distinction between ordinary and extraordinary circumstances is not so clear-cut as we might suppose. These revelations may seem to articulate a veritably Schmittian theme, with the normalization of the exception lurking in the background of such reflections. Yet these three essays actually show that American theorists and politicians resolved the vexed relationship of extraordinary powers and constitutional order in ways that diverged sharply from Schmitt's expectations about liberal crisis government. In chapter 5, "To Save the Country: Reason and Necessity in Constitutional Emergencies," Witt thrillingly recovers a forgotten manuscript of the great German American legal theorist Francis Lieber. One reason American commentators have been drawn toward Schmitt's problematic, notes Witt, is that Lieber's own theory of emergency powers in wartime (a theory built on but also left unfinished by Lieber's son, Norman) was lost. Lieber mounted a strong defense of presidential discretion in wartime and of the use of tools like martial law. But he also zeroed in on how a culture of constitutional government was indispensable to the preservation of the rule of law, especially at moments when emergency powers were being deployed.

Witt here comes close to Dyzenhaus's account of how commitments to the rule of law generate a healthy culture of legality capable of influencing the character and limiting the duration of a state of exception. In chapter 6, "Powers of War in Times of Peace: Emergency Powers in the United States after the End of the Civil War," Downs tells a more ambivalent story. Reconstruction, he writes, blurred the boundary between wartime and peacetime. Radical Republicans wielded war powers as a tool of reform in the defeated South, leaving the country in a twilight zone of neither categorical peacetime nor outright war. The simple truth here is that emergency powers can and have been wielded as a continuation of politics by other means.

That was true, too, during the period stretching from the First World War through the Great Depression and Second World War. As Isaac relates in chapter 9, "Constitutional Dictatorship in Twentieth-Century American Political Thought," a number of US-based political theorists, such as Carl Friedrich and Frederick Watkins, revived the idea of a time-limited dictatorship allowed for in the Roman constitution as a mechanism for preserving liberal constitutional principles during America's prolonged experience of economic collapse and world war. But they also understood that the emergencies of the twentieth century had few precedents. States were different, now possessing vast administrative, regulatory, and judicial functions as well as legislative ones. The kinds of crises that states had to address now included not just war but systemic economic breakdown. Governments often needed to delegate legislative powers to their "constitutional dictators" to revive economic growth, not merely to empower them to uphold the existing regime. Friedrich and Watkins had no illusions about the difficulties involved in squaring such extensive state powers with America's democratic inheritance. Yet they were confident that they had uncovered a government arrangement that would guide America's constitutional order through an extended period of depression and war.

In the final part of the volume, we expand the concept of the exception beyond the juristic framework that Schmitt has given us. To be sure, and as we shall see again and again throughout the book, the state of exception has been given a technical meaning in the political theory literature, especially by Agamben. But even in this literature scope has been given to broader meanings of exception. As Agamben showed, a zone of indistinction was embedded in Schmitt's concept of sovereignty, one in which power is exercised by the sovereign over persons who have no status as juridical subjects. The prototypical example of such an individual, in Agamben's eyes, is the concentration camp inmate, who inhabits a physical space where the state of exception is made visible. The detention center operated by the US Army in Guantánamo Bay has been cited, by Agamben and others, as such a "zone of indistinction" made possible by the state of exception.

Agamben's theory emphasizes the totalizing effects of states of exception as modernity advanced across the nineteenth and twentieth centuries, evident in the multiplication of zones of exception and the utter powerlessness of individuals confined within them. But the authors in part 3 draw different lessons from this spatialized, materialized theorization of exception. In chapter 10, "Frederick Douglass and Constitutional Emergency: An Homage to the Political Creativity of Abolitionist Activism," Mariah Zeisberg demonstrates how emergency, as experienced by blacks in a slave system that increasingly resorted to terror, became a site for innovative, principled, and pragmatic thinking. Slavery and the extralegal methods increasingly used to protect it in the 1840s and 1850s could easily have led to the Constitution's demise, exposing America's republican institutions as nothing more than a Schmittian exercise in liberal hypocrisy. But this was precisely the moment when Frederick Douglass intensified his commitment to America's constitutional regime and called on all abolitionists, black and white, to do the same. In so doing, he helped the opponents of slavery imagine how the American republic might be reborn and placed on a more secure liberal foundation. Zeisberg's focus on Douglass allows her to reveal how political principle, innovation, and courage sometimes erupted in unexpected places, persons, and circumstances.

If Zeisberg illuminates how dynamic and productive popular resistance to the exercise of emergency powers can be, Elisabeth S. Clemens and Gary Gerstle and Desmond King explore the protean character of the state of exception itself, showing how its principles have bled into normal as well emergency practices of liberal polities. In chapter 11, "Delegated Governance as a Structure of Exceptions," Clemens assesses the privatization of the American state as generating a new state of exception in which more and more decision making has been removed from democratic governance. The key concept governing this development is that of delegation—of executive as well as legislative powers—to both executive agencies and, especially, the private contractors whom those agencies engage to provide public services. As Clemens notes, the problem of delegation of legislative powers was first addressed by writers such as Frederick Watkins in connection to situations of public emergency. Yet Watkins did not anticipate how this vision of delegated governance would define the normal, nonemergency actions of the modern American state. Finally, in chapter 12, "Spaces of Exception in American History," Gerstle and King push the spatial idea of the state of exception in new and challenging directions. When conceived as *spaces*, they claim, exceptions are a means of exercising power by denying or circumscribing rights and other legal statuses. More often than not, these spaces—the unincorporated territories of Puerto Rico and the Philippines, the fluid legal space occupied by immigrant aliens, and the ex-Confederate states during the era of Jim Crow—did not depend on a Schmittian-style suspension of law and declaration of emergency powers. Rather, they became durable parts of the polity, powerful, if unacknowledged, tools of liberal governance to this day.

: : :

Taken together, the essays in this book reveal that there is no single or simple solution to the challenges of crisis and exceptions to the rule of law. That is why we need history as well as theory. No legal regime, no matter how perfectly conceived, can count on its principles being enforced or obeyed. Time-bound human judgments and motivations and the balance of forces are essential ingredients of a well-functioning system of laws. Likewise, what rulers can do, even in rule-bound constitutional regimes, is in the end determined not only by the laws but also by what leaders and publics try on or allow against the backdrop of existing traditions and motivations and their relative strength. There is no one-size-fits-all resolution.

Take Roosevelt's 1941 proclamation. In the end, it was a grand fudge of the central issue. The president portrayed his declaration of an unlimited emergency as an action within his remit as head of the executive branch of government—and thus inside the constitutional order—even though emergency proclamations were not authorized by the Constitution. The implications of the proclamation were equally ambiguous: no specific actions were mandated, yet the call for loyal Americans to yield to the demands of national defense was strikingly open-ended and could be taken to allow for extensive new executive powers.

Under certain circumstances, such a proclamation could have been received as a sign of an incipient authoritarian turn in government. But members of Congress and leaders at the state level, as well as the American public, accepted Roosevelt's gambit as necessary and as legitimate within America's constitutional order. They embraced an idea defended soon after the war by commentators such as the political scientist Clinton Rossiter: "[T]he President's initiative is this nation's ultimate weapon of national salvation. The President's power to act as a dictator in a time of crisis may henceforth be regarded as a gift from the sovereign people of the United States!"[12] But for some, at one time or another, this gift has been a curse, has threatened to unleash forces that the constitutional order cannot or will not contain. Nevertheless, it is time we began the process of unwrapping it and examining what lies within.

Notes

1. President Franklin D. Roosevelt, Proclamation 2487, May 27, 1941, *The American Presidency Project*, ed. John Wolley and Gerhard Peters, https://www.presidency.ucsb.edu/documents/proclamation-2487-proclaiming-that-unlimited-national-emergency-confronts-this-country.

2. Franklin D. Roosevelt, "Fireside Chat 17: On an Unlimited National Emergency," May 27, 1941, https://millercenter.org/the-presidency/presidential-speeches/may-27-1941-fireside-chat-17-unlimited-national-emergency.

3. Roosevelt, Proclamation 2487.

4. Clinton Rossiter, *Constitutional Dictatorship: Crisis Government in the Modern Democracies* (New York: Harcourt, Brace, 1963), 267.

5. The use of the qualifying phrase *appears to be* is important. The claim that a state of emergency or exception obtains rests on a judgment that a crisis exists. If an agent (e.g., the president) has the power to decide to make an exception to the rule of law, then what matters politically is his or her judgment. This is true whether or not the crisis actually does obtain. We might better say that the agent's judgment itself establishes the reality of the crisis.

6. Richard A. Posner, *Not a Suicide Pact: The Constitution in a Time of National Emergency* (Oxford: Oxford University Press, 2006).

7. See, e.g., David Dyzenhaus, *The Constitution of Law: Legality in a Time of Emergency* (Cambridge: Cambridge University Press, 2006); Clement Fatovic, *Outside the Law: Emergency and Executive Power* (Baltimore: Johns Hopkins University Press, 2009); Bonnie Honig, *Emergency Politics: Paradox, Law, Democracy* (Princeton, NJ: Princeton University Press, 2009); Nomi Claire Lazar, *States of Emergency in Liberal Democracies* (Cambridge: Cambridge University Press, 2009); Victor Ramraj, ed., *Emergencies and the Limits of Legality* (Cambridge: Cambridge University Press, 2012); and Ryan Alford, *Permanent State of Emergency: Unchecked Executive Power and the Demise of the Rule of Law* (Montreal: McGill-Queen's University Press, 2017).

8. Posner, *Not a Suicide Pact*; Eric A. Posner and Adrian Vermeule, *The Executive Unbound: After the Madisonian Republic* (Oxford: Oxford University Press, 2011); Mariah Zeisberg, *War Powers: The Politics of Constitutional Authority* (Princeton, NJ: Princeton University Press, 2013).

9. David C. Unger, *The Emergency State: America's Pursuit of Absolute Security at All Costs* (New York: Penguin, 2012); John Fabian Witt, *Lincoln's Code: The Laws of War in American History* (New York: Free Press, 2013); and Ira Katznelson, *Fear Itself: The New Deal and the Origins of Our Time* (New York: Liveright, 2013).

10. Carl Schmitt, *Political Theology: Four Chapters on the Concept of Sovereignty*, trans. George Schwab (Chicago: University of Chicago Press, 2005). The literature on Schmitt's political thought is vast. For further references, see esp. Lazar's "What Is the State of Exception?" (chapter 1 in this volume), Atanassow and Katznelson's "Negotiating the Rule of Law" (chapter 2 in this volume), and Dyzenhaus's "Beyond the Exception" (chapter 3 in this volume).

11. For the full story, see John P. McCormick, "The Dilemmas of Dictatorship: Carl Schmitt and Constitutional Emergency Powers," in *Law as Politics: Carl Schmitt's Critique of Liberalism*, ed. David Dyzenhaus (Durham, NC: Duke University Press, 1998), 217–51.

12. Rossiter, *Constitutional Dictatorship*, 269.

Part One
The Challenge of Carl Schmitt

1

What Is the State of Exception?

Nomi Claire Lazar

The "state of exception" has found its way into research across a range of disciplines in the humanities and social sciences. It has become a frame of analysis for everything from refugee camps to the Olympics. In the fifteen years after World War II, a heyday of scholarship on emergency powers, the phrase was used only six times. Between 1970 and 1985, following the Vietnam War, there were a total of fifty-six pieces of scholarship that included the phrase *state of exception*. Between 2002 and 2017, there were more than eighteen thousand.[1] But what is a state of exception, in the American context?

Some countries have legal or constitutional state of exception provisions to deal with emergencies. But, despite legally defined "states of emergency," America does not. And the idea of a moral state of exception—where a leader (as an officeholder) is morally required to act in a way that is also for her (as an individual) morally abhorrent—is incoherent and unnecessary. Such situations are not states of exception but rather tragedies. Then there is the concept of a state of exception that stems from the work of Carl Schmitt. Here, the exception denotes the moment when an enemy, who threatens a way of life, must be recognized and destroyed. It is not legal, and it is not moral but rather political. That this moment exists in turn implies the existence of sovereign power, beyond law, to decide who that enemy is, an act that precludes debate or review. This has led Giorgio Agamben to claim that the stark opposition of this political situation with legality and morality shows that the normative quality of law is illusory. In America as everywhere, the rule of law is just force, liberal normativity farce. Is there, then, a political state of exception in the United States?

I have long argued that, while emergency powers are always dangerous to liberty, those who claim that they represent a manifestation of sovereign power rely on a range of fallacies and empirical errors. There is a plurality of sources of power and its constraint, some institutional or legal, some individual or charismatic, and this plurality operates through time, beyond a moment of decision. As a matter of empirics, this renders the idea of sovereign power in the American context dubious. In addition to formal checks and balances inherent in the Constitution, a range of informal constraints operate to limit executive power. There is nothing in the United States that could accurately be described as sovereign power that creates a state of exception. Of course, political leaders have committed crimes, broken international law, violated human rights, and acted immorally or beyond their power and often escaped punishment for such actions. But no one has, in so doing, succeeded in creating a zone in which normativity *disappeared*, in which punishment was *unwarranted*. To break the law and to silence the law are not the same. Nor is the violation of liberty its negation.

Yet there is a path that leads from a norm- and power-plural republic, by means of emergency, toward a sort of state of exception. A regime that maintains stability through the constraints of a plurality of forms and sources of power relies on civic virtue. Civic virtue supports the election of worthy candidates and outrage at the polls in response to misbehavior. But it is often also members of the public and public organizations who bring cases, who activate the judiciary to enforce the law. To maintain the civic virtue necessary (if not always sufficient) to keep an ambitious executive in check in these and other ways requires, in turn, that the regime type maintain legitimacy. And this depends importantly on government performance. But many emergencies are, or are at least are experienced as, performance failures. Often, that they arose in the first place gives rise to the suggestion that someone was not doing her job. They thus create incentives for political leaders to overperform and overconstrain or else to displace blame away from themselves and toward the regime type. Any such move may threaten faith in republican systems of government and put pressure on civic values. Without civic virtue—a foundational commitment to republican norms and values—what would ultimately constrain executive excess? The Greek political thinkers agreed that sooner or later a democratic republic—even a cleverly designed one like Rome—would disintegrate into populist tyranny. Through its relationship to performance failure and delegitimation, emergency facilitates this process.

Emergencies do not draw back the curtain, then, revealing sovereign power, as Schmitt and Agamben claim. Rather, emergencies contribute to an erosion of faith in republican civic values in part through public desensitization to erosions of rights and concentrations of power. But, beyond this, the persistent and by now ubiquitous rhetoric of a state of exception is itself a tool of destruction because it explicitly strives to undermine belief in these values. By undermining belief in the normative value of the rule of law, it does not describe but actively works to create a state of exception.

1. *The Normative Exception*

In the black letter of the law, a state of exception is a shift in the formal structures of power brought about by a declaration. Its purpose is to provide the executive branch with the necessary means to confront a crisis quickly and effectively. Such legal provisions are described in the constitutions of a number of countries, including Burundi, Chile, Dominican Republic, Ecuador, Equatorial Guinea, Morocco, Paraguay, Peru, Timor-Leste, and Venezuela. While there are no such provisions in the American Constitution, the United States has many provisions for the concentration of power in an emergency along with latent and explicit police and prerogative powers for managing urgent threats to the public welfare. These include the power in Article 1, Section 9, of the Constitution to suspend habeas corpus in time of war or insurrection. There are also a number of statutory provisions at both the federal and the state levels. At the federal level, these include the National Emergencies Act, the International Emergency Economic Powers Act, and the Public Health Service Act. In legal terms, provisions for a state of exception tend not to deviate substantially from provisions for a state of emergency. Both enumerate a range of threats to the public, then enable remedies and provide safeguards. Neither is particularly exceptional. Provisions for managing crises are a normal and well-regulated part of every republican and liberal-democratic legal system.

Yet, despite black letter legality, doesn't the differential normativity of states of emergency or exception undermine the rule of law? If there are different legal structures and different structures of power and rights for different circumstances, then doesn't the rule of law become, quite literally, optional? And because the rule of law sits at the moral core of a liberal democracy—protecting equality before the law, due process, etc.—this question strikes at the heart of American political identity. What does it mean if the protection of the law becomes dependent on circumstance? In a rule-of-law regime individual rights are a bulwark against the moral claims of the majority, a protection against utilitarian pressures. Under the rule of law, the state must respect each person as an end in herself, never using her only as a means to satisfy the needs of the broader community. That is, the exercise of power must respect rights. Yet in a crisis, to protect the public, such constraints on executive power are limited or derogated. Officials may violate privacy through surveillance, restrict freedom of movement during an epidemic or violent incident, commandeer or confiscate property, etc. These rights derogations can be, and normally are, entirely legal, but are they right? That is to say, don't such actions constitute a state of exception from the ethical-political requirements of the rule of law?

This is a misconception. As I argued in *States of Emergency in Liberal Democracies*,[2] rights are never absolute, and no political system imagines them to be. There are always countervailing moral considerations, and often rights conflict with one another too. That such limits are a normal, not exceptional, part of the morality of rights is evident not only in constitutions, which usually contain a variety of clauses and articles on limitations, but even in the more aspirational international rights covenants, such as the International Covenant on Civil and Political Rights. This does not mean that the rule of law is irrelevant. That would imply that the rule of law is a binary condition that either obtains or does not. But the rule of law is a dynamic and aspirational collective commitment. It is a commitment to strive for an optimal, not perfect, realization of its principles.[3] The rule of law is, in David Dyzenhaus's words, a project.[4] In cases where rights conflict with each other or with broader moral norms, the rule of law guides, but does not determine, judgment. *Judgment*, here, denotes both the grounds of a political actor's decision in the moment and the reflection of the people after the fact. Even where rights are ultimately limited, so long as they continue to hold substantial weight in deliberation and judgment, rights holders continue to be treated as ends in themselves, even where they must become means also.

This is true in day-to-day political life as we balance competing rights and needs of citizens: the right to privacy of restaurant owners with food safety for their patrons (i.e., police powers), the right to property with vital, collective transportation needs (i.e., eminent domain), etc. But it can also illuminate the most extreme hypothetical cases—the so-called ticking-time-bomb scenarios where a person, a person's body, may literally become a pure means. Some thinkers, such as Michael Moore, have argued that this must be morally acceptable: "It just is not true that one should allow a nuclear war rather than killing or torturing an innocent person. It is not even true that one should allow the destruction of a sizable city by a terrorist nuclear device rather than kill or torture an innocent person."[5] Such cases, on this view, call for a "threshold deontology" where utilitarian considerations overtake the more duty-based rule of law. But, as Michael Walzer has argued, while genuine, imminent existential terror can require a leader to sacrifice her moral integrity on behalf of her people, this does not mean that her actions are moral per se. Rather, her moral purity is second to the people's existential safety. Wrong does not become right at some threshold; things do not become their opposites. The leader who dirties her hands deserves both thanks and shame. "In an emergency," Walzer notes, "neutral rights can be overridden, and when we override them we make no claim that they have been diminished, weakened, or lost. They have to be overridden... precisely because they are still there, in full force, obstacles to some great (necessary) triumph for mankind."[6] Just as officials must aim to resolve everyday moral conflicts in the spirit of the rule of law, the rule of law continues to provide a moral beacon for leaders facing existential threats. A shining example of how a commitment to the rule of law and participation in the project it generates can guide moral action in a crisis is found in Abraham Lincoln's famous special session message to Congress of July 4, 1861.

America, Lincoln notes, is facing an existential threat and, with it, a threat to the very idea of free government. That threat requires an urgent and decisive response because it is the president's "imperative duty... to prevent... an attempt to destroy the Federal Union." An effective response will press on the rule of law, he admits. For example, habeas corpus has been suspended in many places, perhaps without clear authority. But he has done this with a moral end in view. It is not just that the shared mode of life, the very existence of the United States, is at risk. This mode of life under free government, Lincoln argues, is of fundamental value to persons everywhere because of its intrinsic character. Its "leading object is to elevate the condition of men—to lift artificial weights from all shoulders; to clear the paths of laudable pursuit for all; to afford all an unfettered start and a fair chance in the race of life." If he does not act, the situation threatens not just America but the very idea of constitutional democracy. A prohibition on action here would entail that there was no remedy whenever "discontented individuals, too few in numbers to control the administration, . . . [sought to] break up their government." And this would effectively "put an end to free government upon the earth." If he cannot act decisively, then "a government of the people by the same people . . . cannot maintain its territorial integrity against its own domestic foes." Either he is morally permitted to act, or constitutional democracy is impossible. But constitutional democracy is of profound value, so this is a justification to act.[7]

Lincoln goes on to articulate a legal argument: no law has been violated in any case. The Constitution says habeas corpus can be suspended in certain circumstances, the present circumstances count among them, so it is legally and not just morally justified that habeas corpus will be suspended. The question of whether this power rests with the executive is live, but in this case, where ambiguity has combined with urgent need, Lincoln at minimum had his prerogative power to fall back on.

Observe how, as he carefully makes the case for the actions he has undertaken and those he is about to undertake, Lincoln makes evident his reverence for the rule of law, an extreme reluctance to abuse it, and the heavy burden of necessity, urgency, and the highest moral stakes. He gives reasons; he considers all sides of the matter; he recognizes the limits of his power, his need of Congress, and his duties to the people. He invites Congress to share the burden of both reflection and action, to consider and judge the reasons he has given. In other words, he demonstrates how it is possible to act in an emergency while actively engaged in the rule-of-law project. As he acts to resolve the moral tragedy before him, it is evident to him that his own purity of conscience must be put aside. What guides his deliberations and his reason giving is then precisely a commitment to the rule of law as a collective and collaborative project. What is the best we can do, given the constraints and imperatives, he asks, and how can we do our best together? There is no moral state of exception here. There is only a committed, good faith effort to manage a moral tragedy as *part* of the overall moral project that is the rule of law.

Of course, not everyone who makes use of emergency powers is as fully committed to the rule-of-law project, and not every emergency action is *right*. After Japan's attack on Pearl Harbor in 1941, Governor Poindexter reasonably feared an imminent invasion and so abdicated, transferring power to the military leadership. Lieutenant General Short was promptly relieved of duty and replaced by Delos Emmons, who became the effective but unelected governor of Hawaii. The military leadership issued a variety of directives to control civilian activity, including curfews, blackouts, and restrictions on private communications.[8] There were excesses under martial law in Hawaii, including its temporal extension beyond the scope of any real threat of invasion, and some unnecessarily severe and intrusive measures. The civilian courts remained closed, even after social and leisure places, such as cinemas and gaming halls, were reopened, for example, and civil cases came under summary military jurisdiction when this was patently unnecessary. In one case, a fellow called Spurlock, who had been charged with assault on a police officer and released on bail just prior to the attack on Pearl Harbor, was brought before the court only after the attack and subsequent declaration of martial law. His plea of not guilty was rejected by the military court, which, without trial, sentenced him to probation. But Spurlock, apparently a pugnacious fellow, got in scrap with a civilian just two months later. He was arrested, detained without bail, and then sentenced—again without trial—to five years of hard labor for this misdemeanor. This is a penalty clearly in excess of what a civilian court might have meted out. Spurlock petitioned for a writ of habeas corpus, and the district court found that his rights under the Fifth Amendment had been violated.[9] But the circuit court reversed this. When he then petitioned for a writ of certiorari, he was suddenly released. This happened on a number of occasions, suggesting the military wished to avoid a Supreme Court ruling on military jurisdiction. Each time, the petitioner would be released, and the Supreme Court would decline to consider the constitutionality of military jurisdiction on the grounds that it was moot.[10]

Ultimately, however, the Supreme Court heard *Duncan v. Kahanamoku* and *White v. Steer*.[11] It found that, while itself legal where public safety is at risk, a declaration of martial law did not confer unlimited authority on military command. For example, where the courts can remain open consistent with public safety, military tribunals for civilian crime violate (rather than limit or derogate) Fifth Amendment rights. Further, and perhaps most importantly, military commanders are not judges in their own case. Their actions and decisions are reviewable. On what basis are they judged, we might ask? Fundamentally, on the basis that the actions taken served rather than undermined the rule-of-law project. Thus, in the case of martial law in Hawaii in the period from 1941 to 1944, we see the morality of the rule-of-law project continue in force, with excesses ultimately checked and chastised, even where the law appeared to enable a broad scope of action. Rather, amid some justifiable powers, the military government violated rights, and those violations were recognized as such. The actions of the military in *Spurlock* and similar cases were found to be *illegal* and *immoral*, not *exceptional*, not beyond review. There was no moral state of exception.

2. The Political Exception

There is a third sense of a state of exception, beyond the legal and the moral. This is the political state of exception. Conceptually, a *public emergency*—which is to say an emergency of concern to government— can be defined as a situation in which the state's capacity to respond to threats is itself threatened. Forest fires and hurricanes, nuclear-power-plant meltdowns and epidemic disease not only pose widespread threats to life, limb, and property but may so damage necessary infrastructure and limit human and fiscal resources that the state struggles to prevent or mitigate further harm. Even emergencies that are not initially physical, such as economic emergencies, can lead to persistent fall-on effects such as mass unemployment, destitution, and violence. Because of the threat a public emergency poses to performative legitimacy—which is to say because we expect the state to maintain our physical security and lose confidence in a government that fails to do so—poor emergency management may generate, in turn, political emergencies: threats to the collective way of life. Such threats can also arise independently through civil violence or war.

In his writings from the 1920s and 1930s, the Weimar legal theorist Carl Schmitt distinguished this category under the term *Ausnahmezustand* and contrasted it with a mere emergency, *Notstand*. The former, the true state of exception, is politically existential, surpassing in consequence—not as a matter of scale but as a matter of kind—a public emergency. Not only the well-being of individuals, no matter their number, but also a people and their way of life are at risk. A state of exception, on this conception, is a special and particular case of emergency that generates not just the temporary derogation of rights in the service of the *salus populi* but an entirely different approach to the nature of the political, of power, of the state.

The current flood of interest in the idea of a *state of exception*, and our tendency to refer to a vast swath of emergencies or special measures with this term, is due in part to the rediscovery and translation of Schmitt's work at the end of the twentieth century and its development in the writings of the literary theorist Giorgio Agamben. Schmitt published *Die Diktatur* in 1921, in the chaotic aftermath of the Treaty of Versailles.[12] In this work, he identified two historical types of consolidated power for governing in times of crisis. One type is the "commissarial" dictator, who wields concentrated but temporary power in an identified crisis, specifically to bring about its resolution and the restoration of the constitutional order. An example here is the Roman institution of the dictatorship, where the senate and consuls would appoint a person of known moral standing to resolve a crisis, on the understanding that he must then immediately lay down his power if he succeeds or, if after six months he has failed, lay it down then. This form of dictatorship is constitutional and aims to make itself redundant.[13] Here, the dictator is the agent of the constitution and agrees to take on a specific task.

Other dictators, Schmitt argues, have been not commissars but "guarantors." Sovereign dictators are guardians of the people who stand permanently at the ready. Beginning with *Political Theology* (1922), Schmitt argued that, as a guarantor, the sovereign dictator is always necessary because at any time there may emerge an enemy of the state who seeks to destroy the regime and the people's way of life. The enemy must be quickly and decisively identified and crushed, and the institutions of parliamentary democracy, with its fractious and endless debate, are not suited to this work. Schmitt argued: "The essence of liberalism is negotiation, a cautious half measure, in the hope that the definitive dispute, the decisive bloody battle, can be transformed into a parliamentary debate and permit the decision to be suspended forever in an everlasting discussion." Nor is the exception a clearly delineated ontological category that would allow for a technocratic determination. That is to say, there is no set of criteria against which clear information could be compared to make a definite binary determination: yes, this is a state of exception, or no, this is not. What will count as an exception cannot be established by rules in advance, cannot be discussed and debated in the context of deliberative democracy. A combination of constrained temporality and the lack of defining characteristics means the determination that a state of exception exists must rest on a sovereign, self-emanating *decision*. Norms, Schmitt once said, are applicable only in the normal situation, and, for the legally normal situation to exist, someone must guarantee order from above. It would be deluded to think that the state has no enemies or that they could be dealt with by "cautious half measure[s]."[14] It is in the core nature of political things that some ultimately seek to destroy the regime and the people's way of life. The idea of a state of exception enables the enemy of a people to be taken seriously as the enemy who must be destroyed.[15] It is the job of the sovereign dictator to recognize this and execute this existential task. Liberals, raising reason, fail to acknowledge that their political system necessarily requires—must rely on—raw sovereign power if it is to survive. And this power lurks not just at the fringes but, because the possibility of exception is an omnipresent fact, at the very core of the state. It is in the fact of exception that the potential for violent rupture at the center of all politics, and liberalism's failure to confront this, is most visible.

If law is not the source of power, then liberal democracy is a fraud and rests on a conception of itself that, while it may be rhetorically compelling, is dangerously incoherent. Is not this person by whose grace the law applies and at whose word the law may cease to apply sovereign? As Schmitt asserts in the famous opening statement of *Political Theology*, he is sovereign who decides on the exception. Because an enemy could emerge at any moment, it follows that a guardian, not an agent of the constitution, is permanently needful. Hence, Schmitt moves to reject the category of the commissarial dictator entirely.[16] This sovereign dictatorial power to decide when the law applies and when it does not cannot itself have its source in law because it is through this sovereign power that law is able to persist at all. Without this sovereignty, no constitutional order can persist. This is the political concept of a state of exception according to Carl Schmitt.

For Schmitt, the sovereign's aim is always also "our" aim, which is to say, to protect "us," the friends of the state, from the enemy, "they" who threaten "us." There is no fundamental distinction between the sovereign's interests and "our" own. In Giorgio Agamben's reconstruction of the state of exception, this association is reconfigured. "We" are no longer in union with sovereign power, and the sovereign's aims are not ours. Rather, "we" stand together with "they" against the sovereign who threatens us all. For Agamben, "we" are the multitude, and the sovereign is not our guardian but our vital enemy who seeks to subdue and reduce us to bare life under the cloak of law. Drawing generously on the work of Schmitt and Walter Benjamin, Agamben argues that, because sovereign power can suspend the law at will, this is functionally equivalent to lacking law's protection at all. We are free to be killed without consequence. For Agamben sovereignty means "violence passes over into law and law passes over into violence"[17] and normativity has no place in government. We are all, always bare and vulnerable to sovereign power because the exception is indeterminate. Sovereignty because effectively arbitrary negates the moral substance of constitutional democracy.

Does a state of exception in this political sense obtain in the United States? I have argued at length elsewhere[18] that the Schmitt-Agamben conception of a state of exception is undermined by both logical and empirical difficulties that I will summarize only briefly here. It is certainly true that law cannot rule on its own. Law must be interpreted, extended, observed, and enforced and on rare occasions superseded on the basis of plural and competing norms. And there are certainly times when leaders are called on to act with power beyond the normal scope of their office. But liberal theorists from Locke forward never claimed otherwise. While Schmitt wrote in response to a legal positivism that was perhaps excessively sealed off from politics, most liberals have had a more fluid understanding of the relationship between law and politics.[19] Of course power and law interact. But decisions made on extralegal or extraordinary grounds can be consistent with responsible government too because the moment of decision is situated in a broader temporality. What appears sovereign in an abstract moment looks otherwise when properly situated in the politics and jurisprudence that led up to the decision and the legal and political consequences that follow. The rule of law is not limited to what is written but includes the collective habits of and commitment to principled government in accordance with both written and unwritten conventions and norms. These provide resources to derogate the written law without muting its spirit and to constrain or punish action that silences the law beyond what is strictly necessary. This is not to say that abuses do not occur but rather to underline that, while not all flexibility in laws and institutions is abuse, when abuses occur, they are precisely abuses, potentially subject to both formal and informal punishment.[20] This would be nonsensical from the sovereign power perspective.

Furthermore, the existence of constitutional police and prerogative powers means there is no need for sovereign power in the first place. Police and prerogative are ringed around with jurisprudence, with formal and informal constraints and consequences for ill use.[21] While ultimately a single person may make the decision to act in a crisis (though even this is contestable), such decisions are influenced by, structured by, and in some cases constrained by a mass of experience, informal and formal legal and moral norms, advice, protocol, preordained bureaucratic procedure, and, notably, the banked legitimacy of decision makers. And, after the fact, decisions may be subject to judicial or popular review. All emergency action is surrounded with normative constraint both formal and informal and countervailing sources of power that make clear the fictitious quality of Agamben's image of a sovereign who strips us to bare life. Such sovereign power does not exist in a constitutional republic like the United States with a plurality of sources of power. There must be substantial complicity in the buildup to a momentary exhibition of power. And, after the fact, there are many formal and informal means of holding the decision maker to account, from elections, commissions of inquiry, and criminal sanctions to the threat of infamy.

Attention to the history and jurisprudence of emergency in America—even existential emergency—supports this. We have already seen with the cases of Lincoln and the martial law governance of Hawaii during the Second World War how commitment to the rule-of-law project—a striving to keep the moral end in view as one balances measures to secure the people—can govern a determination of whether extralegal action is right and necessary, even if tragic, or whether it is a violation that must be condemned. No state of moral or legal exception came into existence in these cases. Rights and their bearers maintained their force and their worth, and, where they were violated, this violation was acknowledged, even if only after the fact.

Some will doubtless object that the surge of interest in states of exception is driven not only by the writings of Agamben and the translation of Schmitt but also by recent events. In spaces like Abu Ghraib and Guantánamo, the US government seems to have deliberately set about creating a space outside the law.[22] Surely these are not "normal" spaces. Indeed, some might even question whether prisons are. Agamben argued that, in "the camp," we are stripped of effective legal protection, not the subjects of law but of bare life subjected to its raw, underlying sovereign force. Does this not describe the condition of those in these forms of captivity? And, if these people, some of whom were incarcerated carelessly or mistakenly, are "in a camp," is Agamben not right that the same bare subjection characterizes any of us?[23] And, if indeed we could be stripped of all substantive legal protection at any time, does this not show that legal protection is a sham? That the law is force with window dressing?

But Abu Ghraib and Guantánamo have not been beyond the reach of law. While legal consequences have been tragically too late for some and incomplete or inadequate for others, the abusive actions of Americans at Abu Ghraib were punished as crimes, and some of those who suffered have won civil redress as well. Many who ought to have been held accountable—particularly at higher levels of responsibility—were not. But, in order for that to be a failure of justice, what happened at Abu Ghraib has to be recognized as subject to law; it has to be recognized as crime. The American government may have attempted to create a legal black hole for the prisoners there, but plural power prevented this, however imperfectly.[24]

The same is true of the prison camp at Guantánamo. Here too the executive branch attempted to create a zone of exception where prisoners could "disappear" in a space of torture and inhumanity. But here, too, plural power resisted this. A freedom of information request from journalists resulted in the court-ordered release of Guantánamo prisoners' names.[25] The Supreme Court found, in *Hamdi v. Rumsfeld*, that prisoners could exercise the right of habeas corpus.[26] And claims that the prisoners were not covered by the Geneva Convention were negated by the decision in *Hamdan v. Rumsfeld*.[27] Both cases were driven by the interest and commitment of members of civil society. Again, it seems evident the US government engaged in activities that are contrary to international law. While the prisoners at Guantánamo were not rendered *homo sacer* by sovereign power, they were subjected to abhorrent abuses of their most fundamental rights, abuses that members of civil society and the legal profession worked to redress. State power was not able to create a black hole where the law could not reach, but instead the law did reach there and did shine a light there, even if it was partial and its results irregular, incomplete, and, for some, too late. Whatever criminal actions were undertaken, whatever violations of domestic and international law, the law applied. It was not suspended. The executive branch was not able to create a zone of exception.

Here is an instance of what we might term *zones of legal variance*, where the elasticity characteristic of all law shows itself. In theory the rule of law applies equally to all within its geographic reach and varies in its effects only for salient reasons, which is to say, reasons that increase law's equality. But a just legal system is full of safety valves that respect the complex relationship of justice and mercy, individual rights and the public welfare. At every level of law, there are opportunities for legal variation: from local zoning variances to the pardon power. In every legal system, there are of necessity places and times where the law functions differently. These are morally normal when the rule-of-law project serves to guide that variance and the state takes each person, her rights and interests, seriously, even where that person's interests may be sacrificed for the public welfare, which is always also in her interest. In cases of zoning variance or a pardon, an authority has the power to correct a moral wrong that strict equality before the law—the equal application of a rule—would have generated. But, in other cases, the rules themselves change, apply differently, or else apply differentially to members of a designated class within a delineated space and through a specified time. Whether or not law itself creates these zones of variability, they affect the application of law. So long as a robustly normative rule-of-law project[28] guides these differences, they are right, even when, in extreme cases, they are also tragic.

But some will object, What of those cases—Hawaii, Abu Ghraib—where leaders clearly were not governed by a commitment to the rule-of-law project? Do not these cases of states violating rights show that rights are meaningless, enforced at the whim and discretion of those with the monopoly over justified force? This position is not just logically and empirically wrong but dangerous. It is wrong because a claim that the rule of law is pointless because it is sometimes violated is like a claim that, because murder takes place and murderers sometimes escape detection or conviction, the law against murder is pointless. It may be objected that the analogy does not hold because, in the second place, we have an ordinary citizen who commits a crime while, in the first, we have a sovereign leader with the power to suspend the law itself. But this is circular. Unless we have already chosen to believe that leaders are above the law, the claim is nonsense. Whenever a leader violates the law, she is responsible. When she fails, in the course of her duties, to respect and show commitment to the rule-of-law project, she is culpable. If we fail to or are unable to hold her accountable, that does not absolve *her*. It does not negate the moral force of the rule of law. To claim otherwise—to effectively imagine sovereign power into existence, as the followers of Agamben and his state of exception theory have done—is not just wrong but pernicious. I have suggested that the state of exception has no empirical, normative, or political correlate in the United States. Yet I will now argue that there is a path to something recognizable as a political state of exception in America.

3. The "Theoretical" Exception and Its Empirical Consequences

We expect that some holders of executive power will, periodically, push the limits of legality and morality. It is because we expect this that we have the formal division of powers and a plurality of informal constraints in the first place. In preventing abuse of executive power, the role of civil society is important and perhaps too implicit in studies of emergency power. An exception is the work of Clement Fatovic, who has shown that it was a common view among the American Founders that leaders' republican virtue is the ultimate safeguard in times of crisis. Safety lies in choosing a leader who will not abuse power in the first place. But, as Fatovic concludes, republican virtue cannot stand secure unless it is also, at the same time, anchored in widespread civic virtue.[29] Before a political leader can choose well in a crisis, the people must choose their leader well. The leader knows, too, that her decisions will be judged after the fact against high ethical standards. Anticipation of that judgment should play an important constraining role alongside personal moral standards.

But the public plays a role beyond the polls. Norms—moral or legal—are always latent and potential until they are enforced, put into force. As words, even as laws, they have no independent power. They can do nothing of themselves. It is in every case people who put norms into force, who argue for them, who trumpet them, who insist on them, who call on leaders to enshrine them and courts to recognize and enforce them. From this perspective the people, not sovereign power, are the ultimate guarantor of norms. When the many organs of the state function within normative constraints, it is in part because the people expect and insist on this. Members of civil society hold officials to account through public shaming in the media, through protest, or by accessing the courts. The case of Kaci Hickox provides a fine, recent example. Hickox is a nurse who, having returned from caring for Ebola patients in affected countries in West Africa, was quarantined in response to widespread panic and without scientific justification. She charged that her rights had been violated, despite the claimed emergency, and the courts found in her favor.[30] Through a subsequent lawsuit, she reinforced and secured the rights of those the state of New Jersey might quarantine in the future.[31] But Hickox is a citizen, an active member of the public at large. And constitutional republicanism works when she and her fellow citizens, the public, and not just the branches of government, are engaged with the rule-of-law project. At the point where the public either loses its commitment to or becomes too apathetic to enforce democratic values, including a commitment to the rule of law, the ethical-political enterprise of emergency government is in trouble.

How might this come about? In Atanassow and Katznelson's "Negotiating the Rule of Law" (chapter 2 in this volume), we see that frequent emergency declarations may habituate citizens to concentrated executive power, which may also find its way into constitutional conventions and quotidian legislation. This is exacerbated by the occasional necessity that actions undertaken to prevent an emergency from arising remain secret, which limits the ability of citizens, courts, and legislatures to check excess. But alongside these notable dangers that emergency powers pose to the proper functioning of democracy grows a threat to the perceived legitimacy of the democratic system as such, and this poses its own grave risk to democracy, as I will now show.

Sooner or later republics fail, and tyranny riding a populist wave is a common mechanism. Emergency powers have been present at the deathbed in notable cases, such as Rome and Weimar. Certainly, concentrated power is easy to abuse, but the connection between emergency and democratic failure is not straightforward. As Machiavelli wisely noted in the context of his study of the Roman dictatorship, power can take on a title, but a title alone cannot give power.[32] Rather, emergencies may generate a state of exception by means of delegitimation, undermining popular commitment to foundational norms, which in turn facilitates the rise of populist tyrannies.

Populism, characterized as leading through an appeal for individualized, charismatic legitimacy, grows where a regime's normal stores of legitimacy have begun to run out. Over time, legitimacy is banked from two sources.[33] On one hand there are "underlying orders," which often come to seem self-evident and retreat into the background. Examples include tradition, legal and procedural rules, normative arguments, and, historically, cosmic harmony, divine order, and the order of fate or destiny. Like any claim to justification, whether epistemological, normative, or otherwise, a claim of legitimacy must anchor itself in an already existing cosmological/ontological and epistemological scheme. That is to say, when people come to accept the truth of some claim or the validity of some imperative, it is partly on the basis of its correspondence with other webs of truth or validities accepted already. The first source of legitimacy is thus concordance with an accepted normative order.

The other critical source of legitimacy is performance or capacity. Whether or not a political agent came to power in the procedurally correct fashion, whether or not a regime was properly designed and ratified, and regardless of how committed to and expressive of core values that political actor or regime might be, solid performance will always also be necessary to the maintenance of legitimacy. The criteria for good performance may vary with context, spanning economic growth, food and physical security, and means for the enforcement of justice. And some specific offices may be defined by performance criteria of their own, goals or ends we expect the officeholder to achieve. We attend too little to this role of performance in the study of legitimacy in liberal democracies, focusing instead on procedural and normative aspects. Scholars sometimes assume that performance is more characteristic of authoritative or authoritarian schemes of legitimation, for instance. But no regime can secure consent solely on the basis of underlying norms, whether these are based in tradition, in reason, in constitutional ground rules, or in some other underlying conception of right order. Faith in right order or just procedure always also requires that the government deliver. Governments must, for example, anticipate, prevent, or mitigate harm in accordance with local expectations. When they fail to do so, the people want to hold someone to account.

It is thus important that performance be *communicated*, and thus performance legitimacy is also partly performative. That is, political agents must demonstrate their capacity to manage contingencies and meet public needs so that people trust them going forward. Capacity can be communicated by, for example, not just statistics themselves but the capacity to gather the information necessary to produce those statistics as well as by a variety of semiotic displays such as military parades and national days. By performing, and by communicating a capacity to perform, leaders bank legitimacy for themselves, their party, or the regime.

Legitimacy is not static. Rather, it must be negotiated and renegotiated, banked and spent. Over time, good performance provides a buffer, while failures can eat away at belief in a regime's formative values. For the two wells of legitimacy may not be experienced as distinct. Because foundational political norms are secured, in the first instance, by people's belief in them, even where that belief can be justified on the basis of sound moral argument, erosion of this belief undermines normative power (where power is understood as a capacity to effect or prevent a change). It is critical to the survival of a regime that its normative identity be paramount, that the norms that undergird legitimacy come first, before any other normative or identity commitment. When the consensus around core values of universality of rights, the rule of law, and the democratic process is loosened, the fabric of the civic project may begin to fray. Though they lack any intrinsic connection with foundational values, performative failures may have this consequence.

It is important to note that fraying or tearing the civic fabric is not bad in itself. On the contrary, law and normativity are always growing and developing, and tears in the social fabric have often resulted in moral growth. But occasionally these tears are profound or hard to repair, particularly when performance failures aggravate social cleavage. Normative gaps that resist repair may leave a mounting sense of unease and insecurity. When consensus on shared, foundational norms fades, no one needs to suspend them; they simply lack the power to function. No one enforces them; no one puts them into force.

Now, constitutional democracies have built-in mechanisms for displacing performance failure to help secure the regime and its core values. It is one purpose of elections, for instance, to enable the safe venting of anger and disappointment onto an individual or party in order to protect faith in republican institutions, increasing stability. This safety valve can keep a political emergency from becoming existential for the regime. Consider the example of Hurricane Katrina. Here, various levels of government failed to anticipate and prevent and then failed again to mitigate a disaster. The failure marred the popularity of President Bush and the Republican Party, and this safely insulated the state. It would have been reasonable to blame the form of government: it is a fact that the institutions of liberal democracy work against rational forms of prevention that may better serve the public welfare. Preventive measures are easier to execute in an authoritative regime, such as Singapore, than under the American system of government, where short-term costs with long-term benefits definitely do not serve the electoral interests of sitting politicians. But in the Katrina case the potential cost to the legitimacy of a free and fair democracy was mitigated by the availability of institutions, elected officials, and parties who could take the blame. In this and other ways, well-designed republican institutions and the norms that constitute their core are partly insulated from performative failures.

But this feature can be inverted, and this inversion means emergencies may facilitate a slide from republicanism to populist tyranny: a functional equivalent to a political state of exception. Because emergencies often result from or are exacerbated by a failure of foresight, many emergencies, un- or insufficiently mitigated, may be experienced, as they unfold, as failures of capacity and planning. It follows that public awareness of possible threats—for instance, heightened awareness of the threat of terrorism—creates incentives to overconstrain, so as to minimize the chance an emergency will transpire. Beyond the impact on the public welfare, such a lapse has consequences for legitimacy. And, when there is an emergency, it creates incentives to overperform to compensate for the initial failure. We saw this, for instance, when, in 1970, Pierre Trudeau brought out the army, complete with tanks in the streets of Montreal, in response to the FLQ terrorist crisis. No doubt because he recognized that a show of swagger was necessary to restore perceptions of capacity, he famously told reporters who worried how far he might consider suspending civil liberties: "Just watch me."[34] With less grace, if no less swagger, Chris Christie, then governor of New Jersey, quarantined Nurse Hickox after the Ebola outbreak in 2014. The aim of such overreaction is to perform capacity in the service of restoring depleted legitimacy.

But, if such options to replenish stores of legitimacy are unavailable or seem fruitless, the emergency as a performance failure creates perverse incentives for leaders to displace anger away from themselves and their party toward the regime. In other words, the institutional safety mechanism for performance failure can be inverted. In such cases the leader may insist that it is because of the regime type itself that things are going wrong: institutions are tying her hands, preventing what is needful. Perhaps the leader is being unfairly maligned by the press, by a judiciary that is not "democratic," that is not the people's judiciary. By calling the central importance of liberal and republican norms and institutions into doubt, displacing blame, the leader secures herself. The performance disaster is not her failure but caused by institutions and their constraints. When, in addition, the leader trumpets alternative, partisan ideological norms, these may come to supersede liberal and republican norms in public discourse. Then the violation of those norms will no longer be singular and tragic but rather be understood as righteous. And then the republic is in trouble.

The combination of pressure to devalue republican norms from above and performance failure–driven ambivalence from below is dangerous. Liberal and republican norms recede as other allegiances—lending the appearance of security or collective meaning and identity—take precedence. The overlapping consensus erodes. Through the conduit of performance failure, emergency creates these challenges to the regime's legitimacy, facilitating a slide toward populist tyranny. The civic virtue necessary to check executive power is threatened. The will to enforce norms whose energy is only ever potential fades, and the power of the people yields to sovereign power. Thus, emergency may contribute to the decline or death of democratic republics.

Emergency and the powers it triggers do not reveal the existence of a state of exception. But, because emergency often implies performance failures, which in turn threaten the legitimacy of core values, this may open the way to populist tyranny. In this way, an emergency may lead to a state of exception. The threat of this form of democratic deterioration or deconsolidation probably ebbs and flows in the history of a republic, depending on banked legitimacy and some range of other conditions worth more scholarly attention. Case studies of performative legitimacy levels in republics that live with frequent or extended periods of emergency powers (such as Israel, Egypt, Argentina, and the United States) might be fruitful in this regard.

Finally, we see how the by-now persistent rhetoric of the state of exception, which casts aspersions on liberal and republican norms and in particular on the value of law and the rule of law, helps pave the path to tyranny. Of course it is not the only or the most important factor. But, on the university campuses where political consciousness and activism are traditionally cultivated, the omnipresence of Agamben and his state of exception has impact. The persistent insistence that liberal democracy is a sham, that power is sovereign and not plural, undermines belief in the value of and partnership between liberal democratic institutions and civil society, their joint capacity to enforce norms. This kind of rhetoric may generate a sort of learned helplessness. If law is just force, what reason could there be to fight for the rule of law? If only the deluded think that liberal democracies provide a form of freedom worth defending, why defend it? It would be silly to suggest that Agamben is responsible for the wave of apparent democratic deconsolidation and lower levels of commitment to liberal and democratic norms throughout the world. But it is logical, and worrying, that we find the two occurring together, and they doubtless exacerbate each other. The rhetoric of the state of exception has joined the chorus of threats to the rule-of-law project, the moral core of a republic.

While, strictly speaking, there may be no genuine example of a legal, moral, or political state of exception in the United States, it remains the case that republics do not last forever and that emergency powers have been commonly present at their death. I have been arguing that one reason for this is the pressure that emergencies place on performance legitimacy. This pressure can, over time, help undermine norm-based legitimacy as well, calling the foundational worth of a liberal republic into question. Institutions and norms exist and take on meaning because we believe in them, because we feel compelled by them on various grounds. So the erosion of a foundational commitment to the liberal republican form of government can render republican norms unenforceable. If a state of exception is a condition in which norms and force are uncoupled, and if the force of norms depends crucially on civic engagement, then we ought to take seriously the disruption of civic engagement as a mechanism through which an actual state of exception in the form of populist tyranny could come about. Perhaps the state of exception is, ultimately, a self-fulfilling prophecy.

Notes

1. These figures come from Google Scholar.
2. Nomi Claire Lazar, *States of Emergency in Liberal Democracies* (Cambridge: Cambridge University Press, 2009).
3. See Joseph Raz, *The Authority of Law: Essays on Law and Morality* (Oxford: Clarendon, 1979), 211.
4. David Dyzenhaus, *The Constitution of Law: Legality in a Time of Emergency* (Cambridge: Cambridge University Press, 2006), 3.
5. Michael Moore, *Placing Blame: A General Theory of the Criminal Law* (Oxford: Oxford University Press, 2010), 719.
6. Michael Walzer, *Just and Unjust Wars* (New York: Basic, 2015), 247.
7. Abraham Lincoln, "Special Session Message," July 4, 1861, *The American Presidency Project*, ed. John Wolley and Gerhard Peters, https://www.presidency.ucsb.edu/documents/special-session-message-5.
8. Garner Anthony, "Martial Law in Hawaii," *California Law Review* 30, no. 4 (May 1942): 371–96.

9. *Ex Parte Spurlock*, US District Court for the District of Hawaii, 66 F. Supp. 997 (D. Haw. 1944), June 23, 1944.

10. Garner Anthony, "Hawaiian Martial Law in the Supreme Court," *Yale Law Journal* 27 (1947): 36–37.

11. *Duncan v. Kahanamoku* and *White v. Steer*, 327 U.S. 304, 90 L. ed. 688.

12. Carl Schmitt, *Die Diktatur* (1921; Berlin: Duncker & Humblot, 1994).

13. On the Roman dictatorship, see Nomi Claire Lazar, "Why Rome Didn't Bark in the Night," *Polity* 45, no. 3 (July 2013): 422–44, and "Making Emergencies Safe for Democracy," *Constellations* 13, no. 4 (December 2006): 506–21. See also Andreas Kalyvas, "The Tyranny of Dictatorship," *Political Theory* 35, no. 4 (2007): 412–42; and Marc de Wilde, "The Dictator's Trust: Regulating and Constraining Emergency Powers in the Roman Republic," *History of Political Thought* 33, no. 4 (2012): 555–77.

14. Carl Schmitt, *Political Theology: Four Chapters on the Concept of Sovereignty (1922)*, trans. George Schwab (Chicago: University of Chicago Press, 2010), 63, 19.

15. Carl Schmitt, *Concept of the Political (1932)*, trans. George Schwab (New Brunswick, NJ: Rutgers University Press, 1976).

16. On this move, see John McCormick, *Carl Schmitt's Critique of Liberalism* (Cambridge: Cambridge University Press, 1999), 121ff.

17. Giorgio Agamben, *Homo Sacer: Sovereign Power and Bare Life,* trans. Daniel Heller-Roazen (Stanford, CA: Stanford University Press, 1998), 115, 32 (quote).

18. See Lazar, *States of Emergency in Liberal Democracies.*

19. See the argument in David Bates, *States of War* (New York: Columbia University Press, 2011).

20. Kent Roach, "The Law Working Itself Pure?," in *Guantánamo and Beyond,* ed. Fionnuala Ní Aoláin and Oren Gross (Cambridge: Cambridge University Press, 2013), 201–24.

21. On prerogative power, see Clement Fatovic and Benjamin A. Kleinerman, eds., *Extra-Legal Power and Legitimacy Perspectives on Prerogative* (Oxford: Oxford University Press, 2013). On police power, see William Novak, *The People's Welfare* (Chapel Hill: University of North Carolina Press, 2000); and Ernst Freund, *Police Power, Public Policy, and Constitutional Rights* (Chicago: Callaghan, 1904).

22. Dianne Marie Amann, "Abu Ghraib," *University of Pennsylvania Law Review* 153, no. 6 (2005): 2085–2141.

23. Agamben, *Homo Sacer,* 176.

24. Amann, "Abu Ghraib," 2096ff.

25. Carol Rosenberg, "FOIA Suit Reveals Guantánamo's 'Indefinite Detainees,'" *Miami Herald,* June 17, 2013, https://www.miamiherald.com/news/nation-world/world/americas/article1952557.html.

26. *Hamdi v. Rumsfeld,* 124 S. Ct. 2633 (2004).

27. *Hamdan v. Rumsfeld,* 344 F. Supp. 2d 152, 162, 165 (2004).

28. By *robustly normative,* I mean to exclude forms of rule *by* law, such as Jim Crow, that are not genuinely committed to fundamental principles of equal protection.

29. Clement Fatovic, *Outside the Law* (Baltimore: Johns Hopkins University Press, 2009), 208ff.

30. Dave Sherwood and Colleen Jenkins, "Nurse Kaci Hickox and State of Maine Settle Quarantine Lawsuit," *Scientific American*, November 3, 2014, https://www.scientificamerican.com/article/nurse-kaci-hickox-and-state-of-maine-settle-quarantine-lawsuit.

31. See Marc Santora, "New Jersey Accepts Rights for People in Quarantine to End Ebola Suit," *New York Times*, July 27, 2017.

32. Niccolò Machiavelli, *The Discourses*, trans. Nathan Tarcov and Harvey Mansfield (Chicago: University of Chicago Press, 1998), bk. 1, chap. 34.

33. This account of the two wells of legitimacy summarizes the more extensive argument in Nomi Claire Lazar, *Out of Joint: Power, Crisis, and the Rhetoric of Time* (New Haven, CT: Yale University Press, 2019).

34. It is well worth listening to the full exchange, provided by the Canadian Broadcasting Corporation archive. In hindsight it is extraordinary, the rule-of-law project acted out: https://www.youtube.com/watch?v=-bCxp9JYdOQ.

2 Negotiating the Rule of Law: Dilemmas of Security and Liberty Revisited

Ewa Atanassow and Ira Katznelson

"Many things there are," wrote John Locke in *The Second Treatise*'s chapter on prerogative power, "which the law can by no means provide for; and those must necessarily be left to the discretion of him that has the executive power in his hands, to be ordered by him as the public good and advantage shall require . . . without the prescription of the law, and sometimes even against it."[1] In defense of the Constitution of 1787 and its proposal for a strong executive, Alexander Hamilton similarly averred: "The circumstances that endanger the safety of nations are infinite, and for this reason no constitutional shackles can wisely be imposed on the power to which the care of it is committed."[2]

These assertive statements provoke questions about the capacity of liberal political orders to grapple with emergencies and be true to their rights-based limited government and constitutional orientation. Securing the liberty of their people requires two forms of protection: against foes who wish to defeat, displace, or distort these regimes, and against policy actions that undermine liberalism's core concepts of government by consent, individual and public rights, pluralism of ideas, political representation, and, the premise of these values, the rule of law. The puzzle of how to navigate both imperatives proved persistent throughout the history of the United States, the liberal democracy on which we primarily focus.

Certainly, this conundrum marked the early republic, whose exigencies included the Shays Rebellion, an armed revolt in Massachusetts in 1786 and 1787, the Alien and Sedition Acts of 1798, the War of 1812, a wide array of Indian wars, slave uprisings, and the Mexican-American War from 1846 to 1848. The Civil War, calling the integrity of the republic into question, then raised fundamental and profound tests for order and liberty.

The emergency question took on ever more urgent form during and after the First World War. Emblematically and influentially, Carl Schmitt, the German jurist, later a key legal figure in the Third Reich, set many of the terms for subsequent debates. Questioning the capacities of liberal regimes to deal with emergencies, he argued that their penchant for legalism was politically crippling. Missing the hard-kernel truths of state sovereignty, parliamentary democracy, for Schmitt, hamstrings necessary state action because of its inherent qualities of division, corruption, and absence of a unifying public interest.

The United States soon faced unprecedented challenges from dictatorships claiming to be superior democracies. Rejecting the separation of state and society, bypassing pluralist representative government, and asserting legitimacy by means of vanguard parties professing to express the ethical and political unity of the people, these antiliberal regimes characterized their adversaries as effete and incapable. Alongside the trials of economic crisis, rising totalitarianism, and world war, antiliberal theorists alleged that in the conditions of modern mass democracy liberal societies had become unable to respond to emergency circumstances effectively.

With the abilities of liberal democracy radically put in question in theory and practice, an erudite group of American thinkers sought to design means to confront deep exigencies within the framework of liberal procedures and protections. Writing after the Bolshevik Revolution, the March on Rome, and the shaky start, then collapse, of the Weimar Republic, their effort to provide effective intellectual and institutional foundations for political liberalism is yet to be matched in intellectual passion and power.

The central participants in this effort to buttress liberal democracy all knew and were exercised by Schmitt's writings and by the wider array of fascist and Bolshevik critiques. Led by such eminent scholars as the Leipzig-born Carl Friedrich (who had been taught by Schmitt and, at first, been drawn to his ideas), Frederick Mundell Watkins (Friedrich's graduate student at Harvard), and Columbia University's Lindsay Rogers, this collective rejoinder to the antiliberal critics culminated with the 1948 publication of *Constitutional Dictatorship* by Cornell's Clinton Rossiter, a book that originated as a Princeton doctoral thesis in political science. For these Americans, the central task of robust government at times of emergency is to find means to safeguard the liberal constitutional order even as they temporarily depart from ordinary rules and practices.

Placing problems of emergency and exception in the United States within a comparative consideration of Germany, Britain, and France, Rossiter's *Constitutional Dictatorship* opened with three italicized claims. The first observed how "the complex system of government of the democratic, constitutional state is essentially designed to function under normal, peaceful conditions, and is often unequal to the exigencies of a great national crisis." The second avowed that "in time of crisis a democratic, constitutional government must be temporarily altered to whatever degree is necessary to overcome the peril and restore normal conditions." Third, because of such actions, "the government will have more power and the people fewer rights." This shift is meant to be a necessary but impermanent feature of responses to the emergency. In all, it was this three-part orientation that underpinned the arresting last sentence of the book: "No sacrifice is too great for our democracy, least of all the temporary sacrifice of democracy itself."[3]

Like the other American political analysts who crafted a response to democracy's antiliberal critics, Rossiter was fascinated by the example of the Roman dictatorship, to which he devoted more than half of his book's opening section. Between 501 and 202 BC Rome had witnessed the appointment of seventy-six constitutional dictators, persons granted exceptional powers for a limited period.[4] For Rossiter, this product of "the splendid political genius of the Roman people" remained "invaluable" across the arc of time as "a theoretical standard, as a sort of moral yardstick against which to measure modern institutions of constitutional dictatorship." The model's appealing attributes, he argued, included lasting no longer than six months, being declared and regulated within the constitutional process, and serving to buttress civic virtue as well as legality within a context that Rossiter designated as "a free state blessed by a high constitutional morality."[5]

Republican Rome, however, was not Rossiter's only guidepost. He also was guided by Algernon Sidney's 1680 *Discourses concerning Government*. Sidney advocated the desirability of institutions based on the

Roman model. That set of practices, Sidney explained, had served as a "commission" grounded in the will of the people ultimately to uphold liberty.[6] "I do therefore grant," he wrote, "that a power like to the *dictatorian*, limited in time, circumscribed by law, and kept perpetually under the supreme authority of the people, may, by virtuous and well-disciplined nations, upon some occasions, be prudently granted to a virtuous man," a situation he distinguished from that of "our Author's Monarch, whose Power is in himself, subject to no Law."[7] This set of criteria—transience, lawfulness, and the ultimate supreme authority of the people, not the monarch alone—radically distinguished liberal responses to emergency.

Rossiter understood that to be consistent with liberty a "constitutional dictatorship" system of exceptions must be based on the full constellation of Sidney's conditions: a clearly defined time limit, the rule of law, and virtuous popular sovereignty. What thus came to worry Rossiter was how mid-twentieth-century conditions were making the "limited in time" criterion unlikely, perhaps impossible. He was troubled by their implications for the character and future of constitutional government. Without the temporal stipulation, the laws and mores of liberal democracy would be compromised.

The temporal constraint—the Roman dictator's six-month term of office—had, he appreciated, been "the one important formal limitation" and "the characteristic most clearly distinguishing this dictatorship from all others that have ever existed." This feature went hand in hand with the institution's central motivation, to protect the republican political order and secure its restored operations: "[The dictator's] sacred trust . . . was to maintain the constitutional order, and although to this end he was competent to resort to almost any measure, the Republic which he was chosen to defend could not be altered or subverted."[8]

But what if the dire threat were not temporary? If, as Rossiter emphasized near the close of *Constitutional Dictatorship*, "*[n]o constitutional dictatorship should extend beyond the termination of the crisis for which it was instituted*," what are the implications when emergencies increase in frequency and regularity or come to lack either a prospective or an actual conclusion? In such circumstances, how could an institutional imagination inspired by the Roman example be invented and "successfully used in time of crisis to preserve and advance the cause of liberty?"[9]

This was no distant possibility. Rossiter painfully observed that, in the second half of the 1940s, his country had come to face dramatically altered circumstances: "Dismal and distressing as the prospect may be, it seems probable that in the years to come the American people will be faced with more rather than fewer national emergencies." The penultimate paragraph of *Constitutional Dictatorship* wrestled with this transformation:

> Constitutional dictatorship is today and will continue to be in the stormy years before us, one of the most urgent problems to be solved by the men of the constitutional democracies. It is more than just a problem; it is a compelling and anxious reality. For who in year 1948 would be so blind as to assert that the people of the United States, or any other constitutional democracy, can afford again to be weak and divided and jealous of their elected representatives? The Bomb has settled once and for all the question whether the United States can go back to being what Harold Laski has labeled ... a "negative" state. You can't go home again; the positive state is here to stay, and from now on the accent will be on power, not limitations.[10]

Rossiter's remarkable consideration of constitutional dictatorship thus closed with a profound dilemma. The Roman model taught that exceptions must be short-lived. Yet, under fresh circumstances, they no longer could be transient or interim. In a series of arresting articles published between early 1949 and the close of 1951, Rossiter enlarged his book's closing concerns to the point of ruminating on how the United States could be governed during and after atomic war.[11]

Rossiter underscored that, under the conditions he observed in the late 1940s, constitutional government might be altered as it responds to political and ideological challenges both in war and in peace. Emergencies can be conducive to a process that leads to the development and alteration of the regime, even as it is preserved. The question is not how to prevent change but how to preserve its liberal character and ability to adhere to a constitutional frame.

Seven decades later, we wish to consider the profound challenge discerned by Rossiter: How might constitutional and representative democracies best proceed to stay within a liberal frame while responding to existential threats when the Roman model's and Sidney's temporal condition cannot be realized?

As we pursue this puzzle, we are mindful that it is all too easy to conflate two distinct historical elements: (1) the challenge of exigencies is long-standing, and inherently trying for political liberalism's constitutionalism, rule of law, and insistence on limiting the actions of rulers and (2) the characteristics of our time, which propel distinctive and new challenges. Our aim in this chapter maps onto these features. We wish to ascertain enduring dilemmas and survey the repertoire of solutions elaborated by the liberal tradition, and we should like to think through the implications for present dilemmas and possibilities. Do the tradition's examples and lore help us respond to contemporary challenges and consider responses to the growing zone of security exceptions?[12]

So doing, we are guided, as many before us have been, by the "commission" model that Sidney advanced and by the conditions for its success that he designated. We thus are particularly concerned with how, dating from the mid-1940s, such large-scale developments as atomic weapons, the Cold War, and nonstate terrorism have provided a context, moving from frequency to permanence, that has generated an expanding arena of enduring exceptions, features that Rossiter was among the first to recognize.

If we cannot avoid the zone designated by exception, we reject any leap that identified an inherent or necessary state of exception that negates political liberalism. We can observe instructive refusals to make such a move in the work of the larger intellectual and policy movement of which Rossiter was a part, which stood on the shoulders of the older liberal tradition. This robust American rejoinder to Carl Schmitt and other antiliberal thinkers recommended the expansion of state capacity and the abrogation of the separation of powers through law and liberal procedures only for a limited time, with the purpose of protecting the liberal political order.

We proceed in sections 1 and 2 by exploring the tradition's understanding of and creative solutions to problems of exigency and emergency. By offering a glimpse into the length and diversity of political liberalism, our purpose is less to champion past proposals and solutions than to put institutional imagination on display. We summon past thought and practice to guide understanding of liberalism's long-standing and present dilemmas and galvanize ideas about responses to the contemporary pressures identified in section 3. There, we observe how traditional challenges have accelerated and concentrated since the 1940s without the comforts of temporary existence. We close, in section 4, with proposals for initiatives that might help us cope.

1. Exigencies, Emergencies, and Liberal Exceptions

From liberalism's founding moments, thinkers we have come to designate as liberal placed questions of menace and regime preservation front and center. Their writings were complex and varied as they wrestled with the wish to construct a government of limits and rights that nonetheless facilitated the abilities of rulers to confront danger. The leading example is John Locke's consideration of this sharp conundrum in the *Second Treatise on Government*, a foundational statement of liberal constitutionalism and a significant blueprint for America's founding.

Locke's treatise elevates the rule of law as the *sine qua non* of a well-framed government and identifies the legislature and political representation as the locus of legitimacy and policy decisions while reserving ultimate sovereignty to the people. Accompanying this analysis is a vexing chapter on prerogative powers, a charter for exceptions. Stating the inherent limitations of any legal framework and of the lawmaking body itself when situations demand resolution and speed, it points to the "many things . . . that the law can by no means provide for." Discretionary executive power is required. In Locke's famous formulation: "This power to act according to discretion, for the public good, without the prescription of the law, and sometimes even against it, is that which is called prerogative."[13]

If justified by extreme peril, prerogative power, Locke was quick to insist, must not be arbitrary and must be limited in time, in play only until the legislature can resume its functions. Moreover, executive power to act outside ordinary procedures is both validated and constrained by principles that proclaim the public good and the preservation of society as the supreme law. Ultimately, if the crown violates these strictures, the people have the right to rebel, the final check on predatory rule. For Locke, the ultimate guarantor of the constitutional order is popular sovereignty. Like later liberals, he understood that effective constraint on prerogative power and the stability of a constitutional regime vitally depend on the presence not only of prudent statesmen and conscientious officials but also of vigilant citizens who make judgments concerning the proper exercise of political power under conditions of uncertainty.

Even as Locke's *Treatise*, including the right to revolution, inspired America's founders, many were skeptical of his treatment of prerogative powers, particularly its stark exceptional qualities. The Anti-Federalists were keen to construct a political order without exceptions. Thomas Jefferson sought to limit the range of exceptions to actual times of war, not to a broader range of possibilities. James Madison, who was critical of Locke's limitations on legislative power in emergencies, declared: "The chapter on prerogative, shews how much the reason of the philosopher was clouded by the royalism of the Englishman."[14] Even Alexander

Hamilton, an advocate of a strong executive, did not wish prerogative power to be constrained only by virtue and the right to rebel. Starting from explicitly republican premises, the America founders all sought, even while disagreeing about constitutional details and meanings, to identify institutional solutions, including means to constitutionalize executive power more systematically than Locke had proposed.[15]

The Framers understood that the problem of emergency was far from abstract. The young United States faced recurring threats to its safety from global geopolitics, Native Americans, and internal insurrections by both white citizens and slaves. To "meet the exigencies of the Union" was, in Hamilton's view, among "the principal purposes" that necessitated the Founding and its new constitution.[16]

Thus Hamilton and his *Federalist* coauthors, John Jay and James Madison, called for sweeping federal powers primarily but not wholly within the ambit of the Constitution. Observing that exigencies cannot always be delineated in advance or addressed by regular lawmaking, "Federalist 23" effectively endorsed a form of prerogative power free of "constitutional shackles." Given the infinite variability of circumstances, it insisted: "This power ought to be coextensive with all the possible combinations of such circumstances."[17]

But not without a check on this authority. Recognizing the need for exceptional powers as a stubborn dilemma, Hamilton argued for institutionalizing the means to address this dilemma, by limiting, in one instance, "the appropriations of money for military purposes to the period of two years." Defending a constitutional demand for periodic revision of military expenditures, he highlighted the checks provided by "the spirit of party" and the fear of federal encroachment that would make renewed support for the military a "favorable topic for declamation" and vigorous public debate.[18]

Hamilton stressed more generally the importance of Congress in this domain and repeatedly pointed to legislative consent as precondition for harmonizing state power with legitimacy and governing capacity with freedom. It was Congress, he insisted, that "is the essential, and, after all, the only efficacious security for the rights and privileges of the people, which is attainable in civil society."[19]

Yet, like Locke, Hamilton understood that, just as the parameters of emergency cannot be determined in advance, so the efficacy of institutionalized response would come to depend on situational factors. As executive discretion is contingent and impossible to constrain directly by law, extraordinary executive power must be checked politically both by the other branches of government and by the people.

Federalist solutions, in short, were a combination of institutions and political psychology. Reconciling security and freedom would demand constitutional mechanisms to mobilize and draw on political passions and dynamics. Institutions, the Federalists understood, are not self-sufficient. Concrete policies and outcomes would depend on norms and motivations, both of the people's representatives and of the represented publics, thus on prudence and judgment.

At no point in American history was this dependence more pronounced and more contested than during the presidency of Abraham Lincoln as he navigated the Union's gravest crisis. In Rossiter's view, this presidency was "the paragon of all democratic, constitutional dictatorships," one in which Lincoln assumed, on his own initiative, extraordinary powers, including the suspension of *habeas corpus*.[20]

These capacities Lincoln derived from a broad construction of executive competences and commander-in-chief powers and from unabashed encroachments on Congress, including an eleven-week period in which he governed without the legislature, raising an army and a navy for an undeclared war. Moreover, with the Emancipation Proclamation he also claimed constituent powers and assumed judicial authority. All these were justified *post hoc* before Congress and the people—and so ratified—as instrumental measures necessary to win the war. With appeals to necessity and the gravity of the crisis, Lincoln defended both seizing extraordinary power and exercising it with dubious legality and, on occasion, expressly against the law.

Yet these actions did not illustrate only how, under extraordinary conditions, a constitutional order might need to be suspended in order to preserve it. Crucially, Lincoln used the exceptional circumstances of the conflagration and the "war powers" he believed it gave him as an opportunity to bring the constitutional system closer to its aspirational norms. His purpose was not merely to protect the Constitution but to achieve it.[21]

For all that, Lincoln's emergency politics possessed a clear beginning and an identifiable end. His assertive use of prerogative power had a clear objective and a recognizable time frame. Moreover, after the war's initial eleven weeks, the federal government proceeded largely by doing business as usual, including the congressional elections of 1862 and 1864 and the presidential election of 1864, which put Lincoln's rule and his policies at risk. There was no overarching transfer of powers to the executive from the legislature. Instead, as soon as it was convened, Congress challenged presidential prerogatives and demanded a share in them in that it should authorize most future exercises of exceptional powers.

Along with an "unenthusiastic acquiescence," Congress responded to Lincoln's eleven weeks of dictatorship by forming an investigating commission to inquire into every aspect of the war, setting a vital precedent for the future. Lincoln's presidency further invited and endured vituperative critique from Congress and from the press and American citizens. Notwithstanding a few notable cases, Rossiter notes, "the freedom, indeed, the license of the Northern press, suffered no restriction whatsoever."[22] And the greatest achievement of the war—the abolition of slavery—was not left to stand solely on the basis of a wartime measure but ratified as the Thirteenth Amendment.[23]

Of course, there is much more to be said about the American and, more generally, the long liberal tradition of thinking about governing emergencies. What is clear is that from its beginnings political liberalism has grappled with security. Already in the seventeenth and eighteenth centuries, a central puzzle for realistic liberalism concerning how to secure the state in the world of states without unduly compromising liberty was understood to be fundamentally important for the existence and for the qualities of existence of representative republics. Viewing the problem of emergency as a recurring and inevitable aspect of political life and of sovereign statehood, liberal thinkers and statesmen pointed to the irreducible need for emergency powers and checking institutions and for prudential judgment to guide both. Critics of liberalism, notably Carl Schmitt, believed that liberal constitutionalism was simply technical and legalistic. That charge is incorrect, for political liberalism was from its formation essentially normative and deeply political.

Political liberalism also fashioned diverse institutional solutions that aimed to address inherent tensions and place them within a constitutional framework governed by the rule of law. This long and diverse tradition has experimented with a variety of institutional approaches tailored to circumstances of time and place. As a result, there is a significant repertoire of ideas, impulses, and institutions from which to draw as we consider current conditions.

A core feature of these approaches was their resolute commitment to constitutional arrangements and the rule of law. Their view of how to stay within the confines of liberal law required a sense that key institutional arrangements must be capable of evolving as elements of effective response to exigencies and extraordinary circumstances. The most dramatic changes to constitutional affairs—Emancipation, the New Deal's extension of public authority, and the civil rights revolution—amounting to the re-creation of the Republic, have been based on crucial dramatic changes within the rule of law.[24]

From Locke forward, these designs have been aware of the limits of law and institutional solutions. For all their situational and institutional disagreements, when confronted with the problem of emergency, liberal thinkers have concurred in their ultimate reliance on the people—on attentive citizenry and democratic publics, what Sidney had called "well-disciplined nations." No matter how perfect the institutional design, liberal societies, they recognized, need prudential judgment by leaders and citizens alike. Thus, institutions and policies are to be judged not only by how well they respond to moments of crisis but also by how well they promote virtuous connections of political process and civic culture.

2. *Designing a Commissarial Approach in the 1930s and 1940s*

During the Weimar years and into the Third Reich, it was Carl Schmitt who mounted the most comprehensive analytic and normative assault on the liberal approach to emergencies. Writing in the aftermath of the First World War, this jurist and philosopher argued that constitutional states are unable to grapple with conundrums of security without stepping wholly outside their self-conscious remit. Institutionally as well as ideologically, he considered liberal parliamentary order as ill equipped to deal with the fundamentals of security and sovereignty—a critique that continues to resonate today.[25]

Schmitt's 1921 *Dictatorship* surveyed the institution of the dictator from the Roman paradigm to the emergency provisions of the Weimar constitution. The book's typology distinguished "commissarial" and "sovereign" forms. Exemplified by ancient Rome, the commissarial type is strictly bound by time constraints and carefully defined tasks. It is intended to maintain the existing order. The sovereign form, by contrast, is unlimited in time and boundless in tasks. Rather than preserving, it aims to transform the regime and move history forward by creating a wholly novel form of government.

This analytic distinction was, for Schmitt, also historical. Whereas commissarial dictatorship was a Roman invention, introduced into modern political thought by Machiavelli, the sovereign type, first crystallized in the rule of Oliver Cromwell, issued from the theoretical and practical elaboration of popular sovereignty and its subsequent radicalization in the French and Soviet Revolutions. Propelled by the idea of predestined progress, it represented, as McCormick puts it, "the culmination of the modern historical trend toward totally unrestrained political action."[26]

Both conceptually and historically, the problem of exception, Schmitt argued, had proved "incommensurable" with the rule of law and legal rationalism, which he took to be the essence of liberalism.[27] Because managing an exceptional situation through law usually entails stretching the letter of the law to comprehend cases that are in manifest tension with it, liberal legalism and the very insistence on addressing exigencies through law inevitably eviscerate or hollow out the rule of law. The result is an exercise of arbitrary power under the pretense of legality. Dictatorial powers—at first delegated as commissarial—become sovereign. The regime is transformed from within.

Schmitt thus posed sharp analytic and situational challenges for the generation of Carl Friedrich, Frederick Watkins, and Clinton Rossiter, and also for the present. Continuous emergencies, he had argued, inevitably undermine the liberal order. Commissarial dictatorship, moreover, could no longer succeed because the modern world was different after the political ascendance of radical—especially Soviet—notions of political legitimation.

In the trying circumstances of the 1930s and 1940s, it became imperative for liberals to find answers. As realists reeling from the collapse of the Weimar Republic and the rising tide of totalitarian dictatorships, Friedrich, Watkins, and Rossiter, among other American critics of Schmitt, revisited and elaborated a genuinely liberal approach to emergency that placed responses within the restraining qualities of the rule of law. Their theoretical and policy efforts were self-consciously designed to counter Schmitt's diagnosis of liberalism as incapable. Captured in the title of Rossiter's *Constitutional Dictatorship*, their solution—to theorize a temporary concentration of authority consistent with liberal constitutionalism—was insistently commissarial.

Resurrecting the Roman model, these thinkers explored the character of temporary abrogation, whose central aim would be the protection of the constitutional order itself. This institution could, they believed, be updated and made workable precisely because leaders in liberal democracies were embedded in and answerable to democratic norms and practices. Working with the assumption that a fund of public virtue exists and can be sustained with proper institutions, they believed, crucially, that Algernon's Sidney's conditions—"limited in time, circumscribed by law, and kept perpetually under the supreme authority of the people [in] . . . virtuous and well-disciplined nations"—could be met by modern liberal regimes.

Drawing on the experience of the democracies that fought World War I and on empirical wartime examples of effective government whose powers had been based on temporary assignments to the executive branch by legislatures, these scholars insisted that there must be no departure from the rule of law. Furthermore, they stressed, delegations had to be specific, targeted, and limited in time. Only when such authority existed could exigencies be governed within a liberal frame. Without such an authority, they believed, it would not be possible under conditions of duress to safeguard the standing and rights of citizens, the core intention of the liberal understanding of law. The exception must not become an empty space from which norms are absent.

Cautious optimism characterized this quest. America's theorists of emergency in the 1930s and 1940s understood that Sidney's criteria did not reduce the rule of law simply to the letter but crucially included the spirit of the law, its social meaning and efficacy. Like Sidney, they believed that a commissarial approach comprehends mores, institutional practices, and political culture. To be viable, liberal constitutionalism and any form of constitutional dictatorship must both draw on and quicken this fund of civic spirit. Far from simply legalistic or "technical," as Schmitt had insisted, the liberal approach to emergency relies on a robust public sphere and engaged citizens jealous of their liberties and capable of collective action. For this reason, no simple one-size-fits-all solution could be possible. Commissarial exceptions are always contingent on concrete circumstances, ethical horizons, and political will.

Refusing extralegality as an acceptable orientation, these theorists also rejected patterns of policy that could turn temporary measures into the norm. They proposed to address not just matters of national security but other fear-generating conditions within law-based political processes, chiefly by congressional delegation that helped erect what Rossiter designated as a "positive state." Looking back over the course of the prior two decades and the "startling succession of major emergencies: depression, recession, threat of war, war, inflation, industrial war, and cold war," Rossiter noted the consequence: "an extraordinary expansion of the authority of the national executive in both relative and absolute terms."[28]

This circumstance returned Rossiter to the sweeping puzzle of how to proceed if the Roman and Sidney's temporal condition could no longer be obtained. With temporal limits removed, can liberal norms and values hold in the face of lawmaking that builds exceptions through delegation over time? Under current conditions, is it possible to identify within the ambit of political liberalism effective commissarial alternatives to Schmitt's sovereign dictatorship? This is our central question.

With this history, resources, and guidance, we turn to our own circumstances that badly require institutional and moral means to negotiate dilemmas of liberty and security. None of the solutions of Locke,

Publius, or Lincoln or of the American-based anti-Schmittians were simply satisfactory or able on their own to guarantee the security of and perpetuate the liberal regime. As Sidney's multiple criteria indicate, context matters, as do political actors and publics. What is more, the temporal frame of clear beginning and end was a condition for sustaining constitutional law and a supportive ethos. What happens when this frame no longer exists?

3. Conditions Transformed

Until the mid-twentieth century, liberal thinkers and policy makers shared the Roman model's temporal premise that, even when recurring, emergencies were marked by a beginning and an end. Moreover, as Bernard Manin has underscored, in coping with emergencies, liberals long thought that "liberty may be restricted only for the sake of liberty, not just for the sake of just any kind of common good."[29]

With emergency powers limited in time and content, the repertoire developed by political liberals assumed conditions in which a combination of specification in advance, policy regulation, and post hoc appraisal was thought to be adequate to the purpose. Security measures, including the form of constitutional dictatorship later theorized by Friedrich, Watkins, and Rossiter, could be made compatible with core liberal values, especially the rule of law.[30]

During World War I, Woodrow Wilson became the first president to issue a national emergency proclamation, but it was revoked by statute once the war concluded. With national mobilization, Congress passed laws giving Wilson vast powers over transportation (the Shipping Act of 1916), arms production (the National Defense Act of 1916), private property (the Army Appropriations Act of 1916), the manufacturing and distribution of war necessities (the Lever Act of 1917), and emergency powers to coordinate the federal government (the Overman Act of 1918). As the war closed and the crisis ended, according to Tyles Curley, "the Wilson Administration dismantled the mobilization institutional machinery and wartime dictatorial authorities." The nation's government, Lindsay Rogers observed, "took off its war harness very quickly."[31]

The transformation in conditions did not happen all at once. For Americans, who long had thought that distance from Europe and Asia ensured fundamental security, three developments that came to a head in the 1940s generated a new, deep, and enduring sense of anxiety: a remarkable intensification of violence, the vulnerability of civilians, and the growing opacity of the start and end of emergencies. In World

War II, beyond the horror of concentration camps, more deaths were suffered by civilians than by soldiers. The war culminated in atomic weapons, which, by decade's end, were in Soviet as well as American hands in the context of a threatening superpower conflict. Generating fears of permanent emergency, these developments prompted a significant increase in the quantity and quality of the federal government's security-related actions. These initiatives led to what Rossiter termed an "extraordinary expansion in the authority of the national executive, in both relative and absolute terms," in the face of what seemed like danger without end.[32]

By the early 1950s, it had become clear that "a significant feature of American government during the last fifteen years is the expansion of governmental activity on the basis of emergency,"[33] a change first made dramatically intelligible when President Roosevelt declared a "limited national emergency" on September 8, 1939, a week after the Nazi invasion of Poland, which he extended to "unlimited" status on May 27, 1941, more than six months before Pearl Harbor. These peacetime invocations of presidential power were based on no explicit constitutional provisions and on no congressional delegation. During the war, executive action was placed on a new plane by the passage of war powers acts and other statutes applicable in times of emergency.[34] The Second War Powers Act, legislated in 1942, set the scope and tone by expanding presidential authority "in such manner upon such conditions and to such extent as **he shall deem necessary** in the public interest and to promote the national defense."[35]

On the eve of World War II, the political scientist Lindsay Rogers projected that, "when crisis comes" and "when action must be speedy and drastic, when a wrong decision may be better than no decision at all, the scales always oscillate violently in the direction of the executive." In such situations, he predicted, Congress "must grant enormous powers to the executive."[36]

Clinton Rossiter observed that, after World War I and following a period of intense constitutional dictatorship, normal procedures completely returned in Britain, France, and the United States. But no longer. The 1940 forecast of Harold Lasswell that "we are moving toward a world of 'garrison states'—a world in which the specialists on violence are the most powerful group in society" seemed confirmed, including in the globe's leading liberal democracy. Eight years before he warned Americans about the "grave implications" and "unwarranted influence" of the postwar national security state, Dwight Eisenhower spoke in his January 1953 inaugural address of "freedom . . . pitted against slavery;

lightness against the dark," of "shadows of the night" closing in, while warning how "science seems ready to confer upon us, as its final gift, the power to erase human life from this planet."[37] The most basic exigency had become eternal.

With the combination of Cold War and atomic weapons that provided the basis for this talk, Congress fashioned new delegations, producing what a contemporary, the presidential scholar Albert Sturm, called "a cornucopia of legal authority for the Chief Executive." The result was a situation in which, increasingly, the executive authority to cope with persisting emergencies was placed in the hands of the president. Unlike Rome's dictators, who could neither announce nor extend the period of exception, American presidents began to amass unprecedented capacities to enhance national security. And, whereas earlier such grants, as with the emergency Price Control Act of 1942 and the War Labor Disputes Act of 1943, had termination dates, often extended, many of the new delegations possessed no sunset provisions. After the war, only some of the president's wartime powers were recaptured, and it quickly became clear that "many laws will remain on the statute books permanently," as Sturm observed at the time, "to provide a reserve for future exigencies."[38]

The first enduring example of such legislation was the Atomic Energy Act of 1946—"for the development and control of atomic energy" in the aftermath of Hiroshima and Nagasaki—which placed all fissionable material, domestic as well as military, in the hands of the president and the Atomic Energy Commission, composed of five members that the president would appoint. No private patents would be permitted. "Provision after provision," complained Clare Booth Luce, then a Republican congresswoman from Connecticut, "muzzles free competition and depresses incentive and production in all mining, industrial, patent, and invention fields which impinge at any point on the manufacture of nuclear energy." This legislation, especially for market-oriented conservatives, nevertheless gained the status of a necessary exception. "The bill is full of provisions," noted Senator Eugene Millikin of Colorado, "which I could not subscribe to in any other connection."[39]

This exception zone soon expanded. The 1949 amendments to the National Security Act of 1947 exempted the CIA from ordinary congressional reporting responsibilities for its expenditures and activities. Concerned with subversion, the Internal Security Act of 1950 (passed by a 70–7 margin in the Senate and a 324–8 vote in the House, notwithstanding President Truman's veto on constitutional grounds) created, for the first time, a group of citizens to be treated distinctively with regard to their freedom of association and speech by making it illegal to fail to disclose membership in a Communist organization when working for the government, to contribute funds to such organizations, and to apply for, renew, or use a passport and broadcast or use the mails without making an explicit statement about Communist Party membership. The law required all Communist and Communist-front organizations to register with the federal government and established a subversive activities control board to enforce the act. "Our Constitution is not so weak," the bill's sponsor, Senator Pat McCarran, a Nevada Democrat, insisted, "that it denies us the power and authority to safeguard it."[40] Once-protected speech was relabeled as sedition; once-protected silence became mandatory speech.

So began a long history, now extending more than seven decades, of lawmaking for permanent exceptions regarding atomic weapons, geopolitics, and internal security. By proclamation or delegation, power was centralized in the executive, Congress became secondary with limited oversight, courts in the main were bypassed, and the number of persons involved in making key decisions was sharply restricted, as were open debate and transparency. Citizens became more visible to government through surveillance, and the nation's state became less evident and understandable to citizens through secrecy and the absence of disclosure. And emergency laws tended to become baselines for new laws and new emergency declarations when future threats appear.

America's debacle in the Vietnam War generated pushback marked by congressional hearings and attempts to recoup legislative capacity regarding emergencies. This effort to restore the core features of the liberal tradition was significant. It included the National Emergencies Act of 1976, which terminated long-standing declared emergencies, including the one declared at the start of the Korean War by President Truman in 1950, insisted that future declarations be limited in time, and offered means for Congress to negate future executive declarations by way of a legislative veto. The Foreign Intelligence Surveillance Act of 1978 (FISA) provided procedures for judicial and congressional oversight over foreign intelligence surveillance and created the Foreign Intelligence Surveillance Court to hold closed ex parte sessions to consider issuing warrants under FISA.

The moment passed. The Supreme Court ruled in 1983 that the legislative veto is unconstitutional. Congress soon renewed the practice of deferring to the president. In 1994, it passed the Communications Assistance for Law Enforcement Act, which authorized national, state, and local police forces to conduct electronic surveillance by requiring that telecommunications companies and manufacturers of equipment facilitate these activities. Further, no fewer than twenty-three targeted executive declarations of emergency were promulgated in the quarter century before the terror attacks of 9/11. These actions, the Congressional Research Service had reported in 1990, "increasingly rooted in statutory law," permitted presidents to seize property, organize and control the means of production, assign military forces abroad, institute martial law, oversee all transportation and communication, regulate the operation of private enterprise, restrict travel, and, in a variety of ways, control the lives of US citizens.[41]

Ever since the attacks on the World Trade Center and the Pentagon, the United States has been under a state of national emergency. President Bush's September 14 "Declaration of National Emergency by Reason of Certain Terrorist Attacks" was followed on September 23 by an emergency order "Blocking Property and Prohibiting Transactions with Persons Who Commit, Threaten to Commit, or Support Terrorism." Subsequently, a massive array of instruments of surveillance and security has been deployed through statutes and orders by Presidents Bush, Obama, and Trump. As Judge Richard Posner noted as early as 2006, counterterrorist measures had already included

> the attempt to deny the right of *habeas corpus* to captured terrorist suspects; the interception of phone calls and other electronic communications, such as emails, of U.S. citizens by the National Security Agency outside the limits set by the Foreign Intelligence Surveillance Act; ambitious data-mining projects such as the military's Able Danger project; demands by the FBI under section 215 of PATRIOT Act for records of library borrowings; monitoring of the constitutionally protected speech of radical imams; torture or quasi-torture of terrorist suspects, including U.S. citizens apprehended in the United States rather than on a foreign field of combat such as Afghanistan or Iraq.[42]

Such exceptions have been grounded in executive orders on Detention (2001), *Habeas Corpus* (2001), Terror Detainee Legal Status (2002), Lawful Interrogations (2009), Applicability of Criminal Laws (2010), Periodic Review of Detainees (2011), Border Security and Immigration Enforcement Improvements (2017), Protecting the Nation from Foreign Terrorist Entry into the United States (2017), and Protecting America through Lawful Detention of Terrorists (2018). At a time when partisan polarization is widely thought to be the cause of reduced legislative productivity, Congress has been uncommonly active in passing, among others, the Patriot Act (2001), the Homeland Security Act (2002), the Intelligence Reform and Prevention of Security Act (2004), the Protect America Act (2007), the FISA Amendments Act (2008), the Patriot Sunsets Extension Act (2011), and the USA Freedom Act (2015).[43]

In addition to these, instruments of exception were promulgated without proclamation or legislation. Perhaps most notable was the secret authorization by President Bush of the NSA to eavesdrop on telephone conversations within the United States both on Americans and on others inside the country without court-approved warrants in what the NSA called a "special collections program." Once begun, there was almost no oversight outside the NSA as the agency could pick targets not only without court endorsement but also without agreement by the Department of Justice or other parts of the administration.[44] Later, after the success in killing Osama bin Laden, the SEAL team that carried out the action was converted into "a global manhunting machine" with limited outside oversight.[45]

These policies have cumulatively narrowed legislative power, widened executive prerogatives, and shrunk the secure range of rights possessed by citizens and foreign persons. One does not have to embrace Schmitt's historical and conceptual account to note how conditions of exception have become wider in scope, more heterogeneous in character, and ever more routine and seemingly durable features of liberal democracies. What is new, Samuel Issacharoff has argued, is that after 9/11 the actions of the federal government were justified by an executive claim of powers that are unaccountable and exclusive.[46] Within a week of the attacks, Congress authorized President Bush, in an uncommonly broad delegation, to "use all necessary and appropriate force against those nations, organizations, or persons he determines planned, authorized, committed, or aided the terrorist attacks that occurred on September 11, 2001, or harbored such organizations or persons, in order to prevent any future acts of international terrorism against the United States by such nations, organizations or persons."[47]

Yet, immediately after passage, Bush's in-house lawyer, John Yoo, elaborated a theory that the Constitution had created an executive with extraordinary powers to meet threats of national survival and insisted that this authorization had been superfluous. Writing that "the power to initiate military hostilities, particularly in response to the threat of an armed attack, rests exclusively with the President," he concluded:

"Congress's support for the President's power suggests no limits on the Executive's judgment whether to use military force in response to the national emergency."[48]

To be sure, President Obama did not base his actions on this approach to the separation of powers, which allowed presidents alone to determine when national emergencies exist, how to respond with force, surveillance, torture, unlimited detention, or military tribunals, and whether to set aside laws such as criminal codes in an open-ended manner. Rather, he relied on congressional authorization and delegation in areas that included bulk data collection and the targeted killing of the American citizen and terrorist preacher Anwar al-Awlaki, in Yemen, carried out by a drone strike on September 30, 2011. More recently, President Trump has returned to the unitary executive view.[49]

The liberal centerpiece of law as legislated, implemented, and enforced and of rights that are intended to offer protection against encroachments on basic freedoms is a system, as Carl Friedrich wrote, of "regularized restraint."[50] It is just these arrangements that were transformed by responses to the permanence—not just the recurrence—of emergency. And it was this set of developments that underpinned Giorgio Agamben's elaboration and deepening of Schmitt's critique of liberal capacities. In his 2005 *State of Exception*, Agamben argued that the post-9/11 Bush administration's theory and practice promised so great an expansion to the zone of exception that liberal law itself might become lifeless.[51] Must we be content in our age of emergency with this new normal in which the exception drives the rule?

4. Governing Emergency

As Congress was preparing to approve the Alien and Sedition Acts, James Madison ruminated in a May 13, 1798, letter to Thomas Jefferson: "Perhaps it is a universal truth that the loss of liberty at home is to be charged to provisions against danger, real or pretended, from abroad."[52] This conundrum has sharpened. Some security threats may be pretended, but there can be no doubt about the realities of atomic weapons and active terrorism. Within shifts to the policy landscape, and inside an atmosphere of confusion and often visceral fear, it has become ever more urgent to mount a coherent response by considering how to strengthen the liberal repertoire and discern what Stephen Holmes has designated as "steadying guidelines."[53] Although the puzzles posed by previous generations of liberal thinkers remain and we stand to learn from their conceptual and practical proposals, today's challenges to liberal constitutionalism are not simply resolvable by pointing to, let alone imitating, past solutions. Fresh circumstances have placed great pressure on constitutional constraints, the edges of law, and the distinction between the temporary and the permanent.

We urgently need fresh thought and policy prescriptions to discern how—indeed if—it might be possible, as Bruce Ackerman proposed, to design a doctrine "that allows short-term emergency measures but draws the line against permanent restrictions."[54] In our present context, we are challenged to discern norms that can guide institutional arrangements to reinforce liberal imperatives and compensate, at least in part, for the erosion of once-clearer boundaries and guidelines.

The questions are difficult. Which ideas and practices (i.e., which sets of rules) might best deploy constitutionalism, law, mechanisms of accountability, and such values as due process to serve security and liberty simultaneously without undermining fundamental liberal norms or inhibiting means of learning and correction? Can coordination and remedies be achieved effectively without departing from political liberalism's insistence that rulers give reasons, that decisions be as transparent as possible, and that judgments be rendered as to whether the public good has been and indeed is being served? Can the process of making choices and looking back on those decisions be made consistent with public liberties that give citizens the capacity to examine and critique their leaders? At stake is what Holmes calls "a democratic culture of justification," a central feature of liberal democracies that defines "the difference between a constitutional executive and an absolute monarch": "[T]he former must give reasons for his actions, while the latter can simply announce *tel est mon Plaisir*."[55] Must we abandon the undergirding commissarial ideas of Rossiter and the other American critics of Schmitt in favor of unending sovereign exceptionalism, as Agamben thought had become the case already? How might we work concretely to renew the combination of elements Algernon Sidney considered to be essential? How might we find guidance for political liberalism in often impossibly complex circumstances with difficult-to-predict consequences?

Gaining purchase on these questions requires that we come to terms with the inadequacy of the ordinary mechanisms of rights and responsibility that keep leaders in check in liberal democracies: elections, debate, opinion, interest groups, and social movements. A mix of secrecy and a willingness to step outside the bounds of the normal constitutional order in the quest for security—what Jack Goldsmith has called "secret executive branch interpretation of law"[56]—has placed crucial limitations on these familiar instruments.

The quest for standards to navigate the boundary of the constitutional order and emergency power has a long-standing lineage within liberal thought. "Constitutions," for liberals, "should limit and channel power and at the same time should somehow permit and foster those actions required to achieve the common good, actions that are sometimes quite different from what ordinary times require."[57]

In considering institutional innovations and policy options, we suggest—on the basis of the resources offered by this tradition—four guidelines, each of which continues to possess considerable relevance: (1) Whenever possible, a distinction between temporary action and permanent policy should be insisted on. (2) Neither individual leaders nor institutions should be exempt from continuous oversight. (3) Decisions taken to anticipate and respond to security exigencies should be governed by prudential standards and definitions of necessity. (4) No less important are opportunities for retrospective judgment and appraisal after the fact.

The implications require extended discussion, deliberation, and debate. But what seems clear is that, persisting threats notwithstanding, political actors can continue to recognize the division through the requirement that key legislative acts and delegations to the executive be fixed in time and subject to formal renewal. Such is the case, hardwired in the Constitution, for military expenditures that cannot be authorized and appropriated for more than two years. When legislation characterized by significant delegation has sunset provisions unless renewed, the possibility of debates about necessity and scope in Washington and more broadly by the public become real.

Policies of exception must not portend invisibility or isolation from democratic practices. To the contrary, each branch of government—judicial, legislative, and the executive itself—must have opportunities for information sharing, judgments, and supervision in real time. This desideratum insists on contemporaneous oversight in the tradition of the separation of powers at the heart of America's constitutional design for government that is not predatory.

Further, as the German émigré scholar Francis Lieber (who advised President Lincoln during the Civil War) argued, emergency actions by the government should be appraised by what he called a "reasonable person standard." When necessity is being appraised, he argued, "reason and common sense must approve the particular act," and, "if these conditions are not fulfilled, the act becomes unlawful."[58] Just such a standard has long been part of a reasonableness test in constitutional jurisprudence concerned with the balance between Fourth Amendment protections of privacy rights and the public interest in providing national security.[59]

Perhaps most important, a process of calm learning and evaluation, tied to sanctions when liberal norms have been violated, is particularly valuable for political regimes committed to democratic deliberation and collective choice. Even Judge Posner—who has endorsed extralegal actions, including torture—is open to retrospective investigations, legal as well as political, that assess a price for having stepped outside the rule of law.[60]

This is how Jefferson saw things. On September 14, 1810, he was asked by John B. Colvin: "Are there not periods when, in free governments, it is necessary for officers in responsible stations to exercise an authority beyond the law—and, was not the time of [Aaron] Burr's treason such a period?" "The question you propose," Jefferson replied six days later, "[as to] whether circumstances do not sometimes occur which make it a duty in officers of high trust to assume authorities beyond the law, is easy of solution in principle, but sometimes embarrassing in practice." Noting examples of when "overleaping the law is of greater evil than a strict adherence to its imperfect provisions," he also affirmed that leaders have a "higher obligation . . . of saving our country when in danger." Given this inherent tension, he stipulated, "the officer who is called to act on this superior ground, does indeed risk himself on the justice of the controlling powers of the Constitution." Incurring this risk must go hand in hand with the power of decision. "The line of discrimination between cases may be difficult," he continued, "but the good officer is bound to draw it at his peril, and throw himself on the justice of the country and rectitude of his motives."[61]

In this respect, certainly as compared to Great Britain, the institutional complex of the United States is deficient. The closest American analogue is the FISA Court, but its various limitations, including its secrecy, are legion.[62] By contrast, the constellations of institutions in Great Britain navigate the terrain far from perfectly but with more fluidity and creativity.

The most traditional institution, quite similar in many ways to congressional committees on intelligence matters, is Parliament's Intelligence and Security Committee (ISC), which, like its American counterparts, questions security and intelligence analysts in private, tends to defer to government, identifies closely with the security agencies, and issues only heavily redacted public reports. Notwithstanding, it has on occasion questioned the heads of the security services in public, has defended privacy concerns regarding bulk surveillance, and has reported on the country's drone strikes.[63]

Unlike the United States, Britain possesses a tradition of public inquiries in matters of national security that deserves broader consideration. A recent example is the Iraq Inquiry, led by Sir John Chilcot, whose voluminous 2016 report recapitulated an investigation that lasted some seven years.[64] More original, and demanding close study, is an uncommon, indeed globally unique institution, the Investigatory Powers Tribunal (IPT), a ten-member body that has been in existence since 2000, created by the Regulation of Investigatory Powers Act.[65] Complaints can be made to the IPT by members of the public and NGOs about interception and surveillance by the police or other public authorities or about any conduct by the security agencies. "Particularly in cases brought by NGOs," Sir Michael Burton, the IPT's president, has written,

> it has now become the practice of the Tribunal to hold open hearings, with full open argument, with eminent counsel, expert in Human Rights law appearing before us. We are no longer described as "Britain's most secret court." We have developed this procedure in national security cases of assuming the facts in favour of the claimant. A claimant (including an NGO) is entitled to bring a claim without proof of what he alleges, simply on the basis of reasonable suspicion, and the facts are assumed in his favour, and the Tribunal then considers whether on those assumptions the conduct complained of is lawful.

After open hearings, the IPT reports its decision in an open judgment, and "the legal conclusion can then be applied to the actual facts." This, Burton continued, "gives us a considerable advantage over the statutory Commissioners and the Parliamentary Committee (ISC), because we can hear adversarial argument, balancing the public need for security against the need for public scrutiny, the interests of privacy and free speech." In all, there have been quite dramatic outcomes, leading to rebukes of the government and to "public disclosure of much which was previously closed, particularly the rules and procedures under which the Agencies operated," without, the IPT and the government believe, sacrifices to national security.[66]

There is, however, no one-size-fits-all solution to governing emergency in a liberal frame. Instituting similar procedures in the United States or in other liberal polities would pose distinct legal and political challenges. Likewise, policy responses to present conditions will be variously inflected by expectations, values, and dispositions about the order of political priorities. Navigating tensions between security and freedom is a process, not a matter that can be decisively resolved.

Thus for a liberal state the end of governing exigency cannot be a fail-proof environment from which risk and uncertainty—and therewith liberty—are forever banished. The goal, we suggest, should be to achieve and maintain a resilient framework within which the inherent conundrums of liberty and security can be negotiated and allayed. Only by this pursuit can a commissarial solution appropriate to the time and in accord with Algernon Sidney's conditions be pursued. What we insist is that liberal polities do in fact possess the conceptual and institutional resources to build such a framework by strengthening existing mechanisms of supervision and control and creating new means that build on appealing examples drawn from centuries of liberal thought and practice. On this basis, we submit, there are grounds for cautious optimism.

Notes

1. John Locke, *Second Treatise of Government*, in *Two Treatises of Government*, ed. Peter Laslett (Cambridge: Cambridge University Press, 1990), 374–75 (secs. 159–60).

2. *The Federalist*, ed. George W. Carey and James McClellan (Indianapolis: Liberty Fund, 2001), "Federalist 23."

3. Clinton Rossiter, *Constitutional Dictatorship: Crisis Government in the Modern Democracies* (Princeton, NJ: Princeton University Press, 1948), 5, 314.

4. For an overview, see Nomi Claire Lazar, "Prerogative Power in Rome," in *Extra-Legal Power and Legitimacy: Perspectives on Prerogative*, ed. Clement Fatovic and Benjamin A. Kleinerman (New York: Oxford University Press, 2013), 27–49.

5. Rossiter, *Constitutional Dictatorship*, 15, 28.

6. This formulation significantly predates and anticipates Carl Schmitt's distinction, discussed below, between commissarial and sovereign forms of dictatorship.

7. Algernon Sidney, *Discourses concerning Government* (Indianapolis: Liberty Fund, 1996), 158. See also Rossiter, *Constitutional Dictatorship*, 16.

8. Rossiter, *Constitutional Dictatorship*, 23. "However, there is one feature of constitutional dictatorship which sets it off most sharply from the Hitler variety: it is temporary and self-destructive." Ibid., 8.

9. Rossiter, *Constitutional Dictatorship*, 306, 28.

10. Rossiter, *Constitutional Dictatorship*, 306, 314.

11. See Clinton L. Rossiter, "The President and Labor Disputes," *Journal of Politics* 11 (February 1949): 93–120, "Constitutional Dictatorship in the Atomic Age," *Review of Politics* 11 (October 1949): 395–418, "What of Congress in Atomic War?," *Western Political Quarterly* 3 (December 1950): 602–6, and "War, Depression, and the Presidency," *Social Research* 17 (December 1950): 417–40. At just this moment, other leading political scientists—notably Harold Lasswell and Robert Dahl—were likewise taking note of a garrison zone of national security and atomic weapons that would stretch far into the future. See Harold D. Lasswell, "The Garrison State," *American Journal of Sociology* 46 (January 1941): 455–68, "Does the Garrison State Threaten Civil Rights?,"

Annals of the American Academy of Political and Social Science 275 (May 1951): 111–16, and *National Security and Individual Freedom* (New York: McGraw-Hill, 1950); and Robert A. Dahl, "Atomic Energy and the Democratic Process," *Annals of the American Academy of Political and Social Science* 290 (November 1953): 1–6.

12. In "What Is the State of Exception" (chapter 1 in this volume), Nomi Claire Lazar argues that it is a mistake to perceive exceptions in liberal regimes devoted to the rule of law because they continue to be committed to the separation of powers and plural points of view. Pushback is always possible. Nowhere in American history, she claims here and in important earlier work, does a state of exception exist. Drawing on the model of the Roman dictatorship, of which more is said below, her work has insisted that within liberal regimes these exceptions are not needed because rights and the broader rule of law are intact. By contrast, we underscore how the problem of exceptions has been thought to be hardwired by key liberal thinkers—Locke, the Founders, Lincoln, and the twentieth-century theorists of emergency powers we consider—and how the problem of exceptions has become more pressing. See also Nomi Claire Lazar, *States of Emergency in Liberal Democracies* (Cambridge: Cambridge University Press, 2009).

13. Locke, *Second Treatise of Government*, 374–75 (secs. 159–60).

14. Cited in Clement Fatovic, "James Madison and the Emergency Powers of the Legislature," *Constitutional Studies* 1, no. 1 (2016): 67–93, 75.

15. For a review of the Founders' different types of constitutionalism, see Michael Zuckert and Felix Valenzuela, "Constitutionalism in the Age of Terror," *Social Philosophy and Policy* 28 (January 2001): 72–114.

16. Carey and McClellan, eds., *The Federalist*, 112–13 ("Federalist 23"). See also Sveinn Jóhannesson, "'Securing the State': James Madison, Federal Emergency Powers, and the Rise of the Liberal State in Post-Revolutionary America," *Journal of American History* 104, no. 2, September 2017, 363–85.

17. Carey and McClellan, eds., *The Federalist*, 113 ("Federalist 23").

18. Carey and McClellan, eds., *The Federalist*, 129, 130 ("Federalist 26").

19. Carey and McClellan, eds., *The Federalist*, 138 ("Federalist 28"). See also ibid., 21–26, 112–32 ("Federalist 23").

20. Rossiter, *Constitutional Dictatorship*, 224.

21. Karin Loevy, *Emergencies in Public Law: The Legal Politics of Containment* (Cambridge: Cambridge University Press, 2016). Rossiter notes the "revolutionary" aspect of Lincoln's actions. *Constitutional Dictatorship*, 228 n. 15, 234.

22. Rossiter, *Constitutional Dictatorship*, 237, 232. Compare Benjamin A. Kleinerman, "Lincoln's Example: Executive Power and the Survival of Constitutionalism," *Perspectives on Politics* 3 (December 2005): 801–16.

23. The Thirteenth Amendment is unlikely to have been ratified had President Andrew Johnson, who did not believe that the war truly was over, not put great pressure on the returning southern states. In that sense, the amendment itself was not a wartime measure but a postwar constitutional transformation. See Gregory Downs, *After Appomattox: Military Occupation and the Ends of War* (Cambridge, MA: Harvard University Press, 2015), 43, 82–86.

24. See Bruce Ackerman, *We the People: Transformations* (Cambridge, MA: Harvard University Press, 2000), and *We the People: The Civil Rights Revolution* (Cambridge, MA: Harvard University Press, 2014).

25. For the American reception of Schmitt, see David Dyzenhaus's "Beyond the Exception" (chapter 3 in this volume).

26. Carl Schmitt, *Dictatorship*, trans. Michael Hoelzl (1921; Cambridge, MA: Polity, 2014); John P. McCormick, "The Dilemmas of Dictatorship: Carl Schmitt and Constitutional Emergency Powers," in *Law as Politics: Carl Schmitt's Critique of Liberalism*, ed. David Dyzenhaus (Durham, NC: Duke University Press, 1998), 217–51, 221.

27. Carl Schmitt, *Political Theology: Four Chapters on the Concept of Sovereignty (1922)*, trans. George Schwab (Chicago: University of Chicago Press, 2010), 13–14. See also Clement Fatovic and Benjamin A. Kleinerman, "Introduction: Extra-Legal Measures and the Problem of Legitimacy," in Fatovic and Kleinerman, eds., *Extra-Legal Power and Legitimacy, 1–24*.

28. Rossiter, "War, Depression, and the Presidency," 417. See also Joel Isaac's "Constitutional Dictatorship in Twentieth-Century American Political Thought" (chapter 9 in this volume).

29. Bernard Manin, "The Emergency Paradigm and the New Terrorism" (New York University, 2008, typescript), 143.

30. We can see this postulate underpinning a remarkable 1918 US government document—prepared by the order of the attorney general,- and running to more than one thousand pages—that chronicles "emergency legislation passed prior to December 1917." Excluding matters of military organization and finance, it focuses on statutes together with presidential orders and proclamations that authorized "the taking and control of private property" during the Revolutionary War, the Wars of 1812 and 1847, the Civil War, and World War I. On this account, emergency acts are associated with moments that possess a clear boundary between war and peace. J. Reuben Clark Jr., *Emergency Legislation Passed Prior to December, 1917* (Washington, DC: US Government Printing Office, 1918), 1019.

31. Tyles M. Curley, "Models of Emergency Statebuilding in the United States," *Perspectives on Politics* 13 (September 2015): 697–713, 701; Lindsay Rogers, *Crisis Government* (New York: Norton, 1934), 65.

32. Rossiter, "War, Depression, and the Presidency," 417.

33. Albert L. Sturm, "Emergencies and the Presidency," *Journal of Politics* 11 (February 1949): 121–44, 121.

34. These legislative provisions were summarized in 1945 by the Legislative Reference Service of the Library of Congress in *Acts of Congress Applicable in Times of Emergency*, Bulletin 35 (Washington, DC: US Government Printing Office, 1945).

35. United States Code: Second War Powers Act, 1942, 50a U.S.C. §§ 633–45 (emphasis added).

36. Lindsay Rogers, "Legislature and Executive in Wartime," *Foreign Affairs* 19 (July 1941): 715–26, 716.

37. Dwight D. Eisenhower, "Inaugural Address," January 20, 1953, *The American Presidency Project*, ed. John Wolley and Gerhard Peters, http://www.presidency.ucsb.edu/ws/index.php?pid=9600.

38. Sturm, "Emergencies and the Presidency," 125, 131.
39. *Congressional Record,* 79th Cong., 2nd sess.,1946, 9261, 6086.
40. *Congressional Record,* 81st Cong., 2nd sess., 1950, 15668.
41. Harold C. Relyea, "National Emergency Powers," CRS Report for Congress (Washington, DC: Congressional Research Service, December 10, 1990; rev., April 29, 1991), 2 (an updated version was published in 2007).
42. Richard A. Posner, *Not a Suicide Pact: The Constitution in a Time of National Emergency* (New York: Oxford University Press, 2006), 10.
43. For an analytic account of the endurance of executive orders, see Sharece Thrower, "To Revoke or Not to Revoke? The Political Determinants of Executive Order Longevity," *American Journal of Political Science* 61, no. 3 (2017): 643–56.
44. James Risen and Eric Lichtblau, "Bush Lets U.S. Spy on Callers without Courts," *New York Times,* December 16, 2005.
45. Mark Mazzetti et al., "The Secret History of SEAL Team 6: Quiet Killings and Blurred Lines," *New York Times,* June 6, 2015.
46. Samuel Issacharoff, "Political Safeguards in Democracies at War," *Oxford Journal of Legal Studies* 29 (2009): 189–214, 214.
47. Public Law 107-40, 115 Stat. 224, September 18, 2001, https://www.congress.gov/107/plaws/publ40/PLAW-107publ40.pdf.
48. Cited in Garrett Epps, "Constitutional Myth #3: The 'Unitary Executive' Is a Dictator in War and Peace," *The Atlantic,* June 9, 2011, https://www.theatlantic.com/national/archive/2011/06/constitutional-myth-3-the-unitary-executive-is-a-dictator-in-war-and-peace/239627.
49. Jeffrey Crouch, Mark J. Rozell, and Mitchel A. Sollenberger, "The Law: The Unitary Executive Theory and President Donald J. Trump," *Presidential Studies Quarterly* 47 (September 2017): 561–73.
50. Carl Friedrich, *Transcendent Justice* (Cambridge, MA: Harvard University Press, 1964), 17.
51. Giorgio Agamben, *State of Exception,* trans. Kevin Attell (Chicago: University of Chicago Press, 2005). For a positive assessment arguing that traditional liberal legalism is obsolete, see Eric Posner and Adrian Vermeule, *The Executive Unbound: After the Madisonian Republic* (New York: Oxford University Press, 2011).
52. Cited in Arthur Schlesinger Jr., *The Imperial Presidency* (Boston: Houghton Mifflin, 1973), ix.
53. Stephen Holmes, "In Case of Emergency: Misunderstanding Tradeoffs in the War on Terror," *California Law Review* 97 (April 2009): 301–55, 304. See also Cass Sunstein, *Risk and Reason* (New York: Cambridge University Press, 2004). A distinction between visceral and prudential fear has been made in Jon Elster, "Constitution-Making and Violence," *Journal of Legal Analysis* 4, no. 1 (Spring 2012): 7–39, 7.
54. Bruce Ackerman, "The Emergency Constitution," *Yale Law Journal* 113 (March 2004): 1029–91, 1030.
55. Holmes, "In Case of Emergency," 332. By contrast, Holmes cites George W. Bush announcing to Bob Woodward: "I do not need to explain why I say things. That's the interesting thing about being the president. . . . I don't feel like I owe anybody an explanation." Ibid., 332n72.

56. Jack Goldsmith, "The Irrelevance of Prerogative Power, and the Evils of Secret Legal Interpretation," in Fatovic and Kleinerman, eds., *Extra-Legal Power and Legitimacy*, 214–31.

57. Zuckert and Valenzuela, "Constitutionalism in the Age of Terror," 96–97.

58. Will Smiley and John Fabian Witt, eds., *To Save the Country: A Lost Manuscript of the Civil War* (New Haven, CT: Yale University Press, 2019).

59. FISA directs the FISA Court to follow minimization procedures when policies are assessed that affect individual privacy. In practice, the court has followed a "foreign intelligence exception" to the Fourth Amendment's warrant requirements. See Elizabeth Goitein, "Testimony before the United States Senate Committee on the Judiciary, Oversight and Reauthorization of the FISA Amendments Act: The Balance between National Security, Privacy, and Civil Liberties," May 10, 2016, 5, 4. https://www.brennancenter.org/our-work/research-reports/testimony-fisa-amendments-act-senate-committee-judiciary. Cognate issues have arisen in the administration of criminal law. In *Maryland v. King* (2013), the Supreme Court decided, 5–4, that it is constitutional to obtain a DNA sample from a suspect without a warrant.

60. Posner, *Not a Suicide Pact*, 154–55.

61. John B. Colvin to Thomas Jefferson, September 14, 1810, Founders Online, https://founders.archives.gov/documents/Jefferson/03-03-02-0046; Thomas Jefferson to John B. Colvin, September 20, 1810, Teaching American History, http://teachingamericanhistory.org/library/document/letter-to-john-b-colvin.

62. Elizabeth Goitein and Faiza Patel, "What Went Wrong with the FISA Court?" (New York: Brennan Center for Justice, 2015).

63. Democratic Audit UK, "How Accountable Are the UK's Security and Intelligence Services to Parliament?," Democratic Audit, March 10, 2018, http://www.democraticaudit.com/2018/10/03/audit2018-how-accountable-are-the-uks-security-and-intelligence-services-to-parliament.

64. "The Report of the Iraq Inquiry" (London: Iraq Inquiry, July 2016), www.iraqinquiry.org.uk/the-report.

65. https://www.ipt-uk.com.

66. Talk delivered by Sir Michael Burton in Colchester in the summer of 2018, copy in possession of Ira Katznelson.

3 Beyond the Exception

David Dyzenhaus

A sense of existential threat suffused political rhetoric in the United States after 9/11. But there was never a formal declaration of a state of emergency in which the ordinary law of the land was temporarily suspended to secure the safety of the people. The Bush administration's response was for the most part put on the basis of ordinary law: either statute law enacted as a response to the perceived threat or existing legal instruments, both domestic and international. Legality was thus an essential element of the way in which the administration framed its response to 9/11, as it was during the Obama administration.

In subsequent debates in political and legal theory, the ideas of the German public lawyer and political theorist Carl Schmitt became a commonplace. In the run-up to the election of Donald Trump as president, and since his election, Schmitt's ideas are even harnessed in the media to explain nativist and populist trends in North America, Europe, and Turkey, as a search of the internet sites of newspapers such as the *New York Times*, the *Guardian*, and the *Washington Post* reveals. And, while Trump's policies are often criticized as an assault on the rule of law, his legal advisers and the judges he seeks to have elected to the appellate courts understand their approach to law—one that gathers ever more power unto the president—as what the rule of law requires. While these lawyers are often deeply opposed to the administrative state, they venerate the executive political office at the apex of the state hierarchy.

The reason for Schmitt's emergence from relative obscurity has largely to do with the resource he seems to offer when one is trying to understand the politics of post-9/11 America, in particular, the way in which exceptional or emergency measures have been transmogrified into instruments of ordinary law. This trend of "normalizing" the exception is seen as characteristic of "legal liberalism," a liberal ideology that equates legitimacy with legality and legality with conformity to formal criteria of legal validity.

Schmitt argues that the anti- or apolitical logic of liberalism requires these equations, with Hans Kelsen's "pure theory" of law the chief exemplar. Liberalism requires that the state take no stand on the kind of existential questions about the substance of the good that are the stuff of politics. It does so by making the criterion of the legitimacy of laws whether they have been enacted in accordance with the formal procedures stipulated for enactment and the criterion for the legitimacy of official acts whether the officials have been authorized to act by such laws.

The liberal aspiration is that government according to law will serve liberty by making state action predictable in advance. One will be subject to the rule of law, not to the arbitrary decisions of public officials. In addition, government according to law will serve equality because the formal equality of all before the law is maintained in keeping substantive criteria out of the judgment of whether state action is legitimate. This aspiration is vulnerable to being undermined in two ways. First, it requires that any substantive content that is injected into law by a group that has won political power in the legislature must be deemed to be legitimate as long as the law has been properly enacted. Absurdly, then, illiberal content must be deemed to be legitimate. Second, an official who is authorized by law to act as he deems fit—that is, arbitrarily—is by definition and again absurdly deemed to be acting legitimately.

I said that the critique of legal liberalism was in large part the reason for Schmitt's presence in post-9/11 debates because it is also the case that some political theorists find compelling not only his critique of legal liberalism but also his critique of liberalism itself as the political creed that the state should serve the interests in liberty and equality of those subject to its laws. They agree with Schmitt's claim that "the political" is the site of an existential struggle between friend and enemy, resolved by the decision of the leader or sovereign made on the basis of a vision of the substantive homogeneity of the *Volk*, whose mark of success is that he attracts their acclaim.

I shall show that in any evaluation of the American reception of Schmitt a lot depends on the answer to the question whether his critique of legal liberalism can be disentangled from his critique of liberalism itself. If one thinks that these are two separable critiques, one can accept the critique of legal liberalism and argue that liberalism itself is not affected as long as one sees that in an emergency the appropriate response of the liberal state is not through law. If one thinks that the critiques come as a package, the first critique puts one on the path to the second and to a rejection (even if not wholesale) of the creed.

I already indicated in my description of the first critique that the second is entailed by it. I argue that a "compulsion of legality"—the requirement that the state act legally—is a condition of liberal legitimacy. But, while this is a requirement that the state act in accordance with formal criteria of legality, I also argue that such compliance can both be effective and serve liberal values such as liberty and equality. The formalism I sketch below is not the view that judges should resolve hard legal questions by resort to formal deductive arguments about the content of the law, that is, the view articulated by conservative lawyers in the United States that cloaks a judicial activism that results in the equation of the sovereignty of the people with the sovereignty of the political executive. Rather, it is about the legal forms that political power must follow if it is to be made into law, a process that requires that the law be administered, interpreted, and applied by legal officials so as to serve an ideal of fidelity to legality—to principles protective of the liberty and equality of those subject to the law.

My first section sets out the stages in the American reception of Schmitt. In the second, I describe the extralegal response to emergencies that some of the participants in the present reception advocate. In the third, I set out the reason to avoid using Schmitt other than as a foil through revisiting a debate between him and Kelsen. The fourth section sets out the significance of the fact that the legal orders of advanced liberal democracies differ in their makeup from those of the nineteenth century in that they both provide constraints and offer resources that in combination make it impossible for the executive to consider acting—let alone admit to acting—on the basis of extralegal powers. Finally, I sketch the politics of a legal formalism that informs a substantive liberal response to Schmitt.

1. Five Crossings

Schmitt was not unknown to American scholars before 9/11.[1] As Joel Isaac shows in "Constitutional Dictatorship in Twentieth-Century American Political Thought" (chapter 9 in this volume), lawyers and political scientists who in the 1940s and 1950s studied the history and theory of the use of emergency powers took Schmitt seriously because of his argument in Weimar that the executive enjoyed very extensive powers in terms of Article 48—the emergency powers provision—of the Weimar constitution, a role undergirded by his study of the institution of dictatorship from Rome to his day. Under the guidance of Carl J. Friedrich, the German émigré and political scientist, these scholars used Schmitt as a foil against which to develop a "liberal" theory of "constitutional dictatorship."

In the 1970s and 1980s, a second American reception of Schmitt got underway when a few scholars began to treat him as one of the most important thinkers not only of his period but also of the twentieth century, perhaps even of modernity. Most prominent among them were George Schwab, mainly through his editions and translations of some of Schmitt's major works, but also through an account of Schmitt's thought, and Joseph Bendersky, who wrote the first biography of Schmitt in English.[2]

Both Schwab and Bendersky argued that Schmitt sought to provide the constitutional theory that could save the Weimar Republic and that the same constitutional theory laid the basis for West Germany's successful experiment with constitutional government after the war. On Bendersky's account, Friedrich and the others who used Schmitt as a foil were mistaken—even duplicitous—because the true theorist and defender of liberal constitutionalism was Schmitt.[3]

Schwab and Bendersky's apologetic treatment of Schmitt underplayed his apocalyptic understanding of politics, though it was difficult to understand their esteem without supposing that they themselves were drawn to such an understanding. But that mystic view of politics as existential conflict was celebrated in the 1980s in the third reception of Schmitt by a group of Marxist scholars associated with the journal *Telos*. Perhaps disillusioned with the prospects for class struggle, these scholars found in Schmitt the basis for an understanding of both international and domestic politics as antagonistic struggle. They differed hardly at all from mainstream realist or realpolitik conceptions of the political except in their hope that, when liberalism was seen as an ideology that tried to constrict the sphere of the political, it might become possible to open up the space of politics in ways that would enable dislodging it as the dominant ideology.[4]

In the 1990s, a fourth American reception of Schmitt emerged that shared something with the first in that these scholars sought to show the value in Schmitt's critique of liberal democracy while exposing his understanding of politics as deeply flawed.[5] But, in situating Schmitt as just one important participant in the political and legal debates of Weimar, they also brought to the fore the resources offered by other Weimar-era political and legal theorists, notably Hans Kelsen, Herman Heller, and the lawyers of the Frankfurt school. Kelsen and Heller in particular offered a valuable perspective on Schmitt as they effectively debunked his claims to be a dispassionate legal scholar and exposed his legal theory as a cloak for an elite-driven attempt to harness the forces of populism to the cause of destroying liberal democracy.

Several of the scholars who were part of this reception emphasized the legal aspects of Schmitt's thought. That the apologists and the Marxists had neglected the details of Schmitt's engagement with the public law theorists of his day left rather a large gap in the understanding of his work. In particular, the important exchanges between Schmitt and Kelsen in the early 1930s—when the fate of the Weimar Republic was in the balance—about who was or should be "the guardian" of the Weimar constitution in a time of emergency did not figure in their treatment.[6]

Schmitt's last crossing of the Atlantic in the wake of 9/11 is my focus in this chapter, and it perpetuates the gap. There are three major strands. First, political theorists of the Left—for example, Bonnie Honig and Andreas Kalyvas—continue on the path carved out by the *Telos* Schmittians in an attempt to find in Schmitt's friend-enemy distinction and his concept of the political the clue to a revitalization of democratic politics.[7] They thus accept both critiques sketched above, though they seem to think that they can, as it were, defang the critique of liberalism by preserving the political rights associated with liberal democracy.

Second, lawyers and political theorists use Schmitt as a foil to develop liberal constitutional responses to emergencies. But, unlike Friedrich and the others who were part of the first reception, they accept Schmitt's critique of legal liberalism and thus seek to craft an extralegal or political rather than a legal response to emergencies. Third, an influential group of lawyers accepts Schmitt's critique of legal liberalism and thus a realpolitik understanding of law as the mere instrument of material interests but does not think that the failure of legal liberalism is a big problem, at least in the US political context. In this view, existing political mechanisms for the most part provide an adequate response, and, in the cases in which there is no such response, the costs are not that great.[8] In other words, this third strand differs from the second only in that it supposes that things are fine as they are.

As I now show, all three strands make the mistake of accepting Schmitt's dichotomy between law and politics, or, as he might have preferred to put it, between the political and the legal. My stepping-stone for this argument is the recent collection edited by Clement Fatovic and Benjamin A. Kleinerman, *Extra-Legal Power and Legitimacy*.[9]

2. Liberalism and Extralegal Power

In *Political Theology*, Schmitt says: "The exception was something incommensurable to John Locke's doctrine of the constitutional state and the rationalist eighteenth century." He then makes two claims that seem in some tension with each other: first, that this kind of "rationalist tendency" "ignores the emergency," as exemplified in Kelsen, who does "not know what to do with it"; second, that "liberal constitutionalism" can try to "anticipate" the exception and "can suspend itself" while seeking to "regulate the exception as precisely as possible" by spelling out "in detail the case in which law suspends itself."[10]

One way to respond to the tension in claiming that liberals, on the one hand, ignore emergencies and, on the other, both recognize them and seek to regulate them legally is to suggest that Schmitt was simply mistaken about his target. In the *Second Treatise of Government*, Locke extolled the virtues of the rule of law—of the advantages to liberty of life under "settled, standing" legislated rules common to all in contrast to "the inconstant, uncertain, unknown, arbitrary will of another man." But he also insisted that in emergencies the government has a prerogative or legally unconstrained power to "act according to discretion, for the publick good, without the prescription of the Law, and sometimes even against it."[11] And this account of the prerogative figures prominently in the second strand in the current reception of Schmitt.

Fatovic and Kleinerman adopt the view that liberalism can and should embrace the prerogative, as do other contributors to their collection with only one clear exception.[12] But they also appreciate that from Schmitt's perspective the tension is not between claims that he himself makes. Rather, it is one within liberalism. Liberalism would prefer to ignore the exception because it threatens the ideal of the rule of law. But, when the liberal state is faced with an emergency, it is forced both to respond to it and to respond by legal means. Since the only effective response to an emergency is extralegal, the means adopted are evacuated of any content, leaving state officials to act in substance illegally.

However, their reliance on Locke as the liberal source for the argument that the liberal state is not committed to legalism is problematic for two reasons. The first has to do with the equation these days of *prerogative* power with *extralegal* power. Prerogative power in common law jurisdictions is not extralegal. Rather, it exists as a matter of common law, it can be abolished or superseded by statute, and it is subject to judicial review.[13] Second, the way in which the prerogative has become, as it were, ever more legalized is reflected in the developments sketched in the clear exception in the collection, the essay by Jack Goldsmith, a Harvard law professor, but also a legal adviser to the Bush administration and one of the lawyers who drafted the memoranda justifying components of the War on Terror.[14] Goldsmith presents three main points.

First, Goldsmith argues that the prerogative is "no longer part of a president's justificatory tool kit" since "legal, political and social change" have rendered it "non-operative." The legal world has changed since Lincoln because of the sheer amount of law, including criminal law, that regulates what executive officials may do, with the result that the costs of extralegal action are so high that "the subordinates the president needs to carry out his actions live in a legal culture that insists that executive actions be supported and consistent with law." In addition, the need to rely on prerogative power has "dissipated . . . because of [legally based] expansions in presidential power and in presidential power to interpret the law." But, Goldsmith adds, this "does not mean that a president can legally justify any course of action that suits him; there are still many restrictions and limits, as events of the last decade have demonstrated."[15]

Second, while Goldsmith admits that there is a case for supposing that some executive action in the War on Terror was "without legal authority or contrary to law" in the sense that it was based on "erroneous statutory and constitutional interpretations," he insists that there are "fundamental differences" between such mistaken exercises and exercises of prerogative power. There is a "psychological" difference in that even a highly "tendentious" interpretation of legal authority is "perceived as a less momentous step than prerogative power" because, from both the executive and the public perspectives, "the president . . . still expresses implicit fealty to law and legal constraint." In addition, prerogative power invites "political and public . . . scrutiny," while "tendentious legal interpretation invites legal analysis (and perhaps judicial review)"; that is, they "invite different standards of judgment."[16]

Goldsmith's final point is that the "real evil" is "executive auto-interpretation of the law," which has its most problematic manifestation in "secret executive branch interpretation of the law." He does not think that judicial review is the cure for the obvious problems that inhere in officials themselves determining the legal limits on their activity. But he does think that answerability to Congress, the media, and the public can serve as a considerable check as long as the actions and their legal justifications can be made public. Where publicity is not possible on security grounds, then mechanisms internal to government will have to serve.[17]

Fatovic and Kleinerman approve of Goldsmith's emphasis on publicity as the check on executive action since for them one of the main virtues of extralegal action is that it "occurs out in the open where it is possible to judge and hold accountable." However, they also observe that "accountability becomes possible only when the public understands that a violation has occurred." So they claim that "in the murky legal area . . . where government officials never admit to violating the law because they can construe it to give them whatever power they want to exercise, specialized debates among lawyers could actually obfuscate matters and make accountability to the public even more difficult to achieve."[18]

In his essay in the collection Fatovic elaborates on this point as he focuses on the claim that, when the state acts explicitly against the ordinary law by suspending it in order to rely on extralegal powers, this candor enables the triggering of appropriate deliberative procedures within democratic institutions.[19] His deliberative democratic theory is offered as a counter to Schmitt's claim that the democratic response to extralegal action is to be found in the acclamation by "the people" of the sovereign's decision on and in the state of exception.

However, this is a rather weak response to Goldsmith's case for the irrelevance of the prerogative in the US context. And it is unclear how, given that case, the studies in the collection of the Roman model of emergency powers,[20] of Jewish law,[21] or of the ways in which Hamilton, Jefferson, and Lincoln resorted to the prerogative in previous eras bear on the present.[22] The advanced liberal democracies differ in their legal makeup so radically from even the liberal democracies of the late nineteenth century—owing to the growth of the administrative state—that, interesting as they are in their own right, the studies do not readily provide a basis for answering questions about the present.

I shall come back to this point below. For the moment, I want to note that the compulsion of legality seems to be a permanent feature of advanced liberal democracies. But, as I have recognized in other work, the compulsion can set in motion two very different "cycles of legality." In one—the "virtuous cycle"—the institutions of legal order cooperate in devising controls over public actors that ensure that their decisions comply with the principle of legality that exerts a political-moral discipline on government. In the other—the "empty cycle"—the content of legality is understood in an ever more formal or vacuous manner, resulting in the mere appearance or even the pretence of legality.[23]

If the empty cycle were inevitable, I would have to concede that both Goldsmith and Fatovic and Kleinerman are right in one respect, though in a way that makes things worse overall and that supports Schmitt's argument about liberalism and vacuous legality. On the one hand, Goldsmith is right that the executive will not rely on either extralegal power or prerogative. On the other hand, Fatovic and Kleinerman are right that the exclusive reliance by the executive on a legal response is different from an explicitly extralegal response only in that it takes place in "the murky legal area . . . where government officials never admit to violating the law because they can construe it to give them whatever power they want to exercise."

A lot then turns on Goldsmith's claim that there are "fundamental differences" between erroneous exercises of legal power and exercises of extralegal power. But it is important also to consider a difficulty arising not out of an erroneous exercise of power but when there is an explicit authorization to act that gives such a wide discretion to the actor that he seems to have a free hand. The practice of autointerpretation is an example because, if there is nobody to check my interpretation of the legal limits on my action, there are arguably no limits. However, as I shall now argue, in an analysis of texts by Schmitt and Kelsen, Goldsmith's gesture at fundamental differences contains the seeds of a response to such problems.

3. Debunking Schmitt

In his work on states of exception, Schmitt often seems to be involved in a careful elaboration of the history and theory of the legal constraints on delegated authority to respond to an emergency, that is, of the "commissarial dictator," one who has constitutionally limited emergency powers on commission from the people, by contrast with the "sovereign dictator," who is free from any legal limit. But he also argues that sovereign dictatorship can always assert itself against the law, including the law of the emergency regime, because legally unlimited and illimitable constituent power is always present in a constitution.[24]

This argument comes to the fore in the explicit claim in 1931 in the essays collected in *The Guardian of the Constitution* that the president is the guardian of the constitution, with the result that, when it comes to the limits on executive power under Article 48, they are—to recall Goldsmith's term—to be determined in a process of executive autointerpretation. Schmitt's theory of the judicial role supposes that a judge adjudicates properly only when he subsumes the facts of a case to the determinate content of a statute. The independence of judges depends on such a role being available to them, and they are therefore incapable of resolving the political disputes that face the person who occupies the role of the guardian of the constitution. Such disputes have, Schmitt asserts, to be resolved not by a higher authority but by a "neutral third," in his view the president of the Reich because he alone can take political decisions in the name of the "whole of the political unity" of the German people. On this point, Schmitt rests his final claim that the president has a democratic legitimacy that judges lack.[25]

Kelsen responded that the issue is first and foremost a normative one about the demand for constitutional institutions that control the behavior of other constitutional institutions, a demand that "expresses a requirement of the rule of law, namely the requirement that the exercise of the state's functions be as lawful as possible."[26] If one agrees that it should be met, then it is not open to dispute that "no institution is less suitable to perform this task than the one upon which the constitution confers the exercise, in whole or in part, of the power to be controlled ... No legal-technical principle commands a more universal assent than the demand that no person ought to be judge in her own cause."[27]

Schmitt's argument against courts as guardians of the constitution involves, Kelsen demonstrates, a sleight of hand. First, Schmitt offers an entirely tendentious definition of judicial independence, from which it follows that insofar as there is any political component to a decision it is one that a judge is unequipped to make. Since Schmitt also finds that there is a political moment of decision in any judicial determination, his argument becomes absurdly that the adjudicative function is impossible. That someone of "such extraordinary intelligence ... entangles himself in such manifest contradictions" can only be explained, says Kelsen, by the fact that Schmitt's argument is driven by a "legal-political demand" that the state not have a constitutional court.[28]

Indeed, Kelsen detects in Schmitt the political aim of establishing a total state that will eradicate the pluralism of competitive political parties and social groups in order to bring about the unity of state that he desires based on his idea of the "homogeneous, indivisible unity of the

German people." If neutrality is a requirement to exercise the function of guardian of the constitution, the president is in no better position than judges and moreover lacks the "ethos" of the judicial profession that drive judges toward neutrality. Kelsen thus suggests that in Schmitt's view both parliament and the courts are unconstitutional. His view entails that "the pluralistic system or, in plain German, parliament" is what "severely threatens or disturbs the public security and order in the German Reich."[29]

4. At the Coalface of Administrative Law

Kelsen, as we have seen, debunks the claim that Schmitt is offering a legal analysis of emergency dictatorship. Rather, Schmitt is making a set of political claims about how legal order should be designed if one wishes to establish a substantively homogeneous people. But, even if Kelsen were right that as a result Schmitt "entangles himself in . . . manifest contradictions," we are left with the question whether Schmitt was right that all that liberalism offers in return is vacuous formalism.

In my terms, the compulsion of legality raises an important question about whether a virtuous or an empty cycle of legality will unfold. However, only two conditions need to be met for the virtuous cycle to unfold. First, legal actors must adopt an ideal of fidelity to the principles of legality. Second, to the extent that the legal order in which they operate does not provide the institutional resources for a full realization of that ideal, it should be reformed in ways that will make such realization feasible. If the first condition is not met, if public officials are not fully committed to performing their role honestly and impartially, all bets are off. But the more interesting issue is whether the second condition can be met because in its absence officials find themselves in the uncomfortable position of giving the stamp of legality to acts that are not subject to the rule of law.[30]

It is in this regard no coincidence that several of the scholars in the first American reception of Schmitt were influential in constructing a legal theory of the administrative state at the same time as they were constructing their liberal theory of constitutional dictatorship.[31] For the twentieth-century development of that state is closely bound up with the experiment that countries like the United States and the United Kingdom had to undertake to cope with wartime emergency by enacting legislation to empower public officials to establish and implement complex regulatory regimes. As these scholars knew, official discretion in the situation of emergency rule does not seem qualitatively different from executive discretion in ordinary administrative law, even if much more dramatic both in scope and in subject matter. One can put this point by saying that administrative law is a legal space populated by countless small-scale states of exception in which—to paraphrase Schmitt's infamous opening line of *Political Theology*—public officials are the minisovereigns who get to decide in and on the state of exception.[32] But, once one puts the point this way, there is a lesson to be learned from the coalface of administrative law in common law countries for the liberal constitutional theory of emergencies.

A virtuous cycle in the United Kingdom helps make my point.[33] During the two world wars, the indefinite detention of individuals considered to be risks to UK national security had to follow an administrative procedure set out in cabinet-made regulations. Each decision was subject to an appeal to an executive committee, whose chairman had to inform detainees of the grounds of their detentions so that they could make a case to the committee for their release. The home secretary—the minister in the cabinet responsible for national security—could decline to follow the advice of the committee but had to report monthly to Parliament about the orders he had made and about whether he had declined to follow advice. The committee, however, lacked rule-of-law teeth.[34] Not only did it fail to require the intelligence branch to disclose the real reasons for detentions, but also, even if it thought that someone had been wrongly detained, it could only advise the home secretary of its view.

The majority of the House of Lords in the World War I decision in *Halliday* and the World War II decision in *Liversidge* said that the demands of legality were satisfied by the detention regime and that such regimes were appropriate in wartime emergency.[35] In the common law world, Lord Atkin's sole dissent in *Liversidge* is one of the most famous of the twentieth century, but Lord Shaw's sole dissent in *Halliday* should enjoy as important a place in this cycle of legality.[36]

The Defence of the Realm Consolidation Act of 1914 did not explicitly authorize a detention regulation to be made, so Lord Shaw found the detention regulation invalid. His assumption was that Parliament must be taken to intend that its delegates act in accordance with the rule of law, which meant that it had to authorize any departures from the rule of law explicitly: "[I]f Parliament had intended to make this colossal delegation of power it would have done so plainly and courageously and not under cover of words about regulations for safety and defence."[37]

When civil servants put together the detention regime for World War II, they took note of Shaw's dissent and ensured that the authorizing statute explicitly permitted the establishment of a detention regime by regulation. In addition to this response to a dissenting judge, the government responded to concerns raised in Parliament about the wording of the initial version of the detention regulation. It substituted "reasonable cause to believe" when it came to the grounds for detention for the original proposal of "if satisfied that."

It was on this basis that Lord Atkin held that a court was entitled to more than the government's say-so that an individual is a security risk. The majority disagreed on the basis that it was inappropriate in wartime for judges to go beyond the mechanism explicitly put in place. Lord Atkin thus accused his fellow judges of being more executive minded than the executive.[38]

In my view, *Liversidge* is best understood as the second episode in a virtuous cycle of legality, one in which the writ of the rule of law progressively extends. The first episode is Lord Shaw's insistence in *Halliday* on a "clear statement rule" that the legislature must expressly delegate authority to infringe fundamental rights. It had the result that the explicit authorization to detain was put into the Defence of the Realm Act in World War II. That subjection meant that the question of the content of the regulation as well as the question of whether there should be such a regulation came up for debate in Parliament, instead of being regarded as matters of executive prerogative. Public debate on the former question then led to a substitution in wording.

Here we see at work a process that produces what I term a kind of *legal surplus value*.[39] In order for public policy to become law, it has to be put into legal form. That involves the reduction of a political program to the explicit terms of a statute and thus a conversion of policy into public, legally applicable standards—the legal surplus value. By this I mean that the legitimacy of official action in compliance with the statute does not stem simply from its compliance with a political policy that the legislature has determined to be appropriate. It is also the case that this conversion process adds value because it brings into being a particular type of *public* standard, one that permits the operation of principles of legality and enables claims of right based on legal principle to be adjudicated. And, if, as is often (even usually) the case in the administrative state, the statute delegates in large part to public officials the task of developing the policy of the statute, the officials will be responsible for producing in appropriate form the public standards that will govern their administrative regime. Hence, there is also often an administrative conversion process that mediates between a statute and judicial review of executive action.

In *Liversidge*, Lord Atkin tried to cash out that surplus value by inferring from the substitution and from the very existence of the executive committee that the legislature did intend that some meaningful review of detention decisions was not only possible but also desirable. That is, he tried to show that the first kind of conversion enabled the second kind of conversion, one in which issues arising out of the legislative regime could be properly adjudicated. Moreover, in the leading speech for the majority in *Liversidge*, Viscount Maugham said that, if an appeal against the home secretary's decision "had been thought proper, it would have been to a special tribunal with power to inquire privately into all the reasons for the Secretary's action, but without any obligation to communicate them to the person detained."[40] He too therefore thought that review is possible, even desirable, though he did not think that it was possible in the absence of institutional innovation.

But, if the detention situation were such that judges who insisted on their authority to review would not be able to review effectively, Atkin's dissent could make things worse by adding ineffective judicial review to the charade of legality already in place. In addition, even if, as Maugham suggested, the legislature created an institution "with power to inquire privately into all the reasons for the Secretary's action," there would be an obvious problem if the inquiry had to happen "without any obligation to communicate [the reasons] to the person detained." Finally, if that inquiry were shielded from judicial review, it would seem that the executive was policing itself on decisions that involved drastic deprivations of liberty. One would in substance have executive autointerpretation.

In the 1990s, responding to a decision of the European Court of Human Rights,[41] the UK Parliament put in place the kind of innovation Maugham contemplated when it created the Special Immigration Appeals Commission (SIAC).[42] The SIAC is a three-person tribunal, chaired by a high court judge, with the other two members providing specialist expertise in immigration and security. It was created as a superior court of record, with full authority to review immigration decisions made on national security grounds. The tribunal, whose members have security clearance, has access to all the information on which the executive bases its claims and the services of a special advocate, also with security clearance, to test the executive's case on issues where the individual and his legal representative are excluded because of the sensitive nature of the information.

The big flaw in this regime is that the special advocate is not permitted to communicate with the individual or his legal representative once he has seen the material considered by the home secretary to be "closed"—material that can be considered only in a session from which the individual and his legal representative are excluded. The special advocate can contest the decision of the home secretary, and the SIAC decides issues about disclosure when the special advocate and the home secretary cannot reach agreement, though the home secretary can decide not to rely on information in order to avoid having it disclosed. Since in most—perhaps all—cases the information in the closed sessions is the effective basis for the SIAC decision, the prohibition on communication severely hamstrings the special advocate's ability to test the evidence to the extent that several special advocates have refused to continue in the role and have publicly expressed their disillusionment with it.[43]

The failings of the special advocate system must thus give pause to anyone who wishes to argue that executive action in the context of national security can be made subject to rule-of-law protections. However, Canada has subsequently adopted a more refined version of the special advocate system, one with more scope for reviewing judges to order disclosure of information. That system provides a better basis for challenges by the subjects of control orders, with the result that a Canadian federal court judge has ordered the unconditional release of one high-profile subject of national security measures because the executive withdrew evidence that the judge had ordered could be disclosed without compromising national security, being unwilling to have it disclosed.[44] In addition, courts in the United Kingdom read into the Prevention of Terrorism Act 2005 enhanced procedural protections that review much more effectively the "control order" regime that replaced a detention regime that had been declared incompatible with UK human rights commitments by the House of Lords.[45]

To put the most optimistic gloss on the situation possible, one could say that courts and other institutions in both the United Kingdom and Canada are now grappling with the problem of how to ensure that, both substantively and procedurally, this family of national security measures can be made subject to the discipline of the rule of law. The cycle shows that more due process or procedure makes substantive review possible and that more substantive review seeks the kind of disclosure and testing of information that due process provides. There is then a plausible case for maintaining that a virtuous cycle of legality is not only possible but also actual when it comes to this family of national security measures, despite the problems that remain.[46]

Moreover, the problems that remain are brought to light by the cycle of legality. They are problems that hinder the completion of the cycle and raise the question how and whether further resources can be developed to solve the problem. To the extent that judicial and administrative institutions are unable to find the resources to solve the problem within the legal order as it is, the problem becomes one for legislative politics, for the political institutions of legislative reform. It is in this regard that the first condition of the virtuous cycle becomes particularly important. Public officials must be willing to make the attempt to force the issue onto the legislative agenda. If they do not, they give the stamp of legality and thus of legitimacy to what is in substance a charade.

Notice three related aspects of this process. First, as is illustrated by the part played by dissenting judgments in this section, forcing requires not that the judiciary have the authority to invalidate statutory provisions that are offensive to legality but only that public officials insist on making the public aware that they are unable to perform their role as one of the institutional guardians of legality. Second, it is important that there is a plurality of guardians. In contrast to Schmitt's obsession with the question of who makes the final decision, which implies that sovereignty can be located in one institution or person, all the institutions of legal order are understood as participating in the exercise of sovereignty, and thus all have a guardianship role to play. Third, when the officials point out that they are unable to play this role, they are not bringing any old problem into the public gaze. Rather, they are pointing out a problem of legality—that the society is not living up to its fundamental legal commitments, which is to say, not treating those subject to its laws in a way that respects their interests in liberty and equality. Put differently, the officials are pointing out a problem of political identity for that society, which, on the assumption that it wants to preserve that identity, is faced with the choice between reform that will bring the particular administrative regime into line with the requirements of legality and finding an altogether different political path.

In sum, the issue is not the political versus the legal, as Schmitt would have us believe, and as all the strands in the current American reception of Schmitt seem to accept. Rather, it is a contest between two distinct conceptions of the political. On the one hand, there is the Schmittian conception, in which the political is an existential site of conflict between different visions of the substantive homogeneity of the people and the task of the state is to settle that conflict and then use law as the instrument of the victorious vision. On the other hand, there is the liberal conception, in which the political is a legally constructed space both in that groups contend for power on terms set by the order's constitutional commitments and in that a group that has power exercises it on the condition that the law it makes meets those same commitments.

This latter condition means that the function of law is not confined to the transmission of content by those who have authority to make law to those subject to the law. Because the content of the law is by assumption content that meets the order's constitutional commitments, the legal subject is entitled to contest the application of the law when it is applied or interpreted in a way that appears inconsistent with those commitments. Moreover, as I have sketched above, if officials are unable to find that the law is so consistent, that is not the end of the matter since the issue is then moved from one site of contest to another.

Schmitt's political and legal theory is then a useful foil, but not for the reason that animates the second and third strands within the current American reception—that Schmitt shows that those who wish to defend liberalism should appreciate that liberalism can be preserved only if it is not committed to legal liberalism. Rather, it is useful for a reason quite similar to the one that animates the first strand—that liberalism is committed to legal liberalism and that commitment constricts the space of the political. Moreover, in seeing how (as I would prefer to put it) legal liberalism *shapes* the political by establishing specifically legal terms for political engagement at different levels of the political and legal order, one can do more than appreciate the political nature of the legal. One can also both continue the task begun in the first Schmitt reception by Friedrich and those influenced by him of developing a liberal constitutional theory of emergency response and, with the third reception, explore further how Schmitt's Weimar opponents can help in this task. Both tasks require an appreciation of what we can think of as the politics of legal formalism, as sketched in the next section.

5. The Politics of Legal Formalism

Recall that Goldsmith refers to a "legal culture that insists that executive actions be supported and consistent with law" and that he points out that one difference between a contested exercise of prerogative power and of legal power is that the former invites "political and public . . . scrutiny" while a "tendentious legal interpretation invites legal analysis (and perhaps judicial review)," that is, they "invite different standards of judgment."[47]

On my argument, both the idea of legal culture and the point about different standards require elaboration in accordance with an idea of principles of the rule of law that are both formal, in that they are constitutional principles of legal order, and substantive, in that they conduce to serving the interests of the legal subject, the individual subject to state power. It is because legality requires conformity to such principles that the standards of review that obtain in the legal domain are different from those that obtain in the political domain. It is precisely in this difference that any hope lies for a better political debate about what is appropriate in responding to emergency situations. One might say that the contest in the legal domain is crucial for making vivid to the political domain the interests that both domains are meant to serve and that also underpin the legitimacy claim of each.

In my view, this argument has much in common with the three contributions to this volume that look to the tradition of democratic pragmatism in American thought to counter the logic of Schmitt's exceptionalism,[48] for example, William J. Novak's exercise in recovery of resources in twentieth-century American democratic theory that help facilitate a "more pragmatic and realistic accounting of the close and constant interrelationship of necessity and lawmaking from the earliest days of the republic." All three suggest that democracy is not, as Schmitt thought, the problem but the solution, which, if properly conceived, will show that the exception is not exceptional but a quotidian mode of exercising power in a context of popular rule.[49]

My chapter has provided a similar argument as I suggested that attention to the exception in the quotidian context of administrative law illuminates the way in which the liberal democratic state can and should respond to emergencies on liberal democratic terms. But I differ from Novak in particular in that he takes as his foil not only Schmitt but also the formalist view of public law that he associates with Edwin Corwin and his notion of a "higher law" background to American principles of judicial review, due process of law, and "vested rights" because such notions hamper pragmatist progress.[50] My difference is, however, attached not to Corwin's specific theory but to the wholesale rejection of formalism in public law. As I have suggested above and argued elsewhere,[51] one cannot value the kind of site that law offers for political contest and social experiment in a pragmatist spirit without an appreciation of the importance of legal form.

Such political contest is made possible not only by the conversion of public policy into legal form so that there is a public record of official decisions to which officials can be held accountable. It is also made possible by the fact that the legal form of legislation is shaped by principles such as generality, publicity, and intelligibility as well as by the principles that govern the application of the law (e.g., principles of fairness and impartiality) and, finally, by principles that govern the interpretation of the law, notably the principle that the law should be interpreted in such a way as to serve the legal subject's interests in liberty and equality.

Consider in this regard John Fabian Witt's account of the theory of emergency powers developed by Francis Lieber and his son during and out of the experience of the Civil War as a counter to the claims of the proto-Schmittians of the day who argued that there are no legal limits on executive authority in times of emergency. Witt argues that in the Liebers' theory "the ends of the republic were limited; they were constrained by the existing public values of the regime, embodied in the perspective of the reasonable citizen," that is, the person "whose basic values draw from the constitutive commitments of the republic—commitments whose basic character define the scope of what is reasonably necessary under even the most difficult of circumstances."[52]

I can put my claim as follows. In order for the Liebers to construct their theory or for Friedrich and the scholars he influenced to construct a liberal constitutional theory of emergency, they had to have some idea of fundamental legal commitments or higher law to which both enacted law and the officials who implement it are answerable.[53] That idea need not amount to the target that Novak *et al.* perhaps have in their sights when they name Corwin: the idea of rights as trumps or prepolitical standards of morality that judges can invoke in order to invalidate enacted law whose content they conclude violates the rights. Rather, higher law is no more than the principles of legality that are inherent in what we can think of as the rule-of-law project, the political project that seeks to govern by law rather than by some other means.

Liberalism as a creed is irrevocably committed to that project and thus to legal liberalism and its small *c* constitutionalism. That kind of constitutionalism requires that all public officials have a legal warrant for their actions, not only in the sense that they can point to an enacted authorizing law, but also in that the authorizing law as it is interpreted and applied is law that lives up to the kind of formal principles of legality sketched above. The workings of this kind of constitutionalism are most manifest in the legal regimes of the administrative state, and they show how the exception can become normalized or internalized within regimes of legality in ways that preserve the liberty and equality interests of those subject to law.

To think such a process worth undertaking, one has to adopt as a regulative assumption of institutional design that the point is to channel coercive power so that it is mediated in a way that enables its application to be justified. Proponents of this tradition do not, as Schmitt charged, face the option of either ignoring emergencies or suspending their deepest commitments.[54] Rather, they require, as Friedrich pointed out in 1957, a "progressive realization of constitutionalism." Friedrich, who had observed the travails of the Weimar Republic as a student in Germany before he embarked on a career that made him one of the most influential political scientists in the United States, wrote that, while the Kantian solution of a world state was unattainable, there was nevertheless something to be learned from it. It had "the advantage of providing a developmental model and a pragmatic, if not a practical projection into the future, by which concrete political action programs may be inspired and policy shaped."[55]

: : :

I thank the participants in the Cambridge conference for which this paper was prepared as well as the participants in the London School of Economics Legal and Political Theory Forum and in a seminar at the European University Institute for stimulating discussion and Lars Vinx and the editors of this volume for written comments. In addition, I thank Nomi Claire Lazar for her generous presentation of my argument at the session of the Chicago workshop I could not attend and all those who participated in the illuminating discussion that followed, which the organizers kindly had recorded for me.

Notes

1. For illuminating discussion of the reception of Schmitt in recent years (in America and elsewhere), see Matthew G. Specter, "What's 'Left' in Schmitt? From Aversion to Appropriation in Contemporary Political Theory," in *The Oxford Handbook of Carl Schmitt*, ed. Jens Meierhenrich and Oliver Simons (Oxford: Oxford University Press, 2016), 426–54; Peter C. Caldwell, "Controversies over Carl Schmitt: A Review of Recent Literature," *Journal of Modern History* 77 (2005): 357–87; and John P. McCormick, "Political Theory and Political Theology: The Second Wave of Carl Schmitt in English," *Political Theory* 26 (1998): 830–54.

2. George Schwab, *The Challenge of the Exception: An Introduction to the Political Ideas Carl Schmitt between 1921 and 1936* (1970; 2nd ed., Westport, CT: Greenwood, 1989); Joseph Bendersky, *Carl Schmitt: Theorist for the Reich* (Princeton, NJ: Princeton University Press, 1983).

3. Bendersky, *Carl Schmitt*, 276–77.

4. See esp. *"Carl Schmitt: Enemy or Foe?,"* special issue, *Telos*, vol. 72 (1987).

5. See Peter C. Caldwell, *Popular Sovereignty and the Crisis of German Constitutional Law: The Theory and Practice of Weimar Constitutionalism* (Durham, NC: Duke University Press, 1997); Renato Cristi, *Carl Schmitt and Authoritarian Liberalism: Strong State, Free Economy* (Cardiff: University of Wales Press, 1998); David Dyzenhaus, *Legality and Legitimacy: Carl Schmitt,*

Hans Kelsen and Hermann Heller in Weimar (Oxford: Oxford University Press, 1997); John P. McCormick, *Carl Schmitt's Critique of Liberalism: Against Politics as Technology* (New York: Cambridge University Press, 1997); and William E. Scheuerman, *Carl Schmitt: The End of Law* (Lanham, MD: Rowman & Littlefield, 1999).

6. One hopes that this large gap in the debates will be remedied by the publication in English of the exchange between Schmitt and Kelsen—translated and with an introduction in Lars Vinx, *The Guardian of the Constitution: Hans Kelsen and Carl Schmitt on the Limits of Constitutional Law* (Cambridge: Cambridge University Press, 2015). See also Lars Vinx, *Hans Kelsen's Pure Theory of Law: Legality and Legitimacy* (Oxford: Oxford University Press, 2007).

7. Bonnie Honig, *Emergency Politics: Paradox, Law, Democracy* (Princeton, NJ: Princeton University Press, 2009); Andreas Kalyvas, *Democracy and the Politics of the Extraordinary: Max Weber, Carl Schmitt, and Hannah Arendt* (New York: Cambridge University Press, 2009). The *weltschmerzlich* treatment of Schmitt in Gopal Balikrishnan's *The Enemy: An Intellectual Portrait of Carl Schmitt* (London: Verso, 2000) seems to be another example of this genre, though the account of Schmitt's importance is so vague that readers are left wondering what they are supposed to be anguished or disillusioned about.

8. See, e.g., Eric Posner and Adrian Vermeule, *The Executive Unbound: After the Madisonian Republic* (New York: Oxford University Press, 2011).

9. Clement Fatovic and Benjamin A. Kleinerman, eds., *Extra-Legal Power and Legitimacy: Perspectives on Prerogative* (New York: Oxford University Press, 2013).

10. Carl Schmitt, *Political Theology: Four Chapters on the Concept of Sovereignty* (1922), trans. George Schwab (Chicago: University of Chicago Press, 2005), 13–14.

11. John Locke, *Second Treatise of Government*, ed. Peter Laslett (Cambridge: Cambridge University Press, 1988), pars. 22, 137, 160.

12. See, e.g., Clement Fatovic and Benjamin A. Kleinerman, "Introduction: Extra-Legal Measures and the Problem of Legitimacy," in *Extra-Legal Power and Legitimacy*, ed. Fatovic and Kleinerman, 1–24, 22.

13. See Thomas Poole, *Reason of State: Law, Prerogative and Empire* (Cambridge: Cambridge University Press, 2015).

14. Goldsmith served as assistant attorney general, Office of Legal Counsel, from 2003 to 2004. Two other essays in the collection do not quite support that argument. Mark Tushnet's essay about adjudication after 9/11 in the United States and the United Kingdom seems to conclude that in advanced liberal democracies politics and law are inextricably tangled, with the result that there is no clear distinction possible or even desirable between what he calls "political constitutionalism" (control by democratic politics) and "legal constitutionalism" (control by the judiciary). Mark Tushnet, "Emergency Powers and Terrorism-Related Regulation circa 2012: Perspectives on Prerogative Power in the United States," in *Extra-Legal Power and Legitimacy*, ed. Fatovic and Kleinerman, 198–213, 212–13. And Leonard C. Feldman argues that Locke's account of prerogative does not provide a normative answer to the questions that arise out of the emergencies. Rather, it merely points to the tensions that exist as a matter of

fact in such situations, tensions that will fall to be resolved on a terrain crowded by contesting political and legal claims. Feldman suggests that the right response is "the strong and strategic assertion of rule of law values." Leonard C. Feldman, "Lockean Prerogative: Productive Tensions," in ibid., 75–93, 93.

15. Jack Goldsmith, "The Irrelevance of Prerogative Power, and the Evils of Secret Legal Interpretation," in Fatovic and Kleinerman, eds., *Extra-Legal Power and Legitimacy*, 214–31, 215, 220.

16. Goldsmith, "The Irrelevance of Prerogative Power," 215, 223.

17. Goldsmith, "The Irrelevance of Prerogative Power," 215 (quotes; emphasis removed from third), 226–29.

18. Fatovic and Kleinerman, "Introduction," 22.

19. Clement Fatovic, "Filling the Void: Democratic Deliberation and the Legitimization of Extra-Legal Action," in Fatovic and Kleinerman, eds., *Extra-Legal Power and Legitimacy*, 169–97, 169.

20. Nomi Claire Lazar, "Prerogative Power in Rome," in Fatovic and Kleinerman, eds., *Extra-Legal Power and Legitimacy*, 27–51.

21. Oren Gross, "Violating Divine Law: Emergency Measures in Jewish Law," in Fatovic and Kleinerman, eds., *Extra-Legal Power and Legitimacy*, 52–74.

22. George Thomas, "The Limits of Constitutional Government: Alexander Hamilton on Extraordinary Power and Executive Discretion," in Fatovic and Kleinerman, eds., *Extra-Legal Power and Legitimacy*, 97–116; Jeremy D. Bailey, "The Jeffersonian Executive: More Energetic, More Responsible, and Less Stable," in ibid., 117–38; Michael Kent Curtis, "Lincoln and Executive Power during the Civil War: A Case Study," in ibid, 139–65.

23. For the most recent version, see David Dyzenhaus, "Preventive Justice and the Rule-of-Law Project," in *Prevention and the Limits of the Criminal Law*, ed. Andrew Ashworth, Lucia Zedner, and Patrick Tomlin (Oxford: Oxford University Press, 2013), 91–114.

24. See Carl Schmitt, *Dictatorship: From the Origin of the Modern Concept of Sovereignty to Proletarian Class Struggle* (1922), trans. Michael Hoelzl and Graham Ward (Cambridge: Polity, 2014), 110–11. On the dark formulation of the idea of sovereign dictatorship, see ibid., 119.

25. Carl Schmitt, "The Guardian of the Constitution" (1931), in Vinx, *The Guardian of the Constitution*, 125–73, 79, 117–20, 151–60, 168–73.

26. Schmitt, "The Guardian of the Constitution," 175.

27. Hans Kelsen, "Who Ought to Be the Guardian of the Constitution?" (1931), in Vinx, *The Guardian of the Constitution*, 174–221, 174.

28. Kelsen, "Who Ought to Be the Guardian of the Constitution?," 189–90.

29. Kelsen, "Who Ought to Be the Guardian of the Constitution?," 206–16, 219.

30. My argument thus differs in emphasis from that in Nomi Claire Lazar's "What Is the State of Exception?" (chapter 1 in this volume). Lazar emphasizes the importance of civic virtue over institutional design, whereas my position is that institutional design promotes virtue.

31. See Isaac, "Constitutional Dictatorship in Twentieth-Century American Political Thought."

32. Schmitt, *Political Theology*, 5.

33. For the fuller version of this argument, from which this is adapted, see Dyzenhaus, "Preventive Justice and the Rule-of-Law Project," 103–9.

34. A. W. B. Simpson, *In the Highest Degree Odious: Detention without Trial in Wartime Britain* (Oxford: Oxford University Press, 1992).

35. *R v Halliday, ex parte Zadig* (1917) AC 260; *Liversidge v. Anderson* (1942) AC 206.

36. See David Dyzenhaus, *The Constitution of Law: Legality in a Time of Emergency* (Cambridge: Cambridge University Press, 2006), 24–26; and David Foxton, "*R v Halliday, Ex Parte Zadig* in Retrospect," *Law Quarterly Review* 119 (2003): 445–94.

37. *Halliday*, 292–93.

38. *Liversidge*, 244.

39. The theory that lies behind this idea is due to Lon L. Fuller. See both his discussion of the eight desiderata of the rule of law that impart to law an "inner morality" in *The Morality of Law* (rev. ed. [New Haven, CT: Yale University Press, 1969], 33–94) and his discussion of conversion in "The Forms and Limits of Adjudication" (in *The Principles of Social Order: Selected Essays of Lon L. Fuller, ed.* Kenneth I. Winston [Oxford: Hart, 2001], 101–39, 111–12). For a more elaborate treatment of this theory, see David Dyzenhaus, "Process and Substance as Aspects of the Public Law Form," *Cambridge Law Journal* 74, no. 2 (2015): 284–306, 296–97.

40. *Liversidge*, 220–22.

41. *Chahal v. United Kingdom* (1996), 23 *European Human Rights Reports* 413.

42. Special Immigration Appeals Commission Act 1997.

43. For a comprehensive account, see David Bonner, *Executive Measures and National Security: Have the Rules of the Game Changed?* (Aldershot: Ashgate, 2007,) pt. 3.

44. *Re Charkaoui* 2009 FC 1030 (CanLII) 353 FTR 187.

45. *A and Others v Secretary of State for the Home Department* (2004) UKHL 56 (2005) 2 AC 68. On the activity of the administrative court, see Adam Tomkins, "National Security and the Role of the Court: A Changed Landscape?," *Law Quarterly Review* 126 (2010): 543–67.

46. See Fiona de Londras, *Detention in the "War on Terror": Can Human Rights Fight Back?* (Cambridge: Cambridge University Press, 2011).

47. See the text at n. 15 above.

48. William J. Novak, "The American Law of Overruling Necessity" (chapter 4 in this volume); Stephen W. Sawyer, "Was There an American Concept of Emergency Powers?" (chapter 7 in this volume); and James T. Sparrow, "Charles Merriam and the Search for Democratic Power After Sovereignty" (chapter 8 in this volume).

49. See in particular Sawyer, "Was There an American Concept of Emergency Powers?"

50. Novak, "The American Law of Overruling Necessity."

51. See Dyzenhaus, "Process and Substance as Aspects of the Public Law Form."

52. John Fabian Witt, "To Save the Country" (chapter 5 in this volume).

53. The thought can be pushed even further back, as Straumann has recently shown in his argument that Cicero's maxim *Salus populi suprema lex esto* has long been misinterpreted. See Benjamin Straumann, *Crisis and Constitutionalism: Roman Political Thought from the Fall of the Republic to the Age of Revolution* (Oxford: Oxford University Press, 2016), 35ff. According to Straumann, Cicero meant not that the maxim placed consuls above the law but rather that it offered a supreme principle that governed their conduct in accordance with the law. For the consuls remained subject to law in at least the sense that they were subject to fundamental or constitutional law, which is law that meets two conditions. First, it is more entrenched than other rules and thus less "susceptible to change." Second, it consists of rules that are politically important, i.e., of "great substantive importance in that they govern the institutions through which political power is exercised." Ibid., 36. And Straumann finds that in the Roman Republic the idea of dictatorship was one that was considered subject to such rules and that the claim that it was not so subject—that dictators at times wielded constituent power—is due to a mistaken understanding of Theodor Mommsen that then formed part of the basis for Schmitt's constitutional theory. Ibid., 282.

54. Schmitt, *Political Theology*, 14.

55. C. J. Friedrich, *Constitutional Reason of State* (Providence, RI: Brown University Press, 1957), 90, 89.

Part Two

The American Experience with Emergency Powers

4

The American Law of Overruling Necessity: The Exceptional Origins of State Police Power

William J. Novak

Extemporize all government.

Ralph Waldo Emerson

Necessity, the tyrant's plea, excus'd his devilish deeds.

John Milton

One of the most significant legal-constitutional moments in the history of the American republic occurred in the Confederation Congress on September 26 and 27, 1787. On those dates, the handiwork of the historic Constitutional Convention in Philadelphia was now "laid before the United States in Congress assembled." And the momentous question for the extant official lawmaking body of the US government was what to do next. Under Article 13 of the Articles of Confederation, any alteration of the articles had to be agreed to by Congress and confirmed by the *legislatures* of *every state*. Notably, the Philadelphia convention had already decided on a radically different mode of ratification via conventions in only nine of the original states (arguably contravening the very article on which Congress officially recommended a Philadelphia convention in the first place). So what should Congress do with this document so "laid before" it? Should it independently debate the report anew? Could it amend the proposed constitution? Should it officially vote to approve or disapprove the document? This was a moment of historic constitutional decisionism.[1]

In the end, of course, Congress bent to the prevailing will and urgency of the Philadelphia moment and "resolved unanimously" to transmit the proposed constitution through to "the several legislatures in order to be submitted to a convention of delegates chosen in each state by the people thereof in conformity to the resolves of the Convention."[2] This crucial decision, however, was not uncontroversial. James Madison wrote George Washington that both Richard Henry Lee and Nathan Dane strenuously objected at the time, noting a "constitutional impropriety in their taking any positive agency in the work" as "the new Constitution was more than an alteration of the Articles of Confederation . . . and even subverted these Articles altogether."[3] As Lee argued: "Congress, acting under the present Constitution definitely limiting their powers, have no right to recommend a plan subverting the government. . . . This plan proposes [to] destroy the Confederation of 13 and [to] establish a new one of 9."[4] More than two hundred years later, Bruce Ackerman and Neal Katyal continued to cite Lee for their influential argument about "the Federalist's flagrant illegalities": "How did the Founders manage to win acceptance of their claim to speak for the People at the same moment that they were breaking the rules of the game?"[5]

Despite accusations of illegality, however, the original actions of the Continental Congress were not without contemporaneous justification. Teasing out the substantive terms of that justification remains difficult, however, as this significant legal-historical event remains oddly underdocumented. Consequently, scholars have been left to glean the substance they can mainly from the notes of Melancton Smith (as well as occasional correspondence and newspaper reports). And, while much has been established concerning this momentous two-day constitutional deliberation, one important aspect has been overlooked by modern scholars. For at the very center of the crucial debates recorded by Melancton Smith was a seemingly constant reference by the Founders to nothing less than *salus populi*—"the safety or welfare of the people"—as the primary substantive rationale through which the US Constitution would pass through Congress to the state ratification conventions so as to become the new American law of the land.

The final recorded speaker on September 27—before Congress's resolution to transmit the constitution to the states—was William Grayson, who argued: "If we have no right to amend, then we ought to give a silent passage, for if we cannot alter, why should we deliberate." According to Smith's notes, his opinion was that "they should stand solely upon the opinion of [the] Convention," taking note that "the *salus populi* much talked of." And, indeed, *salus populi* was much "talked of"—the veritable lingua franca of this moment of foundational constitutional necessity. Henry Lee made the connection explicitly, defending Congress's "right to decide from the great principle of *necessity* or the *salus populi*." He concluded: "Necessity justifies the measure." Richard Henry Lee predictably objected: "The doctrine of *salus populi* is dangerous. . . . If men may do as they please, from this argument all constitutions [are] useless. All tyrants have used it." James Madison countered that there was nothing inherently exceptional or extraordinary or tyrannical in the idea of *salus populi*, seeing viable precedents in earlier efforts to strengthen the Articles of Confederation as well as in the "sale and government" of "the western country."[6]

The pivotal role of "necessity" in this crucial founding moment was not lost on later nineteenth-century constitutional commentators. As Thomas Cooley noted in his highly influential *Constitutional Limitations*, the basic exclusion of original states via nine-state ratification was "not warranted by anything in the Articles of Confederation, which purported to be articles of 'perpetual union.'" For Cooley: "[The] radical revision of the Constitution . . . was really revolutionary in character, and only to be defended on the same ground of *necessity* on which all revolutionary action is justified, and which in this case was the absolute need, fully demonstrated by experience, of a more efficient general government."[7]

So what to make of this curious juxtaposition of necessity, *salus populi*, and fundamental law at a crucial moment in American constitutional development? Like Richard Henry Lee, should we view this as a problem or an aporia—an exception to the underlying principles and strictures of liberal constitutionalism and a dangerous precedent more at home in "the mouths of all tyrants"[8]—a tyrant's plea? Or, like James Madison, should we understand this kind of appeal to necessity and an overriding obligation to the people's health, safety, and welfare as a not uncommon—perhaps even a regular or ordinary—feature of everyday, extemporized governance (especially common in popular or democratic polities)? Moreover, what is the relationship of American law to such exercises of power? Do doctrines and rationales like necessity and *salus populi* stand outside the rule of law, looking in, so to speak—as exceptional and emergency political powers antithetical or hostile to any truly legal regime? Or, on the contrary, are such concepts irreducible elements in the very idea of lawmaking—where the political and the legal are always inextricably mixed in a pragmatic conception of democratic governance in the people's interest?

This chapter begins to make a case for the latter perspective, demonstrating the deep and rather unexceptional historical roots of the idea of exception and necessity in American law and democratic governance. It takes its cue from Thomas Kuhn's famous observation about hermeneutics. "Look first for the apparent absurdities in the text," Kuhn counseled, "and ask yourself how a sensible person could have written them. When you find an answer, I continue, when those passages make sense, then you may find that the more central passages, ones you previously thought you understood, have changed their meaning."[9] Rather than seeing necessity and *salus populi* as exceptional anomalies or apparent absurdities in early American jurisprudence, this chapter attempts to take them seriously and to interrogate their pivotal role in some of the baseline concepts in American public law. The original constitutional moment described above was not a totally unique or exceptional occurrence. Rather, in contrast to conventional understandings that try to separate the rule of law and constitutional governance from problems of exception and necessity formalistically, this chapter offers a more pragmatic and realistic accounting of the close and constant interrelationship of necessity and lawmaking from the earliest days of the Republic. This is especially true of the history of the emergence of American police power, which was frequently discussed and often legitimated in the nineteenth century in terms of a law of "overruling necessity" and *salus populi*.

Salus populi—the safety of the people or the welfare of the people—came from the common law maxim, *Salus populi suprema lex est* (The people's welfare is the highest law).[10] *Salus populi*—and its grounds of overruling necessity, public welfare, and the health and well-being of the populace—would go on to become a major principle of American common law and one of the key bases of US police power—a foundation for modern American state power in general.[11] One of its key legal-constitutional consequences was the idea that public right was always supreme, trumping private right. In an early American legal-constitutional historiography centered primarily on notions of individual private, limited governance, and sometimes even laissez-faire, it is perhaps not surprising that the central place of *salus populi* in the very creation of the Republic has been often overlooked. But, from official invocations in the Confederation Congress to the more everyday development of state legislative and administrative power in the nineteenth century, necessity, emergency, and *salus populi* were regular parts of a long and expansive American regulatory history still in need of further recovery and understanding.

1. Anglo-American Rule of Law versus Necessity, Discretion, and Police

One reason for the comparative neglect of concepts of necessity, exception, and emergency in early American history is the powerful hold of an orthodox and formalist conception of a prevailing Anglo-American rule-of-law tradition implacably hostile to the supposedly foreign (or Continental) political influences of necessity, police, and administration. Though renderings of that rule-of-law tradition are notoriously contested and surprisingly diffuse, they frequently turn on three core principles: (*a*) legal supremacy (a rule of law above the rule of men), (*b*) legal determinacy (limiting individual discretion and volition via a system of rules), and (*c*) legal autonomy (a harsh separation and insulation of the rule of law from democratic politics).

The roots of legal supremacy run deep in American lore, perhaps best captured by Thomas Paine's founding dictum: "In America, *the law is king*." Where absolutism and arbitrary government deemed the king "the law" or even above the law, Paine countered: "In free countries the law ought to be king, and there ought to be no other."[12] That basic sentiment was chiseled into the bedrock of American constitutional dogma by a host of admiring law writers and scribes. Edward Corwin's divination of three fundamental doctrines of American constitutional law—vested rights, judicial review, and due process—established the basic metanarrative. To a "higher law" tradition that he traced back to Demosthenes, Corwin grafted a genealogy of great judges, treatise writers, cases, and doctrines that yielded the supremacy of the American rule of law. The main characters in his story are now familiar—from Stoic natural law and Locke's *Second Treatise* to Blackstone and Kent, from *Dr. Bonham's Case* to *Marbury v. Madison*, from Magna Carta to the Fourteenth Amendment, from vested rights to the due process of law. Corwin's perspective was relentlessly textual, court centered, and juridical, yielding a beguiling template for understanding the power and spirit of the American rule of law.[13] The opening lines of Julius Goebel's first volume of the *Oliver Wendell Holmes Devise History of the Supreme Court of the United States* could not resist its allure. "When the first colonies were planted on the North American continent," Goebel began, "the judicial had come to occupy a preeminence in the English constitution." While he admitted that it might be "a little pretentious to speak of a spirit of the laws" operating in colonial America, he forged ahead with the rule-of-law creation narrative: "Nevertheless, one finds [there] that independently of the laws made by men, a complex of principles is unceasingly operative—the supremacy of law, the prescription of certainty, the orderly determination of controversies and, above all, the dominating concept of due process."[14]

In this "suzerainty of the great fundamentals," legal determinacy—"legal certainty"—was the second great guiding principle.[15] For Antonin Scalia, the rule of law was a knowable and predictable "law of rules," the main object of which was to limit personal discretion. Scalia explicitly deployed the central dichotomy of "a general rule of law" versus "personal discretion to do justice," citing Aristotle's *Politics*: "Rightly constituted laws should be the final sovereign; and personal rule, whether it be exercised by a single person or body of persons, should be sovereign only in those matters on which law is unable, owing to the difficulty of framing general rules for all contingencies, to make exact pronouncement." While admitting the actual difficulty, if not impossibility, of the jurist's dream of a truly "gapless" system of such general rules, Scalia's jurisprudence was dedicated, at least in theory, to the ideal of judicial restraint, where "judges [were] bound, not only by the text of code or Constitution, but also by the prior decisions of superior courts." For Scalia, stare decisis, originalism, and textualism were but alternative formulations for what John Manning has called an underlying "anti-discretion principle"—where decisions were ultimately "bound by standards," rules, and sources of authority external to the decider's will.[16] This vision of Promethean justice distinctly *bound* by relatively determinate precedents, rules, traditions, and so-called rule-of-law values was key to separating out law and jurisprudence above and beyond those other *unbound* arenas of open and discretionary decision making—like politics, administration, and police.

But it was Albert Venn Dicey's *Law of the Constitution* that most powerfully stitched these themes together in the epic apologia "The Rule of Law—Its Nature." As Felix Frankfurter captured the impact of Dicey's formulation: "Few books in modern times have had an influence comparable to that produced by the brilliant obfuscation of Dicey's *Law of the Constitution*."[17] Dicey too emphasized the ultimate suzerainty or "absolute supremacy" of the rule of law: "Englishmen are ruled by the law, and by the law alone." And he first defended that rule-of-law tradition squarely in terms of its opposition to discretionary power: "In this sense the rule of law is contrasted with every system of government based on the exercise by persons in authority of wide, arbitrary, or discretionary powers." He found the rule-of-law tradition distinctive or "peculiar" to England and "to those countries which, like the United States of America, have inherited English traditions." "Wherever there is discretion, there is room for arbitrariness," he argued. And that "means insecurity for legal freedom on the part of subjects." Ultimately, Dicey's goal was to contrast the distinctive Anglo-American rule of law with the governance of "most continental states" and particularly the French system of *droit administratif*. For him, administration was too bound up with the kind of potentially abusive and tyrannical discretionary powers of executive action and public officialdom associated in England's past with royal prerogative and Star Chamber.[18] Dicey thus attempted to recenter a relatively autonomous Anglo-American rule of law and a law of the constitution purged for the moment of their inconvenient historical ties to discretion, necessity, emergency, and the politics of administration and police.

Dicey's influential rendering of the nature of the rule of law subsequently spawned a whole host of imitators and acolytes, ranging from the profound to the absurd. In *The Road to Serfdom*, Friedrich Hayek explicitly invoked Dicey's rule of law (excluding "the existence of arbitrariness, of prerogative, or even of widely discretionary authority on the part of government") as the antidote to despotic planning: "Stripped of all its technicalities, [the rule of law] means that government in all its actions is bound by rules fixed and announced beforehand—rules which make it possible to foresee with fair certainty how the authorities will use its coercive powers.... The discretion left to the executive organs wielding coercive power should be reduced as much as possible."[19] More recently, Philip Hamburger's *Is Administrative Law Unlawful?* has reinvoked the Diceyean specter of a reemergent Continental and "absolutist civilian tradition" wherein "administrative officers" are again "outside and above the law" in a wholesale (and ultimately unconvincing) critique of the modern American administrative state.[20]

Such formalist conceptions of an Anglo-American rule of law poised squarely against discretion, administration, and executive action have also infiltrated the more sophisticated debates about the states of exception and emergency discussed in this volume. Giorgio Agamben's influential *State of Exception*, for example, was built squarely on the baseline distinction between law and politics—placing "the state of necessity, on which the exception is founded," precisely at the "limit" or "intersection" or "border" or "no-man's land" between the legal and the political. Agamben's concept of the exception took coherent form through a rigid separation of "public law" from "political fact" and "juridical order" from "life."[21] Of course, Agamben's musings on law, state, and exception were but supplements to *Political Theology*, in which Carl Schmitt too relied on the purported disjunction between liberal law and exceptional statecraft: "the old liberal negation of the state vis-à-vis law" where it is "not the state but law that is sovereign." Schmitt rendered exception and emergency as distinctly outside and apart from the conventional rule of law: "What is argued about is the concrete application, and that means who decides in a situation of conflict what constitutes the public interest or interest of the state, public safety and order, *le salut public*, and so on. The exception, which is not codified in the existing legal *order*, can at best be characterized as a case of extreme peril, a danger to the existence of the state, or the like. But it *cannot be circumscribed factually and made to conform to a preformed law*."[22] While Agamben's and Schmitt's theories of exception and emergency have appeal in terms of the critical leverage they provide against highly abstracted understandings of the rule of law, they risked further reifying the historical reality of such formalisms in the first place.

But, of course, there are alternative avenues to a critical analysis of the American state of exception and the law of overruling necessity. Indeed, the last century and a half of work in American jurisprudence and legal social science has taken exact issue with formalist separations of law and politics, juridical order and life. Whether that work takes the form of historical jurisprudence, sociological jurisprudence, legal pragmatism, legal realism, legal instrumentalism, legal functionalism, law and society, critical legal studies, or sociolegal history, the verdict is essentially the same—that a modern, antiformalist, nonfoundational, postmetaphysical understanding of law confounds the very idea of separating law from politics and/or society. Oliver Wendell Holmes's brilliant deployment of the perspective of the "bad man" in his critical realist "The Path of the Law" turned as early as 1897 on confounding the formalist inside/outside or law/outlaw distinction.[23] Similarly, John Dewey's concept of law was "through and through a social phenomenon; social in origin, in purpose or end, and in application." It could not be talked about in isolation from politics or society or history. It could be discussed only "in terms of the social conditions in which it arises and of what it concretely does there." Unless law was investigated in society and as an irreducibly social and political activity, there were "scraps of paper or voices in the air but nothing that can be called law."[24]

Dewey's critique of a purely intellectualist or formalist approach to law was echoed by Karl Llewellyn's legal realist indictment of the "myth, folderol, and claptrap" that permeated so many formalistic discussions of law and liberalism. Llewellyn's *Bramble Bush* exploded the law/politics distinction: "The doing of something about disputes is the business of law. And the people who have the doing in charge, whether they be judges or sheriffs or clerks or jailers or lawyers, are officials of the law. What these officials do about disputes is, to my mind, the law itself. And rules through all of this are important so far as they help you see or predict what officials will do. That is all their importance, except as pretty plaything."[25] This skeptical, pragmatic, and realist approach to the rule of law became the foundation of modern sociolegal studies in the United States. The legal historian Willard Hurst had little patience with the formalist law/politics binary: "In deciding what to include as 'law' I do not find it profitable to distinguish 'law' from 'government' or from 'policy.'" Robert Cover continued the American tradition of washing the rule of law in "cynical acid," reminding us that legal interpretation took place within a plane of violence, conflict, and coercion—what he famously dubbed "a field of pain and death."[26]

The American pragmatic and legal realist traditions were, in other words, born in direct revolt against the formalism of legal liberalism, classically construed. Pragmatists and realists systematically challenged the idea of an Anglo-American rule-of-law tradition existing somewhere outside and beyond the problems of necessity, emergency, and exception—as a higher, exceptional alternative to foreign or Continental traditions of administration, politics, and police.

2. *Necessity,* Salus Populi, *and the Early Development of State Police Power*

One excellent place to more pragmatically witness and realistically assess the close interrelationship of law, necessity, and public power in American history is in the development of state police power. It is difficult to overstate the significance of this particular legal doctrine and political practice in American history. Police power was basically the crucial site for the expansion of public authority beyond the ancient bounds and jurisdictions of local and municipal self-governance toward a more capacious, centralized, and generalized conception of state regulatory and governing power. In the nineteenth century, this state police power was the preeminent legal-political technology that powered pubic authority well past older common law conceptions of the legitimate range of public action. Police power thus marked the crucial inflection point for the transition from primarily juridical to increasingly legislative and administrative discretion and authority.[27] Finally, this same police power provided the working template for attempts in the early twentieth century to shift the site of a more open-ended legislative, regulatory, and administrative power to the national level. While technically the idea of a truly federal or national police power in American law was constitutionally impossible, the nineteenth-century expansion of state police power was the model for the development of a national plenary power over immigration as well as the subsequent growth and transformation of national taxing, spending, postal, and commerce powers. It would thus seem that the story of the seemingly unstoppable growth of American police power offers great potential for exploring the intersection of law and statecraft, constitutionalism and administration, and precedential rules and the nature of exception.

So what is police power? Basically, *police power* is the name that nineteenth-century American jurists ultimately gave to the powers of a state legislature to pass laws that regulated private interests, properties, and liberties in the more general interest of public safety, health, comfort, order, morals, and welfare. Notably, early American states were actually exercising such powers long before jurists and treatise writers decided on this particular legal nomenclature. Police power was a vibrant and vital political practice long before it was instantiated as a jurisprudential category. Indeed, in its first years of constitutional being—from 1781 to 1801—the state legislature of New York passed police regulations concerning everything from public economy (e.g., lotteries, usury, hawkers and peddlers, etc.), to public morals (e.g., cursing, drunkenness, gaming, etc.), to public health and safety (e.g., firing woods, ship quarantine, the practice of physic and surgery, etc.), to public order and welfare (e.g., beggars, disorderly persons, dogs, poor relief, etc.).[28] Such regulatory powers were seen as necessary and integral parts of the development of general lawmaking authority in a crucial democratic moment as powers once derived from royal prerogative or the High Court of Parliament devolved on newly established American state legislatures.

In many ways, the police power resembles other kinds of government power that are routinely discussed in terms of formal legal categories, for example, the taxing power or the eminent domain power. But what makes the police power more distinct, more problematic, and of more interest to discussions of emergency and necessity (as well as democracy) is its more open-ended, almost unbounded quality. This feature of police power has been a constant topic of jurisprudential discussion and commentary for well over a century. Massachusetts chief justice Lemuel Shaw inaugurated that tradition when he argued classically in *Commonwealth v. Alger* (1851): "[I]t is much easier to perceive and realize the existence of [police] power than to mark its boundaries or to prescribe limits to its exercise." New York's Justice Andrews concurred in *People v. Budd* (1889): "The generality of the terms employed by jurists and publicists in defining this power, while they show the breadth and universality of its presence, nevertheless leave its boundaries and limitations indefinite." Andrews went on to warn against circumscription: "The moment the police power is destroyed or curbed by fixed and rigid rules, a danger is introduced in our system."[29] For Collins Denny, the police power encompassed "one of the most difficult phases of our law to understand": "[I]t is even more difficult to define it within any bounds." And Lewis Hochheimer simply analogized police power to plenary power—the "inherent plenary power of a State."[30] In the late nineteenth century, US Supreme Court justice McKenna described police power as "the most essential of powers—at times, the most insistent, and always one of the least limitable powers of government." And more recently William O. Douglas echoed: "An attempt to define its reach or trace its outer limits is fruitless."[31] Consequently, throughout the nineteenth century and into the twentieth, police power was presented as an inherent and irreducible attribute of governance and statecraft in almost existential discussions of society's relationship to plenary power. As New York justice Woodworth mused as early as 1827, police power was "incident to every well regulated society, and without which it could not well exist."[32]

Significantly for the purposes of this particular volume, the whole development of nineteenth-century American state police power was grounded in larger ideas of "overruling necessity." For most historians and commentators, this unmoored, overruling, emergency, and exceptional quality in police power was intimately bound up with more general European notions of police or *Polizei*. As Marc Raeff, among others, has demonstrated, *Polizeiwissenschaft* celebrated the broad and positive ambitions of governance beyond the traditional public tasks of mere order maintenance and the administration of justice. Indeed, police embraced the more capacious and open-ended task of fostering all "the productive energies of society."[33] Consequently, as Michel Foucault simply put it: "The police includes everything." Maurice Block's *Dictionnaire de l'administration française* (1856) captured something of the vastness of police administration in a list of varieties of police: "morals and religion, sanitary police, police relating to public security, rural and forestry police, police of substance—embracing control over butchers, fairs, markets, prices—industrial and commercial police, police control over carriers, and finally judiciary police, or that pertaining to the administration of justice." Robert von Mohl's *Polizei-Wissenschaft* emphasized three overarching objects of police power relating to "the care of the physical, intellectual and moral needs of the public" with chapters devoted to "the care of the State for population, health, aid to the needy, agriculture, trade, education, and religion."[34] For Foucault, the eleven categories of police in Nicolas Delamare's *Traité de la police* (1722) constituted "the great charter of police functions in the Classical period" with three great aims: "economic regulation (the circulation of commodities, manufacturing processes, the obligations of tradespeople both to one another and to their clientele), measures of public order (surveillance of dangerous individuals, expulsion of vagabonds, and, if necessary, beggars and the pursuit of criminals), and general rules of hygiene (checks on the quality of foodstuffs sold, the water supply and the cleanliness of the streets)."[35]

The relationship of police to a capacious and nearly unlimitable conception of necessitous governance has been the subject of several distinguished commentaries. Indeed, scholars like Nikolas Rose, Mitchell Dean, and Pasquale Pasquino have placed this all-important topic—the nature of the legal and political power of police, broadly construed—at the very center of the history of the making of modern sovereignty, modern governance, the modern state, and even modern empire. Like Rose, Dean, and Pasquino, Mariana Valverde has drawn special inspiration from Foucault in delineating an expansive genealogy of police as power over populations shifted from ecclesiastical pastor to secular potentate: "Police is the direct governmentality of the sovereign as sovereign . . . the permanent *coup d'etat*."[36] For Christopher Tomlins, the police in the police power marks the central component in an insistently expanding and expansive American sovereignty.[37] And, for Markus Dubber especially, the essence of police power is necessity—overruling necessity—the inherently unlimited, extraconstitutional, discretionary prerogative of the sovereign to act quickly and expediently so as to eliminate threats to the health, safety, and security of the people. Indeed, the links between police power and the state of exception, national emergency power, military/martial law, and criminality and incarceration are most direct and inescapable in Dubber's formidable *oeuvre* on this topic.[38]

But one limitation of this otherwise impressive body of work on police is the tendency to separate out the open-ended dimensions of police, policy, necessity, and emergency from the more general operations of ordinary law. Indeed, the separate spheres of law and police is the major trope in both Tomlins's and Dubber's explorations of police in the American context. For Tomlins, law is nothing short of "the American modality of rule," while police is the continental European alternative invoking "a different set of assumptions about social relations." He quotes the German liberal Eduard Lasker: "Rule of law and rule of police are two different ways to which history points, two methods of development between which peoples must choose and have chosen."[39] For Dubber, reviving the "distinction between law and police" is nothing short of urgent because "it brings out the distinguishing feature of law as a mode of governance." Indeed, he claims that the law/police distinction is at the heart of most important academic discussions of a distinctly "liberal" legality in "First Amendment theory, in [Lon] Fuller's distinction between 'managerial direction' and 'law,' in [Friedrich] Hayek's vision of law as a 'rule of just conduct,' and in Herbert Packer's distinction between two models of criminal process, 'managerial' Crime Control and Due Process." For Dubber, this fundamental antinomy is central to the preservation of the liberal idea of a jural or law state (*Rechtsstaat*) distinct from a dangerous police state.[40]

While this robust scholarship has done much to illuminate the central role of necessity, exception, and emergency in the development of police, it goes somewhat astray in positing police as a special sphere of government action and ambition separate from or outside the law. The idea harbors the comforting illusion that law will provide a steady answer and a compelling alternative to the problem of police in the modern state—that it can be used to distinguish good police from bad police easily and to rein in arbitrary and despotic exertions of police power. The idea draws on a deeply rooted set of rule-of-law values that sees law (*Recht, Ius*) as the antithesis of power, sovereignty, coercion, and violence. It also draws authority from an orthodox American legal and constitutional history that too frequently portrays the rule of law as a nay-saying, outside limitation on state power—checking, balancing, dividing, and constraining power—the ultimate liberal (of late, libertarian) guardian of rights to life, liberty, and property against the artificial usurpations of state authority and regulatory government.

But, contrary to this general trend in theorizing police, administration, and exception as transconstitutional or extralegal decisionist and political forces that know no law, they are better understood as part and parcel of the legal history of democratic states. Indeed, far from being strange bedfellows, law and police have been frequent fellow travelers in the development of American state power. Police power originated and was legitimated in law—in the delegations of prerogative and privilege in the charters of the municipalities, villages, corporations, and subsidiary associations that reflected the intimate interrelationships of the state, the law, and the legitimate power to regulate, expropriate, and punish. The official development of the police power as a legal doctrine is almost inseparable from the story of the rise of the judiciary and the common law and American constitutionalism. Indeed, the original phrase *police power* comes from none other than US Supreme Court chief justice John Marshall, much as the concept was most fully worked out by Massachusetts chief justice Lemuel Shaw.[41] In short, though it is common to separate the jural state and the police state, the norm and the exception, as necessary antipodes in a normatively charged metanarrative of the promise and perils of rule, the actual legal history of the American version of the modern democratic state suggests a closer interconnection and interpenetration of sovereignty, necessity, police, and the rule of law.

Indeed, after the pioneering case work of jurists like Marshall, Shaw, and Woodworth, American legal treatise writers explicitly insisted on drawing the connection between the police power and the law of overruling necessity. As Ernst Freund put it in his definitive treatise on *Police Power*: "A government cannot be said to be free and liberal in which there is not a considerable margin between the practice of legislation and constitutional limitations; for a government must have powers to exercise in time of emergency which it would be tyranny to use without such necessity."[42] A decade before Freund, W. P. Prentice organized his entire treatise on *police powers* around the basic idea of "the law of overruling necessity," noting: "The police power inherent in every sovereignty, for the protection of the public welfare, is difficult of exact definition. It has been well said that 'it is easier to perceive and realize the existence of this power than to mark its boundaries or to prescribe limits to its exercise.' Followed through the decisions of the courts, police powers . . . arise under what has been termed 'the law of overruling necessity.'"[43] Platt Potter's notable *Treatise on Statutes* concurred: "There exists another power by which private property may be taken, used or destroyed for the benefit of others, and this is called the *police power*; sometimes called the law of overruling necessity." George Wickersham's pioneering article "The Police Power" began with Prentice's observation that the "law of overruling necessity" was "an exception to all human ordinances and constitutions," and yet, Wickersham concluded, "the entire doctrine of the police power" was "the creation of the courts."[44] The definitive chroniclers of the actual origins and development of nineteenth-century police power and overruling necessity were unanimous that, far from being something outside or foreign to American law, police power was a product of judges and courts and distinctly legal technologies. Platt Potter was unambiguous: "This doctrine of overruling necessity, or police power, was the common law of this state at the time of the adoption of this state constitution. . . . It was brought from England by our ancestors as a part of their system of common law; was adopted by our ancestors as the law of the land; it is not clearly repugnant to the constitution; but being adopted by it, is in effect a part of it."[45]

Indeed, American courts and commentators consistently referred to a canonical line of cases making it "well settled at common law" that in instances of necessity or calamity—for example, fire, pestilence, or war—individual interests, rights, or injuries would not inhibit the preservation of the common weal. As Potter put it: "It was well settled common law, as we find both by the best elementary law writers, and by uniform adjudications in the courts, that in cases of actual necessity,—as that of preventing the spread of fire,—the ravages of a pestilence, or any other great calamity, the private property of any individual may be lawfully taken, used or destroyed for the relief, protection, or safety of the many, without subjecting the actors to personal responsibility."[46] In the *Case of King's Prerogative in Salt-Peter* (1606), Sir Edward Coke made the classic case for necessity and legal exceptions in times of emergency: "By the common law every man may come upon any land for the defence of the realm, and in such case, and on such extremity, they may dig for gravel for the making of bulwarks, for this is for the public, and every one hath a benefit by it. And for the commonwealth, a man shall suffer damage; as for saving of a city, or town, a house shall be plucked down if the next be on fire;—and the suburbs of a city in time of war, for the common safety shall be plucked down; and a thing for the commonwealth a man may do, without being liable to an action." In the equally famous "case of necessity" known as *Mouse's Case* (1608), a tempest threatened a barge and the lives of its forty-seven passengers, requiring the summary ejectment overboard of "a hogshead of wine and other ponderous things," all without compensation or legal redress: "Every one ought to bear his loss for the safeguard and life of a man, for *interest reipublicae quod homines conserventur*; plucking down of a house in time of fire, etc., and this *pro bono publico; et conservatio vitae hominis est bonum publicum*." In *British Cast Plate Manufacturers v. Meredith* (1792), Justice Buller made the rationale and connection to *salus populi* explicit: "There are many cases in which individuals sustain an injury for which the law gives no action; for instance, pulling down houses, or raising bulwarks for the preservation and defence of the king, done against the king's enemies. This is one of the cases to which the maxim applies, '*Salus populi suprema est lex*.'"[47]

Here, then, was the link between necessity, *salus populi*, and, ultimately, the American development of state police power. America's Blackstone, Chancellor James Kent, made that link explicit in his commentaries: "Rights of property must be made subservient to the public welfare. The maxim is, that a private mischief is to be endured, rather than a public inconvenience. On this ground rests the *rights of public necessity*. If a common highway be out of repair, a passenger may lawfully go through an adjoining private enclosure. So it is lawful to raze houses to the ground to prevent the spreading of a conflagration. These are cases of *urgent necessity*; but private property must . . . yield to the general interest."[48] Kent used this rationale to uphold a veritable slew of legislative regulations of unwholesome trades, slaughterhouses, gunpowder, cemeteries, and the like. As Oliver Wendell Holmes accurately noted later in his famous edition of Kent's *Commentaries*, this doctrine was the foundation of the state police power.[49]

The American police power flowed directly from these early legal conceptions of overruling necessity and *salus populi*. If the common welfare and safety of society were the highest law, it followed that, when the preservation of that society was at stake, lesser rules and conventions gave way. As Thomas Cooley reasoned, here individual interest "must yield to that 'necessity' which 'knows no law.'" Any injury to the individual was *damnum absque injuria* (an injury without a remedy) under the reasoning that "a private mischief shall be endured, rather than a public inconvenience."[50] As New York justice Hubbard synthesized these ideas in *Wynehamer v. People*: "The police power is, of necessity, despotic in its character . . . and in emergencies, it may be exercised to the destruction of property, without compensation to the owner. . . . It is the public exigency which demands the summary destruction, upon the maxim that the safety of the society is the paramount law. It is the application of the personal right or principle of self preservation to the body politic."[51] Thus, W. P. Prentice could begin his treatise *Police Powers Arising under the Law of Overruling Necessity* by drawing directly on this long line of well-established precedent, noting that "police powers arising under the law of overruling necessity are no new topic in any practical administration of sovereign authority." The powers were as ancient as those precedents that promoted "'bulwarks for the defense of the realm.'" Here, Prentice concluded, the act of the government was "for the defense of society, or the people whose peace is invaded by any violence."[52] And society must be defended.

The actual development of such "police laws" across almost every conceivable aspect of American life and government and regulation is now the subject of some fairly dense books and treatises. From overruling necessity, *salus populi*, and the common law of public nuisance, the American doctrine and practice of police power grew throughout the nineteenth century into a powerful font of state and ultimately federal regulatory authority. By 1894, Prentice could already trace the development of police laws and statutes through a host of permutations: local administration, metropolitan and market laws, sanitary regulations, mandatory and restraining laws relative to game, intoxicating liquors, and oleomargarine, health and quarantine laws, laws for the protection of purity in water and food and protection against danger from inflammable oils and explosive substances, vital statistics, the regulation of offensive trades and nuisances, building laws, regulations for tenement and lodging houses, licenses, taxes, regulations for occupations, and urban administration. And that was but the tip of the iceberg. Prentice concluded by noting the ever-larger expanse "for the necessary exercise of police powers . . . as new occasions and new demands arise" in a polity where "the object of government and law is the welfare of the people."[53]

3. The Nationalization of Police, Necessity, and Emergency

Of course, one of the truisms regarding this initial development of American police power through older legal conceptions of necessity and *salus populi* was that it remained largely a matter of local, municipal, and state governance. As Gary Gerstle highlighted this peculiar outgrowth of American federalism: "The states operated according to a different governing principle than did the central state." And that principle was "known in judicial circles as 'the police power.' "[54] As John Marshall defended the breadth of such state police power even against the claims of the Bill of Rights: "The Constitution was ordained and established by the people of the United States for themselves and not for the government of the individual states."[55] In *United States v. Dewitt* (1870), the US Supreme Court echoed the antebellum constitutional consensus that the police power was explicitly a state and local rather than a federal power. Closely following Chief Justice Marshall's analysis in *Barron*, Chief Justice Chase held that, though Congress clearly had the authority to regulate interstate commerce, it did not have a general, open-ended national power to pass regulations of internal state police in the interests of public health, safety, and welfare. The police power remained with the individual states and localities, and the national government wielded nothing analogous to the general plenary authority of state legislatures to regulate liberty and property in the public interest.[56]

But, despite this clear, consensual, and formal doctrinal limitation on the legal extent of state police power, larger concerns of necessity and *salus populi*, of course, knew no such bounds. Indeed, as John Witt's work on Francis Lieber and his *Lincoln's Code* make clear, the kinds of national existential issues that faced the Confederation Congress in September 1787 did not dissipate after ratification. To the contrary, as Witt deftly puts the point: "One hundred and fifty years ago, the United States was a world leader in emergency constitutionalism."[57] Consequently, the same kind of emergency, necessity, and extemporizing pressures—*salus populi*—that allowed for the almost unbounded expansion and exertion of state police powers in the nineteenth century underwrote another momentous transformation in the twentieth century as the locus of modern American governing authority moved ineluctably from the local to the national (and arguably from the state legislature to the national executive).[58]

As Samuel P. Hays, among many other historians, has noted, the period between 1880 and 1920 witnessed a thoroughgoing nationalization and systematization of American social and economic life necessitating a distinctly "upward shift of decision-making" power. Leonard D. White surveyed the extent of state centralization even before the onset of the New Deal in 1933: "The evidence of the last thirty years demonstrates a steady accretion of power and influence by the state governments over the administrative powers of local officials especially in the fields of public finance, education, health and highways, as well as a steady extension of federal influence over the states, particularly in the regulation of commerce." In 1923, Leonard Thompson surveyed a similar trend toward "federal centralization," noting that "[s]ince the Civil War there has been a marked tendency for the federal government to increase its activities," provoking "considerable discussion during the last few years."[59] In this respect, one of the more important developments in the transformation of public power in this period was the construction of a *de facto* (if not *de jure*) nationalization of police power culminating in the unmistakable centralization of general-welfare lawmaking authority in the United States—the roots of a modern, central administrative and regulatory state.

This process of nationalization was twofold. First, the police power increasingly became a more positive public law doctrine that defined modern legislative regulatory power. Second, and somewhat more surreptitiously, the police power—and its underlying rationales of necessity and *salus populi*—began to go national.

One of the chief architects of the first transformation was Ernst Freund. Like Francis Lieber, Freund was one of the great, relatively anonymous revolutionaries in American political and legal history, pioneering a modern redefinition of legislative, administrative, and regulatory power. He accomplished this through a range of reform activities, numerous scholarly articles, and four influential treatises on the key legal issues surrounding the creation of the modern American state: *Police Power, Standards of American Legislation, Administrative Powers*, and *Legislative Regulation*.[60] His approach was unmistakably pragmatic, realistic, and functionalist. For Freund, modern socioeconomic change—particularly "the growing power, scope, and complexity of private industrial and social action"—brought an increasing demand for positive state action in the public interest. That action appropriately took the form of written, legislative enactments in areas of police, revenue, and administration that were increasingly positive and public rather than declaratory and private. These regulatory statutes were the hallmarks of a modern state highlighting the expansion of "the functions of government" in pursuit of "the public welfare" and "the public interest."[61]

At the center of this expansion of legislative regulation and the socioeconomic functions of government stood the police power—the major open-ended source of state regulatory authority in American public law. Together with a bevy of other commentaries in this period, Freund's *Police Power* helped free the conception of police power from the limitations of its common law origins and establish it as the public law foundation of extensive legislative regulatory authority.[62] As Freund put it: "[T]he care of the public welfare, or internal public policy, has for its object the improvement of social and economic conditions affecting the community at large and collectively, with a view to bringing about 'the greatest good of the greatest number.'"[63] It was here that an expanded conception of police power did its work, no longer primarily preoccupied with negative common law protections or the simple maintenance of civil and criminal justice, but reconstituted as an instrument for the open-ended positive promotion of public welfare and the satisfaction of public needs and necessities. In this way, Freund transformed the police power from a more limited doctrine of community self-defense and protection hemmed in by traditional common law maxims and local and customary legal procedures into a more positive and open-ended authority to legislate broadly on behalf of the general welfare. Modern legislation and regulation needed to be instrumentally responsive to direct public policy needs rather than constrained by traditional common law conceptions and routines.

By linking the police power with the general promotion of public welfare in a positive legislative state, Freund and his compatriots paved the way for the explosive growth of police power regulation in the Progressive era. Regulatory statute books swelled, case numbers rose exponentially, and expositions on police power proliferated. A new forcefulness and resourcefulness crept into discussions as progressives expanded the scale and scope of American legislative power, calling for the police power to be "more freely exercised and private property more freely controlled to meet the needs of the changed conditions of society." Some progressives saw in the police power "almost unlimited opportunities for adopting whatever legislation the augmenting demands of social pioneers may require."[64]

But legislative police power not only dramatically expanded its scale and scope in this period; it also began a steady and surprising ascent up the levels of American government. While Chief Justices Marshall and Chase were technically and doctrinally correct that the police power *per se* remained a state power, one of the unmistakable developments in modern American legislation and regulation at the turn of the twentieth century was the degree to which Congress insistently expanded its policing powers through the creative exercise of its commerce, taxing, spending, and postal powers. As Charles Evans Hughes told the American Bar Association in 1918, the most significant decisions of the recent Supreme Court involved three aspects of such federal expansion: (*a*) "[t]he extended application of the doctrine that federal rules governing interstate commerce may have the quality of police regulations"; (*b*) "[t]he approval of the cooperation of nation and states"; and (*c*) "[t]he recognition of the sweeping authority of Congress over the relations between interstate common carriers and their employees."[65] In the areas of business, labor, transportation, morals, health, safety, and education, powers and issues that were once the exclusive domain of state and local governments moved up into the purview of the national government in one of the most significant expropriations of political power in American history. And, as Ernst Freund argued in 1920, the role of law and the judiciary in that expropriation was pivotal: "The consolidation of our own nation has proved our allotment of federal powers to be increasingly inadequate; and had it not been aided by liberal judicial construction, our situation would be unbearable."[66]

One of the most important advocates of such an expansive legal construction was Robert E. Cushman. Cushman would eventually go on to write one of the most important treatises on the emergence of independent regulatory commissions on the national level.[67] But first he cut his teeth on the conundrum of federal police power. In one of a series of highly influential articles in the *Minnesota Law Review*, he noted: "The enumeration of the congressional powers in the Constitution does not include any general grant of authority to pass laws for the protection of the health, morals, or general welfare of the nation. It follows, then, that if Congress is to exercise a police power at all, it must do so by a process something akin to indirection." Cushman argued that, if Congress wanted to expand progressive state police power experiments to the national level in an ambitious program to secure the general welfare, it would have to "cloak its good works under its authority to tax, or to regulate commerce, or to control the mails, or the like, and say, 'By this authority we pass this law in the interest of the public welfare.'"[68] That is exactly what Congress did in passing such important national morals, health, safety, and economic regulations as the Pure Food and Drug Act (1906), the Mann Act (1910), the Harrison Narcotics Tax Act (1914), the Child Labor Tax Act (1919), and the National Prohibition Act (1919). Through the spending power and federal grants-in-aid to individual states, Congress was able to wield even more national regulatory authority through the incentive power of the public purse. Consequently, the United States achieved a centralization of national legislative police power authority even before the Supreme Court accepted an expansive interpretation of the interstate commerce clause at the height of the New Deal.[69] Indeed, many of the central components of a modern, positivist, and central legislative and regulatory state were well established in the United States by the time Ernst Freund died and Franklin Delano Roosevelt won election to the presidency in the fall of 1932.

4. Conclusion

The transformation of the police power from its roots in early conceptions of local self-government and common law notions of necessity and *salus populi* into a font of modern legislative, regulatory, and administrative power is one of the epic developments in the history of the American state. And, obviously, a short essay like this can only hint at the actual scale and scope of its implications for everyday American life across the public policy spectrum from issues of public health, safety, and welfare to issues of public utility, public provision, public necessity, and even public emergency. Moreover, it is the contention of this essay that this larger history of the police power is implicated everywhere in trying to understand the larger interrelationship of the American rule of law and the problem of emergency. One closing example might suffice to underscore this important final point.

Between the two historic events that usually frame most discussions of law and emergency—Lincoln's extraordinary wartime presidency and

Article 48 and the rise of Hitler's dictatorship—there was another important episode in the legal expansion of American state powers of emergency. In World War I, the Woodrow Wilson administration launched another extraordinary program of legislative, executive, administrative, and central state action that included such expansive initiatives as conscription, espionage and sedition acts, national prohibition, and the extraordinary experiment in domestic price controls known as the Lever Act or the Food and Fuel Control Act of 1917. As one contemporary critic put it: "The power demanded is greater than has ever been exercised by any king or potentate of earth; it is broader than that which is exercised by the Kaiser of the Germans. It is a power such as no Caesar ever employed over a conquered province in the bloodiest days of Rome's bloody despotism."[70] As Clinton Rossiter enumerated the most important statutory delegations of emergency power to the president, these included "acts empowering [the president] to take over and operate the railroads and water systems, to regulate or commandeer all shipbuilding facilities in the United States, to regulate and prohibit exports, to raise an army by conscription, to allocate priorities in transportation, to regulate the conduct of resident enemy aliens, to take over and operate the telegraph and telephone systems, to redistribute functions among the executive agencies of the federal government, to control the foreign language press, and to censor all communications to and from foreign countries."[71]

But though Wilson's actions have been subject to much scrutiny and commentary, one aspect of this important story has been conspicuously overlooked—the issue of where the Wilson administration turned for historic precedents for this seemingly unprecedented ramping up of American executive and emergency power. One might guess that Lincoln's presidency would suffice. What is surprising, however, is the degree to which, while briefly noting both Confederate and Federal Civil War precedents, the Wilson administration turned instead to another extraordinary historical record of so-called emergency legislation—the legislative record of the American states during the American Revolution.

In 1918, J. Reuben Clark Jr. was charged by Wilson and the attorney-general of the United States with compiling a compendium of historic American emergency legislation dealing especially with regulations "for the public use, benefit, or welfare."[72] The volume included over one thousand pages of historic American statutes. Civil War legislation consumed about fifty of those pages, but most of the rest of the volume—some eight hundred pages—cataloged the extraordinary legislative activities of the Continental Congress and especially the laws of the individual states from Connecticut to Virginia.

Clark began by listing the major wartime congressional acts of the World War I emergency from the Shipping Board Act to the Trading with the Enemy Act. He then detailed Wilson's presidential proclamations and executive orders regarding everything from the manufacture of explosives to the ammonia industry. The accompanying subject digest for these Wilson wartime-era initiatives consumed almost another hundred pages covering matters from accounting, aircraft, alcohol, ammunition, arms, and anchorage to warehouses, war material, the War Trade Board, and wheat.

Then, the vast majority of the eight hundred pages of precedential emergency legislation in the Wilson administration report makes clear the direct links between police power, overruling necessity, and emergency in a much longer American legal history. The American revolutionary state legislatures took center stage. In almost all the states, the legislatures began by taking control of state trade and political economy and aggressively policing fraud and wartime opportunism. Connecticut, for example, early passed an "Act to Encourage Fair Dealing, and to Restrain and Punish Sharpers and Oppressors" that required a license to purchase a wide range of everyday household products. In 1778, at the urging of an actively engaged Continental Congress, commissioners from seven states met in New Haven and agreed to regulate the price of labor, manufactures, internal produce, and imported commodities more aggressively. The Connecticut legislature ordered prices returned to 1774 levels across another encyclopedic list of commodities from "white beans" to "common steel." Beyond such basic economic and price controls, all the revolutionary states aggressively legislated to provide adequately for the militia and the armed services. Maryland, for example, passed ample and detailed statutes to provide for "The Quartering of Soldiers," "To Procure Cloathing for . . . the American Army," "To Secure (or Impress) Vessels and Carriages," "To Procure a Supply of Salt Meat for the Use of the Army," and to provide "For the Service of the United States." The Maryland legislature also frequently and extensively expanded the powers of the governor and council, prohibited the distillation of grain into spirits, and regulated auctions. Other states followed suit with equally aggressive legislative measures distinguished by peculiar local institutions and customs. Georgia, for example, passed a law requiring "Negro Slaves to work on the several Forts, Batteries, or other public Works" within the state.[73]

This catalog of revolutionary American state police legislation could continue ad nauseam. The point is but to underscore the long and close historical relationship among the development of American police power, the problem of overruling necessity, and the conditions of emergency. Much commentary on the American rule of law and the problem of emergency relies on relatively particularized and stylized portraits of executive prerogative, the nature of sovereignty, and the concept of the exception. This essay contends that more can be learned about both the rule of law and the problem of emergency by investigating their historic interaction in the ongoing construction of a modern American state power—the extent and limit of which is neither a simple question nor a merely academic one.

Notes

1. The two best discussions of this pivotal moment are Julius Goebel Jr., "Melancton Smith's Minutes of Debates on the New Constitution," *Columbia Law Review* 64 (1964): 26–43; and Bruce Ackerman and Neal Katyal, "Our Unconventional Founding," *University of Chicago Law Review* 62 (1995): 475–573.

2. *Journals of Congress*, Friday, September 28, 1787, *The Documentary History of the Ratification of the Constitution Digital Edition* (hereafter *DHRC*), ed. John P. Kaminski, Gaspare J. Saladino, Richard Leffler, Charles H. Schoenleber, and Margaret A. Hogan (Charlottesville: University of Virginia Press, 2009), http://rotunda.upress.virginia.edu/founders/RNCN-01-01-02-0009-0002-0022.

3. James Madison to George Washington, New York, September 30, 1787, *DHRC*, http://rotunda.upress.virginia.edu/founders/RNCN-01-01-02-0009-0003-0003.

4. Melancton Smith's Notes, September 27, 1787, *DHRC*, http://rotunda.upress.virginia.edu/founders/RNCN-01-01-02-0009-0002-0012.

5. Ackerman and Katyal, "Our Unconventional Founding," 476–77.

6. Melancton Smith's Notes, September 27, 1787, *DHRC*, http://rotunda.upress.virginia.edu/founders/RNCN-01-01-02-0009-0002-0016.

7. Thomas M. Cooley, *A Treatise on the Constitutional Limitations Which Rest upon the Legislative Power of the States of the American Union* (Boston: Little, Brown, 1868), 8.

8. Merrill Jensen, ed., *Constitutional Documents and Records, 1776–1787* (Madison: University of Wisconsin Press, 1976), 332.

9. Thomas S. Kuhn, *The Essential Tension: Selected Studies in Scientific Tradition and Change* (Chicago: University of Chicago Press, 1977), xii.

10. *Salus populi* (regard for the public welfare is the highest law) is the first maxim discussed in Herbert Broom, *A Selection of Legal Maxims*, 6th American ed. (Philadelphia: T. & J. W. Johnson, 1868), 1.

11. For a fuller elaboration of the role of *salus populi* and police power in nineteenth-century statecraft, see William J. Novak, *The People's Welfare: Law and Regulation in Nineteenth-Century America* (Chapel Hill: University of

North Carolina Press, 1996); and Gary Gerstle, *Liberty and Coercion: The Paradox of American Government from the Founding to the Present* (Princeton, NJ: Princeton University Press, 2015).

12. Thomas Paine, *Common Sense* (1776; Boston: J. P. Mendum, 1856), 46.

13. Edward S. Corwin, *The "Higher Law" Background of American Constitutional Law* (Ithaca, NY: Cornell University Press, 1955), "The Basic Doctrine of American Constitutional Law," *Michigan Law Review* 12 (1914): 247–76, and *"Marbury v. Madison* and the Doctrine of Judicial Review," *Michigan Law Review* 12 (1914): 538–72.

14. Julius Goebel Jr., *The Oliver Wendell Holmes Devise History of the Supreme Court of the United States, vol. 1, Antecedents and Beginnings to 1801* (New York: Macmillan, 1971), 1–2.

15. Goebel, *The Oliver Wendell Holmes Devise History of the Supreme Court*, 1–2.

16. John F. Manning, "Justice Scalia and the Idea of Judicial Restraint," *Michigan Law Review* 115 (2017): 747–82, 749.

17. Frankfurter further attacked Dicey's "sociological sterility," "misconceptions," and "myopia." Felix Frankfurter, "Foreword," *Yale Law Journal* 47 (1938): 515–18, 517.

18. Albert Venn Dicey, *Lectures Introductory to the Study of the Law of the Constitution* (London: Macmillan, 1885), 172–73, 215.

19. Friedrich A. Hayek, *The Road to Serfdom* (1944; New York: Routledge, 2001), 75–76.

20. Philip Hamburger, *Is Administrative Law Unlawful?* (Chicago: University of Chicago Press, 2014), 306. For a blistering critique of this law/nonlaw perspective, see Adrian Vermeule, "No," *Texas Law Review* 93 (2015): 1547–66.

21. Giorgio Agamben, *State of Exception*, trans. Kevin Attell (Chicago: University of Chicago Press, 2005), 1.

22. Carl Schmitt, *Political Theology: Four Chapters on the Concept of Sovereignty*, trans. George Schwab (Chicago: University of Chicago Press, 1985), 5, 21–23, 6.

23. Oliver Wendell Holmes Jr., "The Path of the Law," *Harvard Law Review* 10 (1897): 457–78.

24. John Dewey, "My Philosophy of Law," in *My Philosophy of Law: Credos of Sixteen American Scholars*, ed. Julius Rosenthal Foundation for General Law (Boston: Boston Law Book Co., 1941), 73–85, 76, 78.

25. Karl N. Llewellyn, *The Bramble Bush: Some Lectures on Law and Its Study* (New York: Columbia University Press, 1930), 3–5. See also John R. Commons, *A Sociological View of Sovereignty* (New York: A. M. Kelly, 1965).

26. James Willard Hurst, *Law and Social Order in the United States* (Ithaca, NY: Cornell University Press, 1977), 25; Robert Cover, "Violence and the Word," *Yale Law Journal* 95 (1985): 1601–29, 1601.

27. The tale of these first two developments is basically the subject of my *The People's Welfare*.

28. *Laws of New York, 1781–1801*, 2 vols. (Albany: State of New York, 1802).

29. *Commonwealth v. Alger*, 7 Cush. 53 (Mass., 1851), 53; *People v. Budd*, 117 N.Y. 1 (1889), 14–15, 29.

30. Collins Denny Jr., "The Growth and Development of the Police Power of the State," *Michigan Law Review* 20 (1921): 173–214, 173; Lewis Hochheimer, "Police Power," *Central Law Journal* 44 (1897): 158–62, 158. See also Ernst Freund, *The Police Power and Public Rights* (Chicago: University of Chicago Press, 1904).

31. *District of Columbia v. Brooke*, 214 U.S. 138 (1909), 149; *Berman v. Parker*, 348 U.S. 26 (1954), 32.

32. *Vanderbilt v. Adams*, 7 Cow. 349 (New York, 1827), 351–52.

33. Marc Raeff, "The Well-Ordered Police State and the Development of Modernity," *American Historical Review* 80 (1975): 1221–43, 1226.

34. B. J. Ramage, "Social Progress and the Police Power of a State," *American Law Review* 36 (1902): 681–99, 685.

35. Michel Foucault, "*Omnes et Singulatim*: Towards a Criticism of 'Political Reason,'" *Tanner Lectures on Human Values* (delivered at Stanford University, October 10 and 16, 1979), 248–49, https://tannerlectures.utah.edu/_documents/a-to-z/f/foucault81.pdf, and *Power/Knowledge: Selected Interviews and Other Writings, 1972–1977*, ed. Colin Gordon (New York: Pantheon, 1980), 170.

36. Mariana Valverde, "Police, Sovereignty, and Law: Foucaultian Reflection," in *Police and the Liberal State, ed.* Markus D. Dubber and Mariana Valverde (Stanford, CA: Stanford University Press, 2008), 15–32, 26. See also Nikolas Rose, *Powers of Freedom: Reframing Political Thought* (Cambridge: Cambridge University Press, 1999); Mitchell Dean, *Governmentality: Power and Rule in Modern Society* (London: Sage, 1999); and Pasquale Pasquino, "*Theatrum Politicum*: The Genealogy of Capital—Police and the State of Prosperity," *Ideology and Consciousness* 4 (1978): 41–54.

37. Christopher L. Tomlins, "The Supreme Sovereignty of the State: A Genealogy of Police in American Constitutional Law, from the Founding Era to *Lochner*," in Dubber and Valverde, eds., *Police and the Liberal State*, 33–53.

38. Markus D. Dubber, *The Police Power: Patriarchy and the Foundations of American Government* (New York: Columbia University Press, 2005), and "Policing Possession: The War on Crime and the End of Criminal Law," *Journal of Criminal Law and Criminology* 19 (2002): 829–996.

39. Christopher L. Tomlins, *Law, Labor, and Ideology in the Early American Republic* (New York: Cambridge University Press, 1993), 45.

40. Markus D. Dubber, "Criminal Police and Criminal Law in the Rechtsstaat," in Dubber and Valverde, eds., *Police and the Liberal State*, 92–109. See also William J. Novak, "Police Power and the Hidden Transformation of the American State," in ibid., 54–73.

41. *Brown v. Maryland*, 12 Wheat. 419 (U.S., 1827); *Commonwealth v. Alger*, 7 Cush. 53 (Mass., 1851); Leonard W. Levy, *The Law of the Commonwealth and Chief Justice Shaw* (Cambridge, MA: Harvard University Press, 1957).

42. Freund, *Police Power*, 42.

43. W. P. Prentice, *Police Powers Arising under the Law of Overruling Necessity* (New York: Banks & Bros., 1894), iii. See also W. G. Hastings, "The Development of Law as Illustrated by the Decisions Relating to the Police Power of

the State," *Proceedings of the American Philosophical Society* 39 (1900): 359–554.

44. Platt Potter, *A General Treatise on Statutes* (Albany: William Gould & Sons, 1871), 444; George W. Wickersham, "The Police Power, a Product of the Rule of Reason," *Harvard Law Review* 27 (1914): 297–316, 316.

45. Potter, *Treatise on Statutes*, 446.

46. Potter, *Treatise on Statutes*, 444.

47. *Case of the King's Prerogative in Salt-Peter*, 77 Eng. Rep. 1294 (1606), 1295; *Mouse's Case*, 77 Eng. Rep. 1341 (1608), 1342; *British Cast Plate Manufacturers v. Meredith*, 100 Eng. Rep. 1306 (1792), 1307–8.

48. James Kent, *Commentaries on American Law*, 4 vols. (New York: E. B. Clayton, 1836), 2:338.

49. For Holmes's comments, see James Kent, *Commentaries on American Law*, 12th ed., 4 vols., rev. Oliver Wendell Holmes (Boston: Little, Brown, 1878), 2:441 n. 2.

50. Cooley, *Constitutional Limitations*, 594–95.

51. *Wynehamer v. People*, 13 N.Y. 402 (1856), 451–52.

52. Prentice, *Police Powers*, iii.

53. Prentice, *Police Powers*, 7.

54. Gerstle, *Liberty and Coercion*, 56.

55. *Barron v. Baltimore*, 32 U.S. 243 (1833), 250–51.

56. *United States v. Dewitt*, 76 U.S. 41 (1870).

57. John Fabian Witt, "To Save the Country" (chapter 5 in this volume). See also John Fabian Witt, *Lincoln's Code: The Laws of War in American History* (New York: Free Press, 2012).

58. This basic transformation is a main topic of my current book project, tentatively titled "*New Democracy: Law and the Creation of the Modern American State.*"

59. Samuel P. Hays, "The Social Analysis of American Political History, 1880–1920," *Political Science Quarterly* 80 (1965): 373–94, 391; Leonard D. White, "Public Administration," in *Recent Social Trends in the United States* (New York: McGraw-Hill, 1933), 1391–1429, 1394; Walter Thompson, *Federal Centralization: A Study and Criticism of the Expanding Scope of Congressional Legislation* (New York: Harcourt, Brace, 1923).

60. Ernst Freund, *Standards of American Legislation* (Chicago: University of Chicago Press, 1917), *Administrative Powers over Persons and Property: A Comparative Survey* (Chicago: University of Chicago Press, 1928), *Legislative Regulation: A Study of the Ways and Means of Written Law* (New York: Commonwealth Fund, 1932), and *Police Power*.

61. Ernst Freund, "The Problem of Intelligent Legislation," *Proceedings of the American Political Science Association* 4 (1907): 69–79, 70. See also Francis A. Allen, "Ernst Freund and the New Age of Legislation," in Ernst Freund, *Standards of American Legislation*, 1965 ed. (1917; reprint, Chicago: University of Chicago Press, 1965), vii–xlvi.

62. Hastings, "The Development of Law"; Thomas Reed Powell, *The Supreme Court and State Police Power, 1922–1930* (Charlottesville, VA: Michie, 1932).

63. Freund, *Police Power*, 5–6.

64. Harrison H. Brace, "To What Extent May Government in the Exercise of Its Police Power, Take, Destroy or Damage Private Property without Giving Compensation Therefor?," *Chicago Legal News* 18 (1886): 339–41, 341; Ramage, "Social Progress and the Police Power," 698.

65. Charles Evans Hughes, "New Phases of National Development," *American Bar Association Journal* 4 (1918): 92–110, 93–94.

66. Ernst Freund, "The New German Constitution," *Political Science Quarterly* 35 (1920): 177–203, 181. See also Thompson, *Federal Centralization*, 10.

67. Robert E. Cushman, *The Independent Regulatory Commissions* (New York: Oxford University Press, 1941).

68. Robert Eugene Cushman, *Studies in the Police Power of the National Government* (Minneapolis: Minnesota Law Review, 1919–20), 291. See also James A. Lyons, "Development of a National Police Power," *Tennessee Law Review* 14 (1935): 11–20.

69. Austin F. MacDonald, *Federal Aid: A Study of the American Subsidy System* (New York: Thomas Y. Crowell, 1928); Harry N. Scheiber, "Federalism and the American Economic Order, 1789–1910," *Law and Society Review* 10 (1975): 57–118.

70. Senator James A. Reed, *Congressional Record*, 65th Cong., 1st sess., June 14, 1917, 3597.

71. Clinton L. Rossiter, *Constitutional Dictatorship: Crisis Government in the Modern Democracies* (Princeton, NJ: Princeton University Press, 1948), 243.

72. J. Reuben Clark Jr., *Emergency Legislation Passed Prior to December, 1917 Dealing with the Control and Taking of Private Property for the Public Use, Benefit, or Welfare* (Washington, DC: US Government Printing Office, 1918).

73. Clark, *Emergency Legislation*, 52, 59, 232.

5

To Save the Country: Reason and Necessity in Constitutional Emergencies

John Fabian Witt

One hundred and fifty years ago, the United States was a world leader in emergency constitutionalism. Americans remember Lincoln's suspension of the writ of habeas corpus and the Emancipation Proclamation; some remember his great speech to the Congress on July 4, 1861. Indeed, the American Civil War has become a classic case study for theorists of emergency, from Carl Schmitt a century ago, to Clinton Rossiter in the 1940s, to theorists from left to right today.[1]

Yet debates over emergency constitutionalism in the American Civil War have been missing a key piece of the story. For more than a century, scholars have known that Francis Lieber—the prominent publicist, political theorist, and Lincoln administration insider—wrote a manuscript about emergency constitutionalism after the war ended.[2] When Lieber died unexpectedly, however, the manuscript went missing. It was not to be found in the papers Lieber's family deposited at the Huntington Library. It did not appear in the Lieber manuscripts at Johns Hopkins. And it did not turn up in the collection of Lieber books now in the Judge Advocate General Papers at the Library of Congress.

In the course of research on Lieber, however, I found the manuscript, buried deep in the official archives of his son, G. Norman Lieber, who served as judge advocate general of the United States in the closing years of the nineteenth century. The lost Lieber manuscript, as begun by Francis and developed by Norman, summarizes a fierce strand of thinking about constitutional emergencies, one rooted in controversies from the decades-long struggle that led to the Civil War and its aftermath. Its conception of emergency powers is striking. In keeping with Lieber's famously tough code for the laws of war in 1863, the manuscript on martial law and emergencies defends the Lincoln administration's most controversial assertions of power. It supports the suspensions of habeas corpus, the Emancipation Proclamation, and the use of military commissions.[3]

The Lieber manuscript and the controversies out of which it arose anticipated some of the most daunting features of the Weimar and Nazi jurist Carl Schmitt's work on the same subject. Schmitt famously contended that law gives way to sovereign power in the moment of emergency. As one of the twentieth century's most bitter critics of liberal legal systems, he insisted that the moment of exception revealed the illiberal truth about the supposed sanctity of the law. In the moment of crisis, the hypocrisy of liberal legal order falls away, exposing the brute, inescapable power of the sovereign to remake the state.[4]

The two Liebers (father and son) did not shrink from awesome powers in emergency moments. The elder Lieber grew up in Prussia and celebrated the forcible overthrow of Napoléon as a great moment in world history. The younger man served as a judge advocate in the US army during the Civil War, trying Confederate bushwhackers. Neither shrank from the use of power. But, where Schmitt insisted that emergency powers in the moment of crisis revealed the inevitability of dictatorial authority, the Liebers developed an equally iron-willed but nonetheless deeply liberal theory of constitutions in crisis. Emergency, they argued, does not and cannot throw us back into a nasty and brutish state of nature. With a decade's experience in the very problem about which they were writing, the Liebers contended that a community's most basic values inevitably travel into the very depths of the crisis. In cultures of democratic reason, they insisted, institutions and cultures matter, even in extremis.

1. Emergencies in the Republic of Slavery

The logic of the Lieber manuscript is rooted in the Civil War—but not only in the Civil War. Antebellum Americans participated in a now-long-forgotten controversy over martial law and slavery, one that set the context for the Civil War crisis that followed. In a real way, the story of the Lieber manuscript began in the spring of 1836, when an aging John Quincy Adams took to the floor of the House of Representatives to make a startling argument about Congress and slavery.

The senior congressman's southern colleagues insisted that the federal government lacked the power to reach slavery in the states. Adams had catered to such ideas back when he needed southern votes, but, then again, virtually everyone in American politics agreed that Congress lacked authority over slavery in the states. As James Oakes has recently observed, the consensus on this question was the linchpin of the antebellum political order.[5] But in 1836 Adams gave voice to a dissenting view, articulating an idea that charted a path to the Emancipation Proclamation, still a quarter century in the future. The Constitution, he conceded, might protect slavery from congressional interference in times of peace. But in wartime, he asserted, Congress could interfere with slavery. It could even abolish slavery.[6]

"From the instant that your slave-holding States become the theatre of war, civil, servile, or foreign," Adams said, "from that instant the war powers of Congress extend to interference with the institution of slavery." In a wartime emergency, he later explained, Congress would have "complete, unlimited control over the whole subject of slavery, even to the emancipation of all the slaves."[7]

During the gag rule controversies of the 1840s over antislavery speech on the House floor, Adams repeated the idea again. If Congress could repeal slavery in the event of war, he reasoned, then it could hardly forbid debate on the subject. In the event of foreign invasion, for example, the laws of war authorized martial law; all the "laws and municipal institutions" would be "swept by the board," and the martial law that took their place would, if necessary, authorize the federal government to emancipate slaves.[8]

Adams did not invent the idea from whole cloth. Americans had long worried about the special threat that war posed in a slave society. In 1775, the reviled Lord Dunmore, the last royal governor of Virginia, had issued a proclamation freeing slaves of rebellious Virginians. Ever since, planters and their families worried that an attack on the United States by a European power might take advantage of the presence of several million slaves in the American South.[9]

Unsurprisingly, southern slaveholders rejected Adams's subversive views. In the process, they joined issue in one of the first great debates over emergency constitutionalism in American law.

Samuel Smith Nicholas, a lawyer and judge from Kentucky, issued the most extensive response to Adams. In an 1842 article written under the pseudonym "Kentuckian," Nicholas took on the elder statesman. "I have not the language to express the surprise, not to say horror," he wrote, "with which I have witnessed the promulgation of these opinions." Adams's ideas, he insisted, were "sheer madness." It was outrageous, he asserted, to suggest that "a foreign invader" could create a situation under which either the invader or the United States would be able to do what Congress in peacetime could not do. To think otherwise, he continued, would be to give a leader in wartime the power to "strike dead in the hands of its owners four hundred millions worth of property" and to do so "by his mere proclamation." In Nicholas's view, the Constitution had created a republic organized around a set of core principles—principles that, with his "zeal for his black fellow-citizens," Adams seemed to have forgotten. What Adams proposed, Nicholas objected, would entail nothing short of a complete transformation of the basic identity of the republic. Indeed, he worried that such a transformation might radically invert the basic structure of American social life. Adams's ideas about martial law, he asserted, would "inevitably lead to the enslaving of his white fellow-citizens."[10]

Taken to this extreme, Nicholas's nightmare fantasies were far-fetched. (White slavery in mid-nineteenth-century America?) But his argument carried a nugget of truth. Nicholas contended that to destroy slavery would be to destroy the United States—or at least to destroy the United States as it was then defined. A republic was not merely an aggregation of individuals. It was a creature of its own, constituted by a set of constitutional commitments, one of which was the constitutional protection of slavery. Nicholas knew that altering the constitutional commitment would not rescue the republic, even in extremis. Abolishing slavery could not, by its very nature, save the republic. To the contrary, abolishing slavery would destroy it, or at least transform it into something other than what it had been. The identity of the United States could not survive a martial law that destroyed slavery. Or so Nicholas contended.[11]

In making this argument, Nicholas drew on a long tradition of Anglo-American hostility to martial law. In his 1713 *History and Analysis of the Common Law of England*, Sir Matthew Hale had described martial law as "not a law" at all but rather "something indulged rather than allowed." He denied that martial law applied outside the military; even more, he insisted that its authority "may not be permitted in time of peace, when the king's courts are open." William Blackstone, writing later in the century, contended that martial law was "entirely arbitrary" and therefore utterly inapplicable as common law except inside the military during wartime.¹²

With such great eminences of the English legal tradition as Hale and Blackstone behind them, Nicholas and his fellow critics of emergency authority successfully initiated what would soon become an American tradition. For a half century and more, slave-owning southerners and their heirs would insist that the core commitments of Anglo-American constitutionalism were deeply opposed to martial law and broad emergency authority. In the 1830s and 1840s, their efforts would hold off abolitionist petitions in the Congress. In early 1850, as controversy over the admission of California and a new fugitive slave law raged in Congress, a senator from Mississippi named Jefferson Davis condemned the notion that the president of the United States could "decree that slavery was abolished . . . by virtue of the powers which he held under martial law." ("Does anybody believe it would be submitted to?" Davis asked.)¹³ During the Civil War itself, such arguments would underwrite opposition to the Lincoln administration's Emancipation Proclamation. In the war's aftermath, they would help explain the Supreme Court's decision to block the authority of military tribunals in *Ex Parte Milligan*. In the century thereafter, the arguments against federal military authority that had begun in the defense of slavery would show up in the Posse Comitatus Act of 1878 limiting federal military authority in the southern states, in a riot against black soldiers stationed in Texas during World War I, and in massive resistance to the 101st Airborne's deployment to enforce desegregation of the schools in Little Rock, Arkansas, in 1957. In episode after episode, the special regime of white supremacist authority of the American South sought shelter in a long tradition of Anglo-American liberty.¹⁴

2. *Emergencies and Civil War*

Nicholas and his British predecessors had identified an important truth about constitutions. They believed that martial law posed a threat to the basic character of a regime. And they were right. Changes or exceptions in the law for the purpose of weathering a crisis inevitably threaten to alter the identity of the republic those changes aim to protect. How could it be otherwise? Rational means are instrumentally suited to ends. But they alter those ends, too.

The effects of altered laws on the ends of the state are all the more significant in a republic self-consciously constituted around those very laws. The slavery controversy of the 1830s and 1840s taught the Kentuckian that the very identity of the United States was at stake in the decision of what means were appropriate to rescue the country. If taken too far, such means would undo the very thing that they had been intended to protect.[15]

In the twentieth century, the controversial point of reference for this same basic idea about emergencies and constitutionalism has been Carl Schmitt, the fierce German critic of liberal democratic constitutionalism. Schmitt famously distinguished between *commissary dictatorship* and *sovereign dictatorship*. The former deploys dictatorial power to preserve the state as it is. But the latter uses the sovereign power to redefine the state altogether. And this idea—that emergencies present a radically transformative moment—would have been entirely familiar to the Civil War generation. Americans had been explicitly arguing about it at least since Adams spoke out in the House of Representatives and Nicholas responded. Schmitt's "sovereign dictator" was the transformative leader of Adams's dreams—and of Nicholas's nightmares.[16]

Francis Lieber's role in emergency thinking was to take up the ideas circulating in the antebellum debates and turn them in a new and distinctive direction, one that would prove to be unstinting in its fierce defense of the state in moments of danger yet also pursue a very different path than the one taken by Schmitt.

In his early years in the United States, Lieber adopted southern critics' suspicion of martial law. Born in Berlin in 1798, Lieber came of age in a Prussia under the heel of Napoléon. He battled the dictator at Waterloo in 1815. (He was wounded in the neck and left for dead as the Prussians chased the French back to Paris.) After encountering political difficulties arising out of his liberal views in post-Napoleonic Prussia, he made a pilgrimage to Greece to fight for Greek independence. Eventually he made his way to the United States, arriving in 1827.[17]

Before long, his first-rate German education, his wide learning, and his irrepressible demeanor helped make Lieber a leading American public intellectual. He had the barely controlled megalomania still characteristic of such figures two centuries later. Yet he was unable to find a teaching position in the North, at least at first. Perhaps it was his Germanic habits that turned off the Harvard crowd. His self-aggrandizing personality probably did not help matters. For one reason or another, the only position he was able to find came at the College of South Carolina. In 1835, he and his family moved to the state's capital, Columbia.[18]

In the slave society of South Carolina, Lieber expressed sympathy with the Kentuckian position of Samuel Nicholas. Perhaps it was his long experience with centralized and repressive European states. Or perhaps it had something to do with the fact that he became a slaveholder himself, owning a small number of domestic slaves. Whatever the reason, he adopted the slaveholders' view of martial law. "Martial law," he wrote in the successful *Encyclopaedia Americana* he edited in the 1830s, was made up of rules exclusively for soldiers. It was not an open-ended source of government authority; instead, it was another word for the systems of military law that governed within the command structure of the military.[19] His two-volume *On Civil Liberty and Self-Government*, published in 1853, also limited the authority of the executive in emergencies. It asserted that only Congress could suspend the writ of habeas corpus. (It "need hardly be mentioned," he argued, that suspension "cannot be done by the president alone, but by Congress only.") Lieber described the apparatus of exceptional government—extraordinary courts and military commissions—as the work of dictators and tyrants. In a regime of liberty, he insisted, "every officer, however high or low," was "personally answerable" for the lawfulness of his conduct.[20]

Elements in Lieber's thought tilted away from the Kentuckian tradition. Lieber purported to dislike slavery, notwithstanding that he owned several slaves. He respected John Quincy Adams, whom he had met briefly soon after his arrival in the United States, while Adams was still the president. More importantly, his Prussian upbringing had left a complex legacy. He despised Napoléon's dictatorial rule, to be sure. But he also thrilled to the ideas of his fellow Prussian Carl von Clausewitz, whose writings on war represented the thinking of many Prussians who had chafed under Napoléon's authority. Clausewitz's central idea was that war was the application of pure military force, unconstrained by conventions or laws; such obstacles to force were mere ancillary considerations, insignificant in the scheme of things. And Lieber—who was one of very few Americans to read Clausewitz in the original German—agreed. Warfare and great battles represented the great triumphs of civilization.[21]

After nearly twenty years in South Carolina, Lieber took a new post at Columbia College and moved to New York City. With this move to the North, his attachment to the idea of limits on government authority waned. The Clausewitzian strands in his thinking became more pronounced.[22] Indeed, after war broke out in early 1861, he forged a remarkable connection between two different traditions of thought on state power in the modern world. In what is perhaps his most original breakthrough as a political theorist, he began to connect Clausewitz's fierce teachings about war with John Quincy Adams's ideas about slavery.

The first opportunity for such a connection between Prussian and American ideas presented itself during the controversy that arose in

April 1861 when Abraham Lincoln began to issue orders suspending the writ of habeas corpus without congressional authorization. Opponents of the suspension orders bitterly resisted the orders, decrying them as an unconstitutional expansion of military authority. One such opponent, Chief Justice Roger Taney, famously ordered the president to recognize the writ—an order that Lincoln just as famously ignored.[23]

Lieber's earlier writings served as a rallying point for Taney's allies. Lieber had endorsed the proposition that only Congress could suspend the writ. But an embarrassed Lieber now changed his position.[24] Writing in the *New York Times* under the pen name "Observer," he explained that the authority "to lay aside ordinary legal forms and ordinary legal guarantees of individual freedom, is simply the right of self-preservation." Where once he had criticized martial law as at odds with Anglo-American liberty, now he insisted that "martial law is a tremendous engine of government, essential to its existence." Indeed, martial law seemed to him to be the only thing government could invoke against the "revolutionary faction" that had produced a "state of anarchy."[25]

Lieber's major contribution to the debate was to bring to public attention the most elaborate defense of Lincoln's unilateral suspension orders. The Philadelphia lawyer Horace Binney, an old friend of Lieber's from the 1830s, advanced a novel American theory of emergency constitutionalism. Binney conceded that, in the British tradition, only parliamentary action could authorize the Crown to suspend the writ. But the Philadelphian argued that this approach was badly flawed. The British model permitted arbitrary suspension of the writ for no good reason and even for no reason at all; all that mattered under the British constitution was that Parliament decide to suspend the writ. At the same time, Binney continued, the British approach prohibited unilateral suspension by the Crown—even in the event that such action proved indispensable in a moment of crisis. The British approach to the great writ of habeas corpus was both overinclusive and underinclusive. It authorized unjustified suspensions and prohibited suspensions that were imperative to save the state.[26]

By contrast, Binney celebrated what he saw as the very different approach adopted by the US Constitution. For the framers of the Constitution had grasped the errors of the British model of suspension. Article 1, Section 9, prohibited suspension of the writ except when the necessity of the circumstances so required: "The Privilege of the Writ of Habeas Corpus shall not be suspended, unless when in Cases of Rebellion or Invasion the public Safety may require it." Unlike the British constitution, the US approach authorized suspension only when the necessities of the moment so required. But that was not all. The constraint on suspension in Article 1, Section 9, was the Constitution's only reference to habeas corpus, and that fact contained a further clue to the structure of the suspension power. A constraint on the suspension power necessarily implied a prior power to suspend. It followed for Binney that, unlike its British forerunner, the US Constitution contained an unwritten authority to suspend, one that naturally fell on the president as the government's chief executive officer, vested by the Constitution with the responsibility "to take Care that the Laws be faithfully executed." "The Constitution is itself the authority," Binney concluded, "and all that remains is to execute it in the conditioned case."[27]

Binney offered a nested cluster of ideas in support of his habeas theory. His textual argument rested on the idea that constitutional limits implied prior unwritten powers. The Philadelphia lawyer called on the logic of constitutional democracy, too. As he saw it, the president was the proper location for the power to suspend because the presidency was uniquely accountable to the people. Congressional authorization of a suspension of the writ would diffuse responsibility across the two chambers of Congress and the president, who would of course be required to enforce any congressional suspension. Authority over the writ, Binney wrote, "should obviously be with that department of the government which is the least able to abuse the power, and is the most easily and directly made amenable to responsibility and correction for abuse."[28] And, as Binney and Lieber saw it, that department was undoubtedly the executive department, which would be subject to constraints by both the legislative and the judicial branches.

A third idea behind Binney's suspension power theory was particularly attractive to Lieber. For Lieber believed that no nation could alienate the authority to defend itself. The executive necessarily possessed a suspension power because no constitutional arrangement could strip the authority to protect a state from its empowered officers. A right to self-defense was simply in the nature of what it is to be a state, and, if necessity so required, then the relevant power necessarily followed.

Of course, taken to the extreme, this conception of state power seemed to contradict the entire liberal constitutional project. Constitutional regimes might seem to have little or no significance in moments of crisis. Lieber would be an advocate of the kinds of illimitable state authority later associated with Schmitt.

The fierce strand in Lieber's thinking emerged in the war's second year, as Lincoln began to act on John Quincy Adams's wartime emancipation ideas. Writing in the *New York Times* in April, Lieber asserted that "nations in utmost need are never saved by legal formulas." If the "fundamental law of a nation omits to provide for these exceptional cases," he warned his readers, the people would inevitably seize the power to answer the crisis. "[P]ower will be arrogated," he concluded, "as people arrogate power in cases of shipwreck."[29]

Here was Binney's idea of an inalienable right of self-defense and necessity, one that no law could alienate. And in the United States, with its precarious balance of state and federal authority, the necessity power of the federal government inevitably implicated slavery in the states. The war thus touched off another round of the emancipation debates that Adams and his critics had first taken up two decades before. Senator Charles Sumner of Massachusetts exhumed Adams's emergency emancipation idea; at the very start of the conflict, he urged Lincoln to end slavery as a war measure.[30] On the other side, publishers reissued Nicholas's Kentuckian pamphlet. The Constitution, protested Lincoln's critics, "confers upon the [President] all the powers he has."[31] Emancipation would be the end of the republic—"a destruction of the Government, or such a revolution in its principles as that it does not remain the same." Combined with "martial law, military arrests, trials, and executions," it seemed to promise an end to the antebellum American constitution altogether. One congressman from Kentucky recalled Nicholas's fevered nightmare from two decades before. Freeing "four millions of the black race," said George Yeaman, would "succeed in enslaving twenty millions of the white race."[32]

Late in the summer of 1862, Lincoln moved decisively toward emancipation. On September 22, after the bloody stalemate at Antietam, he announced the Emancipation Proclamation, promising to emancipate slaves in rebel states on January 1. The coming of emancipation, in turn, prompted the Lincoln administration to revisit the laws of war and the martial law tradition. Lincoln's general-in-chief, Henry Halleck, commissioned Lieber to draft a code restating the basic laws of armed conflict. The code Lieber produced took up and defended Adams's position on slavery in the laws of war. In particular, Lieber enthusiastically embraced the basic logic that lay beneath Adams's 1830s speeches and that Lincoln had invoked in defense of emancipation. "Military necessity, as understood by modern civilized nations," he wrote, "consists in the necessity of those measures which are indispensable for securing the ends of the war." Necessity, he explained further, permitted "all direct destruction of life and limb of armed enemies, and of the persons whose destruction is incidentally unavoidable in the armed contests of the war."[33]

Lieber's awesome war power was nothing less than the power to rise to the occasion, whatever that might be. "To save the country," Lieber wrote plainly, "is paramount to all other considerations."[34]

Here, surely, was a dangerously illiberal juncture. Like Schmitt decades later, Lieber seemed to contemplate an emergency power that promised to break through all constraints.

But did it? One of the canonical episodes from the Civil War suggests otherwise. When Lincoln called a special session of Congress on July 4, 1861, he famously put to the assembled members his dilemma in deciding whether to suspend the writ of habeas corpus. He did not believe, he made clear, that he had broken any law in doing so. But what if he had crossed over the legal limits on his office? What if Binney's defense proved wrong and his suspension of the writ had indeed run afoul of the Constitution? What if Chief Justice Taney were right? "Are all the laws, but one," Lincoln asked, "to go unexecuted, and the government itself go to pieces, lest that one be violated?"[35]

Observers today usually read the passage as a justification for overriding legal protections in emergency moments. Lincoln's formulation comes down to Americans as the quintessential wisdom of a practical Lincoln engaged in commonsense reasoning. Pragmatic leaders, goes the idea, test the means at issue by holding them up to the ends at stake and take steps when the ends justify the means. ("If the ends don't justify the means, I'd like to know what in the hell does," goes the quip of one quintessentially practical American official.)[36]

Yet, properly understood, the famous "all the laws but one" passage stands for more than the reductionist pragmatic idea of instrumental reason in the service of the state. When Lincoln asked about all the laws but one, he was also observing that the necessity power and the means-ends relationship between emergency measures and the identity of a state entail a deeper problem than the pragmatic conception allows. For the measures a state takes to rescue itself—the laws it bends or breaks to save itself—redefine the thing being saved. The problem is more acute for collectivities organized neither around some supposed racial or ethnic identity, nor around simple geographic borders, but around a constitutional and legal commitment to certain values. The problem, as Lincoln may have understood, is that a government constituted by law inevitably transforms its own identity when it sacrifices some of those laws to rescue others. The government that comes out the other side is different for having abandoned some of its tenets.

In short, a right to defend the state is not self-defining because the means adopted to do so make and remake the basic identity and values of the state itself. Means and ends are recursive; they have feedback effects on one another. A result is that the necessity power is not self-defining. It entails value judgments and excruciatingly difficult choices.

Lincoln knew this when he asked the Congress in July 1861 whether the republic ought to be allowed to fail so that one of its laws might be saved. And the events of the subsequent four years would remind him of the same point time and again. He agonized over difficult judgments and acted with care and attention precisely because he understood that his conduct as president would reshape the nation for which he cared so deeply. No wall sealed off the ends of the republic from the means it adopted in its defense. The means employed by a regime would help construct the character of the regime itself. And the pervasive fact of feedback loops between means and ends also powerfully shaped Francis Lieber's distinctive approach to emergencies.

3. Milligan, Finlason, and Lieber

Lieber sat down to develop a theory of emergency powers just as pitched battles gave way to the less salient violence of Reconstruction. From the start, a crucial question for the nation was how far into the postwar world the necessity power would reach. Two influential accounts of the question of necessity developed in 1860s Anglo-American constitutionalism.[37]

The first emerged out of Reconstruction itself and found its most prominent voice in the US Supreme Court's decision in *Ex Parte Milligan*. The Indiana resident Lambdin Milligan was a wartime leader of the "Sons of Liberty," a notorious pro-Confederate group operating in the Midwest. In 1864, the United States captured him and charged him in a military commission in Indiana with attempting to deliver guns to Confederate prisoners in prison camps near Chicago and along Lake Erie. Milligan had tried to do this while dressed as a civilian, wearing none of the formal insignia of a legitimate combatant. His conduct therefore constituted a law of war offense, which ordinarily would have sufficed to sustain the jurisdiction of a military commission. But the Union declined to press the law of war basis for the commission's authority. Instead, lawyers for the United States aimed to get a ruling that would permit the continued use of commissions to maintain order more generally in the Reconstruction South. In its *Milligan* decision, however, the Supreme Court imposed new sharp limits on the emergency authority that came with war. It ruled that the war power could "never be applied" in instances "where the courts are open and their process unobstructed."[38]

The Court was not alone. Leading figures soon joined it in reviving limits on martial law and necessity. President Andrew Johnson denounced military tribunals as "arbitrary" and "incompatible" with "the genius and spirit" of "free institutions." Johnson's attorney general,

Henry Stanbery, condemned military tribunals and opined that necessity no longer supplied the grounds for their authority. In Congress, where Republicans controlled the agenda, floor debates moved away from the idea of a broad war power in conquered territories.[39]

In the century and a half since Reconstruction, civil libertarians have celebrated these postwar positions as marking the restoration of civil liberty after the war's end.[40] There is much to be said for this view. But few have paid much attention to the decision's terrible downsides. *Milligan* badly undermined the power of the federal government to deliver on the promises of the Emancipation Proclamation and the Thirteenth Amendment. In cutting back the jurisdiction of the military commissions, the Court was exhuming the legacy of Samuel Smith Nicholas, whose Kentuckian essay from 1842 pitted the South's regime of racial authority against the federal government's martial law power. If the ghost of John Calhoun haunted the Court's subsequent decision in the *Slaughterhouse Cases*, the specter of Nicholas loomed over *Milligan*.[41]

A second theory of necessity's reach emerged at more or less the same time the Court was deciding *Milligan*. But this one, which arose most clearly on the other side of the Atlantic, pressed in the opposite direction. For, if *Milligan* restricted the necessity power that the Lincoln administration had developed during the war, jurists in the British Empire aimed to expand it to terrifying lengths.[42]

A key figure in the British debates was the barrister William F. Finlason, a member of Middle Temple. Finlason argued few cases; instead, for nearly the entire second half of the nineteenth century, he wrote about the law as the chief legal reporter for *The Times*.[43] Most of all, he wrote about martial law. For in 1866, in the wake of an uprising in Jamaica at a place called Morant Bay, he turned his attention to martial law in the British Empire. It soon became his central preoccupation.[44]

Finlason's account of necessity power turned law into a ferocious regime of racial domination. Martial law, Finlason wrote, was the equivalent of "a declaration of a state of war." It suspended the common law and substituted an "arbitrary military power." Not even necessity could constrain it, Finlason insisted. "For what is necessity," he asked with a flourish, "and who is to judge of it?" What mattered, he understood, was the end to which necessary measures were put. Necessary for whom with respect to what? Was necessity to be measured by "reference to the instant exigencies of the particular time or place"? Or was it instead to be determined by reference to "larger considerations" such as the strategic goals of the state? The answer was clear. The common law, Finlason argued, had been built to keep the peace. It sufficed to address "actual outrage or insurrection." Martial law, by contrast, did not deal with events from the past; it was a system of "measures preventative or deterrent."[45]

Preventing uprisings throughout the British Empire necessitated nothing less than a regime of terror—and *terror* quickly became a key term for Finlason. In Jamaica, for example, Governor Edward Jonathan Eyre's forces had turned to martial law because only forceful deterrence would permit Eyre's "inadequate force" to handle and suppress the much larger population of the island colony. Finlason contended that only martial law would allow the colonial regime to employ the kinds of "summary executions" that would "inspire a terror" in would-be rebels. Martial authority could instill in the "rebellious masses" a "terror inspired by the stern and summary severities of military law." Terror was martial law's "very essence." Indeed, in the long run, the terror of martial law was "merciful and humane." By deterring insurrection, martial law would prevent suffering.[46]

For Finlason, only the executive and the military could decide whether martial law was appropriate in the circumstances, and no other body or branch of government could hold the executive accountable. No court could possibly possess the information necessary to review such decisions, so martial law had a presumption of legality. "Persons cannot be criminal," Finlason insisted, for making or following orders, so long as those orders were made "honestly, however erroneously," and "under martial law."[47]

The Liebers saw a third way, between the *Milligan* case's hard-and-fast limits on emergency authority and the brutal martial law power of Finlason. Instead, they offered a tough and uncompromising but nonetheless liberal account of government power in the state of exception.

The elder Lieber began to write an expanded and annotated version of his famous code for the laws of war within weeks of its publication in 1863.[48] In the next two years, as active fighting gave way to military occupation of the South, the martial law sections of the code took on ever greater salience. But, when Lieber died in 1872, the manuscript lay unfinished. His son, Guido Norman Lieber, took up the project, apparently aiming to finish what his father had begun. In the end, however, he left the manuscript unfinished and disorganized, filed deep in his official papers and buried alongside material relating to the Spanish-American War in the Philippines. The manuscript, with the unassuming title "Martial Law Treatise," has lain there unnoticed since the Judge Advocate General transferred its files to the National Archives and Records Administration in the middle of the twentieth century.

The Lieber manuscript's starting point is a distinction between military law and martial law. Military law was, as Wellington had said, "neither more nor less than the will of the general."[49] It was a kind of tyrannical power, conditioned by the imperatives of battle. Earlier writers such as Blackstone and Hale, as well as later military men, like the Duke of Wellington, had assimilated the two forms of authority. Lieber himself, back in the 1830s, had repeated this idea in his *Encyclopaedia Americana* entry on martial law, where he described martial law as a body of law exclusively for soldiers.

But, as the Liebers saw it after the war, military law and martial law were importantly different. The former was the law for soldiers in peace and war alike. But martial law, or *"martial law proper,"* as Chief Justice Chase called it in his concurring opinion in *Milligan*, took up the question of executive and military authority in crisis settings more generally. The key difference between the two regimes was simple. Military law was governed by nothing more than the will of the ruler; the imperatives of order and command in the military setting were such that the will of the command structure was the only possible source of authority. Martial law, by contrast, was subject to principled limits. In particular, martial law was governed by the same principle of necessity that had governed the suspension of habeas corpus in Binney's account. Martial law, the Liebers explained, was simply "the law of necessity applied at home."[50]

Necessity offered vast powers, to be sure. The elder Lieber had written that saving the country was "paramount to all other considerations." The duty of self-preservation, the Liebers said in their manuscript, was "a principle inherent in all politics." Like self-defense for individuals, necessity was a power intrinsic in what it was to be a modern state: "an attribute of sovereignty inherent in all polities." As the Liebers saw it: "[T]he law of necessity can be limited neither by statute, nor by judicial decision." Even if the Constitution itself had aimed to prevent the exercise of the necessity power, such constraints would be ineffective. The necessity power "would nonetheless exist," they concluded, "for the law of necessity cannot be controlled."[51]

But what the Liebers meant by a limitless power of necessity was not, we shall soon see, a power without limits. I will return to this point shortly. For now, we can see the character of the Liebers' necessity power by focusing on the critique they offered of the *Milligan* decision in the Supreme Court.

The Court in *Milligan* purported to confine martial rule "to the locality of actual war," relying on Sir Matthew Hale's old doctrine of a per se bar on martial law whenever the "King's courts are open for all persons." The difficulty with this approach, the Liebers insisted, was that Hale had meant his open-courts rule to apply to military law—the law applicable to the armed forces—not to *martial* law. A state was free to commit itself not to apply its military law in certain contexts. That was a matter of pure discretion, to be decided as prudence and politics dictated. But the inherent emergency power of self-defense was altogether a different beast. As a logical or conceptual matter, it simply could not be "restrained within territorial limits." To try to do so would be a contradiction in terms. If "martial law proper is a law of necessity," the Liebers contended, "its jurisdiction must extend wherever the necessity exists." The fact that courts were open (or not) might serve as a useful proxy for the extent of the emergency. But that fact could not take the place of the underlying determination itself.[52]

The Liebers, in short, contended that nations came with an indefeasible power and right of self-defense, one that could not be alienated or disowned. But it was not a limitless power. It did not authorize mere revenge or capricious actions. Finlason came close to suggesting as much. Schmitt imagined that the will of the sovereign is unbounded; indeed, this very unboundedness is the core of what it means to be a sovereign in his account. The Liebers, by contrast, excluded only per se or a priori limits. Necessity was a license for action. But it was also and always its own constraint. It licensed only those courses of conduct that were necessary. Or, as the Liebers put it in their manuscript, the constraint on the necessity power arose out of the particular "necessity which is looked to for its justification."[53]

Looked at this way, the Liebers were able to identify any number of historical instances of undue force not warranted by the necessity power. They listed the fatal flogging of a British soldier in colonial Senegal in 1782, the military tribunals after the end of a slave rebellion in Demerara on the coast of South America in 1823, and executions after the unrest at Ceylon (now Sri Lanka) in 1848. The execution of a leader of the Jamaican political opposition at Morant Bay in 1865 offered another such instance.[54] In the United States, the Liebers held, necessity would not have warranted military tribunal prosecutions of Confederate leaders such as Jefferson Davis for treason. The Constitution purported to require federal courts for such charges. But, even if necessity could have overridden such provisions, they observed, the civil court had been available to hear such charges. There had been no necessity. And that was the overriding question.[55]

Necessity is, of course, both a warrant and a constraint, a license and a limit. A critical question for any necessity rule is how its license dimension interacts with the limits it imposes. Do the latter give way to the former? Most of all, the necessity standard begs the question whether any measure can be definitively ruled out. *Milligan*'s error, as the Liebers saw it, was to imagine that the defense of the republic could be managed by hard-and-fast rules.[56] But, if necessity's adaptability to circumstance meant that military commissions could not truly be ruled out a priori, could anything be prohibited in advance? Were there ways for a constitutional republic to tie itself to the mast and forswear certain means of self-defense? Or did the inalienable right of self-preservation require a state to push past any such hard-and-fast limit?

Consider the problem of torture under a necessity standard. How can a necessity standard rule out torture or at least rule it out altogether? Surely there must be occasions, even if only hypothetical for the moment, in which torture's use would be required to rescue a republic from destruction. That some philosophers have concluded as much should hardly be surprising,[57] for torture is not categorically different from other domains of necessity reasoning. The logic of necessity rules out per se or a priori prohibitions; no regime of necessity seems to be able to put torture (or anything else, for that matter) utterly and definitively beyond the pale.

Yet the elder Lieber's 1863 code purported to bar torture in all circumstances while nonetheless adopting the philosophy of necessity. It banned "torture to extort confessions." It instructed that "the modern law of war permits no longer the use of any violence against prisoners in order to extort the desired information." Prisoners, it explained, were "subject to no punishment for being a public enemy"; nor was "any revenge wreaked upon him by the intentional infliction of any suffering."[58] Most of the provisions in Lieber's 1863 code contained exceptions and caveats for when necessity so required. Armies could not execute prisoners of war—unless an army's "own salvation" so required in circumstances of "great straits." War was not to touch works of art, libraries, and cultural institutions—so long as the damage was "avoidable." Private property was inviolate—except when "military necessity" so required. And so on.[59]

But no such carve-out haunted the Lieber code's provisions on torture. And Lieber's hard-and-fast Civil War–era rule persisted for decades. In the Philippines, nearly forty years later, violation of the torture rule in the 1863 code produced convictions in courts-martial. The punishments dealt out in those cases were trivial, but they established the principle. Here was a hard-and-fast proposition of law, one that would not bend even in the moment of emergency.[60]

The torture rule's rigidity contains a clue to the deep structure of the Liebers' theory of emergency powers—and to the critical difference that separated it from the contemporary thinking of Finlason, from the historical ideas of Clausewitz, and from the ideas still to come from legal theorists like Schmitt. The problem with torture was that, even where it might *seem* tactically warranted by some necessity calculus, its use in fact would alter the structure and values of the American republic. Emergency tactics, as Ferejohn and Pasquino put it, threaten to "spill over into the operation of the ordinary legal system."[61]

A favorite example of the elder Lieber's involving Indian tribes illustrated the point. Lieber told his students that in wartime Native Americans slowly roasted their prisoners alive. Now, as it happens, he badly misunderstood the ritual and functional value of Indian prisoner-of-war practices. But, regardless, he insisted that a civilized state could not retaliate in kind when at war with Indians. The reason was that a republic like the United States could not simultaneously retain its basic identity and values, on the one hand, and engage in torture, on the other. For a republic to practice torture would alter its identity. Such a republic became something other than the republic it had been at the beginning of the conflict—something more like the Indian tribes against which it fought and against which it defined itself. A state that fought like "savages" became savage itself.[62]

Of course, Lieber's reasoning was full of the usual hypocrisy that attended most Anglo-American thinking about combat with Native Americans. But, accepting that as true, the important point is that the Liebers believed that to resort to torture was irreversibly to alter the identity of the torturer.[63]

At this juncture in the argument, a difficult truth arises. The postwar civil libertarians, like the antebellum critics of martial law before them, understood the risk of a necessity standard as a mode of self-preservation. Former attorney general Jeremiah S. Black grasped the point in arguing the *Milligan* case before the Supreme Court. "A violation of law on pretense of saving a government such as ours," he asserted, "is not self-preservation, but suicide." Justice David Davis's opinion in the *Milligan* case affirmed the same risk. If martial law justified military commissions when the courts were open, Davis contended, then "a country, preserved at the sacrifice of all the cardinal principles of liberty, is not worth the cost of preservation."[64]

It is a noteworthy feature of American history that, from the 1830s on, the nineteenth century's great critiques of martial law and necessity advanced their arguments on behalf of slavery and against the interests of the freed people in Reconstruction. There is an important point in this for the history of emergency powers in the United States. Those powers have been a source of great danger to civil liberties, to be sure. They have underwritten some of our least attractive moments. Just think of Japanese internment during World War II or the Red scare panic in the aftermath of World War I. But emergency powers and the necessity principle have also sustained some of the country's best moments, too. As John Quincy Adams grasped in the 1830s, emergency powers and the necessity principle would be the source for the Emancipation Proclamation. They would sustain federal power in Reconstruction. And their slow diminution in the 1870s helped undo the new liberty of the freed people.[65]

Regardless of the context, however, Buchanan and Davis left unmentioned that, in a true crisis, the risk to the values and identity of the republic is on both sides. That is what a crisis is. For, if necessity truly seems to demand recourse to some terrible tactic, it follows that *not* engaging in that conduct will also have grave consequences. Not acting in such circumstances inevitably reshapes a republic, too. Feedback loops and recursive redefinitions of the community will take place whether or not the community takes action inconsistent with its initial values in order to preserve itself. That is precisely why the crisis is a crisis. But this is not so much a critique of the Lieber perspective as it is a deeper understanding of it. For the moment of crisis demands complex judgments that weigh competing and incommensurable values against one another. Lincoln's crisis moment of all the laws but one yields no clear answer in the abstract, only hard all-things-considered answers in particular contexts. So too with the Liebers' manuscript.

The most remarkable piece of the lost Lieber manuscript is the solution it offers to the dilemma of the republic in the moment of crisis, beset on all sides by risks to its fundamental commitments and principles. The Liebers understood full well that moments of necessity were junctures of radical instability. To decide on the steps to be taken in a moment of crisis is to redefine the identity and values of the community since there is no acoustic separation walling off the identity of the regime from the tactics adopted to protect it. A republic's laws, institutions, and practices constitute its identity. The Liebers were in a position to see as much thanks to debates over slavery and martial law from the 1830s and 1840s on.

It was at this point that the Liebers made the most analytically interesting move in the manuscript. Their account offered an idea about necessity that did not appear in the 1863 code but that supplied an account of why permitting torture would differ from other alterations of the laws in moments of crisis.

As the Liebers put it, the way to determine whether an act was permitted under martial law's necessity standard was to ask not whether an act of the state official in question was necessary or whether it was required as judged by the common sense of a reasonable citizen. No, the critical feature of the law of necessity was that "reason and common sense must approve the particular act" in question. The acts of officials in moments of crisis, the Liebers wrote, "should be adjudged to be necessary in the judgment of a moderate and reasonable man."[66]

Here was a vitally important addition to the analysis: the *moderate and reasonable man*. In 1863, when the elder Lieber drafted his fierce code, he left the standard of necessity underspecified. That code offered precious few resources for evaluating whether necessity warranted a proposed course of action or whether instead the proposed course of action would itself undermine the republic. How was one to tell whether some course of conduct was self-preservation or suicide? The great difficulty was that the necessity standard alone does not supply a definition of the ends to which means may be put. And so long as there are no limits on the ends to which means may be applied—so long as the identity of the state may be radically remade in the process of evaluating the means necessary to rescue it—then there will be no limit on the means that will prove necessary.

The torture example made clear that the Liebers rejected the illimitable power approach to necessity—and the standard of a reasonable and moderate man explained how. The Liebers identified limits on the means that necessity might warrant because (and only because) they believed the American republic to be constituted around an identifiable set of values—values that together formed a standard of temperate reasonableness. For Schmitt, the sovereign dictator exercised a kind of radical freedom in the moment of exception precisely because that moment offered an opportunity to reinvent the ends of the state. But, for the Liebers, the ends of the American republic were limited; they were constrained by the public values of the regime, embodied in the perspective of the moderate and reasonable citizen.

The Liebers' reasonable citizen was not merely a self-interested rational actor. The Liebers filled in the reasonable citizen with substantive values such as an opposition to torture and a commitment to moderation. Doing this gave determinacy to the necessity inquiry; it offered the resources for distinguishing self-preservation from suicide and thereby allowed a republic to rule out certain courses of conduct.

By the same token, the reasonable citizen was no sovereign dictator; she did not choose in an act of pure will from outside the institutions, practices, and norms of the social formations in which she was embedded. (If she did, there would be no grounds for excluding torture a priori.) Nor was she merely a biological creature programmed for survival alone. (Once again, the torture bar would make no sense if she were.) No, the Liebers' citizen was a different kind of subject altogether, one shaped and molded by the values of the community—what the legal theorist David Dyzenhaus recently has called the "political culture" that exerts itself even in moments of emergency. The Liebers posited that even the moment of crisis is saturated by a system of norms and principles. The Liebers, father and son, articulated a view like that of the political philosopher Nomi Lazar when she argues that "normal ethics do not cease to function" during moments of emergency. The Liebers shared Lazar's basic view that the basic logic of the republic travels into the moment of crisis and exerts influence over events. And, as they saw it, the carrier of that logic was the reasonable citizen, whose basic values draw from the constitutive commitments of the republic—commitments whose basic character defines the scope of what is reasonably necessary under even the most difficult of circumstances.[67]

Put this way, the Lieber manuscript reached both backward and forward. Looking back, it tweaked the seventeenth-century prerogative power idea associated with John Locke. Locke asserted that the prerogative was restricted to the advancement of "publick good and advantage"; his executive power authorized the executive to act without or against the law so long as those actions promoted "the preservation of all." In the Liebers' theory, by contrast, the reasonable citizen principle connected the necessity standard not to the preservation of the citizen's life but to the preservation of the collective values and constitutive commitments of the republic.[68]

At the same time, the manuscript anticipates a central thread in the twenty-first-century emergency literature. It rebuts the bitter nihilism of Finlason's state of terror and anticipates the critique of Schmitt's state of exception offered by scholars like Dyzenhaus, Lazar, Benjamin Straumann, and others.[69] And it foreshadows the contention of the British legal theorist Thomas Poole, echoing the American lawyer Philip Bobbitt, that the logic of *raison d'état* is inescapably contingent on the particular kind of regime in which the claim of necessity arises.

4. Conclusion: Between Self-Preservation and Suicide

Would arguments about emergency constitutionalism look different today if the Liebers' manuscript had not been lost? What if a generation and more of American experience with emergency constitutionalism had been remembered through Lieber alongside Lincoln, rather than in the strains of Samuel Nicholas's Kentuckian essay, refracted through Justice Davis's opinion in *Milligan*?

Many an informed observer has been tempted to say that the lasting contribution of American debates on the problem of emergency constitutionalism is Justice Robert Jackson's ringing dictum from the era of the Second World War. The Constitution, Jackson wrote in his *Terminiello v. City of Chicago* dissent in 1949, "is not a suicide pact." Assistant Secretary of War John J. McCloy said much the same thing a few years earlier about the internment of Japanese Americans along the West Coast. "If it is a question of the safety of the country [and] the Constitution," he wrote, "why the Constitution is just a scrap of paper to me."[70]

Jackson's suicide pact and McCloy's scrap of paper have been the American short form for the ideas of Continental theorists led by Schmitt. On this view, leaders will set the law aside to reveal naked power in the moment of emergency. Recent commentators such as Eric Posner and Adrian Vermeule argue that we ought not expect anything different.[71] But the nineteenth-century tradition embodied in the Lieber manuscript offered a further insight. The suicide pact conception of the emergency asks us to imagine some unconstructed collectivity conceptually prior to the Constitution such that setting norms aside for the purpose of saving the collectivity might be the coherent thing to do. It contemplates a collectivity that has some brute existence outside shared language, values, institutions, and commitments. Such a collectivity might—in principle—be able to step outside its practices since those practices would by hypothesis be contingent rather than constitutive.

What the Lieber manuscript grasps, and what an increasingly powerful strand of the emergency literature contends, is that this way of thinking about the problem of emergency has the problem backward. Our imagined communities are constituted by law, and this makes the project of saving the country (as the elder Lieber put it in 1863) radically more complex. Saving the country may indeed be paramount. But deciding what it means to save the country—deciding which courses of conduct effectively destroy it in the name of saving it—entails an excruciating exercise of judgment about the character of the country. The Liebers' insight is to see that the practices of the country itself already supply the ingredients of that difficult judgment. Decision in the moment of emergency is an act of judgment from within the regime, not from without. How could it be otherwise?

Commentators have long associated Lincoln's alternative dictum— "all the laws but one"—with the suicide pact concept.[72] But Lincoln came closer than either Jackson and McCloy, on the one hand, or Schmitt, on the other, to capturing the distinctive dilemma of emergencies in a republic of laws. His formulation asks us to figure out what it would mean to save a *constitutional* community. The Liebers saw that this special problem in the theory of emergencies highlighted the prescriptive limits that a constitutional order must establish to preserve itself, even in the midst of the exception. They saw, too, that, as a descriptive matter, the constitutional values of the regime could not help but condition and shape the course of the emergency.

The persistence of values and traditions does not, of course, mean that there will be easy answers when emergency looms. But to derive answers one needs to have the questions right. Before the twentieth century took hold, in an era when the constructedness of American national identity was still clear, the two Liebers developed a theory of the republic in existential crisis—a theory that, like its flawed but endearing authors, was fiercely uncompromising and deeply humane.

: : :

Many thanks to Bruce Ackerman, Greg Downs, Beverly Gage, David Dyzenhaus, Gary Gerstle, Joel Isaac, Oona Hathaway, Ira Katznelson, Duncan Kelly, Jeremy Kessler, Nomi Lazar, Bill Novak, Noah Rosenblum, Steve Sawyer, Scott Shapiro, Will Smiley, Matt Waxman, and Mariah Zeisberg for comments on this and other versions of this project. I am grateful to Michael Cotter, Berit Fitzsimmons, David Miller, Lauren Miller, Rob Nelson, Conor Reynolds, and Brandon Thompson for excellent research assistance on this and related projects.

Notes

1. For the work of emergency theorists who dwell on the American Civil War, see, e.g., Edward S. Corwin, *The President: Office and Powers, 1787–1957*, 4th ed. (New York: New York University Press, 1957); James G. Randall, *Constitutional Problems under Lincoln* (New York: D. Appleton, 1926; rev. ed., Urbana: University of Illinois Press, 1951); William Rehnquist, *All the Laws but One* (New York: Knopf, 1998); Clinton Rossiter, *Constitutional Dictatorship* (Abingdon: Routledge, 2002); Trevor Morrison, "Suspension and the Extra Judicial Constitution," *Columbia Law Review* 107, no. 7 (2007): 1533–1616; Michael Stokes Paulsen, "The Constitution of Necessity," *Notre Dame Law Review* 79, no. 4 (2004): 1257–97; Kim Lane Scheppele, "North American Emergencies," *International Journal of Constitutional Law* 4, no. 2 (April 2006): 213–43; Brook Thomas, "Reconstructing the Limits of Schmitt's Theory

of Sovereignty: A Case for Law as Rhetoric, Not as Political Theology," *UC Irvine Law Review* 4, no. 1 (2014): 254–60; Stephen I. Vladeck, "The Field Theory: Martial Law, the Suspension Power, and the Insurrection Act," *Temple Law Review* 80, no. 2 (2007): 391–439, and "Emergency Power and the Militia Acts," *Yale Law Journal* 114, no. 1 (2004): 149–94; Samuel Issacharoff and Richard Pildes, "Between Civil Libertarianism and Executive Unilateralism," in *The Constitution in Wartime*, ed. Mark Tushnet (Durham, NC: Duke University Press, 2005), 161–97; and Daniel A. Farber, "Lincoln, Presidential Power, and the Rule of Law," Public Law Research Paper (Berkeley: University of California, Berkeley, March 2018).

2. For published fragments of the underlying manuscript, see G. Norman Lieber, *Meaning of the Term Martial Law as Used in the Petition of Right and the Preamble to the Mutiny Act* ([New York?]: n.p., 1877), 2–3 and n.; "Martial Law during the Revolution," *The Magazine of American History with Notes and Queries* (New York) 1 (1877): 538–41, and "What Is the Justification for Martial Law," *North American Review* 163, no. 480 (1896): 558. Francis Lieber also described his plans for the manuscript in correspondence during the second half of the Civil War. See Francis Lieber to Henry Halleck, June 2, 1863, and Francis Lieber to Charles Sumner, May 24, 1863, Francis Lieber Papers, Huntington Library, San Marino, CA (hereafter Huntington Lieber Papers).

3. Francis Lieber and G. Norman Lieber, *"Martial Law Treatise"* (n.d., manuscript), Guido Norman Lieber Collection, Judge Advocate General Papers, Record Group 153, National Archives and Records Administration, Washington, DC. See generally Will Smiley and John Fabian Witt, eds., *To Save the Country: A Lost Manuscript of the Civil War* (New Haven, CT: Yale University Press, 2019); John Fabian Witt, "A Lost Theory of American Emergency Constitutionalism," *Law and History Review* 36, no. 3 (2018): 551.

4. Carl Schmitt, *Political Theology: Four Chapters on the Concept of Sovereignty*, trans. George Schwab (Chicago: University of Chicago Press, 2005), and *Dictatorship*, trans. M. Hoelzl and G. Ward (Cambridge: Polity, 2014). See also Giorgio Agamben, *Homo Sacer: Sovereign Power and Bare Life*, trans. Daniel Heller-Roazen (Stanford, CA: Stanford University Press, 1998), and *State of Exception*, trans. Kevin Attell (Chicago: University of Chicago Press, 2005).

5. See James Oakes, *The Scorpion's Sting: Antislavery and the Coming of the Civil War* (New York: Norton, 2015), 22–23.

6. John Fabian Witt, *Lincoln's Code: The Laws of War in American History* (New York: Simon & Schuster, 2012); William W. Freehling, *Road to Disunion*, 2 vols. (Oxford: Oxford University Press, 1991–2008); Oakes, *The Scorpion's Sting*; Leonard L. Richards, *The Life and Times of Congressman John Quincy Adams* (Oxford: Oxford University Press, 1988); Richard H. Sewell, *Ballots for Freedom: Antislavery Politics in the United States, 1837–1860* (New York: Norton, 1980); Worthington Chauncey Ford, *The Writings of John Adams*, 7 vols. (New York: Macmillan, 1913–17), 5:125–26; Samuel Flagg Bemis, *A Diplomatic History of the United States*, 4th ed. (New York: Holt, Rinehart & Winston, 1955), 175n.

7. Adams quoted in Worthington Chauncey Ford and Charles Francis Adams, *John Quincy Adams, His Connection with the Monroe Doctrine (1823) by*

Worthington Chauncey Ford, and with Emancipation under Martial Law (1819–1842) by Charles Francis Adams (Cambridge, MA: John Wilson & Son, 1902), 73, 75–76. See also *Cong. Globe*, 24th Cong., 1st sess., appendix at 433 (1836).

8. Ford and Adams, *John Quincy Adams*, 77. See also "The Beginning of the End," *Harper's Weekly*, September 14, 1861, 578; and William Lee Miller, *Arguing about Slavery: John Quincy Adams and the Great Battle in the United States Congress* (New York: Vintage, 1998).

9. "Proclamation, November 7, 1775, by His Excellency the Right Honourable John Earl of Dunmore," Library of Congress, https://www.loc.gov/item/rbpe.1780130a; Maya Jasanoff, *Liberty's Exiles: American Loyalists in the Revolutionary World* (New York: Knopf, 2011), 47–49; Alan Taylor, *The Internal Enemy: Slavery and War in Virginia, 1772–1832* (New York: Norton, 2013); Witt, *Lincoln's Code*.

10. *Martial Law by a Kentuckian* (Louisville: Louisville Journal, 1842), 6–7.

11. Nicholas's objection was a reprise of the fundamentally conservative tradition of Roman dictatorship—conservative in the sense that it aimed above all to restore the status quo ante. See John Ferejohn and Pasquale Pasquino, "The Law of the Exception: A Typology of Emergency Powers," *I.CON* 2, no. 2 (2004): 210–39. For a contemporary echo of the resistance to a necessity power that would transform the nation at the expense of the Constitution, see Saikrishna Prakash, "The Constitution as Suicide Pact," *Notre Dame Law Review* 74, no. 4 (2004): 1302–9.

12. Sir Matthew Hale, *History and Analysis of the Common Law of England* (London: J. Nutt, 1713), 40; William Blackstone, *Commentaries on the Laws of England*, ed. Wilfrid Prest, vol. 1, *Of the Rights of Persons*, ed. David Lemmings (New York: Oxford University Press, 2016), 265.

13. *Appendix to the Congressional Globe*, 31st Cong., 1st sess., 23, pt. 1:151, https://books.google.com/books?id=tQ3nAAAAMAAJ&pg=PA151&lpg=PA151&dq=jefferson+davis+%22decree+that+slavery+was+abolished%22&source=bl&ots=qj0GjNHKhu&sig=ACfU3U3A5Ktq1-eozlcxCnUOz3-8Qums6A&hl=en&sa=X&ved=2ahUKEwjx49Gnv5TlAhXxQ98KHYSPDC8Q6AEwAXoECAMQAg#v=onepage&q=jefferson%20davis%20%22decree%20that%20slavery%20was%20abolished%22&f=false.

14. Miller, *Arguing about Slavery*; *Daily National Intelligencer*, February 19, 1850; "The Rightful Power of Congress to Confiscate and Emancipate," *Monthly Law Reporter* 24 (1862): 27; Aziz Rana, "Freedom Struggles and the Limits of Constitutional Continuity," *Maryland Law Review* 71, no 4 (2012): 1015–51; Steven G. Calabresi and Christopher S. Yoo, "The Unitary Executive during the Second Half-Century," *Harvard Journal of Law and Public Policy* 26, no. 3 (2003): 720; Chad L. Williams, *Torchbearers of Democracy: African American Soldiers in the World War I Era* (Chapel Hill: University of North Carolina Press, 2010); Robert Haynes, "The Houston Mutiny and Riot of 1917," *Southwestern Historical Quarterly* 76, no. 4 (1973): 418–39; Mary L. Dudziak, *Cold War Civil Rights: Race and the Image of American Democracy* (Princeton, NJ: Princeton University Press, 2000), 115–51.

15. On the United States as a legally constructed community, see Akhil Reed Amar, "A Few Thoughts on Constitutionalism, Textualism, and Populism,"

Fordham Law Review 65, no. 4 (1997): 1658; Laurence H. Tribe, "America's Constitutional Narrative," *Daedalus* 141 (Winter 2012): 34; and Aziz Rana, "Constitutionalism and the Foundations of the Security State," *California Law Review* 103, no. 2 (2015): 337. See also John Fabian Witt, *Patriots and Cosmopolitans: Hidden Histories of American Law* (Cambridge, MA: Harvard University Press, 2007).

16. Schmitt, *Political Theology*. See also David Dyzenhaus, *Legality and Legitimacy: Carl Schmitt, Hans Kelsen, and Hermann Heller in Weimar* (Oxford: Clarendon, 1997); David Dyzenhaus, ed., *Law as Politics: Carl Schmitt's Critique of Liberalism* (Durham, NC: Duke University Press, 1998); Oona Hathaway and Scott Shapiro, *The Internationalists: How a Radical Plan to Outlaw War Remade the World* (New York: Simon & Schuster, 2017); Paul W. Kahn, *Political Theology: Four New Chapters on the Concept of Sovereignty* (New York: Columbia University Press, 2012); Jan-Werner Müller, *A Dangerous Mind: Carl Schmitt in Post-War European Thought* (New Haven, CT: Yale University Press, 2003); Eric A. Posner and Adrian Vermeule, *Terror in the Balance: Security, Liberty, and the Courts* (New York: Oxford University Press, 2007), and *The Executive Unbound: After the Madisonian Republic* (New York: Oxford University Press, 2011); and Sanford Levinson, "Preserving Constitutional Norms in Times of Permanent Emergencies," *Constellations* 13, no. 1 (2006): 59.

17. Frank Freidel, *Francis Lieber: Nineteenth-Century Liberal* (Baton Rouge: Louisiana State University Press, 1947); Witt, *Lincoln's Code*; Charles R. Mack and Henry H. Lesesne, eds., *Francis Lieber and the Culture of the Mind* (Columbia: University of South Carolina Press, 2005); David Bosco, "Moral Principle vs. Military Necessity," *American Scholar* (Winter 2008): 25–34; Paul Finkelman, "Francis Lieber and the Modern Law of War," *University of Chicago Law Review* 80, no. 4 (2013): 2071–2132.

18. Freidel, *Francis Lieber*; Witt, *Lincoln's Code*; Mack and Lesesne, eds., *Francis Lieber*.

19. Francis Lieber, "Martial Law," in *Encyclopaedia Americana, 13 vols.* (Philadelphia: Carey & Lea, 1830–35), 8:308–9. Lieber cited Matthew Hale's argument that martial law was no part of the common law but only "indulged by the law rather than constituting a part of it."

20. Francis Lieber, *On Civil Liberty and Self-Government*, 2 vols. (Philadelphia: Carey & Lea, 1853), 1:131.

21. Witt, *Lincoln's Code*; Carl von Clausewitz, *On War*, trans. and ed. Michael Howard and Peter Paret (Princeton, NJ: Princeton University Press, 1989); Michael Howard, *Clausewitz: A Very Short Introduction* (New York: Oxford University Press, 2002).

22. Freidel, *Francis Lieber*; Witt, *Lincoln's Code*.

23. Amanda L. Tyler, *Habeas Corpus in Wartime: From the Tower of London to Guantanamo* (New York: Oxford University Press, 2017), 159–66. See also Mark Neely, *Lincoln and the Triumph of the Nation: Constitutional Conflict in the American Civil War* (Chapel Hill: University of North Carolina Press, 2011), and *The Fate of Liberty: Abraham Lincoln and Civil Liberties* (Oxford: Oxford University Press, 1992); Randall, *Constitutional Problems*; Daniel A.

Farber, *Lincoln's Constitution* (Chicago: University of Chicago Press, 2003); Michael Stokes Paulsen, "The *Merryman* Power and the Dilemma of Autonomous Executive Branch Interpretation," *Cardozo Law Review* 15, nos. 1–2 (1993): 81–111; and Seth Barrett Tillman, "*Ex Parte Merryman*: Myth, History, and Scholarship," *Military Law Review* 224, no. 2 (2016): 481–540.

24. "Dr. Lieber on the Writ of Habeas Corpus," *New York Times*, April 6, 1862, https://www.nytimes.com/1862/04/06/news/dr-lieber-on-the-writ-of-habeas-corpus.html.

25. Observer, "The Rebellion and the Constitution," *New York Times*, November 30, 1861, https://www.nytimes.com/1861/11/30/news/rebellion-constitution-free-constitution-not-incompatible-with-state-war-habeas.html?pagewanted=1.

26. Horace Binney, *The Privilege of the Writ of Habeas Corpus under the Constitution*, 2nd ed. (Philadelphia: C. Sherman & Son, 1862).

27. Binney, *Privilege of the Writ*. See also Akhil Reed Amar, *America's Constitution: A Biography* (New York: Random House, 2005), 122; and William Baude, "The Judgment Power," *Georgetown Law Journal* 96, no. 6 (2008): 1854.

28. Interestingly, this is the opposite of the phenomenon described by Prakash in the early republic state constitutions that allocated emergency authority to legislatures in the first instance and to executives only derivatively. See Saikrishna Prakash, "The Sweeping Domestic War Powers of Congress," *Michigan Law Review* 113, no. 8 (2015): 1352–53. The view Binney held looks more like the presidentialist view articulated by Michael Paulsen. See Paulsen, "The Constitution of Necessity."

29. "Dr. Lieber on the Writ of Habeas Corpus." See also Richard Salomon, "The Unsuspected Francis Lieber" (MA thesis, City University of New York, 2018), 14–15.

30. David Donald, *Charles Sumner and the Rights of Man* (New York: Knopf, 1970), 16–17, 54.

31. *Cong. Globe*, 37th Cong., 3rd sess. 1421 (1863) (statement of Rep. Johnson).

32. *Cong. Globe*, 37th Cong., 3rd sess. 133 (1863) (statement of Rep. Yeaman).

33. Witt, *Lincoln's Code*, 220–49; Matthew J. Mancini, "Francis Lieber, Slavery, and the 'Genesis' of the Laws of War," *Journal of Southern History* 77, no. 2 (2011): 325–48; James F. Childress, "Francis Lieber's Interpretation of the Laws of War: General Orders No. 100 in the Context of His Life and Thought," *American Journal of Jurisprudence* 21, no. 1 (1976): 34–70. The quotation comes from Article 15 of the Lieber Code, reprinted in Witt, *Lincoln's Code*, 377 (app.). All citations to the Lieber Code are to the version reprinted as an appendix to Witt, *Lincoln's Code*, which corrects errors that have crept into copies of the code over the years beginning with a private printing in 1863 and restores the official version published by the Union in the spring of 1863.

34. Witt, *Lincoln's Code*, 376 (app.), art. 5.

35. "Message to Congress in Special Session, July 4, 1861," in *Collected Works of Abraham Lincoln*, ed. Roy Basler, 9 vols. (New Brunswick, NJ: Rutgers University Press, 1953), 4:421, 430.

36. Rehnquist, *All the Laws but One*; Neely, *Lincoln and the Triumph of the Nation*; Farber, *Lincoln's Constitution*; Randall, *Constitutional Problems*; Philip Bobbitt, *Terror and Consent: The Wars of the Twenty-First Century* (New York: Anchor, 2009), 351 (quote).

37. Gregory P. Downs, *After Appomattox: Military Occupation and the Ends of War* (Cambridge, MA: Harvard University Press, 2015); Chandra Manning, *Troubled Refuge: Struggling for Freedom in the Civil War* (New York: Knopf, 2016); Gregory P. Downs and Kate Masur, "Echoes of War: Rethinking Post–Civil War Governance and Politics," in *The World the Civil War Made*, ed. Gregory P. Downs and Kate Masur (Chapel Hill: University of North Carolina Press, 2015), 1–21.

38. *Ex Parte* Milligan, 71 U.S. 2 (1866). See Neely, *The Fate of Liberty*; Charles Fairman, *Reconstruction and Reunion, 1864–88*, 2 vols. (New York: Macmillan, 1971); and Rehnquist, *All the Laws but One*.

39. James D. Richardson, ed., *A Compilation of the Messages and Papers of the Presidents, 1789–1897*, 10 vols. (Washington, DC: US Government Printing Office, 1897), 6:312–14, 432; Henry Stanbery, "The Reconstruction Acts," in *Official Opinions of the Attorneys General of the United States, vol. 12* (Washington, DC: W. H. & O. H. Morrison, 1870), 182–206, esp. 199–200. See also Lisset Pino and John Fabian Witt, "The Fourteenth Amendment as an Ending" (paper presented at the conference "The Many Fourteenth Amendments," Miami, February 2018); *Cong. Globe*, 40th Cong., 3rd sess. 121 (1869) (statement of Sen. Doolittle) ("No plea of 'war necessity,' no 'logic of events,' nothing in the war or in the purpose of the war, can lead me to think for one moment that I am not bound by the Constitution as a Senator upon my oath and upon my conscience"); *Cong. Globe*, 40th Cong., 2nd sess. 775 (1868) (statement of Sen. Johnson) ("[I]n the vocabulary of the Constitution there is no such word as 'necessity'"); *Cong. Globe*, 40th Cong., 1st sess. 3 (1867) (statement of Rep. Chanler) ("For a military commander, created under a past special necessity, to be allowed . . . to hold within his grasp the rights and destinies of the people whom he may be sent to rule over is inconsistent with the principles of the Declaration of Independence"); *Cong. Globe*, 39th Cong., 2nd sess. 167 (1867) (statement of Rep. Wright) ("If the Congress of the United States can place military governors over ten States of this Union in the absence of any constitutional right to do so, why may they not place a military governor over every other State, until at last we shall be merged into an absolute monarchy or a military despotism?").

40. Charles Warren, *The Supreme Court in United States History*, 3 vols. (Boston: Little, Brown, 1922), vol. 3; Neely, *The Fate of Liberty*; Randall, *Constitutional Problems*.

41. *The Slaughterhouse Cases*, 83 U.S. 36, 94 (1873). For *The Slaughterhouse Cases* and Calhoun, see Charles Black Jr., *A New Birth of Freedom: Human Rights, Named and Unnamed* (New Haven, CT: Yale University Press, 1997), 72; and William E. Forbath, "Lincoln, the Declaration, and the 'Grisly, Undying Corpse of States' Rights': History, Memory, and Imagination in the Constitution of a Southern Liberal," *Georgetown Law Journal* 92, no. 4 (2004): 747.

42. Lauren Benton and Lisa Ford, *Rage for Order: The British Empire and the Origins of International Law, 1800–1850* (Cambridge, MA: Harvard Uni-

versity Press, 2016); Mark Condos, "Licence to Kill: The Murderous Outrages Act and the Rule of Law in Colonial India, 1867–1925," *Modern Asian Studies* 50, no. 2 (2016): 479–517.

43. Rande W. Kostal, *A Jurisprudence of Power: Victorian Empire and the Rule of Law* (Oxford: Oxford University Press, 2008); Gad Heuman, *The Killing Time: The Morant Bay Rebellion in Jamaica* (Knoxville: University of Tennessee Press, 1994); John Fabian Witt, "Anglo-American Empire and the Crisis of the Legal Frame (Will the Real British Empire Please Stand Up)," *Harvard Law Review* 120, no. 3 (2007): 787–91; Michael Lobban, "William Francis Finlason (1818–1895)," in *Oxford Dictionary of National Biography* (2004), https://doi.org/10.1093/ref:odnb/9462.

44. William Francis Finlason, *A Treatise on Martial Law: As Allowed by the Law of England: In Time of Rebellion* (London: Stevens & Sons, 1866), *Commentaries upon Martial Law with Special Reference to Its Regulation and Restraint* (London: Stevens & Sons, 1867), *A Review of the Authorities as to the Repression of Riot or Rebellion* (London: Stevens & Sons, 1868), and *The History of the Jamaican Case* (London: Chapman & Hall, 1869).

45. Finlason, *A Treatise on Martial Law*, xi–xxxi. See also David Dyzenhaus, "The Puzzle of Martial Law," *University of Toronto Law Journal* 59, no. 1 (2009): 17–19.

46. Finlason, *A Treatise on Martial Law*, xxxi. See also Heuman, *The Killing Time*.

47. Finlason, *A Treatise on Martial Law*, xvi.

48. See Francis Lieber to Henry Halleck, June 2, 1863, and Francis Lieber to Charles Sumner, May 24, 1863, Huntington Lieber Papers.

49. Arthur Wellesley, Duke of Wellington, *The Dispatches of Field Marshall the Duke of Wellington, K.G. during His Various Campaigns*, 13 vols. (London: John Murray, 1836–39), 6:43. See also Smiley and Witt, eds., *To Save the Country*, 239.

50. Lieber and Lieber, "Martial Law Treatise," in Smiley and Witt, eds., *To Save the Country*. Note that Lieber did not treat necessity and martial law as two different powers, the former extraconstitutional, the latter not. For this latter approach, see Vladeck, "The *Field* Theory."

51. Witt, *Lincoln's Code*, 376 (app.), art. 5; Lieber and Lieber, "Martial Law Treatise," in Smiley and Witt, eds., *To Save the Country, 15*. See also Joel Prentiss Bishop, *Commentaries on the Criminal Law*, 2 vols., 3rd ed. (Boston: Little, Brown, 1865), 1:506, sec. 910. The Liebers observed that even the *Milligan* majority conceded as much.

52. Lieber and Lieber, "Martial Law Treatise," in Smiley and Witt, eds., *To Save the Country, 98*.

53. Lieber and Lieber, "Martial Law Treatise," in Smiley and Witt, eds., *To Save the Country, 30*.

54. Lieber and Lieber, "Martial Law Treatise," in Smiley and Witt, eds., *To Save the Country, 43*; J. R. Maddicott, "Thomas of Lancaster, Second Earl of Lancaster, Second Earl of Leicester, and Earl of Lincoln (c. 1278–1322)," in *Oxford Dictionary of National Biography* (2008), https://doi.org/10.1093/ref:odnb/27195 (describing the "show" trial and execution of Thomas of

Lancaster); *The Trial of Lieutenant-Colonel Joseph Wall, Late Governor of Goree, at the Old Bailey, on Wednesday, January 20, 1802; for the Wilful Murder of Benjamin Armstrong, a Serjeant of the African Corps, July 10, 1782* (London: Sabine & Son, [1802]); Joshua Bryant, *Account of an Insurrection of the Negro Slaves in the Colony of Demerara, Which Broke Out on the 18th of August, 1823* (Georgetown, Demerara: Printed by A. Stevenson at the Guinea Chronicle Office, 1824), 60–61; J. Forbes, *Recent Disturbances and Military Executions in Ceylon* (Edinburgh: William Blackwood & Sons, 1850), 18–22; William Nassau Molesworth, *The History of England from the Year 1830* (London: Chapman & Hall, 1873), 3:400–401.

55. Witt, *Lincoln's Code*.

56. Lieber and Lieber, "Martial Law Treatise," in Smiley and Witt, eds., *To Save the Country*, 21.

57. See, e.g., Jeff McMahan, "Torture, Morality, and Law," *Case Western Reserve Journal of International Law* 37, no. 2 (2006): 241–48. Some but hardly all philosophers. See Charles Fried and Gregory Fried, *Because It Is Wrong: Torture, Privacy and Presidential Power in the Age of Terror* (New York: Norton, 2010); and Jeremy Waldron, *Torture, Terror, and Trade-Offs: Philosophy for the White House* (New York: Oxford University Press, 2010).

58. Witt, *Lincoln's Code*, 377 (app.), art. 16; 385 (app.), art. 80; 383 (app.), art. 56.

59. Witt, *Lincoln's Code*, 383 (app.), art. 60 ("great straits"); 380 (app.), arts. 35, 36, 38 (art, libraries, and private property).

60. Witt, *Lincoln's Code*, 327–65; Paul A. Kramer, *The Blood of Government: Race, Empire, the United States, and the Philippines* (Chapel Hill: University of North Carolina Press, 2006), and "The Water Cure: Debating Torture and Counterinsurgency—a Century Ago," *New Yorker*, February 25, 2008, https://www.newyorker.com/magazine/2008/02/25/the-water-cure; "Trials or Court-Martial in the Philippine Islands in Consequence of Certain Instructions," S. Doc. 57-213, 57th Cong. 2nd sess. March 3, 1903, 26.

61. Ferejohn and Pasquino, "Law of the Exception," 235.

62. Witt, *Lincoln's Code*, 184, 236.

63. Francis Lieber, "Law and Usages of War," no. IV, December 17, 1861 (Notebook no. 4), box 2, Francis Lieber Papers, Johns Hopkins University. Compare Ferejohn and Pasquino, "Law of the Exception," 223.

64. *Ex Parte* Milligan, 71 U.S. 2, 81, 126 (1866).

65. Witt, *Lincoln's Code*; Downs, *After Appomattox*; Manning, *Troubled Refuge*; Downs and Masur, "Echoes of War."

66. Lieber and Lieber, "Martial Law Treatise," in Smiley and Witt, eds., *To Save the Country*, 47.

67. David Dyzenhaus, *The Constitution of Law: Legality in a Time of Emergency* (Cambridge: Cambridge University Press, 2006), 212; Nomi Claire Lazar, *States of Emergency in Liberal Democracies* (New York: Cambridge University Press, 2013). A lawyer's version of Lazar's thesis emerges in Morrison, "Suspension and the Extra Judicial Constitution." On the ways in which the standard of reason invokes the values of the relevant community, see Robert C. Post, *Constitutional Domains: Democracy, Community, Management* (Cambridge, MA:

Harvard University Press, 1995), "The Social Foundations of Privacy: Community and Self in the Common Law Tort," 77 *California Law Review* 957 (1989): 957–1010, and "Federalism, Positive Law, and the Emergence of the Administrative State," *William and Mary Law Review* 48, no. 1 (2006): 1–183.

68. John Locke, *The Second Treatise of Government*, in *Two Treatises of Government*, ed. Peter Laslett (Cambridge: Cambridge University Press, 1960), 375, par. 159.

69. Benjamin Straumann, *Crisis and Constitutionalism: Roman Political Thought from the Fall of the Republic to the Age of Revolution* (Oxford: Oxford University Press, 2016), 42–43; David Dyzenhaus, "The Safety of the People Is the Supreme Law," *New Rambler*, October 25, 2016, https://newramblerreview.com/book-reviews/classics/the-safety-of-the-people-is-the-supreme-law.

70. *Terminiello v. City of Chicago*, 337 U.S. 1 (1949) (Jackson, J., dissenting). See also Roger Daniels, *The Japanese American Cases: The Rule of Law in Time of War* (Lawrence: University Press of Kansas, 2013), 9; Greg Robinson, *By Order of the President* (Cambridge, MA: Harvard University Press, 2003).

71. See Posner and Vermeule, *Terror in the Balance*.

72. See, e.g., Rehnquist, *All the Laws but One*.

6

Powers of War in Times of Peace: Emergency Powers in the United States after the End of the Civil War

Gregory P. Downs

In April 1879, fourteen years after the Confederate surrender at Appomattox and eight after the readmission of the last Confederate state, congressmen still debated the persistence of the exceptional war powers the Civil War had birthed. In a fraught special session called after the previous Congress failed to pass a budget for the army or the legislative, judicial, or executive branches, partisans fought over an effort to repeal an 1865 law that limited (but seemed to acknowledge) the use of the military to keep the peace on election day. Although congressmen defended and attacked the law on the basis of republican theory, electoral-day violence, taxation, and other issues, much of the debate—and of the government shutdown that called Congress back into special session—turned on the question of whether a law passed during wartime applied to a period of legal peace. "Grant that the war power, if you please, like charity that covers a multitude of sins, justifies all these acts, what war is going on now in this country?" Arkansas senator Augustus Garland asked. Republicans, he charged, "are shedding or attempting to shed . . . the blood of war in time of peace": "You cannot run this country in time of peace in a war harness. . . . If the necessity that brought forth this law existed, but has departed, let this law depart with it."[1] Republicans, however, denied that the law had anything to do with war powers, even if it did regulate military-civilian relations and was passed in time of flagrant war. It was not a "war measure," one senator replied, but an effort to define soldiers' authority after the war was over.[2] Other Republicans called the military's role in protecting elections a simple application of the military's role as *"the police force of the nation."*[3] Some argued that the 1865 act built on 1850s expansions of military power to enforce the Fugitive Slave Law. Republican senator James Blaine, who led the effort to save the law, looked to more recent but to his mind more definitive explanations for the law's constitutionality. The act was justified by the constitutional overhaul of the Thirteenth, Fourteenth, and Fifteenth Amendments even though all had been ratified after the law had been passed. "We thought there had been something gained on this question in a costly war and in amendments to the Constitution," he said. To Blaine and many Republicans, war had altered the nature of peacetime; to map normal powers in the 1870s, one should look not to the 1830s or even the 1850s but to the new authorities in the new constitution.[4]

These 1879 debates brought to a close a decade-long argument about the nature and definition of emergency powers in wartime. During the Civil War, Republicans and Democrats fought bitterly over the limits of war powers, then after Appomattox over their duration. By 1871 Democrats and Republicans agreed that wartime had concluded. Rather than ending debates about war powers, however, this acknowledgment sparked arguments about what war powers actually are and what remnants of wartime carried over into the new peace. Democrats—many of whom had once questioned the existence of emergency powers—now clung to a hard-and-fast definition of wartime in order to delegitimize ongoing civil uses of the military. Peacetime would be measured by resemblance to the 1840s or 1850s; any new reliance on military power over civilians was, by definition, a product of the Civil War and thus of war powers. Some Republicans—even those who had once championed war powers—now argued that the military's role was either a legitimate fruit of the Civil War, a necessary response to new emergencies, or a justifiable extension of constitutional and early republic practices.

By reconstructing the agonizing conflicts over Civil War emergency powers in the 1870s, we can rethink the endings and endpoints of the Civil War and the redefinitions of peace during wartime that made the exit to normalcy so challenging. Democrats and Republicans fought over these norms and habits, the anomalies shifting into systems, in 1870s floor fights about enforcement statutes that permitted federal supervisors, commissioners, and marshals to call out the military as a *posse comitatus*, granted the president authority to suspend the privilege of the writ of habeas corpus and declare states of insurrection, and permitted the military to guard polling places. Beyond those statutes, the arguments also turned on statutorily distinct events where the army intervened to sweep away allegedly insurgent Democratic state legislators or instate allegedly legitimate Republican legislators and governors. Which of these were normal efforts to keep the peace, and which violated conceptions of the government's proper peacetime powers altogether?

Because of the regional nature of the Civil War and Reconstruction, the debates also turned on geography, in ways that presage Gary Gerstle's arguments about the spaces of exception in later US history.[5] Once the United States readmitted the final rebel states in 1870–71, did the federal government retain any special powers in the former Confederate states? Or was every act in the South a precedent for a similar act in the North? Once again consistency was no virtue. Democrats charged Republicans with *both* extending a special charter of war powers over the South *and* unleashing powers that could be utilized in the North (as in fact army troops were used in New York City elections). Republicans claimed *both* that the South was in a special state of emergency *and* that Congress derived the power to use the military to keep the peace from statutes applicable everywhere in the country. In these arguments about whether the powers against the South could spread North, the vexing issue of force and the West frequently confounded debates as western—especially Texas—Democrats saved military funding in order to ensure protection in their ongoing wars against the Comanche and other tribes.

If the 1870s debates frustrate a wish for a single, clear history of war powers, they point to several intriguing ways of narrating that history. After the Confederate surrender, many Democrats embraced a simple narrative: war powers, however unpleasant or even unconstitutional, existed from necessity during the Civil War but expired either at Appomattox, or at President Johnson's 1866 proclamations of peace, or, perhaps, at the 1868–71 restoration of rebel governments. After the moment of expiration, the army could be used only to assist legislatures (or governors in the absence of the legislatures) in putting down insurrections or disturbances or enforcing federal court orders. Even in those cases, many Democrats preferred to rely on militias. By these lights almost every use of the military in the 1870s was illegitimate, contributing to a breakdown in firm and obvious barriers separating the powers of the government in war from those it possessed in peace.

Republicans, however, advanced several competing narratives of the role of military power over civilian life and laws. Drawing on early national deployments of the army against insurrections, the Burr conspiracy, and other crises, they argued that the military had always kept the peace. At their most expansive, they claimed that deposing or sustaining state governments in the 1870s was a normal, peacetime use of the military to support the survival of republican forms. They did acknowledge limits. Some believed that only the president could deploy the army and some that he could do so only when responding to local authorities. These Republicans drew clear lines: The army should not normally remove public officials from office or try civilians in front of military commissions.

But some Republicans looked to broad powers in the face of those crises, rooting those powers in the Civil War's constitutional revolution, not its state of exception. Like Blaine, they argued that the Civil War had in fact been a revolution that permitted the use of the powers of war to remake peacetime. Pointing to the expansiveness of the Thirteenth, Fourteenth, and Fifteenth Amendments, they claimed that laws and actions that would previously have been unconstitutional in peacetime were now constitutional. Why else would one bother to amend the Constitution? They argued that the peacetime of the 1870s could never resemble the peacetime of the 1850s because they operated under different constitutional regimes. War had changed peace forever.

Still other Republicans used the antebellum expansion of military power to enforce the 1850 Fugitive Slave Law to justify new martial powers. That law created a new federal police power for marshals and commissioners. Attorney General Caleb Cushing's 1854 memo authorized those officials to call on the military as a *posse comitatus* to enforce federal law, even over the objection of state officials. In 1866, Republicans turned those powers against slavery in the Civil Rights Act. In 1870s laws, and in memos from secretaries of war, Republicans increasingly separated the military's power as a *posse comitatus* from prior restraints. No longer did army officers need to wait for authorization from Washington; no longer did requests need to come from a legislature or a federal judge. Instead, deputy commissioners or deputy supervisors—often short-term appointees during crises—or even sheriffs or mayors could call directly for military aid. In this history of war powers, the 1870s resembled not the 1860s but the 1850s, when the United States established what we might call a commissioner state that could call on the army as its police.

Between 1870 and 1879, Congress fought over the military in a series of bitter debates that raised questions about war powers and peacetime.

In 1870 and 1871, Republicans passed enforcement laws that extended the authority to call on the army as a posse and, in 1871, authorized the president to suspend habeas corpus to protect voting rights. In 1875, Republican efforts to preserve some military power in peacetime led to a nearly forgotten but immensely controversial effort to put four states back under martial law. The 1876 election represented one flash point in this debate as Democrats now in control of the House of Representatives tried to slash the army's size and block the military from sustaining pro-Reconstruction state governments, leading to months when the army operated without pay. Then, in 1878 and 1879, Democrats launched more wide-ranging attacks on what they called wartime uses of the army, passing the *posse comitatus* amendment in 1878, and attempting to repeal the 1865 election law and undo other electoral protections in 1879 budget fights that led to a government shutdown and multiple vetoes by President Rutherford B. Hayes.

The 1870s, therefore, are a particularly propitious, if complex, moment to analyze the "fundamental conundrum" that Gerstle and Isaac raise: "What are constitutional regimes like that of the United States permitted to do in situations in which the survival of the regime appears to be at stake?"[6] This question structured a good deal of the political fighting in the 1870s and revealed that the answer could never be solely philosophical but was inherently political. Whether the regime faced a challenge to survival was not an empirical but an ideological question and one that would be particularly fraught at the precise moments of crisis. The difficulty of defining either necessity or the powers that could be utilized in an exceptional moment confounded everyone's attempts at consistency. How participants understood the means could not be separated from their competing views of the ends.

This period also directs our attention to the endurance of exceptional powers once the exceptional moment has passed. What happens to war powers when wartime is over? On further examination, some of the quick divisions between wartime and peacetime or between normalcy and exception seem to dissolve. Politicians could not agree on either what war powers were or when wartime ended. They frequently shifted arguments to defend their ultimate goal of sustaining (for Republicans) or overthrowing (for Democrats) civil rights in the South. To add to the complexity, many of these debates were shaped by congressional procedure, especially the process by which the House and the Senate reconciled legislation passed in different forms by each chamber. Given politicians' shifty, motivated reasoning on the Constitution and war powers, it may be tempting to dismiss the whole period as an anomaly in an otherwise fairly clear narrative of the efforts to regulate war powers in the United States.

But this messiness is precisely what makes the 1870s debates so potentially useful for scholars of wartime and other states of exception. Without any kind of clear, objective standard of war powers, politicians had to invent their theories on the fly, theories that they drew from European and US legal writings but also from their understanding of the necessity to take action. That necessity was the postemancipation crisis in the southern states, where planters and their accomplices launched violent counterinsurgencies to displace federal power and reassert their dominance over the four million newly freed ex-slaves.

Republicans therefore extended war powers for a rare purpose: to create transformative social change. Debates about the government's exceptional powers were always debates about the proper way to reconstruct a postwar, postslavery society. Short of war, how could a nineteenth-century government force its views on a resistant population? Instead of simply stabilizing a system under strain, war powers were deployed to create a new system, a system of civil rights replacing one rooted in slavery.

While we currently live in a cultural moment attuned to war powers' reactionary functions, the 1870s suggest their liberatory potential. In a literature that often assumes war powers' efficacy, the 1870s provide examples of their inadequacy to prevent the rollback of civil rights. In a moment when we associate war powers with the "discretionary powers that may be exercised by the executive branch of government, in particular by the president," as Gerstle and Isaac note, we see Congress fighting over its ability to seize the reins of war powers.[7] Holding the anomalies of the 1870s in our minds as we contemplate the development of war powers and exceptional powers in the twentieth and twenty-first centuries may help us see war powers as more contingent, contextual, and calculated than they appear in responses to external emergencies.

: : :

War powers emerged as one guiding principle of government power in the early days of the Civil War. As John Fabian Witt explored in *Lincoln's Code*, the Civil War itself was fought under evolving but meaningful powers and constraints of wartime as a state of exception. The turn to military force to override normal peacetime law developed in the war's first weeks. On April 27, 1861, Lincoln authorized Lieutenant General Winfield Scott to suspend the writ of habeas corpus along the

Eastern Seaboard to prevent Confederate sympathizers from sabotaging the army or drawing Maryland into the Confederacy. Supreme Court chief justice Roger Taney argued that only Congress, not the president, had the power to suspend habeas corpus in emergencies and lamented that the army had, "by force of arms, thrust aside the judicial authorities and officers."[8] Democratic politicians—including the extraordinarily able Marylander Reverdy Johnson—often critiqued war powers as tyrannical, unconstitutional, and proof "that our fathers fought during the Revolution in vain."[9] Lincoln argued that his use of war powers actually protected the Constitution by simultaneously saving the country and preserving a peacetime state of normalcy that could be returned to at war's end.[10] After Lincoln broadened the suspension in September 1862, his officers used their powers more widely than he likely intended, arresting the Democratic politician Clement Vallandigham, suppressing the *Chicago Times*, and trying more than three thousand individuals before military commissions, mostly in the South.[11]

Lincoln soon began to use these powers forcibly to restructure the country's political and social order through attacks on slavery, most notably in the Emancipation Proclamation. In General Orders No. 100, drawn up by the lawyer Francis Lieber, the army claimed that martial law over the Confederate states meant the "substitution of military rule and force" for "domestic administration and government." Although the military should be "strictly guided by the principles of justice, honor, and humanity," it had enormous powers of necessity, including the authority to free slaves.[12] In his 1863 proclamation of amnesty, Lincoln aimed to remake southern state governments by leveraging his power of amnesty to nudge white southern rebels to create new loyal governments that would end slavery. Throughout 1864, he struggled against recalcitrant white Louisianans, beleaguered generals, and his own Congress to create functional governments. Although war powers could not deliver all he wanted, they permitted the military to treat the rebel states as occupied lands, overrule and supplant their local elected officials, try civilians in front of military commissions, and order the emancipation of hundreds of thousands of slaves by presidential proclamation.

As US forces cornered the Confederate armies in March 1865, the question arose, Would the end of fighting mean the end of war powers? In early April, Confederate general Robert E. Lee indeed asked for "peace" that would restore normal law in the rebel states, but Ulysses S. Grant offered only a "surrender" that implied the continuance of military rule.[13] The United States intended to hold its war powers after the Confederates stopped fighting. Later in April, Major General William T.

Sherman did offer peace to surrendering Confederates in North Carolina, a peace that would have curtailed the military's authority to overrule local judges, free slaves, strike down oppressive state laws, arrest and try criminals, replace local officials, and press governments to ratify the Thirteenth Amendment. But President Johnson and the cabinet overruled the offer, arguing that peace had yet to come.

Reconstruction thus proceeded on a continuation of a wartime state of exception. In a postsurrender invasion of the South, the army declared that it recognized "no authority but its own."[14] It began to spread over the South, moving from roughly 120 outposts in March 1865 to more than 630, covering not just cities but plantation district market towns and railroad crossings, including places like Gillisonville, Grahamville, Pocotaligo, and McPhersonville in South Carolina. On the ground, soldiers and ex-slaves together created a revolution as soldiers rode onto plantations and read the Emancipation Proclamation and, crucially, provided access to federal government resources for ex-slaves seeking to claim their rights. As ex-slaves brought news of ongoing slavery, whippings, denial of wages, and other forms of mistreatment, they taught officers of the need to take control of legal cases through Freedmen's Bureau agents and sometimes provost courts and military commissions. President Johnson both supplemented and restrained military power by appointing provisional governors to call constitutional conventions in most rebel states. Using the threat of continued martial law, he all but forced the former Confederate states to repudiate debts incurred during the war, end slavery by state law, and ratify the Thirteenth Amendment "without delay."[15] Backed by eight rebel states held under martial law, the Thirteenth Amendment became the law of the land in December 1865.

For President Johnson, this marked a potential end to the war. Instead, Congress effectively said no when it refused to consider elected rebel state congressman and referred the status of the Confederate states to a joint committee on Reconstruction. While keeping southern representatives from their seats, it overrode Johnson's vetoes of both a civil rights act that turned the commissioner and marshal powers of the 1850 Fugitive Slave Act toward the new end of protecting freed people's civil rights and an act extending the Freedmen's Bureau. At the end of its term, Congress passed the Fourteenth Amendment and held open the possibility of sustaining war powers in rebel states to ensure smooth sailing for the ratification process in those states. When northern voters backed Republicans in the fall midterm elections, it placed all rebel states except Tennessee under military supervision and required them—under martial law—to provide the crucial votes to ratify first the Fourteenth and then—for some—the Fifteenth Amendments. As this constitutional revolution—a forcible and permanent transformation of the political order—came to fruition, Democrats reacted with fury and with a creative reinterpretation of history. They now, for the first time, described the use of war powers from 1861 to 1865 as appropriate and constitutional but their invocation after 1865 as outrageous and illegitimate. Military Reconstruction was, one critic said, "nothing less" than a "declaration of war against ten States of this Union."[16] Republicans replied that it was a continuation of war, not a new declaration.

That state of war ended in most Confederate states between 1868 and 1870 as they returned to Congress and to a state of peace. With their seating in Congress, the Department of War dissolved the military districts, and army commanders shifted toward supporting, not overruling, state governments. No longer did they displace officials, try cases, invalidate laws, issue new state laws, or make arrests under their own orders. While the military remained on the ground, commanders hoped simply to respond to requests for assistance from state and federal civil officers.

Congressmen debated the meaning and duration of wartime and war powers as they assessed the unusual case of Georgia in 1870. Georgia had remade its constitution in 1868, and Congress seated one set of its representatives, but not both, in summer 1868. But, in the fall of 1868, state legislators expelled all the black members of the legislature, and Ku Klux Klan chapters and other paramilitary organizations spread from Tennessee across the state, suppressing black votes in the presidential election. Then, in 1869, Republicans refused to seat its representatives and kept Georgia in a state of wartime while pondering what to do over a bitter four-and-a-half-month debate. "We have endeavored to protect law and property there by the force of provisional State law, by the force of provisional congressional law, and by the force of the armies of the United States," the Vermont Republican senator George Edmunds said, "[but] we have totally failed. . . . Then what are we to do?"[17] Here, we see the necessity argument laid bare. The necessity stemmed from a lack of other available modes to protect freed people's (or white loyalists') rights.

The endurance of wartime raised the possibility of a broader military supervision across the South. The problems in Georgia might empower the government even in states already returned to peace. The Missouri Republican senator Charles Drake proposed using the Georgia case to authorize the president to invoke martial law—including military commissions—if a governor or legislator requested aid. Most Republicans, however, considered that a violation of peacetime. But they did work to construct a narrower version of the Georgia bill that would expand some government powers. Striking out military commissions and tying habeas corpus suspensions to the general power to put down insurrections, they created a framework for peacetime law enforcement. Although some dissident Republicans denounced the use of the military's power in a "time of peace," the bill carried the Senate. "I do not want to violate the constitution," a North Carolina Republican said. "But we want something."[18] But House Republicans wished to treat Georgia separately, not as a part of a broader enforcement crisis. Therefore, Senate Republicans looked for other interim remedies for the state. Senator Matthew Carpenter of Wisconsin—who had penned an 1865 pamphlet on martial law for the army and had argued for the extension of wartime in the 1868 *McCardle* case in front of the Supreme Court—saw a simple solution: avoid tearing apart the constitutional limits on the powers of peace by extending the war. Carpenter told the Senate to move slowly on Georgia because its return "consummates reconstruction, and closes the civil war." Once peace returned, so too would "the rights and blessings of peace, chief of which is constitutional protection."[19] Even this provoked controversy, and House Republicans never agreed to these terms. But Congress essentially sustained Georgia in its state of wartime by adjourning without resolving the state's status.

Meanwhile Congress took up the issue of peace powers in a separate 1870 enforcement act. Although the initial bill simply made it a federal crime to restrict black men's votes by force, fraud, or intimidation, Republican senators reached back to the failed Georgia bill to empower the military to make arrests at its own discretion. Again some Republicans rebelled, arguing that the war had "compelled" them to "subordinate the elections" to the "military power" in the past but that it was their "duty" as "soon as practicable to go back to the old system." Under pressure, Republicans backed away from provisions that allowed the army to hold suspects for trial and compel them to testify, but they did give federal courts the authority to overturn state elections, authorize the president to call out the army to prevent possible violations of the law, and outlaw conspiracies in disguise to intimidate voters.[20] In conference, House Republicans feared the implications of granting the president power to call out the military to prevent potential violations of the law rather than to respond to existing violations, so the final bill allowed him to use the military only to help execute judicial processes. These guardrails around military power reassured some Republicans that they were exiting wartime but worried others that they were unilaterally disarming. "Peace on what terms?" an unhappy Republican senator asked. "The terms upon which we intend to have it, and the only terms upon which peace can be had, are that every citizen of the United States, without regard to color, shall have an equal opportunity to vote." This formulation extended wartime potentially indefinitely. Later in the term, Republicans modified a naturalization bill to empower the marshals and US attorneys to intervene on election days in New York City under their expansive reading of the peacetime powers created by the Fifteenth Amendment.[21]

On February 1, 1871, nine years, nine months, and eighteen days after President Lincoln called for volunteers to fight the Confederacy, Congress seated Georgia's final representative, ending the wartime state of exception and, in that sense, the Civil War. "Let us have peace," a Democratic senator called out.[22] With the closing of the military district of Georgia, the wartime powers that had grown over the past decade seemed to come to an end.

But now Republicans faced the daunting problem of peace. Across 1870, increasingly fierce paramilitary groups counterattacked in the Carolinas and Georgia and across the South. The day after the US Army departed Laurensville, South Carolina, thousands of mounted whites raided the town, killing twelve black men, including one legislator. In North Carolina, Democrats intimidated voters from coming to the polls and carried the legislature easily; almost immediately the new legislature impeached the Republican governor and expelled him from office. Altogether, Democrats claimed four state legislatures and elected a Klan leader as governor of Tennessee. Tellingly, President Grant's message to Congress in December 1870 insisted both that the "work of reconstruction" would soon end and that the federal government must defend with vigilance the "free exercise of the elective franchise" against "violence and intimidation."[23]

If the wartime powers of Reconstruction were extinguished by 1871, what powers remained to protect the "elective franchise" against "violence and intimidation"? And did Reconstruction actually depend on war powers? These were the questions Republicans wrestled with for the next four years. After Grant asked Congress to act against the Klan, Republicans in 1871 debated extending new peacetime powers to the president and granting him broader authority to declare martial law, suspend habeas corpus, and deploy the military against conspiracies without a request from a legislature, governor, or federal judge. But moderate Republicans forced Congress to strip away a direct reference to martial law and limited the president's power to suspend habeas corpus to the next two years. Some Republicans, like Senator Henry Wilson, pushed back against these limits and embraced a sweeping vision of necessity. "I reverence the Constitution," Wilson said, "but man is more than constitutions."[24] In 1871, Grant used his new peacetime powers against the Ku Klux Klan in South Carolina, moving one thousand soldiers into the state, including the Seventh Cavalry from the Great Plains. In October, he ordered members of the Klan to disperse and then suspended the writ of habeas corpus in nine counties. Eventually, the federal attorney indicted more than six hundred alleged Klansmen. The Klan's actions "amount to war, and cannot be effectually crushed on any other theory," the attorney general wrote. But, in court, prosecutions moved slowly. In 1872, Congress passed one final enforcement bill, a rider to an appropriations act that allowed federal supervision of elections in rural areas but did not permit supervisors outside cities to make direct arrests. Still, by 1874, the army had intervened 350 times, and Congress had created forty-seven different regulatory provisions that Republicans later—in an effort to mask the slippage between war and peace powers—dispersed across the federal code to make them harder to excise.[25] But Republicans divided over the righteousness of using these powers in peacetime; in 1872, Republicans like Charles Sumner and Lyman Trumbull—opposites on many issues but fellow travelers on limiting the deployment of wartime powers during the peace—backed the Liberal movement out of the Republican Party. After the Panic of 1873 produced staggering unemployment, Democrats in 1874 won control of the House of Representatives for the first time since the Civil War.

While Republicans nervously waited for that new Congress to take power, they faced a wave of violent threats in the South in the fall and winter of 1874–75 that raised questions about whether the United States remained in a state of emergency or perhaps had entered a new state of emergency. Louisiana White Leagues defeated the metropolitan police in the so-called Battle of Liberty Place and drove the governor from office. Only after the army forced Democrats to retreat did the governor resume power. In the winter, Democrats tried to claim the state legislature by physically seizing control of the meeting, expelling Republicans, and seating Democrats. In response, Lieutenant General Philip Sheridan denounced the "banditti," and commanders on the spot sent troops to protect the Republican legislature and drive out some Democratic claimants. After insurgents in Alabama killed and wounded almost one hundred men in Eufala, and mobs in Vicksburg, Mississippi, forcibly drove a black sheriff from office, legislators debated how to protect civil rights in a time of peace. Meanwhile, in Arkansas a bewildering series of events allied a formerly Republican governor with Democratic legislators who sought to institute a new, reactionary constitution.

To congressional Democrats, the warlike actions were the army's march into Louisiana's legislative chamber and Sheridan's request to arrest "banditti." These were "declarations of war by a rash general of the United States Army against an innocent people . . . ten years after peace has been declared."[26] Desperate to forestall Republican use of the army, Democrats emphasized that this was a time of "profound peace—not in a time of war." Therefore, the military's actions created a precedent for the entire nation. If the army could be used in Louisiana after its readmission, then "it may be New York to-morrow; it may be Massachusetts the day following; it may be in Congress of the United States on the 4th day of March next."[27] For the apostate Republican Carl Schurz, who had joined the Liberal insurgency and allied with Democrats in Missouri, it was all evidence that time had unfortunately normalized war powers: "I cannot close my eyes to the fact that the generation which has grown up to political activity during and since the war . . . has but too much been accustomed to witness the bold display of arbitrary assumption of military power."[28] Wars changed the cultural expectations of what was normal, what needed to be justified.

But other Republicans identified the warlike actions as white Louisianans' use of terror and force. They defended the military's intrusion in Louisiana as a normal peacetime means of keeping the peace. "It is well enough to use the Army and Navy to enslave men; but when you use the Army to enforce law, when you use the Army to protect the liberty of citizens in a State, it is an outrage, and tyranny," the Republican John Logan said sarcastically.[29] Others described Louisiana Democrats as "invaders" and noted that "it was not a time of peace."[30] Even the generally moderate John Sherman said: "[I]t is manifest that the excited parties to this contest in the State of Louisiana are rather in a condition of war, of force, of violence, than a condition of calm discussion."[31] Others simply pleaded necessity. "But for 'Federal bayonets' may I not well ask what the condition of this nation would be to-day?" one asked.[32]

Fearful of what lay ahead, Republicans attempted unsuccessfully to use the lame-duck session from December 1874 to March 1875 to expand the federal government's powers of peace. Both senators and congressmen introduced bills to protect states against vigilante invasion. The House version drew on the now-expired Ku Klux Klan Act and permitted the president to suspend habeas corpus and made it a felony to go into a state to interfere with elections or to conspire to overthrow the government or to use firearms near registration or election sites.[33] "When civil authority in all branches is cast down, then military authority is to step in," the Indiana Republican John Coburn said. "Somebody in great emergencies must be trusted, somebody must be clothed with power, somebody must act, somebody must take the responsibility, or the nation will die."[34] But the bill ran up against the peacetime question of whether it would be applicable to every state in the nation, an outcome that northern Republicans could not stomach. Therefore, in a move that seemed to straddle war and peace, Republicans rewrote the bill so that it applied only to Alabama, Arkansas, Louisiana, and Mississippi, permitted the suspension of habeas corpus only in specific districts under armed confrontation, barred the use of military commissions, and expired in two years. Democrats in turn tried to amend it to apply to Massachusetts and Ohio.

For Democrats, the deployment of this measure against four southern states made this bill a continuation of wartime measures. "Ten years have elapsed since it was declared from the highest official authority known to civil government that the war was over," Congressman C. W. Milliken from Kentucky said. "Then if it is over, why are not each of the States free and independent as before the war?"[35] Democrats complained that the reliance on the military treated the South as "India is to England or Poland to Russia."[36] War powers had become normalized. This bill was "one of the scions which sprang from the reconstruction policy which . . . is now attempted to be palmed off as a constitutional prerogative of Congress," one congressman complained.[37] More philosophically, Kentucky's James Beck described war powers constantly bleeding into peacetime as "parties are driven on by an irresistible necessity to the perpetration of acts which they would have shrunk from, when the first departure was taken."[38] For the Republican George Willard, the distinction between war and peace lay in the difference between "actually existing rebellion" and an "imaginary one." In wartime, it might be acceptable to use the army to put down imaginary as well as real threats, but, in peacetime, only real emergencies demanded responses: "We can have no supremacy of the law so long as the law is not left to its normal and constitutional methods of enforcement."[39]

But many Republicans dismissed the notion that the South was at peace. The aptly named Julius Caesar Burrows acknowledged: "It is true, sir, a full decade has gone by since the overthrow of armed resistance to Federal authority; yet it is past contradiction that in many portions of the South there has not been an hour since of substantial peace."[40] Others compared the peace in the South to the peace that "reigned in Warsaw when Poland's bravest and best lay dead and ghastly in the streets of the city"⁴¹ or to the "peace of death and the quiet of the grave."⁴² But the broadest—and in some ways clearest—defense came from Pennsylvania's Charles Albright. In the "emergency" they faced, what choice did they have? "Of what use is a constitution that makes a promise to the ear and breaks it?" he asked. "It may be unpleasant and undesirable to employ the military, but how else will you give effect to the constitutional amendments or enforce the laws when resisted?"⁴³ Despite bitter opposition, House Republicans passed the modified bill and beat back efforts to strip away the habeas corpus clause. But the Senate did not take up the legislation, and the act died.⁴⁴ In the closing days, what passed was the ill-fated Civil Rights Act of 1875, which seemed to outlaw discrimination in a wide range of areas; it quickly fell into disuse.

If the early years of the 1870s marked a period of Republican expansion of the powers of peace, 1875 marked its end. From then on, the fight would be about sustaining, not adding to, what wartime powers still endured. Politics, not constitutional debates, had put a brake on the military's authority. As Democrats prepared to organize the House of Representatives, Democratic White Lines launched a campaign of terror in Mississippi. Undermined by his own attorney general, and fearful of impeachment and electoral defeat, Grant did not send troops until it was too late. In black majority Yazoo County, where the Republican governor had won by 1,800 votes in 1873, Democrats now prevailed 4,044 to 7.⁴⁵

The often-misunderstood election of 1876 was a turning point but still not an end point for the military's role in the South. During the election, federal marshals and the army stationed troops "practically every place on the map" in South Carolina—where rifle clubs massacred black Republicans at Hamburg and Ellenton—and in scattered stations in other states. After election night, three southern states produced competing election returns, one for the Republican Rutherford B. Hayes, one for the Democrat Samuel Tilden. In the confusion, there was talk of civil war. President Grant recalled troops from the West to defend Washington, DC, and stationed soldiers near the capitol buildings in South Carolina and Louisiana to protect the threatened Republican governments there.

After a commission and then Congress awarded the White House to Hayes, the new president withdrew the Army from its position around the state houses in Louisiana and South Carolina in April. "The time had come to put an end to bayonet rule," Hayes later wrote. "I saw things done in the South which could only be accounted for on the theory that the war was not yet ended." Republican governments in Louisiana and South Carolina collapsed, and Democrats assumed the statehouses. But the army did not withdraw from the South. In Louisiana the movement was from the Orleans Hotel to a camp outside the city, in Columbia from the grounds of the statehouse to the barracks four blocks away. Although troop levels fell starkly from 1876 to 1877, a handful of soldiers remained in the South, including 123 in Louisiana and 165 in South Carolina. What ended in 1877 was the use of the military to prop up Republican state governments, not the use of the military altogether.[46]

The year 1877 marked the beginning, not the end, of Democratic efforts to roll back powers of peace to something like an 1840s level. In 1877, House Democrats tried to slash the army from twenty-five thousand to seventeen thousand men and to forbid the use of any federal funds to support a state government that had not been recognized by Congress. "The day is near at hand when we shall repeal all this military legislation which has sprung up under a semi-revolutionary condition of affairs, and permit us to return where the Constitution intended," a Democratic representative said. But Senate Republicans blocked the bill, and President Hayes did not call Congress back into session to finish the budget. Thus no bill passed, nor did any funds for the army. Soldiers were not paid for months at a time.[47]

But the question of the military's role in peacetime could not be narrowed to the ex-Confederate South. While Congress was in recess and the army unpaid, the Great Strike tested the role of the army. When the strike fanned out from Maryland and West Virginia, several states—including those with Democratic governors—requested help as their militias failed to put down strikers or clear railways. Hayes generally pressed those states to follow the precise antebellum procedure for requesting aid before sending troops. His secretary of war pointed to this bipartisan reliance on the military as proof that "it must now be accepted as a fact, which experience has demonstrated, that Federal troops may be required not only for the protection of our frontiers, but also to preserve peace and order in our more populous interior."[48] Some Democrats indeed defended the president's response to legislative or gubernatorial requests as straightforwardly constitutional; others denounced both Hayes and their party's governors for not relying on militias. "I do not hold to the doctrine that because there is a little riot in Baltimore it is the duty of the Federal Army to be called in," one Democrat said.[49]

In 1878, Democrats tried, with mixed success, to restore what they believed was an antebellum definition of peacetime by stripping away the powers of the army. The New Yorker Abram Hewitt, a leading figure in Sam Tilden's failed 1876 campaign, aimed to handcuff the army that he believed had cost his friend the White House. Despite bitter objections from western Democrats, especially Texans, he aimed to cut the army from twenty-five thousand men to twenty thousand. Democrats amended the bill to outlaw the use of the army as a *posse comitatus* and levy fines and jail terms on violators.[50] One hundred times, James P. Knott complained, the army had been used "without one scintilla of authority": "[N]ow, when this country is in the enjoyment of profound peace, is a fitting time for us to say that this practice shall no longer continue; that the Army of the United States shall be amenable to the civil law."[51] Both sides accused the other of hypocrisy—Democrats had once celebrated Caleb Cushing's 1854 memo affirming the use of the army as a *posse comitatus*; Republicans had in 1856 used an appropriations bill to try to prevent the army from supporting a proslavery territorial legislature in Kansas. After intense debate, the amended army bill narrowly carried the House, first by eight votes, then by thirteen.[52] In the Senate, the Delaware Democrat Thomas Bayard Sr. carried on a family tradition of denouncing war powers and demanded the "reaffirmation of these old doctrines on the use of the military."[53] Although Senate Republicans struck out the penalty, the conference committee retained it, at Democratic insistence, even as it also sustained the army at twenty-five thousand men.[54]

This amendment—often referred to as the Posse Comitatus Act even though it was simply an amendment to the appropriations bill—made it a crime to use the military as a posse to enforce the law except in cases "expressly authorized by the Constitution or by Act of Congress." Democrats believed that they had found a foothold against expansive use of the military and perhaps a bar to certain types of deployment—like sending troops as a posse on the request of a marshal or a commissioner without a judicial order or prior approval from Washington. "Thus we have this day secured to the people of this country the same great protection against a standing army which cost a struggle of two hundred years for the Commons of England to secure for the British people," Hewitt crowed. "[The] Army of the United States in time of peace should be under the control of Congress."[55] But the ultimate issue had not been resolved. The shadow that *posse comitatus* casts today may be reflected in the creative efforts of military lawyers since the 1970s to utilize it in order to save the army from politically charged work in the drug wars and border enforcement.[56]

The clearest evidence that the Posse Comitatus Act did not resolve the issue of war powers is in Democrats' determination in 1879 to undo what they believed were enduring powers of war that that act had not touched. Because that act exempted uses expressly authorized by Congress, Democrats sought to strip away legislation that they believed embedded war powers into peacetime. Particularly, they went after an 1865 election law that permitted military presence at polling places and, later, sections of civil rights and enforcement laws of 1866, 1870, and 1871. This effort sparked the bitter 1879 shutdown of government. After Democrats added amendments to government funding bills that would repeal an 1865 law that regulated—and seemingly permitted—the use of the army on election day, the House and the Senate could not agree to fund the government, and Congress dissolved without a budget and then had to call in the newly elected Congress in a special session.

In the ensuing special session, Democrats now controlled both the House and the Senate for the first time in two decades and aimed to force through their changes. When the Republican James Garfield called their efforts a "revolution against the Constitution and the Government of the United States," the New York Democrat Fernando Wood asked "whether, after the experience of fourteen years since the war has subsided, [Garfield] is yet prepared to continue a war measure in a time of profound peace in this country." In turn, Garfield denounced Wood for supporting the military's use to return slaves but not to "maintain the purity of our own elections and keep the peace at our polls."[57] Once again Democrats trotted out their arguments about the end of wartime. "[Democrats] do not intend to allow a vicious and anomalous precedent which was fastened upon the country in time of trouble to become one of the fundamental maxims of the Government," a Kentucky Democrat argued.[58] Derisively pointing to the ways in which Republicans acknowledged peacetime, Alabama's William Lowe said, to "laughter and applause": "The war is over everywhere except in Congress."[59] Republicans meanwhile responded with their own well-honed arguments about "necessity" in an "emergency."[60] "Behind the constitutional exercise of voluntary powers there sleeps the war power of this nation, ever ready to preserve its constitutional existence, to enforce its laws, to defend its undying transmittal to the latest generation," Iowa's Moses McCoid said. Force did not destroy freedom; force saved freedom, and peace thus depended ultimately on the threat of the powers of war.[61]

Republicans also advanced the idea that war powers had permanently transformed the nation. Wartime created an exceptional state during which Republicans had redefined normal political power through constitutional amendments. Democrats confused the powers of war, which were limited, with the implications or effects of the war, which were not limited. The Massachusetts Republican senator Henry Dawes said that Democrats "have openly avowed that they have come back to stay for the purpose of wiping out every vestige of the legislation for the last eighteen years growing out of *the war.*"⁶² A return to peacetime did not mean a return to the *status quo ante*; it meant a dependence on newly defined legal powers, powers of peacetime forged in the new realities of war. The war, as James Blaine reminded his colleagues, had changed the Constitution and thus changed the nature of peacetime. Despite his reputation for weakness, Rutherford B. Hayes blocked Democratic plans to strip away the military's role in peacetime by using his veto repeatedly. As Democrats and Hayes warred over additional bills and additional vetoes, the government remained shut down. Over the next year, Democrats and Republicans continued to fight over the role of the military in civilian governance. After vetoing yet another act, Hayes wrote in his diary: "It is for the victors to say what shall remain. Not for the vanquished."⁶³

But in many ways Hayes's comment was inaccurate. Although Democrats did not gain everything they wanted, they did set guardrails around the use of the military in the states. (Territories remained a different question, constitutionally and politically.) Although President Grover Cleveland deployed the army against Pullman strikers in 1894, over the opposition of the state's governor, in many respects the military retreated into its pre-1850 role during peacetime. Without the military to provide a counterbalance, southern Democrats launched increasingly blatant, violent efforts to intimidate African Americans. By the early twentieth century, Jim Crow segregation and disfranchisement turned parts of the Fourteenth Amendment and the civil rights acts into hollow shells.

: : :

The longer one looks, the more difficult it becomes to pin down the relationship between wartime states of emergency and the federal government's actions in the years after Appomattox. The problem lay not in the theory but in the condition of things. Republicans edged against the limits of peacetime not because they opposed them in principle but because they wished to sustain Reconstruction. Democrats firmed their opposition to the use of the military not because they necessarily abhorred war powers per se but because they abhorred Reconstruction.

The 1870s were at once peacetime and not quite peacetime, in ways that suggest analogies to other extended periods after conflicts when some exceptional powers remain. These liminal moments may be particularly useful places to assess how wars do and do not permanently transform US society. Democrats were not wrong to wonder when, if ever, the Civil War would end, but Republicans, too, were not wrong to ask whether peacetime meant acquiescence to oppression. As war and peace became moving targets in their debates, they became stand-ins for deeper arguments about Reconstruction and black civil rights. Yet Republicans countered that peace could itself be a useful myth, a way of making one's policy preferences the only legitimate policy, a way of delegitimizing opponents. Had the peace of the 1840s—and especially of the 1850s—been quite so peaceful? Beyond that, did the constitutional amendments—passed with the help of martial law—not create a new definition of peacetime?

In the long sweep of the history of war powers in the United States, the 1870s stand as both a prelude and a peculiarity. In some ways, the US debates about the precise end of wartime presage the struggles to define the completion of World War II and, particularly, the War on Terror, just as Civil War era tools like military commissions were precedents for later usages. From this perspective, one can see heartening signs of civilian, constitutional resumption in the Democrats' efforts to both end wartime and shear away war powers, and one can also find useful reminders about the utility of war powers in Republicans' defenses during the 1870s. The 1870s may suggest, if not quite an answer, at least the right questions.

From other viewpoints, the 1870s appear far stranger. A domestic civil war may pose challenges of war powers that are distinct from those posed by an external war. Determining how to govern parts of the United States under military rule proved bafflingly complex, though in many ways governing external regions in the Spanish-American War or the War on Terror proved no simpler. The relationship between civilian and military power was always charged during the domestic debates because of the possibility that actions taken in Georgia would be a precedent for future ones in Ohio. Thus, war powers could never be easily separated from peace powers.

Examining war powers in the 1870s may also help us ask probing questions about the nature of the US government more broadly. Did the United States possess sufficient authority and force to carry out its obligations to its citizens? In debates over the persistence of war powers, this question of state sufficiency troubled both sides. Would rolling back war powers shear away the government's efficacy? Or simply restrict its actions to legitimate fields? War powers endured because those questions seemed unanswered, even by the Fourteenth Amendment.

Republicans hoped to answer the question both by using war powers and then by discarding them. They aimed to hold an exceptional state long enough to transform, not preserve, society, then return to a constitutional time that was both normal and also transformed. In this way, they hoped to use the state of exception to radical ends without trapping themselves in a state of never-ending radical time. Democrats' triumphant rollback of military power in the late 1870s at once reaffirmed the constitutional limitations on the military and consigned freed people to generations of Jim Crow segregation. In this tension, we see the doubleness of Reconstruction as an exceptional moment in US history, one in which both the powers and the outcomes were exceptional. If so, we might ask whether peace was defined in US history, at least until the middle of the twentieth century, as a stable white supremacy, as oppression.

Notes

1. *Congressional Record*, 46th Cong., 1st sess., April 22, 1879, 665.
2. *Congressional Record*, 46th Cong., 1st sess., April 24, 1879, 804.
3. *Congressional Record*, 46th Cong., 1st sess., June 20, 1879, 2199.
4. *Congressional Record*, 46th Cong., 1st sess., May 9, 1879, 1188.
5. Gary Gerstle and Desmond King, "Spaces of Exception in American History" (chapter 12 in this volume).
6. Gary Gerstle and Joel Isaac, introduction to this volume.
7. Gerstle and Isaac, introduction to this volume.
8. *Ex Parte Merryman*, http://teachingamericanhistory.org/library/document/ex-parte-merryman.
9. Bernard Christian Steiner, *Life of Reverdy Johnson* (Baltimore: Norman, Remington, 1914), 107.
10. Roy P. Basler, ed., *Collected Works of Abraham Lincoln, 8 vols.* (New Brunswick, NJ: Rutgers University Press, 1953), 6:261–67.
11. See the somewhat different estimates in Mark E. Neely Jr., *The Fate of Liberty: Abraham Lincoln and Civil Liberties* (New York: Oxford University Press, 1991), 168; Gideon M. Hart, "Military Commissions and the Lieber Code: Toward a New Understanding of the Jurisdictional Foundations of Military Commissions," *Military Law Review* 203 (Spring 2010): 1–77, esp. 4; and John Fabian Witt, *Lincoln's Code: The Laws of War in American History* (New York: Free Press, 2012), 267–68.
12. "General Orders No. 100: The Lieber Code," http://avalon.law.yale.edu/19th_century/lieber.asp; Witt, *Lincoln's Code*.
13. Ulysses S. Grant, *Personal Memoirs of U. S. Grant*, 2 vols. (New York: C. L. Webster, 1885), 2:483–85; Horace Porter, *Campaigning with Grant* (New York: Century, 1897), 463–64; Brooks D. Simpson, *Let Us Have Peace: Ulysses S. Grant and the Politics of War and Reconstruction, 1861–1868* (Chapel Hill: University of North Carolina Press, 1991), 82.
14. *The War of the Rebellion: A Compilation of the Official Records of the Union and Confederate Armies*, 127 vols. (Washington, DC: US Government Printing Office, 1880–1901), ser. 1, 47, pt. 3:538.
15. William C. Harris, *Presidential Reconstruction in Mississippi* (Baton Rouge: Louisiana State University Press, 1967), 52–54; Paul H. Bergeron, ed.,

The Papers of Andrew Johnson, 16 vols. (Knoxville: University of Tennessee Press, 1967–2000), 9:325, 329.

16. *Congressional Globe*, 39th Cong., 2nd sess., February 16, 1867, 1440–41.

17. *Congressional Globe*, 41st Cong., 2nd sess., March 15, 1870, 1957–60.

18. *Congressional Globe*, 41st Cong., 2nd sess., March 18, 1870, 2068, March 21, 1870, 2089–92, 2645–48, 2722–24, 2826–29, and April 19, 1870, Appendix, 291–93.

19. *Congressional Globe*, 41st Cong., 2nd sess., April 5, 1870, 2428–30.

20. *Congressional Globe*, 41st Cong., 2nd sess., May 18, 1870, 3568, May 19, 1870, 3607–9, 3613, May 20, 1870, 3657, 3668–69, 3678–79, 3683–84, 3688.

21. *Congressional Globe*, 41st Cong., 2nd sess., May 24, 1870, 3755, May 25, 1870, 3805–6, 3808.

22. *Congressional Globe*, 41st Cong., 3rd sess., February 1, 1871, 873, February 13, 1871, 1184.

23. *Congressional Globe*, 41st Cong., 3rd sess., December 5, 1870, 5–6.

24. *Congressional Globe*, 41st Cong., 3rd sess., January 18, 1871, 571, 575, and February, 15, 1871, Appendix, 125; *Army and Navy Journal*, September 2, 1871, 35; Robert W. Coakley, *The Role of Federal Military Forces in Domestic Disorders, 1789–1878 (Washington DC: Center of Military History, 2011)*, 308–10; William Gillette, *Retreat from Reconstruction, 1869–1879* (Baton Rouge: Louisiana State University Press, 1982), 25–26, 53; Charles W. Calhoun, *Conceiving a New Republic: The Republican Party and the Southern Question, 1869–1900* (Lawrence: University Press of Kansas, 2006), 20–22, 26–33; James E. Sefton, *The United States Army and Reconstruction, 1865–1877* (Baton Rouge: Louisiana State University Press, 1967), 222–24; Brooks D. Simpson, *The Reconstruction Presidents* (Lawrence: University Press of Kansas, 2009), 155–57; Allen W. Trelease, *White Terror: The Ku Klux Klan Conspiracy and Southern Reconstruction* (New York: Harper & Row, 1971), 374–80; Richard M. Valelly, *The Two Reconstructions: The Struggle for Black Enfranchisement* (Chicago: University of Chicago Press, 2004), 106–7; Eric Foner, *Reconstruction: America's Unfinished Revolution, 1863–1877* (New York: Harper & Row, 1988), 454–57; Lou Falkner Williams, *The Great South Carolina Ku Klux Klan Trials, 1871–1872* (Athens: University of Georgia Press, 2004), 44–47; Xi Wang, *The Trial of Democracy: Black Suffrage and Northern Republicans, 1860–1910* (Athens: University of Georgia Press, 1996), 49–133; *Annual Report of the Secretary of War* (Washington, DC: US Government Printing Office, 1871), 2–4, 16–17; Robert Goldman, *A Free Ballot and a Fair Count: The Department of Justice and the Enforcement of Voting Rights in the South, 1877–1893* (New York: Fordham University Press, 2001).

25. Coakley, *The Role of Federal Military Forces in Domestic Disorders*, 311–13; Gillette, *Retreat from Reconstruction*, 29–37, 41–43; Sefton, *The United States Army and Reconstruction*, 228; Valelly, *The Two Reconstructions*, 1; Williams, *The Great South Carolina Ku Klux Klan Trials*, 44–47, 85–88, 100, 123; Foner, *Reconstruction*, 457; Robert J Kaczorowski, *The Politics of Judicial Interpretation: The Federal Courts, Department of Justice and Civil*

Rights, 1866–1876 (Dobbs Ferry, NY: Oceana, 1985), 87–90; Trelease, *White Terror*, 399–418; Wang, *The Trial of Democracy*, 93–133; Stephen Budiansky, *The Bloody Shirt: Terror After Appomattox* (New York: Viking, 2008).

26. *Congressional Record*, 43rd Cong., 2nd sess., February 27, 1875, Appendix, 25.

27. *Congressional Record*, 43rd Cong., 2nd sess., January 8, 1875, 334.

28. *Congressional Record*, 43rd Cong., 2nd sess., January 11, 1875, 371.

29. *Congressional Record*, 43rd Cong., 2nd sess., January 13, 1875, 427.

30. *Congressional Record*, 43rd Cong., 2nd sess., January 15, 1875, 492.

31. *Congressional Record*, 43rd Cong., 2nd sess., January 22, 1875, 652, 660.

32. *Congressional Record*, 43rd Cong., 2nd sess., January 6, 1875, 275.

33. *Congressional Record*, 43rd Cong., 2nd sess., February 18, 1875, 1453.

34. *Congressional Record*, 43rd Cong., 2nd sess., February 26, 1875, 1834–35.

35. *Congressional Record*, 43rd Cong., 2nd sess., February 10, 1875, Appendix, 38.

36. *Congressional Record*, 43rd Cong., 2nd sess., February 10, 1875, 1151.

37. *Congressional Record*, 43rd Cong., 2nd sess., February 10, 1875, 1141, 1147.

38. *Congressional Record*, 43rd Cong., 2nd sess., February 27, 1875, Appendix, 142.

39. *Congressional Record*, 43rd Cong., 2nd sess., February 26, 1875, 1838.

40. *Congressional Record*, 43rd Cong., 2nd sess., February 27, 1875, 1924.

41. *Congressional Record*, 43rd Cong., 2nd sess., March 2, 1875, Appendix, 190.

42. *Congressional Record*, 43rd Cong., 2nd sess., February 26, 1875, 1855.

43. *Congressional Record*, 43rd Cong., 2nd sess., February 26, 1875, 1840, 1846–48.

44. *Congressional Record*, 43rd Cong., 2nd sess., February 27, 1875, 1935.

45. Coakley, *The Role of Federal Military Forces in Domestic Disorders*, 328–30; Gillette, *Retreat from Reconstruction*, 96, 102, 107–27, 139–49, 158–63; Sefton, *The United States Army and Reconstruction*, 222–46.

46. Heather Cox Richardson, "Hemingway, South Carolina, and Reconstruction," The Historical Society, 2013, http://histsociety.blogspot.com/2013/01/hemingway-south-carolina-and.html; Coakley, *The Role of Federal Military Forces in Domestic Disorders*, 333–39; Calhoun, *Conceiving a New Republic*, 141–45; Sefton, *The United States Army and Reconstruction*, 247–51; Valelly, *The Two Reconstructions*, 95; T. Harry Williams, ed., *Hayes: The Diary of a President, 1875–1881, Covering the Disputed Election, the End of Reconstruction, and the Beginning of Civil Service* (New York: D. McKay, 1964), 269–70; Vincent P. DeSantis, "Rutherford B. Hayes and the Removal of Troops and the End of Reconstruction," in *Region, Race and Reconstruction: Essays in Honor of C. Vann Woodward*, ed. J. Morgan Kousser and James M. McPherson (New York: Oxford University Press, 1982), 417–50.

47. Clayton D. Laurie and Ronald H. Cole, *The Role of Federal Military Forces in Domestic Disorders, 1877–1945* (Washington, DC: Center of Military History, 1997), 33–46, 66.

48. *Congressional Record*, 45th Cong., 2nd sess., May 22, 1878, 3679.

49. *Congressional Record*, 45th Cong., 3rd sess., February 1, 1879, 964.

50. *Congressional Record*, 45th Cong., 2nd sess., May 27, 1878, 3760.

51. *Congressional Record*, 45th Cong., 2nd sess., May 27, 1878, 3846–47.

52. *Congressional Record*, 45th Cong., 2nd sess., May 27, 28, 1878, 3852, 3878.

53. *Congressional Record*, 45th Cong., 2nd sess., June 8, 1878, 4301–5.

54. The army's statutory size had been roughly thirty thousand but had been held to twenty-five thousand by appropriations bills, so Blaine offered simply to accept the new standard of twenty-five thousand as both a statutory and an appropriations limit. *Congressional Record*, 45th Cong., 2nd sess., June 15, 1878, 4647.

55. *Congressional Record*, 45th Cong., 2nd sess., June 15, 1878, 4684–86.

56. Gary Felicetti and John Luce, "The Posse Comitatus Act: Liberation from the Lawyers," *Parameters* 34, no. 3 (2004): 100; Candidus Dougherty, " 'Necessity Hath No Law': Executive Power and the Posse Comitatus Act," *Campbell Law Review* 31, no. 1 (Fall 2008): 1–50; Guido Norman Lieber, *The Use of the Army in Aid of the Civil Power (Washington, DC: Government Printing Office, 1898)*, 10–13; Coakley, *The Role of Federal Military Forces in Domestic Disorders*, 342–48; Calhoun, *Conceiving a New Republic*, 157–60; Charles Doyle, *The Posse Comitatus Act and Related Matters: The Use of the Military to Execute Civilian Law* (Washington, DC: Congressional Research Service, 2012), 19–20.

57. *Congressional Record*, 46th Cong., 1st sess., March 29, 1879, 115, 117–19.

58. *Congressional Record*, 46th Cong., 1st sess., April 16, 1879, 470.

59. *Congressional Record*, 46th Cong., 1st sess., April 5, 1879, 257.

60. *Congressional Record*, 46th Cong., 1st sess., April 3, 1879, 213.

61. *Congressional Record*, 46th Cong., 1st sess., April 5, 1879, 267.

62. *Congressional Record*, 46th Cong., 1st sess., April 16, 1879, 470.

63. Heather Cox Richardson, "Lessons from the First National Shutdown," *New York Times* Room for Debate, December 18, 2013, http://www.nytimes.com/roomfordebate/2013/12/18/the-history-and-lessons-of-congressional-crises/lessons-from-the-first-national-shutdown; Calhoun, *Conceiving a New Republic*, 160–65, 172–73, 191, 196–97, 229–30; Lieber, *The Use of the Army in Aid of the Civil Power*, 16–17; Heather Cox Richardson, *Wounded Knee: Party Politics and the Road to an American Massacre* (New York: Basic, 2010); Valelly, *The Two Reconstructions*, 66–68; Simpson, *The Reconstruction Presidents*, 222; Williams, *Hayes*, 195 (Hayes quote), 219; Wang, *The Trial of Democracy*, 134–215.

7

Was There an American Concept of Emergency Powers? John Dewey, Carl Schmitt, and the Democratic Politics of Exception

Stephen W. Sawyer

> From the outset I viewed American pragmatism as the third productive reply to Hegel, after Marx and Kierkegaard, as the radical-democratic branch of Young Hegelianism. Ever since, I have relied on this American version of the philosophy of praxis when the problem arises of compensating for the weaknesses of Marxism with respect to democratic theory.
>
> **Jürgen Habermas**

"But how did Dewey fit in," Habermas queried, "the embodiment of that democratic wing of the Young Hegelians that we had so sorely lacked in Europe? After all, Dewey's way of thinking stood in strident contrast to the Greco-German pretension, the high tone and elitist gesture of the Few who claim a privileged access to truth against the many." By his own admission, Habermas considered the intrusion of Dewey on an elite American university campus (in this case summoned forth through the incantations of Richard Rorty) in a conference on interwar German philosophy "so obscene that I quite lost my cool."[1] He repented. But at times it would appear he was almost alone. And perhaps for good reason. Who could blame scholars of this tumultuous century for finding relatively little in Dewey's political thought, especially on such weighty topics as exception, to which only the Greco-German pretentions of Carl Schmitt would seem to provide privileged access?

Considering Dewey's aversion to interwar German philosophy, it may be surprising to some that Rorty won Habermas over—as this chapter's epigraph suggests. Perhaps it might even inspire one to consider Rorty's insight that "determining truth is just the intuition that we make our new beliefs conform with a vast body of platitudes, unquestioned perceptual reports and the like."[2] That is no doubt a step too far for many. But, as far as the state of exception is concerned, Schmitt's high tone continues to speak incontestable truths when it comes to sovereign exception (admittedly his elitist gestures are more convincing than most). "Sovereign is he who decides on the exception," Schmitt opens his *Political Theology* dramatically in a stand-alone one-sentence paragraph, before solemnly starting at the line: "Only this definition can do justice to a borderline concept." Exception *is* the expression of sovereign power. And thus political conceptions ignorant of the abstract need not apply. Those who should—and do—apply counter Schmitt from *this* side of the ostensibly impenetrable, fast-growing walls of legal limits. Raise them higher! we are told: the answer to exceptional power surely lies in *our* constitution or in a fundamental higher law to which officials must be answerable and to which we must eternally return.

No doubt Dewey, the American philosopher, is a third wheel in this conversation. He cares little for "doing justice to a concept," and his Young Hegelianism is hopelessly unhelpful in the search for a fundamental higher law. As he quizzically pondered in response to the liberal British legal theorist A. V. Dicey: "[B]ut why should such a fact be thought to have any bearing at all?"[3] So doesn't such blatant disregard for the limits of legal norms in understanding modern politics simply exclude him from this constellation? Or is it precisely here, in his rejection of such absolutes—his Hegelian sense that "nothing, including an a priori concept, is immune from cultural development"[4]—that his political insights gain purchase?

While scholars of exceptional circumstances have overwhelmingly looked to an interwar Continent to find insights into exceptional powers, this chapter asks whether there might also have been some resources in American political philosophy itself for grasping the problem of exception. Granted, Dewey's pragmatic politics do not traffic in metaphysics: "sovereignty," for him, "is a social fact, something existing *within* social activities and not outside of them."[5] We may therefore be unsurprised to discover a radical difference from Schmitt in his conceptualizing politics as an exceptional capacity to solve social problems. Indeed, from this interwar pragmatic perspective, Schmitt *and* a formal liberal "higher law" share a common problem: they have accepted the *idea* of exception before the "concrete facts and relations involved have been faced and stated on their own account."[6] In the realm of emergency, Dewey's is therefore a method that is also a politics: as method, it shuns the idea that the "sovereign" exists to be uncovered and upheld in crisis moments, by decision or formal constitution; as politics, it remains open to the endless possibilities for the exceptional exercise of public power confronted with both existential and quotidian problems.

I

Schmitt twice offered an unflinching definition of sovereign power in his *Political Theology*: in the first (1922) edition and the second (1934). In the latter, a new opening to his *definitive* statement, Schmitt announced that he was investigating not just two types of legal thinking on the state, as he had in the first edition, but three. Beyond the normativist and the decisionist positions, he argued, it was also necessary to reconsider what he referred to as the "institutional" approach. On this third legal form, he insisted: "Whereas the normativist in his distortion makes of law a mere mode of operation of state bureaucracy, and the decisionist, focusing on the moment always runs the risk of missing the stable content inherent in every great political movement, an isolated institutional thinking leads to the pluralism characteristic of a feudal-corporate growth that is devoid of sovereignty."[7]

Schmitt roared at this third "institutional" conception and against the feudal-corporatism of these "pluralists" who emptied politics of sovereignty. Seeking a means of reasserting the time-honored notion, the second edition—published at the outset of the rise of the Nazi power in 1933—was hardly alone in critiquing pluralism and its attempt to evacuate sovereign power from political theory during this critical decade. Between Schmitt's two editions, stretching from 1922 to 1933, the once-dominant pluralist thought was crumbling. "The single most striking feature of the pluralist movement," David Runciman has argued, "is the abrupt way in which it ends."[8]

The decline of pluralism was just one of the intellectual contexts within which Schmitt penned his theory of the exception and Dewey reformulated his understanding of the same idea through his "democratic state." But, as they both highlighted in their works in this period, it was an increasingly important one. In the late 1920s and early 1930s, Schmitt and Dewey shared the conviction that the pluralist balance of associations and state that had offered a new ballast to liberal constitutionalism in the late nineteenth century and the early twentieth was insufficient. They therefore confronted a common problem: how to conceive of the increasingly extraordinary capacities of the modern state necessary in an age of unprecedented military capacity, international corporations, businesses, and labor movements.

From the United States to England, Germany, and France, the problem was raised across the political spectrum—Dewey in the United States and Schmitt on the Continent marking perhaps two extremes. Between them, there emerged a new attentiveness to the various ways that exceptional circumstances enabled the polity to act on itself. From *ceaseless experiment* to *decisionism*, a renewed interest in necessary breaches of formal legal strictures began to take form as a means of thinking about modern state power. For some, including Schmitt, the solution sat outside liberalism,[9] while for others, like Dewey, the response required an even more radical conception of liberalism, one that embraced the sociological foundations of the democratic ends of state action. Each elaborated the problem in its own way by targeting the frailties of the previous pluralist solution, each challenged a formal liberal constitutionalist conception, and each turned to its own conception of the state's exceptional powers to respond to it.

Schmitt's critique of the pluralist and pragmatic state was perhaps best captured in an essay published a few years before the second edition of *Political Theology* in *Kant-Studien* in 1930, "State Ethics and the Pluralist State."[10] Schmitt opened his essay citing Ernest Barker's 1915 "The Discredited State."[11] Barker's work had achieved some renown in Germany, just as he had been fundamental in importing and translating founding German texts for English pluralism.[12] Schmitt's new interest in the falling fortunes of pluralism in the 1920s pushed him to outline his own critique of those confused theorists who had attempted to sideline the idea of sovereignty as the central concept of modern political life. "Even in very strong states," Schmitt opined, specifying: "[I]n the United States of America and England ... the traditional concepts of the state have been strongly criticized since the war; the state's old claim to be the sovereign unity and whole has been shaken." He then quickly followed with a quote from a French jurist from 1907 that, in these works, "[t]he state is dead."[13]

The opening salvo in this piece may be astonishing to contemporary ears. Schmitt takes for granted that the United States and England are "very strong states" while insisting that it is the famously statist French who have declared the state dead. A more complete reversal of our contemporary assumptions about "strong" versus "weak" statehood on the Continent versus the Anglo-American liberal polities is hard to imagine.[14] Coming to terms with how this central theorist of the state could have a vision so radically opposed to our contemporary conception may offer keys to challenging some of our assumptions about the political and the exception in the American past.

David Dyzenhaus has offered insight into Schmitt's 1930 critique of pluralism by highlighting his paradoxical embrace of Kant's liberalism. While his antiliberalism is often interpreted as being hostile to pluralism "because it denies the state a role as guarantor of political unity," Dyzenhaus writes, Schmitt is in fact specifically targeting Laski and Cole's pluralism more than the doctrine of pluralism as a whole. For Schmitt, Dyzenhaus suggests, the problem with Laski and Cole is not so much their pluralism as the fact that the radical individualism on which their pluralism rests cannot be justified through their own political theory. For Schmitt, "the appropriate response to the fact of pluralism has to be pluralistic," and therefore any embrace of pluralism requires a recognition of the profound multiplicity of "the empirical world."[15] In such a framework, grounding one's pluralism in an unshakable conception of the individual as the foundational subject of political modernity was logical nonsense.

This argument took further shape in Schmitt's attack on the American pragmatist William James. "If pluralist social theorists such as Cole and Laski adhere mainly to the empirical," Schmitt argued, "they do so as pragmatists and thereby remain consistent with their pragmatic philosophy. . . . [Laski] transposes the pluralist world view of the philosophy of William James to the state." He later returned to his critique of James, arguing: "In the system of 'political theology' the pluralism of James's world view corresponds to the age of today's democratic national states, with their pluralism of peoples who are disposed towards the state on the basis of their nationhood." This critique of pragmatism followed a pattern similar to that of the critique of pluralism. Leaving aside for the moment the verity of Schmitt's suggested lineage and the more complex question of the relationship between pragmatism and Laskian pluralism, we should note Schmitt's suggestion that the problem with the pragmatic vision of the national state was not its pluralist foundations but rather that pragmatists did not recognize the full implications of their own pluralist theory. "The state really does appear to be largely dependent on various social groups, sometimes as a victim, sometimes as the outcome of their agreements, an object of compromise between social and economic power groups, a conglomerate of heterogeneous factors, parties, interest groups, combines, unions, churches, etc. reaching understandings with one another. In the compromise of social powers, the state is weakened and relativized, and even becomes problematic, as it is difficult to determine what independent significance it retains."[16]

Pluralist theory, Schmitt argued, did indeed problematize the state in its relationship to a whole range of other associations. But, he argued, one could draw the conclusion that this rendered the state weak or even "dead" only if one also maintained the "theological" assumption that individuals remained within a state by some natural predilection. If one examined the "concrete" foundation of state unity instead of taking it for granted, one was forced to draw the logical conclusion that state unity through the nation could be *decided* only by a constituent, sovereign act. It was therefore precisely *through* an embrace of pluralism, instead of its rejection, that Schmitt opened the door to decisionism. For him, the liberal polities of the United States and Britain were strong states precisely *because* they continued to wield power amid their pluralism. In other words, if these central states managed to wage wars and assert domestic order amid such extreme relativity, it was precisely the consequence of their exceptional power.

Central to Schmitt's claim was a redefinition of the substance of the state as opposed to other associations. In his view, the state was not one association among many. Instead, it was different from other associations because the *political*, out of which it was built, did not itself have a substance. Unlike a sports club that practiced a sport, a religious group that practiced a certain religion, or a fraternal order that engaged in specific social activities, the state consisted of the political, which had no specific restrictions: "Among pluralist theorists of the state as nearly everywhere, an error prevails that generally persists in uncritical unconsciousness—that the political signifies a specific substance, next to the substance of other 'social associations.'" For Schmitt, "the political more accurately describes the degree of intensity of a unity." Because "the political has no specific substance, the point of the political can be derived from any terrain, and any social group, church, union, business, or nation becomes political, and thus related to the state." The political, then, did not simply provide the foundation for one group among many; rather, it was the overarching unity that constituted the relationship between the different groups. "Power creates consensus," Schmitt concluded before continuing his critique of pragmatic philosophy: "Viewed pragmatically and empirically, the question then is, Who has at his disposal the means for producing the 'free' consensus of the masses."[17] As Schmitt suggested, pluralism invited the need to determine the concrete moment and site where unity was effectively established amid the variety of associations.

In sum, Schmitt's critical embrace of liberal pluralism was grounded in three essential elements. First, it was radically relativist. Second, it was rooted in concrete action. And, third, the political necessarily lacked any consistency of its own, appearing instead as a spectrum of intensity amid the various individuals and social groups within a given state. Radical relativism, concrete actions, and a nonsubstantial vision of the political—oddly enough, Dewey's own critical engagement with pluralism concurred with all these arguments.

2

In his essay "The Historic Background of Corporate Legal Personality," Dewey penned one of his most stinging critiques of pluralism. And, while he regularly brought the conversation back to its import for the American context, that essay directly engaged with the German, French, and English conceptions of legal personality. Challenging these European conceptions, Dewey clearly stated regarding pluralist theories of legal personality: "[W]e often go on discussing problems in terms of old ideas when the solution of the problem depends upon getting rid of old ideas."[18] At the heart of his formulation of the problem was therefore an attempt to set aside such "old ideas."

Dewey began then with the observation that the legal personality of groups and states was central to pluralist theory. He then, however, took his own swing at this legal cornerstone of pluralist conceptions of the state. "The question, of legal personality," he argued, "has been enormously complicated by the employment of a wrong logical method, and by the introduction of irrelevant conceptions, imported into legal discussion (and often into legal practice) from uncritical popular beliefs, from psychology, and from a metaphysics ultimately derived from theology." Building on his own critique of his political theology, his pragmatic argued—and paradoxically in keeping with Schmitt—that the key to solving the problem of legal personality was turning toward an understanding in which "a thing is—is defined as—what it does."[19]

Dewey offered only a sketch of what he meant in this essay, but he did nonetheless hint that he would not solve the problem on Schmittian terms since he insisted that the problem of overcoming theology could not be achieved by resurrecting the notion of the "will" of a given legal personality, including a state. A given group, he argued, could not be "conceived or defined in terms of something intrinsic" because *will* does not capture an essence but rather "denotes certain empirically detectable and specifiable consequences."[20] In other words, a will was not inherent in but a consequence of a given group or even a state.

Just one year later, *The Public and Its Problems* elaborated Dewey's earlier critique of legal personality and pluralism to provide a more robust conception of the state. Here too, like Schmitt, Dewey focused on an embrace of pluralism as a radical relativism, a response to concrete problems, and a nonsubstantial vision of the political. Reiterating the critique of political theology that he had penned the previous year, he wrote: "That the state should be to some a deity and to others a devil is another evidence of the defects of the premises from which discussion sets out."[21]

Like Schmitt, Dewey embraced the plurality of social groupings and the social individual who inhabited them. Furthermore, he concurred that the plurality of interests and associations did exist below an organization that superseded them. But, while he paralleled Schmitt's critique of pluralism, he broke from the Schmittian perspective at the final, crucial moment—the moment when Schmitt sought to make national unity amid pluralism the foundation of an exceptional moment of decision. Here, Dewey looked in another direction, emphasizing the overlapping, direct and indirect interests that empirically brought any *public* into existence. Instead of positing *the people*, as Schmitt had, he understood this larger interest as *the public*. *The public* famously captured those interests that spread beyond any one immediate grouping: "Those indirectly and seriously affected for good or for evil form a group distinctive enough to require recognition and a name. The name selected is The Public."[22] The public, then, came into existence through the effects and consequences of the interactions of social individuals and groups—if it existed as a legal personality, it was by neither concession nor fiction nor will; it was but as an empirical fact of social existence emerging out of the contingent problems of social life and the necessity of solving them.

The public was, therefore, not a concession granted by the state, as with other associations. Instead, it was itself the product of consequences instead of a formal legal arrangement: "The consequences which call a public into being is the fact that they expand beyond those directly engaged in producing them." The public therefore could not act in itself but needed a third party to manage the consequences emerging from the conflicts and problems of its common interests. Like Schmitt's concept of the political, the problem of the public did not emerge out of its own substance; in Dewey's case, the public was the consequence of a problem on some specific occasion. In this way, Dewey effectively turned the pluralist ideal on its head: the state derived from the problem of a given public instead of the state granting a concession to or making a legal fiction of a given group to solve a social problem. "This public is organized and made effective," Dewey argued, "by means of representatives who as guardians of custom, as legislators, as executives, judges, etc., care for its especial interests by methods intended to regulate the conjoint actions of individuals and groups. Then and in so far, association adds to itself political organization, and something which may be government comes into being: the public is a political state."[23] Through his emphasis on *the public*—as opposed to *the people*—Dewey expressed his own attempt to push beyond pluralism while salvaging a meaningful conception of the state. He shared this ambition with Schmitt at the same time that he chose a very different means of resolving it. He elaborated a vision of the state that was at once democratic and released from the aporia of being rooted in the people as a unified concept.

By turning his back on the notion of the people as the foundation of the state, he sidestepped one of the key tensions driving Schmitt's claim that modern popular sovereignty could be incarnated only in a great leader who decided in the name of the people as a whole. As Schmitt famously argued, popular representation took two forms: "symbolic figuration" and "mandate."[24] In this conception, the symbolic representation of the people required a figure that transcended the individual features of its popular source in order to incarnate the sovereign people as a whole, while the mandate required an attentiveness and similitude to specific groups and individuals that challenged this transcendence. Schmitt argued then that the aporetic relationship between these two forms of representation were reconcilable only in a great leader who could capture the singular will of a unified people and decide in their name.

It should be noted that, in itself, Schmitt's conception of a symbolic figuration and a mandate are not necessarily antidemocratic. To illustrate this point from a conceptual perspective, it may be worth taking a brief look at how a more recent democratic theorist has elaborated a democratic theory directly out of Schmitt's conception. Pierre Rosanvallon has elaborated Schmitt's aporia for the history of modern democracy by suggesting that the notion of the people captures a larger tension at the heart of all democratic organization rooted in what he refers to as the "unfigurable people": "By making will sacred and opposing it to the order of nature or of history, modern politics grants the people the power at the same time that the emancipatory project that it contains renders the social more abstract. There is therefore a contradiction between the political principle of democracy and its sociological principle. The political principle consecrates the power of a collective subject at the same time that it is rendered less coherent and visible by its sociological principle."[25] Rosanvallon thus mobilizes Schmitt's concept while at the same time defanging it, rendering the sociological principle of the people forever fleeting: the realization of the democratic society may therefore be driven by an attempt to realize a full image of itself (political principle) while always and necessarily coming up short (sociological principle).

Yet Rosanvallon's phenomenological adaptation of Schmitt's distinction does not necessarily shield him from Schmitt's conclusions. A Schmittian could formulate a critique of this solution along the following lines: suggesting that the relationship between the people as a political principle, on the one hand, and the people a sociological principle, on the other, and defining the relationship of those two principles through their incapacity to coincide instead of through their ultimate synthesis does not in itself overcome the basic fact that the origin of the formal principle of the people is not accounted for. If one suggests that the people emerges as the subject of political modernity merely through either revolution or a constitution, one could still argue—or at least one's theory is not equipped to explain away—that it must have been instantiated by a force of will at some historical occasion. In fact, it is precisely because the people at once exist conceptually and are also fleeting that a latent power—a power that may or may not be invoked—always exists. From this perspective, the continuity of the aporia that Rosanvallon posits is dependent on the goodwill of those who choose not to invoke the principle at the expense of the diversity of sociological experience.

Dewey's conception of the public as the foundation of the democratic state directly addressed this same problem but, again, resolved it differently. Dewey proposed another, more radical solution when he observed that it was only by erecting a constant democratic principle, rooted according to Schmitt in a symbolic order, that a tension emerged with the sociological reality of individual social particularities in the first place. If, however, one replaced any figuration of the people with a "contingent public" that formed only through varied social problems, then the sociological principle of individual variety was no longer in tension with an overarching symbolic figuration because the very philosophical foundation of the polity was rendered historically variable. Therefore, it was precisely the process of abstraction as political principle that Dewey avoided by turning entirely toward the sociological principle of the public. The state took shape through the delegation of authority by the public to officials who were charged with solving their specific problems at a given moment. From this perspective, the political state was sociological and historical all the way down.

Like Schmitt, then, Dewey also argued that the unity of the state could not be founded on a metaphysical ideal: it emerged in a given moment out of a given public. He therefore argued that even the state itself, or those who decide, was the product of a contingent public that was generated by the problem posed and existed only as long as the problem remained untreated: "Special agencies and measures must be formed if they are to be attended to; or else some existing group must take on new functions." The state as organized public could of course act to preserve the public interest: "From this point of view there is nothing extraordinary in the preeminence of the claims of the organized public over other interests when once they are called into play,"[26] Dewey insisted. He thus sought to downplay at the very outset the idea of discretionary or extraordinary public measures over private interests by removing the very formal legal limits on state authority from the equation.

Of course, this was also precisely the point around which Schmitt anchored his theory of the state. The state's capacity for preeminence in managing the organized claims of the public was proof to Schmitt that the state could be rooted only in a sovereign's decision to preserve unity. Dewey, however, turned in a different direction, insisting: "[T]hus it happens that the state, instead of being all absorbing and inclusive, is under some circumstances the most idle and empty of social arrangements." The state could therefore hypertrophy and atrophy in keeping with the specific needs of the publics. In other words, unity was a problem and a consequence, not the a priori guarantee of a state's legitimate existence. In this way Dewey overcame "the temptation to generalize from these instances" and at the same time refuted the pluralist conclusion that "the state generically is of no significance."[27]

Dewey was therefore determined to remove the substance of the state while maintaining its power to act: "There is no a priori rule which can be laid down and by which when it is followed a good state will be brought into existence. In no two ages or places is there the same public. . . . The formation of states must be an experimental process."[28] Again like Schmitt, he criticized the pluralists who suggested that the state was of no particular significance in solving social problems and that individuals would ultimately be able to manage the conflicts between competing claims. Conflict could at times be managed at other scales, but such problems could always potentially become public. When the intensity of the conflict outstripped the strict circle of immediate relations and spread beyond to other groups or associations involved, it became a matter that required the delegation of officers of state. In this instance, the public organized itself—that is, it formed a state—to manage these problems.

The similarities with Schmitt's framing of the problem of state power were a symptom of the broader critique of pluralism and "the return of the state" that was taking place across the 1920s and the early 1930s. But those similarities go beyond a general dissatisfaction with basic pluralist claims. For both Dewey and Schmitt, the overarching power—or the political—that breathed life into the state did not have an essence. "[T]he State must always be rediscovered," Dewey argued. "Except, once more, in a formal statement of conditions to be met, we have no idea what history may still bring forth." Similarly, both embraced a radical relativism turning their backs on a normative conception of the proper relationship between associations or states. Finally, they both left the proper relationship between state and society to be determined in specific concrete situations.[29]

So where does the essential difference between Schmitt and Dewey lie? There was, indeed, one issue on which they profoundly disagreed: the conclusions to be drawn from this diagnosis. Schmitt insisted: "[T]he issue itself, [was] the problem of a people's political unity." In this way, he correctly surmised that the only way to reestablish a coherent theory of sovereignty within the pluralist paradigm was to ground the political in he "who decides on the exception."[30] Dewey agreed with the logic of the conclusion, but he disagreed with the terms on which the conclusion needed to be drawn. Yes, any attempt to resurrect sovereignty in the context of radical pluralism required a return to the concept, be it dictatorial, theological, or metaphysical. And it was precisely for this reason that he turned in the opposite direction, embracing an even more radical position, entirely jettisoning sovereignty and the people as a principle of political unity. "Sovereignty," he wrote in his philosophy of law, "[is] at best an expression of the working of a vast multitude of social forces, and at worst a pure abstraction."[31] Through this refusal of popular sovereignty as a foundation of legislative power, Dewey shed the limits of liberal constitutionalism, like Schmitt, while at the same time returning to the quotidian, singular, and often exceptional social problems confronted in the process of self-rule. Thus, instead of the sovereign deciding the exception, he reversed the proposition: "General theory might indeed be helpful; but it would serve intelligent decision only if it were used as an aid to foreseeing factual consequences, not directly per se."[32]

At the center of Dewey's solution was, therefore, his refusal to root decision in a final figuration of the people, in a presupposed unity of the people as the basic political principle of the state. In his view, Schmitt may have been correct that, the moment one established the unity of the people as superior to all other forms of organization, the right to serve the people by establishing its unity took precedence. For Dewey, however, neither this coherence nor its consonant will existed as such. Rather, even the most intense and dangerous problems of public life as well as the scale at which they needed to be decided were contingent. Thus, once the problem was resolved, the powers it had accumulated ceased to exist as such. The state official's energy, directed toward a new problem, could decrease in intensity as the conflict dissipated, to the point that often the state was the "most idle and empty of social arrangements."[33]

This state was born in its capacity to solve variable and endless sets of problems that emerged through the association of individuals. These (infinitely multiple) decisions were not the revelation of a basic unity and loyalty that separated the entire community from another: "Somewhere between associations that are narrow, close and intimate and those which are so remote as to have only infrequent and casual contact lies, then, the province of the state. We do not find and should not expect of find sharp and fast demarcations."[34] Dewey pushed the capacity of public decision making to its extreme, denying that any one decision at any one moment could harken back to a foundational unity. The public was the ever-shifting, multiple, overlapping, and profoundly historical set of relations that presented a consistently differentiating set of problems.

Dewey made this relationship more explicit by tackling the problem of law and constitutionalism—the sphere of predilection of Carl Schmitt—directly. In "My Philosophy of Law," he reformulated his critique of legal personality in terms that could be applied to constitutional and public law more generally. "The question of what law *is*," he wrote, "reduces itself to a question of what it is believed regulations and practices *should be*. According to traditions that are highly influential, determination of the end and standard is intimately bound up with determination of an ultimate source—as is obvious when the Will or Reason of God, or the ultimate and intrinsic Law of Nature, is held to be the source of law." To this idea, Dewey responded that it was, in fact, neither "the work of legislation" nor "judicial decisions." Rather: "[L]aw is through and through a social phenomenon; social in origin, in purpose or end, and in application."[35] With this statement, he offered a direct response to the formal legal and constitutional law arguments that had been raised against the tragedies of European war by arguing that the law and the state remained profoundly sociological practices.

3

As I have discussed, Schmitt established the decision in exceptional circumstances as the foundation for political sovereignty. As I have also pointed out, this position was seductive and powerful both for its intellectual coherence and for its political applicability in a moment of crisis. However, it also signed the death warrant of democratic life by shutting down the possibility of a nondespotic decision as the foundation for state power and arguing that any mode of organization outside the decision of a singular unifying will was a mere shell game of self-deception. So how might we understand attempts during the same moment to build a theory of everyday decision within American pragmatic philosophy that did not undermine the possibility of a democratic politics? In other words, what could a regime that placed the nondespotic exigencies of modern democratic society and the institutional processes of a democratic politics at its center look like? Through his critical response to pluralism, Dewey provided at least a partial response to this question. Pushing quotidian problems to the fore while denying the power of the unique decision, his search for the public was also a search to avoid the Schmittian trap of fetishizing *the* despotic decision.

The democratic state required multiplying the moments and wills that could serve as arbiters for negotiating the serial and sometimes exceptional challenges that emerge in self-rule. But could such a conception respond to the immediate challenges of exceptional circumstances? Was Dewey's pragmatic conception of the democratic state up to the task of actual exceptional situations? In his work on Dewey's politics, Gary Bullert has argued that his philosophy was able to provide a coherent response to the many, very real emergencies of his day. In particular, he challenges the idea that pragmatism was "incapable of functioning adequately in a wartime emergency."[36] Dewey's long life forced him on a number of occasions to confront the sharp realities of attempting to live by and govern through pragmatic theory in times of emergency. A consummate public intellectual, Dewey remained deeply engaged in the exceptional circumstances of his time mobilizing his understanding of the democratic state.

Among the emergencies Dewey confronted pragmatically were US involvement and the expansion of executive powers under Wilson during

World War I. In 1917, as Wilson sent American soldiers to the European theater, Dewey argued that the president's decision was justified. In doing so, however, he contradicted a general tendency toward pacifism that he had supported in previous decades. He also solicited the ire of a large portion of the intellectual left, most famously Randolphe Bourne, among others, who turned against Dewey's pragmatism, arguing that he had abandoned the very workers and ideals of international democracy that he had previously held dear.[37] Richard Westbrook, one of Dewey's biographers, suggested as well that during this World War I moment "Dewey's own scientific judgment faltered."[38] In many respects, Westbrook defends Bourne's critique, suggesting that Dewey's pragmatism fell short on its own progressive grounds.

As insightful as Bourne's and Westbrook's claims may be when placed in the context of leftist progressivism and the international worker's movement, when Dewey's support of Wilson is understood in dialogue with theories of emergency and exceptional circumstances, especially those of Schmitt, a different perspective emerges. In his short 1917 essay "The Future of Pacifism," for example, which Westbrook argues "lacked a convincing demonstration,"[39] Dewey does provide an analysis of how his support of the war relates to a pragmatic conception of executive power. Moreover, he does so in terms that were fundamentally different from Schmitt's, denying that Wilson's decision was rooted in the inflation or supremacy of executive power:

> Indictment of professional pacifism for futile gesturing may seem to rest upon acceptance of the belief in the political omnipotence of the executive; it may seem to imply the belief that his original step committed the nation irretrievably. Such an inference however is merely formal. It overlooks the material fact that President Wilson's action had the sanction of the country.... [T]his brings us back to the basic fact that in a world organized for war there are as yet no political mechanisms which enable a nation with warm sympathies to make them effective, save through military participation.[40]

We see here some of the key foundations of Dewey's pragmatic approach to exceptional powers. Recalling his legal pragmatism, Dewey critiques "merely formal" notions of office and invokes "basic" and "material fact." The heart of his claim is to place Wilson's decision within its specific context. While it may appear "idealistic," as Bourne argued, it is also a very real attempt to understand how Wilson could accumulate such powers and make such a decision without legitimating it through an abstract or formal legal principle.[41] Action was necessary, Dewey argued, since it was "sanctioned" by the country; the problem was that there were no clear means for defining this action. Wilson's decision was, in his view, not about extending executive power in exceptional circumstances but instead a product of the disjuncture between the actual political mechanisms available and the ends of achieving a new peace that he—and other Americans including Wilson—sought to achieve. As Westbrook himself noted, for Dewey this was "a critical moment when democratic hopes required concrete formulation into specific purposes."[42] The concreteness and specificity of his claims suggest that, while he remained vague on exactly what this allowed Wilson to do and not to do, it was because from a pragmatic perspective his actions could not be formally bound or rooted in an abstract notion of the foundations of political power. Instead, he was attempting to treat executive decision as a specifically, temporally limited, ends-oriented problem. To recognize the legitimacy of Wilson's action, he turned in the opposite direction of a formal decision, looking toward the highly contextualized set of possible resources and responses available for committing a country to military engagement. In his view, military action was the only mechanism available to attain the immediate ends of making the nation's "sympathies" effective.

The argument in favor of Wilson's decision and against an a priori pacifism pushed further away from decisionism and toward a radical contextualism when Dewey argued against Jane Addams's claim that the pacifist alternative to war was not passive isolationism but rather "that the United States should play a 'vitally energetic role' in a political reorganization of the world." He fully embraced Addams's conviction, but he questioned whether pacifism was the best means for achieving this long-term end of bringing "into existence those new agencies of international control." He argued against such pacifism that Wilson's decision to go to war was the most effective means of bringing this massive shift in international governance to fruition. In fact, it was precisely the war itself, he argued, that revealed at once the profound interrelations between nation-states and the limits of previous notions of "isolated nationality, big or small." The war provided the opportunity to accommodate the political system within a new international order, revealing whether these forces "are to continue to work furtively, blindly, and by those tricks of manipulation which have constituted the game of international diplomacy." For this reason, Dewey regretted the pacifists who refused to see that the war actually created an opportunity to participate in the construction of a new form of international governance that was in keeping with the ambition of just social forces. At the same time, taking a jab at those who found comfort in the early modern political theories of figures like Hobbes, he decried the military men who "continue to think within the lines laid down in the seventeenth century, in the days when modern 'sovereign' nations were formed." The facts of governance had changed, and the president's decision to participate in war was not by any means an expression of sovereign power. It was instead an attempt to reconcile current politics and political means with the "forces which are actually shaping the associations and organizations of men."[43]

So, while Westbrook may be right that Dewey's case sits somewhat uneasily alongside some aspects of his prewar pacifism, this may not be the only context within which to understand his support of Wilson's decision. Indeed, there are a number of elements in these articles that confirm the power of his pragmatism for understanding political action in times of emergency. For Dewey, the decision was sanctioned neither by the formal invocations of the sovereign nor in relation to formal legal limits. As a result, the decision could be understood only through a process of radical contextualization in which the executive decisions could not be judged according to formal, a priori legal or abstract rules. There is no doubt that this was a radical politics: it suggested that, even in the realm of war, the truth, content, or legitimacy of an executive act was ultimately grounded in its ends. It was necessary to understand the social forces that generated the war and the ends that needed to be achieved—in this case, a push beyond isolated nationalism and the construction of new transnational modes of governance. Moreover, Dewey's argument against narrow nationalism and the opportunities for a "political reorganization of the world" directly challenged the idea that a homogeneous people should be at the center of all political decision and understanding. In his view, Wilson's decision was a step toward creating new opportunities for governance at different scales that would be more in keeping with the social forces of the moment.

James Livingston has argued that Bourne's (and Westbrook's) critique of Dewey's support for entry into the war ignores Dewey's key idea "that the relation between ought and is, values and facts, ethical principles and historical circumstances, was a great deal more complicated."[44] With his support of Wilson, Dewey turned in the opposite direction from a defense of executive decisionism. Navigating between values and facts, he offered a deeply contextualized conception of the democratic state during an extreme moment of emergency politics. Far from establishing formal constitutionalism, a unified and singular will, or sovereignty as the foundation for wartime emergency powers, his aim was to embrace the social ends of the polity and popular sanction as a legitimate foundation for executive action.

Conclusion

This chapter has suggested that Schmitt and Dewey shared key elements of intellectual context in their formulation of emergency powers and executive decision, building their idea of exceptional politics out of a critique of the pluralist moment. Schmitt brought down the basic pluralist and, he argued, pragmatist arguments by suggesting that they misunderstood the nature of political association as opposed to all other forms of social organization. Drawing what he considered the real consequences of a radically relativist pluralist theory of the state, he held that, if the state existed as a political form, then it was the product of a decision and, therefore, dominated all other forms of associative life. The exceptional decision therefore became at once the proof and the foundation that sovereign power was ultimately founded on a singular will and could be wielded by only one individual.

Paradoxically, while he embraced this critique of pluralism, Dewey pursued a very different response. For him as well, the radical relativism of pluralism did not entirely solve the problem of the state. Like Schmitt, he conceded that, as a public authority, the state did have a distinct role to play, which set it apart from other associations. This meant, however, not that it was necessary to hand over all power to an all-powerful executive, but rather, to the contrary, that it was necessary to dissolve any distinction between the state and society at all. This of course did not mean that the state ceased to exist; rather, in his view, it was indicative of the fact that it formed around social problems, each one of which was particular, singular, and exceptional. Decision-making power was no longer the marker of sovereignty or the singular action that made the state a state; rather, it became a means of achieving specific social ends. As Dewey argued: "The new public which is generated remains long inchoate, unorganized, because it cannot use inherited political agencies. The latter, if elaborate and well institutionalized, obstruct the organization of the new public. They prevent that development of new forms of the state which might grow up rapidly were social life more fluid, less precipitated into set political and legal molds. To form itself, the public has to break existing political forms." The state then could properly hug the social terrain only by consistently renewing itself—or, in the case of World War I, by engaging in war in order to pursue the social ends of democracy and new international governance in the early twentieth century. "A state," Dewey insisted, "is ever something to be scrutinized, investigated, searched for. Almost as soon as its form is stabilized, it needs to be re-made."[45]

Notes

1. Jürgen Habermas, "'. . . And to define America, her athletic democracy': The Philosopher and the Language Shaper; In Memory of Richard Rorty," *New Literary History* 39 (2008): 3–12.
2. Richard Rorty, "A World Well Lost," *Journal of Philosophy* 69 (1972): 649–665, 661.
3. John Dewey, "The Historic Background of Corporate Legal Personality," *Yale Law Journal* 35, no. 6 (April 1926): 655–73, 673.
4. Rorty, "A World Well Lost," 665.
5. John Dewey, "My Philosophy of Law," in *The Later Works: 1925–1952*, vol. 14, *1939–1941: Essays, Reviews, and Miscellany*, ed. Jo Ann Boydston (Carbondale: Southern Illinois University Press, 1988), 115–22, 120.
6. Dewey, "The Historic Background of Corporate Legal Personality," 673.
7. Carl Schmitt, *Political Theology: Four Chapters on the Concept of Sovereignty*, trans. George Schwab (Chicago: University of Chicago Press, 1985), 3.
8. David Runciman, *Pluralism and the Personality of the State* (Cambridge: Cambridge University Press, 1997), 139.
9. Perhaps Schmitt's most famous statement of this critique came in 1933 when he referred to his rejection of nineteenth-century liberal democracy as the death of Hegel: "Only when the Reichspräsident, on the 30th January 1933, named the leader of the National-Socialist movement, Adolf Hitler, as the German Chancellor, did the German Reich recover a political leadership, and the German state find the strength to annihilate Marxism, as the enemy of the state. . . . On this day, one might thus say, 'Hegel died' [because] the political unity of the present [Nazi] state is a tripartite summation of state, movement and people. It differs from the ground up from the liberal-democratic state schema that has come to us from the nineteenth century." Carl Schmitt, *Staat, Bewegung, Volk* (Hamburg: Hanseatische Verlagsanstalt, 1933), 11–12. On Schmitt's relationship to liberalism, see Laurence Paul Hemming, "Heidegger's Claim 'Carl Schmitt Thinks as a Liberal,'" *Journal for Cultural Research* 20, no. 3 (2016): 286–94.
10. Carl Schmitt, "Staatsethik und pluralistischer Staat" (State ethics and the pluralist state), *Kant-Studien* 35 (1930): 28–42.
11. Ernest Barker, "The Discredited State," *Political Quarterly*, no. 5 (February 1915): 101–21.
12. Barker included his translation Troeltsch's 1923 lecture "Natural Law and Humanity in World Politics" in Otto von Gierke, *Natural Law and the Theory of Society, 1500–1800*, trans. Ernest Barker (Cambridge: Cambridge University Press, 1934).
13. Carl Schmitt, "State Ethics and the Pluralist State," in *Weimar: A Juris-*

prudence of Crisis, ed. Arthur J. Jacobson and Bernhard Schlink (Berkeley and Los Angeles: University of California Press, 2000), 300.

14. For a contemporary reconsideration of this question, see Peter Baldwin, "Beyond Weak and Strong: Rethinking the State in Comparative Policy History," *Journal of Policy History* 17, no. 1 (2005): 13–33; Desmond King and Robert C. Lieberman, "Ironies of State Building: A Comparative Perspective on the American State," *World Politics* 61, no. 3 (2009): 547–88; Ann Orloff and Kimberly Morgan, eds., *Many Hands of the State* (Cambridge: Cambridge University Press, 2017).

15. David Dyzenhaus, "Putting the State Back in Credit," in *The Challenge of Carl Schmitt*, ed. Chantal Mouffe (London: Verso, 1999), 75–91, 77–78.

16. Schmitt, "State Ethics and the Pluralist State," 302, 308, 303.

17. Schmitt, "State Ethics and the Pluralist State," 303.

18. Dewey, "The Historic Background of Corporate Legal Personality," 657.

19. Dewey, "The Historic Background of Corporate Legal Personality," 663–64, 660.

20. Dewey, "The Historic Background of Corporate Legal Personality," 663.

21. John Dewey, *The Public and Its Problems: An Essay in Political Inquiry*, ed. Melvin L. Rogers (Athens, OH: Swallow, 2016), 77.

22. Dewey, *The Public and Its Problems*, 84.

23. Dewey, *The Public and Its Problems*, 84.

24. The distinction between *Stellvertretung* and *Repräsentation* is developed in Schmitt's *Political Theology*.

25. Pierre Rosanvallon, *Le peuple introuvable: Histoire de la représentation démocratique en France* (Paris: Gallimard, 1998), 12 (my translation).

26. Dewey, *The Public and Its Problems*, 78.

27. Dewey, *The Public and Its Problems*, 79.

28. Dewey, *The Public and Its Problems*, 83.

29. Dewey, *The Public and Its Problems*, 83.

30. Schmitt, *Political Theology*, 5.

31. Dewey, "My Philosophy of Law," 119–20.

32. Dewey, *The Public and Its Problems*, 52.

33. Dewey, *The Public and Its Problems*, 79.

34. Dewey, *The Public and Its Problems*, 91.

35. Dewey, "My Philosophy of Law," 117.

36. Gary Bullert, "John Dewey on War and Fascism: A Response," *Educational Theory* 39, no. 1 (Winter 1989): 71–80, 71.

37. For Randolphe Bourne's critique of Dewey during the war, see, e.g., his "Twilight of Idols," *The Seven Arts* 11 (October 1917): 688–702.

38. Robert B. Westbrook, *John Dewey and American Democracy* (Ithaca, NY: Cornell University Press, 1991), 203.

39. Westbrook, *John Dewey and American Democracy*.

40. John Dewey, "The Future of Pacifism" (1917), in John Dewey, *The Middle Works, 1899–1924*, vol. 10, ed. Jo Ann Boydston (Carbondale: Southern Illinois University Press, 1980), 266.

41. For Bourne's critique of Dewey, see Westbrook, *John Dewey and American Democracy*.

42. Westbrook, *John Dewey and American Democracy*, 202.
43. Dewey, "The Future of Pacifism," 267, 269–70.
44. James Livingston, "War and the Intellectuals: Bourne, Dewey, and the Fate of Pragmatism," *Journal of the Gilded Age and Progressive Era* 2, no. 4 (October 2003): 431–50, 443.
45. Dewey, *The Public and Its Problems*, 41, 81.

8

Charles Merriam and the Search for Democratic Power After Sovereignty

James T. Sparrow

Sovereignty was an idea ripe for pragmatist reappraisal when Charles E. Merriam came of intellectual age at the turn of the twentieth century. This was because progressives did not understand emergency to be a special problem requiring absolute solutions—or absolutes of any kind, for that matter. Far from constituting the exception, emergency came closer to identifying the underlying condition on which society now operated. The market society that had matured in the long nineteenth century constantly revolutionized the world through recursive dynamism, revealing a yawning void of endless flux and bottomless uncertainty behind the seemingly solid fabric of a materialist society. The most consistent and penetrating pragmatist thinkers made no categorical distinction between the regular business of everyday administration and the occasional emergencies that only *seemed* to pose an exceptional challenge—that is, before an innovative solution could be devised. A reengineered democracy was the only frame within which that condition could be managed without further accelerating the unaccountable concentrations of power that constantly rocked the world.[1]

To justify their statecraft, progressives relied on a political philosophy derived from pragmatism. This philosophy rejected the formalism of the nineteenth century's classical liberalism, adopting a science-inspired stance toward truth as provisional, improvised, experimental, and relative to the task at hand. Modern life had broken so fundamentally from the bounds of tradition that it regularly made a mockery of common sense and received wisdom, not to mention religious and philosophical truth. There were no absolutes—or at least none that could solve modern problems and keep them solved. From the existential ordeal of the Civil War to the ruinous corruption of the Gilded Age to the global apocalypse of the Great War, shibboleths such as states' rights, property rights, and diplomatic insularity without entanglements fell before the necessities of national union, stable prosperity, and international peace.[2] Formal axioms and precedents yielded to the social facts and functional solutions of legal realism.[3]

Everywhere the "social problem" was posed by what the progressive avatar Graham Wallas eventually termed "the Great Society", whose thoroughgoing, if strained, interdependencies were constantly heightened by trade, migration, communications, boom, and bust.[4] In place of the private interest maximized by individuals through the invisible hand of the market under classical liberalism, the pragmatists sought out a public interest pursued by the social individual, enabling collaborative solutions through a "creative intelligence" that could constantly reassemble the new formations necessary to update self-government for the modern age. Anywhere progressives could find a way to summon a countervailing force against concentrations of unaccountable power they did so, calling the resulting constituency they mobilized *the public*—a postmetaphysical improvement on the old romantic ideal of *the people*.[5] As progressives challenged formal constructs like sovereignty through political experimentation, they left them behind conceptually as their cash value dwindled at every scale of political reform.

Merriam played a central role in the progressive discounting of sovereignty's cash value. He emerged at the dawn of professional political science, first as a leading American political theorist, then as an aldermanic boy wonder on Chicago's South Side. By the 1920s, he established himself as the dean of the ascendant Chicago school of political science. He also presided over a very large portion of policy-facing social science in the interwar period as a consequence of his founding role at the Social Science Research Council, his leadership on Hoover's *Survey of Recent Social Trends*, his entrepreneurial role in the Public Administration Clearinghouse, and eventually his pole position at the center of New Deal planning from 1933 to 1945.[6] To understand the doomed fate of that planning tradition, the fatal flaws in the imperial presidency shaped by Merriam's role in executive reorganization, and the inadequacies of the "world jural order" that he advocated at the dawn of the United Nations, we must recover his gradual elision of sovereignty, particularly as it pertained to emergency. As he sought out a distinctively modern and democratic principle of politics that could safeguard it from formalism, neoabsolutism, and other atavisms, he replaced sovereignty with authority in order to place society ahead of power. We live with the consequences of that substitution to this day.

∴

The concept of democratic power and its ramifications lay at the heart of Merriam's Columbia University dissertation, published as *The History of the Theory of Sovereignty since Rousseau* (1900). Merriam selected Jean-Jacques Rousseau as his point of departure because he had transformed the concept of sovereignty with his notion of the general will. Although he had begun from the individualistic assumptions undergirding natural rights and the social contract, Rousseau drew conclusions that identified the taproot of power in collectivity, not individuality. Not only was the general will, like earlier sources of sovereignty, indivisible, infallible, and unlimited in its pursuit of the general good, but the individual enjoyed no absolute rights against it. Indeed, the very idea of representative government itself was "shattered" because, unlike power, will could not be transferred. This meant that "there is but one possible bearer of sovereignty, the people; but one form of State, the democratic." It also meant that there was no limit that could be placed on the political community, no matter how despotic its will might become.[7]

"Rousseau," the young Merriam observed, "accomplished for the people what Hobbes had done for the ruler." He, too, had authorized a worldly god. But this one was driven by an infinity of hydras' heads, not commanded by the singular crowned sovereign of Thomas Hobbes's *Leviathan*. Through a complete inversion, Rousseau had "absorbed the government in the people," whereas Hobbes had "absorbed the entire personality of the State in the ruling body, the government."[8] This conceptual reversal unleashed forces capable of decapitating the ancien régime, unleashing the Terror, whiplashing it back in Thermidor, and distributing it across the Continent and beyond for an Age of Revolution. The political force of the general will was more than historical or theoretical. Its potency could not have been lost on Merriam as he scanned the newspapers in New York and Paris. In those years, populism terrorized the African American population of the South and profoundly destabilized the electoral base of the Democratic Party, capturing the presidential nomination for William Jennings Bryan in 1896, and scaring Republican voters and political professionals alike into securing a lock on national politics that would last a generation.

Over the course of the century that had transpired between Thermidor and Merriam's entry into graduate school, a procession of thinkers from Kant to the jurists of the *Rechtsstaat* had grasped after a version of sovereignty that could put the revolutionary genie back in the bottle.[9] By the time he got to the thought of his progressive contemporaries, the very notion of sovereignty had become the object of great skepticism. Modern political science and law had decided that the concept of "sovereignty has really no place . . . and should be banished from jurisdiction nomenclature altogether." Hugo Preuss proposed dispensing with the concept of sovereignty altogether, and replacing it with "authority" (*Herrschaft*) produced by the interdependence, coordination, and hierarchy of wills within the law. Merriam clearly admired his Berlin mentor's approach to municipal law and acknowledged that "semi-sovereignty" and other forms of incomplete sovereignty somehow served a function for international lawyers and for empire more generally, despite the apparent logical contradiction.[10] In later years, he would follow Preuss in turning to authority to do the work sovereignty formerly had.

Thanks to the historical process of ideation unleashed by popular sovereignty, it was possible to distinguish, as Merriam did in his conclusion, between three aspects of sovereignty: (1) superiority over other organs of government, as exercised by a king; (2) supremacy of a political community over individuals and associations within its territory, as established (*a*) legally by a constitutional regime such as Parliament, (*b*) politically yet prelegally by a political society such as a constitutional convention, and (*c*) communally by the broad body of the whole society whose will must be obeyed, as in public opinion, mass uprising, or worse; and (3) external independence or complete freedom of action relative to other political societies.[11] His typology of sovereignty thus distinguished three distinct sources of independence in politics, each of which depended on particular configurations of state organization.

This conceptual separation that distinguished sovereign from state and government produced an ideational pincer movement. On the one hand, successive thinkers could not help but "derive the power of the sovereign from the people as a whole," despite failed countervailing efforts to locate its origins in divine command, nature, reason, or tradition. On the other hand, this same articulation of the theory of popular sovereignty, proceeding through affirmation as well as refutation, produced an overall "movement toward" an "absolutist conception of sovereignty" that was increasingly unconstrained by divine, natural, or traditional limitations and surprisingly abetted by contract and by organicisms of both romantic and scientific varieties as much as by competing absolutist alternatives such as order, will, or truth. Both trends flowed from the separation between state and government forced on the world by the popular sovereignty of the French Revolution.[12]

The modern conception of ultimate power had become "irresponsible," or absolute in the sense of being "legally despotic," because there remained no power above the political community—not even God or nature. After the Revolution had shattered absolute monarchy and science had dispelled metaphysics as mythology, the only source of a sovereign power that could be independent because it was unchecked, universal, continuous, and indivisible was a political community organized "for the purpose of social control" and self-determining "the ends it will follow out and what means it will devote to these purposes . . . forcibly [compelling] the execution of its plans."[13] The division and separation of powers within constitutional government that had once been understood to limit its power now were revealed as an unchecked source of it.

In addition to explaining the escalating power of modern constitutional states, the distinct facets of sovereignty explained a range of logical puzzles, from the possibility of federal government (but not a federal state), to the supremacy of functionally specific agencies without the fragmentation of the government or the nation, to the operation of partial or semisovereignty in international law. More significantly for Merriam, their distinction and articulation could allow new modes of government to be devised to meet the endless challenges of the modern world. If it was true that "the indivisibility of sovereignty has been purchased at the price of sovereign statehood" in international law, then that only freed up statesmen to harness emergent sources of social power more directly to meet the ever-shifting political crises produced by market society, globalization, and empire. They could build any number of government agencies at multiple scales without canceling out the organization of power.[14]

Merriam considered the recognition of the "double organization" of political power in state and government to be a breakthrough, enabling "American public law" to advance "beyond that of the States of Europe." On this question he showed the influence of his Columbia dissertation adviser John W. Burgess, one of the founding fathers of modern political science. By distributing government powers among any number of agencies to meet virtually any requirement of the public welfare (including individual liberty and personal rights), it allowed for a simultaneous concentration of sovereignty in "the national state"—which, he agreed with his adviser, "is the safest repository for irresponsible power."[15] The mixture of power and decentralization afforded by the federal government—if not by the impossible federal state—ended the paradox of self-canceling power that had crippled the theorists of "dual sovereignty" and the *Bundesstaat* while unleashing the widely dispersed energies of a nation that could now be unified in its diversity. It freed state builders to reach past encrusted structures of tradition by recombining, multiplying, and more efficiently arraying Preuss's "extended series of 'social persons' . . . all associated in a complicated system of reciprocal rights and duties." The distribution of power also harnessed the "long chain of unions and associations . . . all heaped from . . . the social element or material found in every individual" that the German legal jurist Otto von Gierke had taught a generation of transatlantic political scientists to recognize as fundamentally constitutive of the *Rechtsstaat*.[16]

While the young Merriam was sufficiently daring to attempt grounding sovereignty in the social individual, he could not yet bring himself to dismantle sovereignty altogether or dissolve it into society itself. He wondered whether it was clear, in 1900, *what* exactly would replace the "idea of monarchical sovereignty" and *where* precisely one would locate "this ultimately controlling power" produced by the totality of political arrangements in a modern community of interdependent social individuals.[17] Even if it was the ultimate source of power, how could the community transcend its "inchoate condition" to assert its will? "The question is raised," Merriam worried, "whether the power that has no legal or governmental organs of expression may properly be termed *political*."[18]

The more troubling question Merriam did not raise was whether the inchoate potential of the ultimate sovereignty generated by the modern interdependent community could be hijacked precisely because it was prepolitical. Indeed, it might be more vulnerable to capture than had been the case in the more segmented societies of the medieval and early modern world. What if the political community neglected popular wishes, as Congress had under "Uncle Joe" Cannon's regime of Republican rule around the turn of the twentieth century? What were the remedies should the legal organs of government pervert the general will, as southern populists did in creating Jim Crow regimes? Were there any protections against the machinations of social persons—such as the proliferating interest groups, corrupt political machines, or ruthless trusts that ran so much of politics in the late Gilded Age—who might conspire to subvert the will of the people?

This vulnerability of modern society to preemption surfaced in Merriam's treatment of Hobbes, whose inversion of the social contract he had left behind in his introductory chapter before moving on to Rousseau. In *Leviathan*, the monarch owed no responsibility to his subjects because neither people nor state existed beforehand to delegate powers to him. On the contrary, it was the monarch who constituted the person of the sovereign and generated "common power" by convening the people to form the commonwealth, thereby rescuing them from the war of all against all. "Sovereignty and its subjects are created simultaneously . . . not delegated or alienated by the people," as the Monarchomachs had claimed in their responses to Bodin. Because "the people never possessed the supreme power," they "had no right to dispose of it." This was a vision of sovereignty "far more absolute than Bodin." It was flawed, in Merriam's view, because of its narrowly individualistic and voluntaristic grounding of power in the social contract. Yet, if a modern version of the *Leviathan* could be imagined from the starting point of the social individual or from the premise of a sovereign who could mobilize political society on principles better attuned to the interdependence of modern society, what would prevent political animals from acting to arrogate authority and instituting a new absolutism?[19] It was a possibility Merriam apparently did not want to consider or could not imagine.

This oversight coincided with a gaping empirical and conceptual hole in *The History of the Theory of Sovereignty*. That hole was the functions of the state and the command of the sovereign in war, a recurring human pestilence that turn-of-the-century international lawyers and utopian visionaries hoped to banish through law and science. Merriam's thesis appeared at the universalist apogee of imperial reform, toward the end of the "century of peace" established among the European powers after Waterloo. What appeared to intellectuals within the metropole as a century of peace presented itself to millions of colonial subjects as rapine, conquest, and globalizing violence. By the time of the Berlin Conference of 1884, the great powers had agreed on a frame of international law within which they could respect each other's sovereignty while extending it indefinitely across the globe all the better to conquer and uproot the peoples of the non-Western world.[20]

Although the typology of sovereignty that Merriam formulated in his conclusion culminated in independence within international society, very little of the train of conceptualization he analyzed took up the empirical problem of international society and its proclivity to armed conflict. He indulged barely any reference to, much less discussion of, the actual wars that had necessitated new conceptions of sovereignty. Yet his major touchstones all emerged from major conflicts. He acknowledged that it was the English Civil War that had inspired the "naturrecht absolutism" of *Leviathan* yet devoted no attention to Hobbes's treatment of the Long Parliament in *Behemoth* or to the challenge Cromwell posed to prior concepts of sovereignty. The point of departure for Merriam's treatment of popular sovereignty was Rousseau's general will. In his telling, the Revolution merely enacted Rousseau's idea in a fashion that required no extended discussion of the politically disorienting progress of violent conflict from Terror to Thermidor to empire. Merriam's American Civil War came down to the collapse of the ideas of dual sovereignty and concurrent powers that the Founders had improvised and Massachusetts senator Daniel Webster had famously defended during the Nullification Crisis. These venerable ideas were brought down by the irresistible logic of Senator John C. Calhoun of South Carolina, whose famous claim about sovereignty—that "to divide it is to destroy it"— apparently "led straight to the trial of arms in the Civil War." The German-American jurist and political philosopher Francis Lieber developed a very similar theory to reformulate the Union on a national rather than a state level. Of Lieber's unitary sovereignty Merriam warned that "despotism is despotism, whether it comes from Prince or People." But he did so without any discussion of the violence that had prompted Lincoln to suspend *habeas corpus* or any mention of Lieber's adaptation of the laws of war and the bloody reasons for them.[21]

The culmination of modern sovereignty theory in the writings of the great jurists and scholars under whom Merriam had studied in Berlin fell into place without any discussion of war in the statecraft of Bismarck. It was as if the war-born empire had simply grown through a process of integration as smooth as the theoretical evolution of the debate over the *Bundesstaat* and its transcendence by the more advanced notions of sovereignty developed in the writings of the political theorist and public lawyer Georg Jellinek and the abstruse distinctions of the *Kompetenz-Kompetenz* doctrine. These two concepts allowed for forms of self-limitation (through the "competence" of legal self-determination) and distribution (through federalism) without extinguishing the supremacy of the political community. Yet this vision of sovereignty was almost entirely inward looking, even if it had emerged from the often-bellicose relations between German states. At no point did Merriam relate it to the outward face of German imperial sovereignty, which in less than half a decade would authorize protogenocidal violence against the Herero peoples of South West Africa and a decade after that would unleash world war.

To be fair, not many other thinkers of the time picked up on the problem either. Yet these oversights make it clear that Merriam was not ready to confront the Achilles heel of his democratic theory of power. For, if liberty was ultimately a function of sovereign discretion, not the reverse, then sovereign independence within the globe was prior to other forms of control and power, whether social or not. Democratic power could not survive without a theory of the outward face of sovereignty.

: : :

It took Merriam three decades to move from decomposing the concept of sovereignty, as he had in his dissertation, to decommissioning it altogether as a central construct of politics. The occasion to do so arose when he began writing his magnum opus, *Political Power* (1934), during the academic year 1932–33—in Berlin of all places, "in the midst of a furious struggle for the possession of the symbols and substance of political power (the German Reichstag election of 1932)" that brought the Nazis to power.[22] By the time Merriam finished writing and published his book in 1934, the Nazis had already used the pretext of the Reichstag fire to seize power by pressuring President Paul von Hindenburg to dissolve the government under the authority of Article 48 of the Weimar constitution. Merriam made a pointed and portentous reference to the Reichstag in the opening paragraph of the introduction. But he made no mention of emergency, much less exception, when invoking what may have been the greatest crisis of democratic sovereignty in history, despite the fact that its smoldering shell still haunted Königsplatz. Indeed, neither emergency nor sovereignty would make much of an appearance anywhere in the book. This was not due to ignorance or indifference. Only a few pages into his introduction, at the point where he posed the question of the political, his only citation was to "Carl Schmitt, *Das Wesen des Politischen*"—a mistranscription of the 1932 publication *Der Begriff des Politischen* that revealingly substituted an inaptly metaphysical "essence" (*Wesen*) for Schmitt's "concept" (*Begriff*) of the political.[23]

In the opening paragraphs of *Political Power*, Merriam made clear that his theoretical omission of emergency was intentional. He intended to make a statement with *Political Power*, to clarify the break with the past that he had been steadily making over the preceding three decades. Indeed, the break was so great that he abandoned all the most venerable categories on which his field had always relied: not a chapter could be found on sovereignty (whether popular or absolute), the state, constitutionalism, the law, the nation, or international relations. Instead, his guiding concern would be to "set forth what role political power plays in the process of social control." In good pragmatist fashion, he argued that it was necessary to rethink power in light of the many new facts and situations that social science had brought to light. He looked beyond the institutional categories of government as mere aftereffects of political life: "The power does not lie in the guns, or the ships, or the walls of stone, or the lines of steel. Important as these are, the real political power lies in a definite common pattern of impulse."[24]

Merriam situated ultimate political compulsion in the lowest possible pragmatist denominator, "power situations," instead of the seat of power or the moment of decision. Formal constructs such as the state merely invoked abstract phantasms to recapitulate received wisdom and political tradition. The "monopoly of legality" that could be exercised by a legislative body was not only circular in its logic but also insufficient to explain other phenomena of power, such as the seemingly paradoxical fact of "law among the outlaws" amply documented and examined in chapter 3 of *Political Power*. It was necessary to keep away from the "narrowly juristic point of view," look beyond the mere "instrumentation of politics through institutions," and train attention instead on the "border lines" of politics to discern its principles.[25]

The border line that Merriam chose to privilege was one of the most venerable in Anglo-American political theory, namely, the one thought to separate state from society—precisely the analytic site at which his dissertation had left off. For Merriam, as for so many progressives, power was fundamentally social. His *The History of the Theory of Sovereignty* had pointed out the social preconditions without which sovereignty would be impossible—in the impulse to make contracts and keep them in Hobbes and in the habit of obedience that was the glue for the pure utilitarianism of the English legal theorist John Austin.[26] Despite his search for a distinctively political dimension defining power, his conceptualization of it always led back to society.

All the essentials of political community were, according to Merriam, "rooted deep in the inner life of the individual and the associations of individuals which we term society." Time and again, his treatment of the political emphasized social "integration"—a new "mark of distinction" for power—as the hallmark of the modern world. "Political power," he wrote, "possesses a peculiar and undefinable integrating quality, important for the individual personality and for the social group of which he is a part." At all levels of society—from the inner recesses of the individual personality "adjusting" to shifting social needs to the greatest association of them all, the state—interdependence defined the terms on which common action could be based. Merriam admitted that the "blanket power" of sanction was "recognized in the political relationship alone." But, while, much like traditional sovereignty, the power of society was absolute and unlimited in the sanctions it could impose, it was also grounded on such thoroughgoing social integration that no single source of command could fix its ultimate location.[27]

With power now grounded in "authority" and fundamentally dependent on modern social integration, older hallmarks of the political lost their conceptual priority or exclusivity. Merriam recognized that the "fatherhood of power" was "found in violence," which could operate on a purely individual basis or even among nonhumans such as bees or mammals. But violence was insufficient on its own and left groups vulnerable to conquest and dissolution. Instead, his starting point was that the "birth" of political power in human relationships flowed from three fundamental situations: (1) "social group tensions" producing a need for "organized political action," (2) "personality types adjusted and adapted in social living," and (3) "power hungry leaders" ready and able to match their needs to those of the other personality types, producing the relationship of authority in the process.[28]

Recasting the political around social power had major implications for the state. The "mold in which the modern state was cast a few centuries ago," Merriam announced, was "broken" and desperately needed to be "adapted to modern social forces." The state enjoyed a monopoly on violence "by common consent," commanding the supreme authority, but it constantly had to counteract the corrosive effects of violence and demoralization if it wished to maintain the loyalties of its members, from which it drew its strength. The nature of its power lay not "solely in the monopoly of brute force," pace Weber, "but in the organization of community action on wider or other scales than those of most associations of which the individual is a member." Merriam ventured an unnerving speculation, wondering how "some bold hand" might remake the maps of the modern world "in accord with the social facts of the present time," invoking the specters of Hitler, Mussolini, and Stalin. But he also pointedly cited the *Survey of Recent Social Trends* to suggest how one might direct the reorganization of power in a fashion more informed by collective intelligence.[29]

Because science enabled increasingly sophisticated and precise modes of social control, it was the most important element in the ever-widening scope of authority.[30] All the "emerging trends of power" itemized in the last chapter of *Political Power* pointed to science in one way or another. Scientific experts were the most capable of manipulating "the politico-economic, technological network of services and functions." Only they could reengineer and redistribute control by drawing on their deep knowledge to direct the progressive integration of their groups. Consequently, experts emerged as a new kind of third estate, serving as critical "power brokers" between rulers and "consumer-producers" because they were capable of creating "new types of control, new inventions in construction, new adventures in imagination and in administration as well, directed toward the formation of new power points, new power centers."[31]

Authority, then, replaced sovereignty as the arch stone of modern political power. The essential person exercising unlimited and unified will within Merriam's politics was the expert, whose "characteristics of equilibrator, stabilizer, general director, . . . governor" allowed her or him to be a distributed regulator, employing sanctions delimited by function rather than juridical boundary: "These 'sanctions,' as they are called, may in fact be juristically without limit. . . . Thus the political differs not merely in the type of penalty, but in the universality or generality of penalties available for the regulation of conduct."[32] Power situations delivered increasingly effective results in direct proportion to the level of generality attained. This was because the Great Society could become more extensive only through ever-greater integration and articulated control.[33]

Authority was thus the glue of the political community and the ultimate arbiter of the political. In "every unit" of organization there was "a control system" organized around "a central sun of authority" whose limits were defined not by territory or juridical boundary but by "the functional radius of the group." Consequently, power situations and the authority they generated would scale up to whatever level of interdependent generality social order and political control could sustain. If in the future "the growth of modern intercommunication and modern interrelation" were to progress, "a world state" could, he noted, "remove the territorial boundaries" and make the political community genuinely unbounded in a way that no other human association was.[34]

Political power in the future would increase not only as it became unbound but also as it operated through mechanisms that were increasingly nonviolent. The sophisticated, targeted, and indirect mechanisms of control that Merriam observed unleashing the "new functionalism of power" promised that it would rely less and less on violence as authority shifted to a new synthesis of "constructive intelligence" enabling ever greater integration.[35] Although he ominously cited Aldous Huxley's recently published *Brave New World* (1932), H. G. Wells's *Shape of Things to Come* (1933), and Samuel Butler's *Erewhon* (1872) to warn of the impending revolution in society and politics, Merriam insisted that whatever pattern of global reconstruction might emerge would have to establish its "more valid principle of authority" on the grounds of a "more complete universalization."[36]

Even as fascist plans for violent conquest cast shadows over Asia, Africa, and Europe, Merriam thought that the view for the long term was not as gloomy as one might conclude. While "powerful nationalisms" would allow leaders to simplify patterns of loyalty for a while, the resulting integration and centralization would ultimately lead to a "jural order leaving no disputes between groups unjusticiable." At such a stage of world development, a "wide variety of pluralisms" would "assert and express themselves within the framework of a larger unity," producing "freer" association and a "far richer social life than hitherto possible." Even though "the battle against disorganization may for a time prevent the full freedom which later periods will see," nothing less than a "neo-individualism" or "neoanarchism" beckoned to "the anti-authoritarian of the new day."[37]

Emergency assumed a less sinister aspect, with power generated by situations held together by integral authority. It was simply the most extreme kind of problem a polity would have to solve together. This was made clear at the very outset of *Political Power* when Merriam asked: "How shall we define 'the political' so clearly and sharply as to set it apart from all other and competing forms of social control?" He made no mention of emergency, decision, friend, or foe. Ignoring Schmitt's categories even as he cited him as the sole authority on the political, he hastened to reject any crisp salient separating the political from the other dimensions of social life: "The truth is that only confusion will be created by trying to draw too sharp and exclusive a line between political and all other forms of organization."[38]

Rather than setting the political on the throne of analytic categories, thereby crowning political will the master principle of human life as Schmitt did, Merriam chose to reverse the direction of causality. To solve the great challenges posed by depression and war, his experts would use the tools of medicine, economics, or psychology to blend government with industry and science, "uniting power and responsibility" to address crises of class, race, and religion that were bigger than the nation itself. Consequently, "the sharp distinction between so-called 'economics' and so-called 'politics'" would "disappear, merged into . . . social engineering or management" capable of operating the new controls.[39]

Even more revealing than his confidence in the saving neutrality of experts was Merriam's conceptual taming of emergency itself, the legal construct in Article 48 that had opened the door to the Nazi seizure of power, and the pretext in Schmitt that allowed the sovereign to decide on the exception to the rule of law. (Emergency also made it much easier to divide friend from foe, Schmitt's foundation for the political.) Throughout *Political Power* Merriam mentioned occasions for emergency, but he gave them no priority. Indeed, he deemed emergency so inconsequential that he neglected to mention it explicitly as one of the "marks of distinction" setting the political aside from other dimensions of human life. Instead, he listed diverse instances of emergency—"famine, fire, flood, or in modern days disease and industrial security"—as occasions demanding "leadership," which he deemed a "vague" and "residual quality" essential to political relationships.[40]

Merriam failed in *Political Power* to provide a conceptual criterion for distinguishing between democratic and undemocratic government on his functional basis. Again and again he pointed to the similarities between democracy, fascism, and communism. Provocatively, he listed Hitler, Lenin, and Gandhi together more than once as examples of charismatic leaders breaking old political molds through bold mass politics—even though he clearly rooted for the home team of democracy. In his discussion of the "credenda" of democracy—which he identified as "the will of the majority expressed through some institutional form of consent"—he seemed to anticipate later theories of totalitarianism by noting that Marxist ideology "repudiated" not only the values of democracy but also the democratic "organization of government itself." Yet a few sentences later he rushed past the "bitterness of the controversy between the Marxians and the democrats" to insist on "the unavoidable conclusion that they are fundamentally democratic in basic assumptions" such as equality, fraternity, and "the emphasis on mass sentiment as the ultimate point of departure and control as against an elite in whatever form." These democratic orientations were "inherent" in communism, even if "responsibility on the part of the rulers to the ruled is obscured by the dictatorship of the so-called proletariat."[41]

Such equivalencies abounded throughout *Political Power*, initially lending it a provocative frisson, but after a few years casting a more equivocating shadow over it. What appeared boldly scientific in 1934 might have seemed to betray an abiding intellectual appeasement a decade later. Only a few years' experience during that fateful decade would cure Merriam of such conflations, inspiring him to affirm the democratic faith that so many other pragmatists embraced as their scientific naturalism collapsed on itself from within and Axis geopolitics assaulted their assumptions from without.[42]

: : :

The events of the 1930s made it increasingly impossible to ignore the mounting threat posed by fascist victories around the world. Merriam could no longer sustain the surface aloofness that *Power Politics* had affected in order to raise the banner of an unblinking and objective social science. It would have required a close reading of that text to see that his timely obsession with the revolutionary energies of mass politics, combined with his perennial optimism, pointed to the eventual "burning out" of fascism. But such a close reading would not be required to grasp the normative commitments of his next foray into political theory. They were emblazoned boldly on the book's title: *The New Democracy and the New Despotism* (1939). In this book Merriam confronted the problem of totalitarianism head-on. In the process he dove headlong into a deeper philosophical crisis within democratic theory. Disillusionment with the repression and jingoistic excesses of the Great War, compounded by the teetering emergence and collapse of new democracies across Europe in the following years, prompted many progressives to retreat from the open-ended and relativistic pragmatism of their earlier years into a more normative "democratic faith" defined against totalitarianism.[43] Others retreated further still to an astringent liberalism skeptical of any reformist incursions (such as New Deal planning) that might open the door to modern tyranny.[44] Despite the mounting revulsion against totalitarianism, by 1939 Merriam still had not succumbed to the retreat from pragmatic philosophical commitments but instead reaffirmed them.

The very chapter structure of *The New Democracy and the New Despotism* counterposed democracy against its historical antagonist, "mastery and slavery."[45] Merriam divided the book into discrete sections devoted to the two antitheses, distinguishing them by working outward from their opposing principles. The new democracy flowed from the "dignity" and "perfectibility of mankind," the "consent of the governed," and "consciously directed and peaceful social change." The new despotism fed off of "economic inequality" and violent repression, masking it in the superiority of the "Master Race" or the nation, the nobility of "the few" who could be trusted to run "the Party," and the heroic charisma of "the Superman"—which was nothing more than a new "Caesarism."

Merriam devoted the bulk of his book to drawing out the implications of his view that democratic power was more effective than its alternatives. He devoted a fulsome 180 pages to outlining the full breadth of democratic practices in the modern world. Contrary to the new despots' caricature of corruption, decadence, and enervation, democracy was quite competent to meet the demands of the modern world, whether shaped by emergency or not. Contrasting the failure of the *Kaiserreich* with the success of the democracies in the previous world war—visible in the rapid and effective US mobilization—he observed that decisiveness was not a quality reserved only for exceptional individuals. Indeed, in the case of Napoleon, it could be seen as a liability. (This certainly would prove equally true of Hitler, whose military genius lost its luster after the winter of 1942–43—a revealing repeat of Napoleon's tragic folly.) True decisiveness rested on the configuration of social organization and thus was as much "a matter of special social tension and unity of community purpose at a particular time, as it is of particular forms of organization."[46]

The functionalist frame of *Political Power* remained in place, but now Merriam draped it in the vestments of democracy. Rather than exploring the similarities in power situations on which power-hungry democrats and dictators might act to establish their authority, he contrasted their principles of action. No contrast was more starkly drawn than the one between the fascist idea of exception and the democratic approach to emergency. The Continental notion of exception was, Merriam recognized, simply a modern updating of a very old metaphysic of divine right that did not in fact implicate genuine democracy of any variety, whether driven by parliamentary or by mass politics. Although the fascists draped themselves in demagogic vestments that seemed to invoke the general will, in fact both their words and their actions revealed their determination to shut down democracy in order to create a new ruling class of supermen that repudiated the very notion of equality at all levels, from the social and economic to the ideological and spiritual.

Rather than shrinking from democratic power, as the emerging totalitarian synthesis demanded, Merriam embraced it, arguing that only an amplified demos could meet the challenge of the day. This was apparent in the section he devoted to the problem of "decision"—which fell not within the "new despotism" at all, as one might expect, but rather at the very heart of his democratic theory. In keeping with this approach, this section "Democracy and Decisionism" appeared at the crux of a chapter titled "Validation of Democratic Assumptions," which was devoted to the "New Democracy" section's central concern: "the consent of the governed." Far from representing the outer limit of democratic self-government, much less its Achilles heel, emergency and exception were at its heart—in the ever-unsettled, evolving, open field of contestation within which citizens resolved their plural and unlimited differences under the cope of the democratic state.

There was nothing special about emergency in the democratic state. It certainly was not the fountainhead of sovereignty, as Schmitt or the realists might have it, nor was it the negative specter haunting the very prospect of democracy that constitutionalists or other kinds of liberals might imagine. It emphatically did not require the cabining of executive power. Indeed, all Merriam's thought and experience had taught him that executive power was absolutely "necessary to make democracy work under modern conditions."[47] In Merriam's view, the real danger lay in the invitation that emergency provided to an "anti-democratic politics" indulged by elites determined to reinvigorate aristocratic politics. The threat lay not in some totalitarian *state* but instead in an overflowing of the political through one-party polarization and domination of society.[48]

Merriam's critique of decisionism, and of the concept of exception from which it flowed, was rooted in his abiding skepticism of sovereignty. Since his dissertation Merriam had argued that the very notion of sovereignty itself was the supreme antidemocratic *Geist* whose final exorcism from the state was necessary to complete the banishment of arbitrary, hierarchical, categorical, top-down authority from modern society. This skepticism of any arguments positing even the momentary inevitability or necessity of absolute power made him immune to the elisions of the totalitarian synthesis.

Seen from the pragmatic point of view, it was Merriam who was the realist. Indeed, one could argue that antitotalitarian thinkers—from reformed progressives like Walter Lippmann to reformed radicals like James Burnham—were themselves captured by the totalizing and mystifying move made by Schmitt and the theorists of *total war*, a term that had, after all, been brought into the world by General Erich Ludendorff. They were, in a sense, terrorized into accepting the awesome, Leviathan-like image of unlimited sovereign force and all-penetrating social control that the Nazis, fascists, and Communists projected. Consequently, they presumed that only its opposite—the "limited state"—could be its antidote.

Such a view ultimately rested on an inverted, monstrous fantasy of popular sovereignty rather than a historical, measured, discerning understanding of how self-rule had actually operated within American society. The fantasy rested on reifications of political violence that were themselves the mirror image of liberal order grounded in rational law and timeless human nature.

By insisting on the complete segmentation of politics from the economy, thoroughgoing liberalism created only a new absolutism of property. The advocates of a limited state were overreacting to "Marx and Mussolini," who themselves both "overemphasize the role of violence as a contributory factor in modern advancement." The proper response was emphatically *not* to place the state in a utilitarian straightjacket: "The doctrines of Mill and Marx alike have overemphasized the role of ill-defined 'economic' factors in our civilization—the one as the basis for 'collectivism,' the other as a basis for 'individualism.' The basic troubles of our time are not fundamentally 'economic' only, but are scientific and technological, territorial-racial, sociopolitical, philosophical, psychological, as well. Our problems involve forms of behavior, value systems, ideas, and institutions beyond the bounds of 'economics' in any ordinary use of that term."[49] Law and private interest provided no ultimate solution to despotism. In the long run, far more power *and* liberty could be generated through a graduated, nonviolent, provisional adjustment of policy to societal requirements as directed by the hurly-burly of popular rule and mixed government within equal freedom.

The core question for Merriam was not whether democracy could respond successfully to emergency—clearly it could—but how effectively the "organization of violence" could be balanced against the "organization of consent."[50] This was the role of the expert authority in *Political Power*. If, as Franz Neumann would observe in his *Behemoth* a few years later, the Nazis had seized power by *hollowing out* the German state and supplanting it with a parallel party structure that progressively infused German society with principles of domination and decisionism, then the United States could respond only by *suffusing* the state with democratic social power and collaborative problem solving.[51] The model here was the Tennessee Valley Authority, whose "grassroots democracy" summoned all the hydraulic force of an entire societal watershed to lift a beleaguered region into the modern world.

The violent decisionism that Schmitt placed at the center of his conception of the political could ever generate only significant new increments of power through parasitic or predatory exploitation of modern society. Even the total application of violence could not coerce everyone all the time. But, where fascist political theory posited a total foundation of exception for state power that fit perfectly with its monistic conception of political will and its ultimately static vision of social order, a democratic political theory required a suppler understanding of the place of violence and decision within the social production of political authority. "Violence in this sense is not a rule of uniform action," Merriam observed, "but a rule of *differential exception*."[52]

Differential exception was only a starting point, not a fully developed concept. Merriam was so intent on defending the democratic potential of administration that he never managed to identify a principle as clear as individual utility, national interest, or even friend versus foe that would specify the nature of the public interest. Only such a specification could clarify how differential decision might be deployed to attain the ends of democratic government. Functionalist assumptions still underlay Merriam's integral organicism even if its behavioral sources had been yoked to democratic values. At this critical place in his theory of democratic power, it might have been useful to return to the distinction between government and sovereignty that Merriam had traced as a young scholar. Doing so would have clarified the principles by which criteria could be used to decide where and how coercion might be combined with consent. It might also have helped specify the mechanisms by which citizens could ensure that expert administrators would remain accountable without ceding their authority to make decisions within their competency.

The "constructive intelligence" of cooperation in the new democracy, which now stood in for the integral functionalism of *Political Power*, accounted for the unity Merriam had once attributed to sovereignty but now located in the Great Society envisioned as a boundless democracy. This shift in underlying causation enabled him to emphasize as he never had before the democratic priority of rights, freedom, and even the dignity of man—the very first passage of his main chapter, "The Validation of Democratic Assumptions." The "defense of human liberty depends in large measure on public administration," he claimed, with due respect for the continuing role of judicial agencies. And, far from building the inflexible bureaucracy of the Weberian iron cage, democratic administrators combining "the spirit of science and the spirit of democracy" would provide "one of the greatest guaranties of daily liberty and security" in their "adjustment of broad rules to the specific problems of individual life."[53]

If the great challenge for democracy was not emergency or exception but rather the balance of coercion and consent within the democratic state, how could the essential equipoise be guaranteed? What was crucial, according to Merriam, was the existence of "clearly defined channels" where executive and popular will could meet and communicate. These lines of communication enabled the operation of flexible, multiply reinforcing, even competitive sources of review and insight—such as from businessmen and labor, multiple branches of the military and civilian administration, policy-oriented politicians, etc. The history of democratic governance in the United States suggested that this was eminently possible.[54] In contrasting democratic against despotic principles of power, Merriam contained power-hungry leaders in a cooperative matrix of authority whose susceptibility to violent or divisive will he discounted.

The democratic state's resemblance to other, antidemocratic governments was ultimately superficial, Merriam now claimed. The mass spectacle of fascist society and the theater of mass obeisance under communism may have borne a family resemblance to the mass participation of modern democracies—a point made over and over again in *Political Power*, but in support of a very different interpretation. Now the crucial difference lay in the principles operating to balance coercion and consent, with democracies always seeking ways to minimize violent conflict and maximize techniques of cooperation or bounded competition in service of equal freedom, while the new despotisms did the reverse.

The prospect of differential exception provided useful alternatives for the conceptualization of democratic emergency: most notably, practices grounded in countervailing powers and transparency and ideas derived from pragmatic and historical gradations of compromise and judgment rather than timeless and categorical axioms authorizing absolute authority, exceptional decision, or even classic balance of power. By defining decision points differentially according to the nature and location of the myriad emergencies that will arise and distributing them in a fashion that would promote accountability, review, coordinated action, collective learning, improved rule making, and above all compromise and power sharing—if not at the moment of the emergency, then before and afterward—democracies may rise to the challenges of the modern world without canceling themselves out. If the necessary balance between liberty and equality could be established, the fusion of coercion and consent could proceed with a muscular, unlimited efficacy. Indeed, it would be limited only by the degree of its democratization and perfectly equal to the necessity of any emergency.[55]

While differential exception was a start, it did not deliver on a full theory of democratic emergency. Indeed, Merriam's argument was limited by some glaring blind spots. His analysis of authoritarianism in *The New Democracy and the New Despotism* indulged a striking oversight that would not have been lost on Lippmann or the others then producing the embryonic totalitarian synthesis. There was no entry in its index for either the Soviet Union or Stalin, reflecting his neglect of Soviet-style totalitarianism—although there *was* a single reference to the Soviet purge trials that equated them with Röhm's "night of the long knives," indicating his recognition of the underlying similarities.[56]

Merriam's preoccupation with the cultivation of democratic practices pushed his political imagination away from the problems of sovereign contestation then reorganizing the planet through conquest and total war. Perhaps the friend-foe distinction need not necessarily apply to politics, but it certainly could be applied, particularly within the democratic register of a people's war. Once that became the basis for the mobilization of entire societies for total war, what would it do to the democratic state? How would it shape the new states whose practices of self-determination might emerge from the ashes? Merriam did not venture to pose, much less answer, such questions.

: : :

In neglecting such questions, Merriam jeopardized his own legacy. The conclusions he drew about the best solution to the crisis of democracy then engulfing the globe strike the contemporary reader as particularly inadequate. The only answer to fascism, he claimed, was to establish a "jural order, by force if necessary," to outlaw war as an instrument of national policy while getting to the root of the matter by establishing machinery for domestic (economic) security to guarantee democracy "in everyday life."[57] His wartime lectures on democratic government—which he worked up into a final major book, *Systematic Politics* (1945)— culminated in a chapter on the "future of government" pointing toward a "world jural order" of "the united peoples" that would establish a "clearer conception of authority" promising, as the last line concludes, "free men—in free states—in a free world." Now sovereignty was merely a level of generality within *order*, Merriam's updated term for *social integration*. Because it was subordinate to the "commonweal," sovereignty did not "imply omnipotence"; it was merely "the high point in the political hierarchy" that served as "a symbol of intent to decide as well as deliberate."[58]

By 1946, Merriam was advocating a specific mode of world government—run, unsurprisingly, by atomic scientists, the ultimate experts in charge of the ultimate instrument of sovereignty. The problem of democratic sovereignty had assumed global dimensions and existential stakes. Only "deliberate and systematic planning" that fused—indeed conflated—"physics and politics" could harness the unlimited energy of the atom to bring the "end of military security as a political problem" and "eliminate violence as a means of settling disagreements."[59]

Merriam's progressive erasure of the problem of democratic sovereignty had major consequences. The United Nations was, after all, born of a military alliance. In the end it would only reinforce a global order defined by sovereign nation-states, despite Merriam's claim that "nations never were omnipotent either in fact or in law."[60] Regardless, the potential of the United Nations as a world government or even a global constabulary soon fell before the prerogatives of two hypersovereigns squaring off for a cold war. What is worse, Merriam's innovations were essential to that outcome. His beloved atomic scientists and the broader institutionalization of atomic power on which US hypersovereignty rested may have enjoyed the highest form of technoscientific authority in the modern world. Certainly, the Manhattan Project would be difficult to imagine without the Tennessee Valley Authority and the broader New Deal planning Merriam had done so much to advance. But from the very beginning the scientists were easily controlled by General Leslie Groves, a rather old-fashioned sort of sovereign. After a few years of atomic fear, anti-Communist investigations, and discipline imposed by the loyalty-security apparatus, they posed no alternative to the national security state. This was a form of government—really a state within a state—whose secrecy, bureaucracy, and scientific authority proved virtually impenetrable to democratic scrutiny.[61] And it was directed by an imperial presidency whose streamlined efficiency, centralized control, and insulation from congressional supervision owed as much to Merriam's role in executive reorganization as it did to the war powers that protected it for several decades. Perhaps this was an irony that Merriam pondered silently as he sat on the Loyalty Review Board, his last post in Washington.

While Merriam cannot be blamed for the postwar tsunami of national security politics, he cannot be excused for failing to account for it. This failure was an unavoidable consequence of his refusal to confront the problem of democratic sovereignty. His behavioralism had completed the conceptual separation of sovereignty as societal power from government as organization. It was a conceptual distinction that he had begun in his dissertation and that then exploded through his pragmatic recasting of state sovereignty as symbol verging on myth. With political power grounded in the evolving requirements of the social individual and experts distributed through the body politics to balance coercion and consent, freedom could be located within power without either canceling out the other. Merriam freed himself up to reimagine government in ways that adapted democratic social ideals, energies, and practices to the very managerial and scientific developments that both fascist and liberal critics claimed were incompatible with mass democracy. This was the reason why he would emphasize centralization so often in his mature work, most notably in his role in New Deal planning and reorganizing FDR's executive branch in the late 1930s—not because he was a secret hypocrite about unchecked power or obsessed with the efficiencies of hierarchy and concentration (both of which merely flowed from generality) but because he believed that the functional integration within which generality could be attained ensured that power would ultimately have to be responsible. It was also why he placed his ultimate trust in regulation by experts: because they attained integration through generality on a rational basis, "in the universality or generality of penalties available for the regulation of conduct."[62]

But dissolving sovereignty into democratic power came at a price that Merriam refused to acknowledge. His service in New Deal planning may have shown a way to reorganize the political energies unleashed by his distributed sovereigns, the experts. But, significantly, it was the national executive that served as the focus of this reorganization. The timing for this elision could not have been worse. By discounting emergency, particularly as it emerged through war, Merriam had placed his postsovereign conception of democratic political power under the greatest possible strain. Envisioning the cooperative organization of social life around the new forces unleashed by technoscientific interdependence had allowed him to innovate, directly shaping the centralized executive structure on which both the late New Deal and the emerging imperial president would rely in equal measure. Marshaling the powers of surveillance and social knowledge to guide government policy directly allowed agencies to adjust social resources to the needs of citizens. But it also left the definition of needs (and thus of ultimate ends) in the hands of Merriam's democratic experts without allowing for a transparent or collaborative mechanism by which to balance interests. The perils of democratic administration could be seen as organized interests steadily captured crop policy under the US Department of Agriculture, watershed planning for electrical generation, flood control and nitrate production under the Tennessee Valley Authority, atomic power under the Atomic Energy Commission, and defense contracting from 1940 on. The secrecy and constitutional insularity of war powers served only to cement expert immunity in the national security state. The result was a conception of planning whose object (whether human or not) was the national resource, whose agent was the scientific expert reorganizing social cooperation along "functional" lines, and whose objective was maximizing the efficiency of aggregate output for a monistic conception of the national interest.

The universal quality of Merriam's democratic power was, then, its ultimate strength and its greatest liability. In place of the pragmatist horizon of open-ended objectives freed from metaphysics or even consensus, national defense simplified democratic purposes to a unitary conception of public interest—*the* national interest—that would brook no contingency or irony in its solidarity. Merriam had not considered that emergency, particularly in war, could free democratic power up for undemocratic application on a vaster scale than ever before imaginable. In that sense, his democratic state had indeed proved superior to the new despotism, but only to reinscribe power within the ultimate sovereign weapon: a democratic nation indefinitely mobilized for total war with no end to emergency in sight.

Notes

1. See William J. Novak, "The American Law of Overruling Necessity" (chapter 4 in this volume); and Stephen W. Sawyer, "Was There an American Concept of Emergency Powers?" (chapter 7 in this volume).

2. Bruce Kuklick, *The Rise of American Philosophy: Cambridge, Massachusetts, 1860–1930* (New Haven, CT: Yale University Press, 1977); Louis Menand, *The Metaphysical Club: A Story of Ideas in America* (New York: Farrar, Strauss & Giroux, 2001); James Kloppenberg, *Uncertain Victory: Social Democracy and Progressivism in European and American Thought, 1870–1920* (New York: Oxford University Press, 1986); Daniel Rodgers, *Atlantic Crossings: Social Politics in a Progressive Age* (Cambridge, MA: Belknap Press of Harvard University Press, 1998); Trygvie Throntveit, *Power without Victory: Woodrow Wilson and the American Internationalist Experiment* (Chicago: University of Chicago Press, 2017).

3. Morton Horowitz, *The Transformation of American Law, 1870–1960: The Crisis of Legal Orthodoxy* (New York: Oxford University Press, 1992), esp. chaps. 5–7.

4. Graham Wallas, *The Great Society: A Psychological Analysis* (New York: Macmillan, 1914). See also George Herbert Mead, "The Social Self," *Journal of Philosophy, Psychology, and Scientific Methods* 10, no. 14 (July 1913): 374–80. For a recent restatement, see Axel Honneth, *Freedom's Right: The Social Foundations of Democratic Life* (New York: Columbia University Press, 2014), 42–67, 253–335.

5. See Sawyer, "Was There an American Concept of Emergency Powers"?

6. Barry Karl, *Charles Merriam and the Study of Politics* (Chicago: University of Chicago Press, 1974); John Gunnell, *The Descent of Political Theory:*

The Genealogy of an American Vocation (Chicago: University of Chicago Press, 1993); Alan Brinkley, *The End of Reform: New Deal Liberalism in Recession and War* (New York: Knopf, 1995); Patrick Reagan, *Designing a New America: The Origins of New Deal Planning, 1890–1943* (Amherst: University of Massachusetts Press, 1999).

7. Charles Merriam, *The History of the Theory of Sovereignty*, Studies in History, Economics and Public Law, vol. 12, no. 4 (whole no. 33) (New York: Columbia University Press, 1900), 33.

8. Merriam, *The History of the Theory of Sovereignty*, 34–35.

9. Andrew Jainchill, *Reimagining Politics After the Terror: The Republican Origins of French Liberalism* (Ithaca, NY: Cornell University Press, 2008); Stephen W. Sawyer, *Demos Assembled: Democracy and the International Origins of the Modern State, 1840–1880* (Chicago: University of Chicago Press, 2018).

10. Merriam, *The History of the Theory of Sovereignty*, 209–10, 220.

11. Merriam, *The History of the Theory of Sovereignty*, 224–27.

12. Merriam, *The History of the Theory of Sovereignty*, 36–37.

13. Merriam, *The History of the Theory of Sovereignty*, 222–24.

14. Merriam, *The History of the Theory of Sovereignty*, 116–17, 207–9 (see esp. 208 n. 3).

15. Merriam, *The History of the Theory of Sovereignty*, 182 n. 1.

16. Merriam, *The History of the Theory of Sovereignty*, 116–17, 208.

17. Merriam, *The History of the Theory of Sovereignty*, 207 n. 2, 220–21.

18. Merriam, *The History of the Theory of Sovereignty*, 222.

19. Merriam, *The History of the Theory of Sovereignty*, 24–28.

20. Antony Anghie, *Imperialism, Sovereignty, and the Making of International Law* (New York: Cambridge University Press, 2007), xi, 69; Michael Geyer and Charles Bright, "Global Violence and Nationalizing Wars in Eurasia and America: The Geopolitics of War in the Mid-Nineteenth Century," *Comparative Studies in Society and History* 38, no. 4 (1996): 619–57.

21. Merriam, *The History of the Theory of Sovereignty*, 169, 171 (and 168–173 generally). See also John Fabian Witt, *Lincoln's Code: The Laws of War in American History* (New York: Free Press, 2012).

22. Charles Merriam, *Political Power: Its Composition and Incidence* (New York and London: Whittlesey House/McGraw-Hill, 1934), 3.

23. Merriam, *Political Power*, 8 n. 7. Special thanks to John McCormick for noting this slip on Merriam's part.

24. Merriam, *Political Power*, 3–4, 7–8.

25. Merriam, *Political Power*, 7, 11. Compare James T. Sparrow, William J. Novak, and Stephen W. Sawyer, eds., *Boundaries of the State in US History* (Chicago: University of Chicago Press, 2015), 1–15 (editors' introduction).

26. Merriam, *The History of the Theory of Sovereignty*, 24–28, 131–48.

27. Merriam, *Political Power*, 11.

28. Merriam, *Political Power*, 15.

29. Merriam, *Political Power*, 326, 222, 280 n. 1.

30. Merriam, *Political Power*, 279, 289, 320.

31. Merriam, *Political Power*, 292, 295, 305.

32. Merriam, *Political Power*, 11.

33. Echoing John Dewey, *The Public and Its Problems* (New York: Henry Holt, 1927), 98.
34. Merriam, *Political Power*, 289, 9.
35. Merriam, *Political Power*, 320.
36. Merriam, *Political Power*, 311 n. 16 (for Huxley et al.), 314.
37. Merriam, *Political Power*, 285, 322.
38. Merriam, *Political Power*, 8, 9.
39. Merriam, *Political Power*, 316.
40. Merriam, *Political Power*, 10.
41. Merriam, *Political Power*, 39, 311, 122 (quotes).
42. Edward Purcell, *The Crisis of Democratic Theory: Scientific Naturalism and the Problem of Value* (Lexington: University Press of Kentucky, 1973).
43. Purcell, *The Crisis of Democratic Theory*; Benjamin Alpers, *Dictators, Democracy, and American Public Culture: Envisioning the Totalitarian Enemy, 1920s–1950s* (Chapel Hill: University of North Carolina Press, 2003).
44. Walter Lippmann, *An Inquiry into the Principles of the Good Society* (Boston: Little, Brown, 1937); David Ciepley, *Liberalism in the Shadow of Totalitarianism* (Cambridge, MA: Harvard University Press, 2006).
45. Charles Merriam, *The New Democracy and the New Despotism* (New York: McGraw-Hill, 1939), 6. Subsequent quotations in this paragraph are from section titles in the table of contents.
46. Merriam, *The New Democracy and the New Despotism*, 136–37 (see generally 132–45).
47. Merriam, *The New Democracy and the New Despotism*, 127.
48. Merriam, *The New Democracy and the New Despotism*, 236–40. Compare Franz Neumann, *Behemoth: The Structure and Practice of National Socialism* (New York: Oxford University Press, 1942).
49. Merriam, *The New Democracy and the New Despotism*, 6–8.
50. Merriam, *The New Democracy and the New Despotism*, 340–45.
51. Neumann, *Behemoth*, esp. pt. 1, chap. 1.
52. Merriam, *The New Democracy and the New Despotism*, 345 (emphasis added).
53. Merriam, *The New Democracy and the New Despotism*, 131, 124.
54. Merriam, *The New Democracy and the New Despotism*, 140, 133.
55. Merriam, *The New Democracy and the New Despotism*, 183–86.
56. Merriam, *The New Democracy and the New Despotism*, 111–12.
57. Merriam, *The New Democracy and the New Despotism*, 187.
58. Charles Merriam, *Systematic Politics* (Chicago: University of Chicago Press, 1945), 37–38, 344–45.
59. Charles Merriam, "Physics and Politics," *American Political Science Review* 40, no. 3 (June 1946): 445–57, 446, 454, 457.
60. Merriam, *Systematic Politics*, 279.
61. Ira Katznelson, *Fear Itself: The New Deal and the Origins of Our Time* (New York: Liveright, 2013), 431–56.
62. Merriam, *Political Power*, 11.

9

Constitutional Dictatorship in Twentieth-Century American Political Thought

Joel Isaac

Despite their rejection of Carl Schmitt's famous claims about the nature of sovereign power, many liberal thinkers today nevertheless accept his diagnosis of the inherent weaknesses in traditional liberal accounts of the rule of law.[1] According to Schmitt, liberals insist that every act of sovereign power must be grounded in the law. In other words, the central thesis of liberalism is that every use of state power must be justified, ultimately, by an appeal to the constitution. In Schmitt's view, this kind of liberal constitutionalism was an evasion, for it dodged the quintessentially political question of *who* had the power to implement—or, conversely, to suspend—the constitution.[2] How could liberals explain the existence of this power, which one sees again and again in those moments of emergency when the rule of law is limited or suspended altogether? On the one hand, appealing to the law to explain the world-creating power to implement the legal order would beg the question. On the other hand, accepting that an extralegal sovereign power was needed to establish the rule of law undermined the liberal theory of constitutional government, which insisted that all uses of coercive power by the state had to be grounded in the law of the land. This sounds like a purely conceptual puzzle in legal theory, but, as many liberals have admitted, it is a puzzle with real-world consequences. From Schmitt's perspective, liberal regimes are prone to dangerous delusions about the exercise of state power precisely because they are in denial about the nature of that power. The actions of the American government after the attacks of September 11, 2001, are widely taken to have made this weakness in the liberal worldview manifest once more. All manner of lawless actions have been taken by a government that considers itself the epitome of the liberal order.

Much liberal jurisprudence and political theory has been devoted to overcoming, outflanking, or dissolving the problems Schmitt placed in the path of liberal constitutionalism. The overriding aim of these responses has been to square constitutional principles with the need for effective emergency powers while at the same time resisting one of two extremes to which liberal regimes are prone: either the unwitting slide into permanent emergency conditions or, alternatively, the creation of a constitutional straitjacket making discretionary action by government so difficult that the state is unable to protect its citizens in emergencies.[3]

How to forge a constitutional state that can avail itself of extraordinary executive powers when it needs them without opening the door to a power that can be destructive of the rule of law? The most compelling answers to this question try to show that the exercise of extraordinary powers by the executive does not have to involve a Schmitt-style "state of exception." Emergencies, that is to say, need not be understood in terms of a stark dichotomy of norm and exception, for prerogative powers can and have been incorporated into liberal democracy. The exercise of the police power by the administrative state is an example of how this has been done.[4] So too is Locke's thoroughly empirical and pragmatic account of the criteria of legitimate use of the prerogative and of the measures that can be taken to check it when it is abused.[5] If, as many theorists have argued, there can be emergencies without states of exception, then Schmitt's treatment of emergencies as revealing the extralegal foundations of sovereign power is not as destructive or as unavoidable as it seems. The chapters by Nomi Lazar and David Dyzenhaus in this volume offer arguments against Schmitt from just this vantage point.

To speak in general terms, then, we can say that there are two approaches to emergencies in contemporary political theory. One follows Schmitt's path toward a radical theory of sovereignty, a theory that threatens to explode the pretensions of liberal constitutionalism. The other leads toward a liberal-pragmatic account of derogations from the rule of law in constitutional regimes. In this chapter, I aim to show that the present split between Schmittians and liberal constitutionalists occurred much earlier than hitherto supposed and on grounds that, while not identical to those cited in the current literature, resonate powerfully with more recent attempts by liberals to rethink, in the wake of Schmitt's critique, the discretionary power of the executive. In particular, I shall try to connect aspects of the present non-Schmittian theory of emergency with an earlier liberal account of *constitutional* dictatorship. The idea of constitutional dictatorship is old; its roots can be traced back to the Roman republic. The version of this idea examined in this chapter is of more recent provenance: it was developed by a group of political scientists working at North American universities from the late 1930s to the early 1950s. One of them, Carl J. Friedrich, was a German émigré who had encountered Schmitt's teaching firsthand. The others were connected to Friedrich in one way or another.

Going back to this mid-twentieth century theory of constitutional dictatorship demands that we also return to an older version of Schmitt's famous account of sovereignty. An important point of reference for Friedrich and his followers was Schmitt's study of the history and theory of dictatorship, *Die Diktatur*, which went through two editions in the 1920s.[6] On the face of it, the notion of constitutional dictatorship would appear to be akin to what Schmitt refers to in his 1920s study as "commissarial dictatorship." As we shall see, this reading would then strongly suggest that the missing element of the North American[7] theory is Schmitt's critical concept of "sovereign dictatorship," whose implicit inclusion in the commissarial theory and later historical emergence in the eighteenth century *Die Diktatur* carefully described.[8] Although this crucial notion in Schmitt's theory certainly is absent in the literature on constitutional dictatorship, it would be a mistake, I shall argue, to conclude that the North American theorists were simply trying to banish all the unsettling elements of state theory—sovereignty, decision, state of exception—from public law.[9] A Schmittian is entitled to that view on Schmitt's own terms, but at issue here is a more fundamental clash of perspectives: a clash as marked as that between those who follow Schmitt in insisting that all emergencies must be states of exception and those who reject exceptionalism as an analytic framework for emergencies.

As we shall see, the pivot of Schmitt's analysis of dictatorship in modern political thought was the joining together during the eighteenth century of two ideas: first, the notion of dictatorship as a *commission* of the sovereign and, second, the ideology of *popular sovereignty*, in particular the notion of the sovereign will of the people as something distinct from its representation or exercise in any constituted organ of government.

The fusion of these two concepts, Schmitt explained, played a key role in the Jacobin phase of the French Revolution and went on to inform ideas of class dictatorship during the rise of Communist regimes in Europe in the era of the First World War.[10] In contrast with this Schmittian view, American political and legal theorists of the interwar and post–Second World War decades were deeply wary of the distinction between sovereignty and government that had fueled putatively "democratic" or "proletarian" dictatorships in the nineteenth and twentieth centuries. In their theory of the state in general and of dictatorship in particular, these American writers were trying to find a way (conceptually) to reabsorb sovereignty back into government or at least neuter its putatively revolutionary content. If, in a broad sense at least, the people were what the jurist Max Radin called an "intermittent sovereign," their will was not to be conceived as a protean and revolutionary force, operating at all times in the background of the constitutional state.[11] Insofar as the claim was that the people's sovereignty was a *legal* power—and the very notion of sovereignty was conceived by constitutional lawyers, including Schmitt, as in some sense or other a juridical concept—the American theorists of dictatorship were adamant that the sovereign will of the people was expressed by the laws produced and enforced by government. To speak of the sovereign was, on this view, to use a technical term that picked out an authority defined by the fact that it is bound by no positive laws—that it is "supreme."[12] *There was simply no room for the categorical disjuncture between sovereignty and government that opened the way for Schmitt's theory of sovereign dictatorship.*

Hence, there was a genuine clash of perspectives between Schmitt's theory of dictatorship and the literature of the mid-twentieth century on constitutional dictatorship. As I have said, this clash in some ways anticipates the more recent controversy between liberal, anti-Schmittian theories of emergency and Schmittian accounts of the state of exception. In the opening section, I provide a brief survey of the theory of constitutional dictatorship and the criticisms it has attracted in recent scholarship. Next, I examine Schmitt's theory of dictatorship and the rival view of the American theorists. Having drawn this contrast, I turn, finally, to the deeper intellectual roots of the mid-twentieth-century idea of constitutional dictatorship.

1. *The Theory of Constitutional Dictatorship*

The locus classicus of the American theory of constitutional dictatorship is Clinton Rossiter's *Constitutional Dictatorship*, first published in 1948.[13] For many years it was the most comprehensive study of the problem of emergency powers in Anglo-American political science, and it remained a vital source for writers on this topic until the glut of studies after 2001.[14] Giorgio Agamben has rightly connected Rossiter's book to two prior treatments of the problem of constitutional dictatorship in the Anglophone literature: Frederick Watkins's 1940 essay on the topic in *Public Policy* and the second and third editions of the Harvard political scientist Carl J. Friedrich's textbook *Constitutional Government and Democracy*.[15] These texts have been cited elsewhere in the recent literature, although not as frequently or as thoroughly as one might expect given their explicit discussion of the theoretical difficulties surrounding the idea of constitutional emergency powers.[16] Agamben is certainly right that these three works form a natural set. Rossiter's book draws on the studies of Watkins and Friedrich; indeed, Rossiter thanks Watkins for his "criticism, help and encouragement" in the preparation of the manuscript.[17] Watkins, in turn, was a graduate student of Friedrich's in the 1930s; Friedrich was the editor of *Public Policy* and, presumably, commissioned Watkins's essay. His and Watkins's respective treatments of the problem of constitutional dictatorship were structurally similar.[18]

These authors typically began their accounts by recording the tension between two principles. Constitutionalism, as Watkins noted, was "a system of government whereby rulers are subjected to the restraining influence of law."[19] One of the central means by which this subjection was achieved was the division of powers. Yet, when the existence of the constitutional state was under threat, those powers would need to be concentrated in order to allow for effective response to the emergency. Constitutionalism would have to give way, temporarily, to absolutism. This requirement, Friedrich observed, had become particularly pressing in an age of industrialism and mass warfare as class conflict and total war taxed the powers of the state to maintain order as never before.[20] There was no way around the need, on occasion, for massive and centralized state power. A paradoxical demand was thus placed on modern constitutionalism: to uphold the rule of law by limiting and dividing power—this being the essence of constitutional government—while also periodically having recourse to despotism. To many, this seemed like a recipe for wild swings between dictatorship and democracy. "Is there in all republics this inherent and fatal weakness?" Rossiter asked rhetorically. "Must a government of necessity be too *strong* for the liberties of its people, or too *weak* to maintain its own existence?"[21]

In their key texts on the problem of constitutional dictatorship, Friedrich, Watkins, and Rossiter went on to provide assessments of the institutions within the constitutionalist tradition that might allow for temporary absolutism. Indeed, their principal purpose was stocktaking rather than theoretical innovation. In Friedrich's and Watkins's studies, the focus was on the strengths and weaknesses of different constitutional measures for coping with emergency. Rossiter's book was more narrowly concerned with the assessment of the history of crisis government in four national contexts: those of Weimar Germany, France, Great Britain, and the United States. Nevertheless, all three authors identified a similar set of contrasts and problems.

Each invoked the institution of dictatorship in the Roman Republic as an example of a successful regime of—carefully circumscribed and temporally limited—constitutional absolutism. Importantly, none thought that Roman dictatorship provided a concrete model for constitutional absolutism in the modern state. In Friedrich's and Watkins's accounts, the principal function of the Roman example was to provide a contrast with the early modern rendering of the dictator as a commissioner appointed by the sovereign "out of the fullness of [the prince's] authority."[22] This concept of dictatorship as a commission was a product of the modern doctrine of sovereignty. The role of the commissar was modeled on papal precedent; the royal commissioners drew their authority from the *plenitudo potestatis* claimed by the prince.[23] In the eyes of the writers on constitutional dictatorship, the Roman dictator was not someone given sovereign command to undertake a very specific task to intervene in the causal order of a political community. Roman dictators, they claimed, had a more general, less specific legal power to act with discretion—and, where the competence was defined legally, there was room to set limits on the office of the dictator.[24] As we shall see below, this was one of many attempts made by the twentieth-century political scientists to resist Schmitt's account of modern dictatorship.[25]

For present purposes, it will suffice to note that Friedrich, Watkins, and Rossiter argued that the two major modern institutions for concentrating executive power—martial rule and the state of siege—were much closer to the Roman constitutional model of dictatorship than to the early modern commissarial concept of the dictator. Although, as Friedrich wrote, "it is undeniable that both martial rule in common-law lands and the state of siege on the Continent of Europe are derived in part from institutions similar to the commissionership," unlike the latter, and "like the Roman Republican dictatorship, martial rule, emergency powers, and the state of siege are all conceived in terms of maintaining a constitutional system rather than destroying it."[26] The absolutist system of commissioners expressly undermined the medieval constitutional order, but martial law and state of siege were measures designed to protect the existing constitutional order by giving the executive the necessary (military) powers to defend it. All three writers weighed the comparative merits of martial law and state of siege as mechanisms for temporarily concentrating executive power in emergencies. Critically, they also examined what they agreed was perhaps the central feature of dictatorship in twentieth-century constitutional states, namely, what Friedrich and Rossiter called *legislative dictatorship* or what might otherwise be described as a *war government* with full executive and legislative powers. This institution, once again, was to be understood on the Roman model: not as a means of creating a new order but as protecting the authority of an existing one even as it changed the character and jurisdiction of that order. The assessment of legislative dictatorship was in fact at the heart of the theory of constitutional dictatorship, but we can grasp its fundamental importance only once we have a clearer view of Schmitt's rival view and of the central issues in American legal and political thought in the interwar years.

For now, it remains to fill out the description of the literature. The texts summarized above were by no means marginal and brief essays for the three authors we are discussing. *Constitutional Dictatorship* was Rossiter's first contribution to the debate, but it was not his last. In the three years following its publication, Rossiter released a string of articles and one book in which he built on his account of emergency powers. The focus of his publications was on practical challenges facing America's political system in the age of the Cold War. Two key pieces dealt with emergency government after a nuclear attack.[27] Others took up related issues in American constitutional and political theory: presidential war powers, the effects of a permanent war footing on relations between the executive and the legislature, the protection of civil liberties in the face of heightened security fears.[28] Of central importance in many of these essays was the problem of legislation in an emergency: a requirement that under modern conditions seemed unavoidable yet had to be reconciled with the commitment to defending a putatively stable or freestanding constitutional order.

Friedrich's meditations on constitutional dictatorship in the 1940s had a more immediate object than the generalized crisis of democracy in the interwar years. As the director of the then Civilian Training School at Harvard during the war, Friedrich was responsible for overseeing the training of military officers to carry out the functions of civilian government in areas under the occupation of US military forces, especially those in the Pacific. One of the central problems he confronted was how military government by the army of a liberal regime could pave the way for self-rule and constitutional government by the occupied state. His answer—at least in the 1940s—was that the normative framework of constitutional dictatorship showed how military government could be conceived as a guardian of a constitutional order then coming into being.[29] The examples of occupied Germany and Japan were at the forefront of his mind.[30] As with Rossiter, this way of elaborating on his formal theory of dictatorship placed him in contact with existing discussions of military government and the rule of law in occupied territories.[31] By the mid-1950s, he was ready to show how *raison d'état*, of which the use of exceptional measures to defend the state in an emergency was an example, could be reconciled with the constitutionalist tradition.[32] His reflections on emergency dictatorship and constitutional reason of state in the 1940s and 1950s were part of a larger attempt to create a political science of the constitutional state. The fundamental premise of that science of the state was that constitutionalism was born in the struggle to control the standing fact of the bureaucratic expansion that accompanied the rise of the absolutist state.[33] In an age of military occupations and powerful administrative states, the practical dimensions of this project were obvious to Friedrich and his interlocutors.

A year before his essay on dictatorship appeared in *Public Policy*, Watkins published a close case study of Article 48 of the Weimar constitution and its place in the downfall of the republic.[34] Yet his programmatic essay on constitutional dictatorship was less a gloss on his case study than it was a coda to his earlier book-length essay *The State as a Concept of Political Science*, which he wrote as a graduate student under Friedrich's guidance. The purpose of this essay was to defend a "realistic" concept of the state. This was an intervention in the debates between Hobbesian or Rousseauian theorists of indivisible sovereignty, on the one hand, and the pluralist critique of the doctrine of sovereignty, on the other. Watkins shared with the pluralists a deep skepticism of the juristic view of the sovereign state as the "highest power," from which the powers and identity of all other associations were derived.[35] The state had, in practice, no monopoly on the use of force. But nor could the modern state be considered merely one association among many, for any realistic appraisal of its emergence showed that "the concentration of power is the fundamental phenomenon underlying the concept of the state."[36] The idea of the sovereign state was thus a "limiting concept" that was useful in characterizing the heightened concentration of power within a given territory—a process that had gripped Europe as the medieval system of rule disintegrated. Actually existing states tended to approximate more or less closely this ideal.

Armed with this gradualist notion of sovereignty, Watkins described constitutional dictatorship as itself an "extreme or limiting case." There was nothing special about how emergencies demanded the concentration of power, except insofar as they expedited the process and might ingrain its effects. No doubt a perfect constitutional dictatorship was impossible, Watkins averred, but perfect justice and absolute power were not things that could be had from a system of political rule in the first place. Accordingly, the "problem of constitutional dictatorship" was "very far from being . . . hopeless." Because "analogous problems are being solved every day in other fields of law, it is hard to believe that constitutional principles alone are indeed incapable of achieving flexibility in the face of emergency needs."[37]

In this section, I have tried to show that the literature on constitutional dictatorship had its own distinct targets and was integrated into a larger set of concerns in political science and constitutional law than has perhaps been appreciated. I think there is more to these texts than the credulous belief that Schmitt's problem with sovereignty and dictatorship can be solved easily. In particular, there is a concern with executive lawmaking in emergencies—what the theorists of constitutional dictatorship called *legislative dictatorship*—that puts them fundamentally at odds with Schmitt's way of posing the problem of dictatorship in the modern state. Rossiter and his colleagues were interested in the problem of concentrating powers—specifically legislative powers—by delegation, and their way of framing the problem encouraged them to move sharply away from the interlocking ideas of sovereignty and commission that were at the heart of Schmitt's account. In making this move, Friedrich, Watkins, and Rossiter were following the precedent of a number of other American writers of the period who were interested in issues of executive lawmaking, sovereignty, and the rule of law. In the next two sections, I try to bring out this crucial contrast between Schmitt and the American theorists.

2. Schmitt on Sovereign Dictatorship

We have already observed that, when viewed through a Schmittian lens, the midcentury theory of dictatorial crisis government contains a hole at its center. In none of the accounts of constitutional dictatorship is there any serious attempt to grapple with what Schmitt saw as the critical issue. This was the problem of sovereign dictatorship, an institution that took on world-historical importance in the French Revolution and that had continued to maintain a grip on political thought and practice from Napoleon to the Bolsheviks. To appreciate what the theory of constitutional dictatorship was supposed to achieve, we need a fuller understanding of Schmitt's key idea.

Schmitt's concept of sovereign dictatorship was composed of three distinct elements. The first was the idea of the dictator as a *commissar*, as an agent commissioned or mandated to undertake a very specific task. This, as I have said, involved the sovereign delegating powers to subordinates who act as their agents. The second concept was that of *popular sovereignty*. This is of course the idea that the people are the direct source of all constituted powers and therefore a "constitutive power" (in the terms of the Abbé Sieyès, who coined the concept, the *pouvoir constituant*), subject to no laws or constitutional restraints. The third element, which served as the hinge for the theory as a whole, was the notion of *dictatorship* itself, which, as Schmitt was eager to stress, had a juridical as well as a purely political meaning.

Dictatorship was not to be understood as merely lawless and despotic power. For its aim was to hold in suspension a norm whose authority dictatorial rule was designed to guarantee. Strictly speaking: "The justification for dictatorship consists in the fact that, although it ignores existing law, it does so in order to save it." As Schmitt explained, this made dictatorship a linchpin of the modern theory of the state. Exceptions to the norms of justice had to be made for the sake of making possible the implementation of law. Accordingly, there had to be both a highest authority that could determine when exceptions could be made—namely, the sovereign—and a mechanism for creating conditions in which the law can be implemented: the commission of a dictator with a brief to resolve the emergency and restore the rule of law. Hence, the pivotal role in the theory of the state played by dictatorship: the concept of dictatorship pointed toward the definition of sovereignty, as rooted in the exception, and also to the crucial distinction in jurisprudence between "the norms of justice and the implementation of law."[38]

It was Jean Bodin, writing in the sixteenth century, who began to bring the three elements of sovereign dictatorship together. A corollary of Bodin's seminal definition of sovereignty as "the absolute and perpetual power of a commonwealth" was that a clear distinction could be made between the sovereign and those given a mandate to carry out duties on its behalf. While those mandatees might be public officeholders given proprietorial rights over their office, Bodin focused his attention on commissars: those delegated by the sovereign to undertake specific tasks on his or her behalf.[39] The appointment of royal commissars was in fact one of the principal tools used to break down the medieval hierarchy of hereditary offices and consolidate power in the hands of the absolutist prince. In any case, the theoretical framework provided by the contrast between sovereign power and its commissars led Bodin to the conclusion that dictators—an institution with which he, along with all Renaissance humanists, was familiar from Roman sources—were not sovereigns but commissars. For, as the example of the Roman Republic strongly suggested, dictators, who in the usual case were military commanders, were commissioned by the highest constituted authorities to address specific crises and restore the rule of law. Here we have in clear view the relations between dictatorship and sovereignty and between dictatorship and commission. We can spot here in Bodin a distinction between sovereignty and government that, as Richard Tuck has recently emphasized, was to prove crucial to the theory of modern mass democracy once the notion of popular sovereignty took hold of the political imagination in the eighteenth century.[40]

Schmitt tells, it should be said, a somewhat similar story. If Bodin was the first to articulate a theory of commissarial dictatorship as an institution of the sovereign state, it was Hobbes who connected the idea of (what would later be called) popular sovereignty with dictatorship. In Hobbes's account of the covenant between persons in the state of nature that establishes the state: "Sovereignty emerges from a constitutive act of absolute power, made through the people." To escape the state of nature, the people agree to obey a sovereign who dictates for them what their opinion on matters of public interest will be. As Schmitt notes, this argument "calls to mind the system of Caesar and of a sovereign dictatorship based on absolute delegation."[41] Nevertheless, Hobbes's sovereign is not a sovereign dictator for he or she does not suspend the law in order to save it; he or she simply *makes* the law. What is needed for sovereign dictatorship, Schmitt insists, is a conception of popular sovereignty in which the people, as the source of all constituted authority, are conceived as distinct from how they are represented in civil institutions. In other words, sovereign dictatorship is possible when all the representational architecture is stripped out of the modern theory of popular sovereignty. This radicalizes the notion of the commissar, for now it is possible for a dictator to present himself or herself as "a commissar of the people"—but now of a people conceived as unmediated and unorganized, as a pure will that can give to itself any constitution it desires. To be a commissar of this constituent power is a quite different affair from being the commissar of the prince who claims divine right to supreme earthly power within a given territory. The unmediated and unformed character of the constituent power means that its authority to suspend the existing order can be appealed to not just during emergencies but whenever "the existing order is seen as an inhibition to the free exercise of the *pouvoir constituant*—so that new revolutions and a new appeal to the *pouvoir constituant* are always possible."[42]

We are now in a position to see how the theoretical elements just described work together to produce sovereign dictatorship. First, the sovereign is conceived not as a prince with a mandate from God but as the unrepresentable and inalienable constituent power or general will of the people. Second, the constituted powers of government, including the institution of dictatorship, are conceived as commissioned by the sovereign, by the constituent power. Third, a revolutionary situation arises in which a constituted power dissolves the current constitutional order in the name of the constituent power, the free exercise of which (it is claimed) is being inhibited by the existing order. This revolutionary power presents itself as a commissar of the people, of the constituent power. But even though it acts with what Schmitt calls a "minimum of constitution"—for it recognizes the constituent power of the people and aims to resolve the crisis—it does so *in the name of an order that does not yet exist* and that therefore cannot yet authorize this dictatorial rule. The dictator appeals to the constituent power, but only this dictator has the power to determine what its will is. In this situation, dictators who act only on the authority of the constituent power are sovereign. They are at once commissars (of the people) and sovereigns, insofar as they are the only judge of their authority.[43]

Schmitt seems to have thought that the possibility of sovereign dictatorship was inherent in the very institution of dictatorship. He finds expressions of this form of rule both in Caesarism and in Hobbes's theory of the state, and he shows in detail how state theory since the Renaissance crafted the various components of political philosophy and jurisprudence that together constitute the concept of sovereign dictatorship. Whatever its antecedents, Schmitt was unequivocal that the transformation of the idea of dictatorship into its modern, revolutionary guise was the work of French-speaking Europe in the eighteenth century. Gabriel Bonnot de Mably extended the Roman model of dictatorship to encompass the nullification of the function of all other magistrates and then defended the thesis that in revolutionary conditions representatives of the people must be given sweeping powers to control the executive. The key inspirations for the exercise of sovereign dictatorship were, however, Rousseau and Sieyès, for they made it possible to conceive of the people as a force apart from the operations of government (even if Sieyès insisted that the constituent power could be exercised only by a constituted or representative power). These ideas were then amply borne out by the actions of the National Convention and the Committee on Public Safety during the French Revolution. The National Convention was a sovereign dictator.[44]

3. From Sovereign Dictatorship to Legislative Emergency Powers

If sovereign dictatorship set the terms of Schmitt's inquiry, it is hardly present in the mid-twentieth-century accounts of constitutional dictatorship. This is not to say that Friedrich, Watkins, and Rossiter were not concerned about the possibility of a constitutional dictatorship degenerating into unconstitutional tyranny. On the contrary, although all three theorists were eager to enumerate the constitutional limitations and safeguards that could help check the exercise of emergency powers in times of crisis, they were quick to recognize that the fundamental problem in the theory of constitutional dictatorship was the evident lack of *any* purely legal guarantee that extraordinary powers would not be abused by political leadership. Existing constitutional provisions, they insisted, were inadequate to prevent the misuse of emergency powers, and the tendency of contemporary governments appeared to be that "under crisis conditions a continuous state of emergency arises."[45] "There can no longer be any question," Rossiter wrote, "that the constitutional democracies, faced with repeated emergencies and influenced by the examples of permanent authoritarian government all about them, are caught up in a pronounced, if lamentable trend toward more arbitrary, more powerful, and more 'efficient' government."[46]

Yet this sober realism about the tendency of crisis government to drift into a permanent state of emergency flatly refused to entertain Schmitt's account of the transformation of a commissarial into a sovereign dictatorship. For the American writers, there was simply no story to be told about how the standard Bodinian commissarial role of the dictator was radicalized by the ideology of popular sovereignty in the eighteenth century. We have already recorded the fact that Friedrich, Watkins, and Rossiter drew on the example of the Roman republic precisely in order to reject the assumption that dictators were commissars given a specific mandate by the sovereign. By handling martial rule and the state of siege in constitutionalist as opposed to commissarial terms, they left no place for Schmitt's story about popular sovereignty and Jacobin rule in the eighteenth century. Indeed, the distinction between using extraordinary means to maintain a constitution, a legal order, and using them to maintain the state was critical. For, as Friedrich wrote, "the word 'state' is itself a propaganda tool of the absolutist," one that hid "the fact that order for its own sake is being substituted for constitutional, legal order as the primary objective of the exceptional concentration of powers." In reality, these approaches were "quite distinct": "This distinction, therefore, is not one of formalities, such as might be suggested by the terms commissioned and non-commissioned (sovereign) dictatorship, but one of objectives, properly designated by the terms constitutional and unconstitutional (unrestrained) dictatorship."[47] Here, Friedrich was quite explicitly repudiating Schmitt's contrast and replacing sovereign dictatorship with "unrestrained" dictatorship as the central theoretical challenge to be faced in the modern theory of dictatorship.

To this the response may be, So much the worse for the theory of constitutional dictatorship. It had been one of the main points of Schmitt's identification of sovereignty with the decision on the exception that the constitutionalist attempt to repress the concept of sovereignty in public law was bound to fail. Friedrich's complaint that the idea of the state was a propaganda tool of the absolutist hardly met this challenge. Nevertheless, we should take seriously the plain fact that the theorists of constitutional dictatorship found Schmitt's palette of concepts unappealing given the challenges facing constitutional order as they saw them in the 1930s and 1940s. What seems evident from the writings of Friedrich and the others is that, with its linking of sovereign and mandatee, the notion of commission was considered inadequate to the task of making sense of the legislative aspects of emergency powers.

The fact that emergency government might need to make law, whether by simply invoking executive prerogative in order to rule by decree or by exercising lawmaking powers delegated to the executive by the legislature, transformed the problem of dictatorship for the American theorists. Even on Schmitt's own terms, it made no sense to characterize dictators *qua* commissars as *legislators*. The function of dictators in Schmitt's analysis was to provide the means to *implement* law, not make it: their tasks were always concrete and defined by a very specific remit to intervene in the causal order of society. This was true even when the remit was given by the protean constituent power. Of course, as we have observed, a sovereign dictatorship will make a new order, but its job is not to make laws within an existing constitution. We might say that, whereas Schmitt's points of reference were the Committee of Public Safety and the Bolshevik dictatorship of the proletariat, the theorists of constitutional dictatorship took their bearings from the war governments of the Allied powers during the First World War and the Depression-era regimes in the United States and Great Britain modeled on those governments. These democratic regimes wielded effectively dictatorial power, yet they also made law. Notions of commission and sovereign here were less salient than were mechanisms for delegation of powers within the constitutional architecture, executive rule making, and administrative justice.

During the war, a series of acts of legislative delegation to the executive marked a watershed in the history of constitutional government. This was true even of France, which ostensibly had recourse to the long-standing constitutional emergency measure of the state of siege, initially created in the early 1790s, and further entrenched in constitutional law after 1848. Yet the state of siege declared by President Poincaré on August 2, 1914, was unprecedented, for it placed not a single city but, for the first time, the whole country under emergency rule, which lasted for the duration of the war. The executive assumed some, but not all, functions of the Parliament, while the Parliament itself allowed the cabinet to take the lead guiding legislation. In Britain, the war cabinet was given even stronger powers through the Defense of the Realm Act (DORA) of August 1914. DORA, in Rossiter's words, "delegated to government out-and-out legislative power." The king-in-council—the war cabinet—was given full power to make and enforce law as the situation required. This was, as the political scientist Lindsay Rogers stated, "a marked departure of Anglo-Saxon legal traditions." In short, Rossiter concluded, DORA "established a virtual state of siege, brought the entire scope of English life and liberty under the control of government, exalted the Cabinet, and deflated Parliament."[48] In the United States, similarly sweeping powers were granted to President Wilson by a series of congressional acts. The executive was empowered to rule by decree in order to face the demands of mass mobilization and total war.

By far the largest part of Rossiter's *Constitutional Dictatorship* was taken up with the discussion of legislative dictatorship in the First World War and the precedents it set for democratic crisis government during the 1930s and 1940s. Friedrich and, especially, Watkins also zeroed in on this issue in their studies of dictatorship. "Basically and ordinarily," wrote Friedrich in emphasizing the importance for constitutional theory of the wartime revolution in emergency government, "constitutional dictatorship applies to executive action. But under modern conditions where a complex industrial society is extensively shaped by correspondingly complex statutes, emergencies are likely to require adequate powers for the legislative change as well as administrative action. Most modern constitutions are silent on the subject."[49] It is striking and important that Friedrich underscored the need for complex or technical legislation. The issue here is not, as it might have been for Schmitt, whether the constituent power, acting through a dictatorship, can under emergency conditions begin legislating or constituting new powers as it sees fit. Rather, it is that new and highly targeted laws, focused on managing aspects of mobilization for total war, will be needed during emergencies and that the ordinary process of legislation—of parliamentary government—will simply be inadequate to the task. The question was then one of how the executive—the emergency government—was going to make law: this was a practical question of the exercise of the legislative capacity and the constitutional bounds placed on it, not a moment in which a governing committee would became a Jacobin political demiurge, as Schmitt imagined. Friedrich, Watkins, and Rossiter rejected the possibility that pure executive prerogative should provide the basis for such legislation. They did so partly because of the sheer lack of controls in such a mechanism but also because the complex nature of the legislation involved needed the considered cooperation of legislature and executive and the careful specification of aims and remits. In taking this view, they were not, I think, engaged in wishful thinking by imagining that a sovereign dictatorship could somehow be restrained by the pretense that jurisdictional boundaries still existed for the dictator. Instead, they were resolutely theorists working against the background of the legislative dictatorship of the First World War and, behind that, the rise of the administrative state, with its vast delegation of legislative powers to executive agencies. They were empirical theorists of a new kind of legislative capacity.

Frederick Watkins gave the most sophisticated theoretical account of this position. First, he pointed out that, although the "main problem" in the theory of constitutional dictatorship, as it had been discussed in modern political theory, was the need to secure "emergency action in the field of administration," the "conditions of modern life" were such that "emergency breakdown is also possible in the process of legislation." Parliaments and other representative bodies had to act on behalf of large and often extremely diverse constituencies. Decision making in such bodies was typically slow, subject to pervasive partisanship, and often inconclusive. At the same time, modern legislatures had to deal with "a mass of highly technical legislation" as a result of which they had to "adopt more elaborate and cumbersome methods than the direct assembly of a small urban community." Consequently: "Like all highly specialized procedures, the legislative methods of the modern nation state are relatively incapable of meeting the needs of unusual situations. The resulting dangers of emergency breakdown can be met only by providing alternative forms of emergency legislation. This is the problem of legislative dictatorship."[50]

It was obvious to Watkins that legislative dictatorship would have to be exercised by the executive. Only executive authorities were "always in a position for immediate action": "[S]ocial necessities require . . . that the complex administrative machinery of a modern state be kept constantly in motion." The only question was on what grounds the executive would exercise the power of legislative dictatorship. But this was the critical issue for constitutional theory because there were "serious forces of resistance" felt whenever the possibility was raised of extending emergency authority into "the realm of legislation." The source of these concerns was the resistance of constitutionalist political thought to the idea of including lawmaking powers within the prerogative of the executive. For the granting of this kind of power was seen as fueling the abuse of centralized authority: "Not even the need for effective emergency action has been able fully to overcome a reluctance so deeply rooted in the traditions of modern constitutional government."[51] Moreover, as Watkins was quick to admit, such "caution is based . . . on a good deal of genuinely painful experience." In France, Charles X's abuse of legislative emergency powers granted to him by the Charte of 1814 made liberals wary of including lawmaking powers within the executive prerogative. Still, during the nineteenth century, various ways of making legislative dictatorship part of the royal or executive prerogative were trialed. Either they were more carefully circumscribed than in the Charte, or, as was the case with Lincoln in the American Civil War, a convention arose whereby in emergencies the executive acted "illegally"—outside its constitutionally defined competence—and it was subsequently given retrospective legitimacy by an act of indemnity passed by the legislature. The problem with this kind of legislative "dictatorship by usurpation" was that it gave "the impression that extraordinary needs can only be satisfied by extralegal means." Not only did this erode the commitment to the rule of law. It also left the (necessary) exercise of emergency legislative dictatorship constrained by little more than "the mere accumulation of constitutional precedents, which must in the very nature of things be few a far between."[52]

Legislative dictatorship by prerogative was therefore off the table. The only remaining alternative, for Watkins, was the kind of legislative dictatorship that had been piloted as a tool of democratic crisis government during the First World War: dictatorship by delegation. The legislature would have to delegate specified elements of its lawmaking powers to the executive formally. This seemed to Watkins the form of legislative emergency power most compatible with constitutional government. For, although the emergency executive would be endowed with the ability to issue decrees having the force of law, the limits of these powers could be strictly defined in the enabling act, and those powers of legislation could be recalled by parliament at any time. In addition, enabling laws seemed to Watkins to provide a means for legislators paralyzed by the conflicting demands of constituents and special interests to empower the executive to provide leadership when it could not. Of course, delegated powers could be abused like any other, but they seemed the most amenable to control.

We need to record here that Watkins framed the problem of legislative dictatorship as one of delegation from popular assembly to executive bureaucracy. It is hard not to notice that this formula left no place for the idea of dictatorship as a commission from sovereign to mandatee. And it is true that, like Friedrich and Rossiter, Watkins did not think about the problem in this way. His framework was that of the delegation of legislative competences to executive authorities that, under extraordinary circumstances, were in a better position to realize the purposes of the legislature. The model here, it seems evident, was the discretion given executive agencies to regulate complex new public utilities. Agencies like the Interstate Commerce Commission and the Federal Trade Commission regulated trade and transportation services on the delegated authority of the US Congress. Watkins took a tour through the First World War and New Deal agencies that operated in the same fashion. The problems and tasks of the legislative dictatorship by delegation were similar to those of the administrative state. From this perspective, Schmitt's analytics of popular sovereignty radicalizing the notion of the dictatorial commissioner would have seemed a diversion from the real issue, one that was already well-known in the literature of administrative law.

Confirmation of this reading can be found in Watkins's concluding remarks on dictatorship by delegation. The interwar decades had seen the emergence of a powerful new doctrinal obstacle to the executive legislation: jurists in France and the United States had opposed legislative delegations to the executive on the ground of the Roman constitutional principle of *potestas delegata non potest delegari*—a person or body to whom a power had been delegated could not delegate that power in turn to another. The legislature had been delegated the power to make law by the American people; it could not therefore redelegate that power to the executive. This nondelegation doctrine had in fact played very little part in American constitutional law even when agencies like the Interstate Commerce Commission and the Federal Trade Commission had been established.[53] But this principle became the basis of the Supreme Court's decisions to strike down the National Industrial Recovery Act and other emergency New Deal enabling laws. As Watkins put it: "The continuing authority of an ancient Roman maxim could hardly have been expressed in a more uncompromising or in more dramatic form."[54] He worried that the drift toward eliminating legislative dictatorship by delegation would rob constitutional regimes of a powerful, if imperfect, tool for defending constitutional order. It was nonetheless an axiom of his analysis of constitutional dictatorship, as it was of the studies of Friedrich and Rossiter, that the theoretical challenges of dictatorship faced by modern democracies turned on these matters of delegation and executive legislation and that questions of popular sovereignty and the extraordinary commission of the dictator were much less central to the problems at hand.

4. The Idea of Constitutional Dictatorship in Context

If this is a plausible reconstruction of the theory of constitutional dictatorship, it may still be thought to be an aberrant vision of the problem of modern emergency government. In closing, then, I will try to demonstrate that these views were embedded in American political and legal thought of the period.

We can begin our account of the context of the theory of constitutional dictatorship with the concept of sovereignty. As I have said, Friedrich, Watkins, and Rossiter were visibly resistant to the kind of reasoning about the relations between sovereignty and commissionership that propelled Schmitt's theory of sovereign dictatorship. While they recognized that any adequate description of democratic or constitutional government would have to treat the will of the people as, in some sense, the highest authority for all law and government, they and their contemporaries sought to detach the determining power of the popular will, as an empirical fact about a political community, from the theory of the state sensu stricto. Their aim was, in other words, to bring the concept of sovereignty and the state fully into public law and thus to remove the contrast between sovereignty and government that seemed to open the door to radical, and totalitarian, visions of democratic rule.

In his *Concept of the State in Political Science*, Watkins took an unusual route to this position. I noted above that he treated the idea of sovereignty not as a representation of any actually existing state of affairs—as an actual force in the state—but as a "limiting concept" in political science. This trained the analysis of modern politics on the tendency of the modern state toward ever-greater concentrations of power. But this process of concentration could be empirically described, and the state, as but one of many important theoretical constructs in political science, was a useful generalization or placeholder for describing this process. By far the most popular path to stripping the concept of sovereignty of its invidious content, however, was to insist on its purely technical character as a term in public law and, thus, to insist that the juristic notion of sovereignty captured everything important that could be said about sovereign power. A whole series of publications in the 1920s took precisely this view. On the one hand, the defenders of the juristic concept of sovereignty tried to push back against the idea that what A. V. Dicey and James Bryce had called "practical" sovereignty, or the actual location of the preponderance of power in a political community, had any kind of juristic meaning, for this was only mere fact, sheer might, which could of course act in the world as it wished. On the other hand, they were not defenders of the pluralist theory of the state because they were committed to the idea that the state did indeed have a distinct legal personality that held the highest authority in a political community.

A flavor of this 1920s literature on sovereignty can be found in Westel W. Willoughby's writings on the state. Under the clear influence of German public lawyers such as Georg Jellinek, Willoughby depicted the general theory of public law as a kind of constitutional algebra, in which concepts like sovereignty were axioms from which particular legal truths could be deduced.[55] Sovereignty was nothing more and nothing less than "the name given to the supreme will of the state which finds expression in legally binding commands." It was "a faculty or quality of statehood" that connoted "legal omnipotence rather than physical power." Willoughby was emphatic on this last point. Sovereignty was an idea "purely of legal competence and jurisdiction": "No element of actual power (as distinguished from will), or of moral right, or of political expediency is involved."[56]

These arguments were developed further toward the end of the decade by the constitutional historian Charles McIlwain and the University of Pennsylvania law professor John Dickinson. Spotting an ambiguity in Bodin's famous definition of *sovereignty*, McIlwain contended that the meaning of *power* (*potestas*) in Bodin's definition was not sheer might or the unconstituted, extralegal power of the people but rather simply the juristic notion of the "highest authority." He laid out his view of sovereignty as follows:

> The upshot of this is that "sovereign power" as distinct from any other power is the highest *legal* power in a state, itself subject to no law. And this being so, the term "sovereign" has no proper application beyond the domain of law. It is a purely juristic term and it should convey a purely juristic idea. It has no proper meaning if carried beyond the sphere of law and into the sphere of mere fact. Sovereignty is authority, not might. The sovereign power is the highest legal authority qua legal not qua actual. In a state of mature development actual power and legal authority might be identical or nearly so, but they seldom are and for various reasons. But in any case the important thing to note is that the only really "sovereign" power is that made so by law.[57]

McIlwain drew the logical conclusions from this principle. Bryce's view that there were two kinds of sovereignty—the legal and the practical—had to be rejected. Insofar as the practical sovereign was that person or body of persons who could make his or her will prevail with or against the law—that person, that is to say, to whom obedience was actually paid—then this was just the operation of sheer power, for which the notion of authority was superfluous. Of course the sovereign—the highest legal power—was often controlled by these purely political forces, but that did not stop it from being the legal authority that was itself subject to no other positive laws. Indeed, McIlwain believed that the thoroughly juridical character of sovereignty was its most beneficial feature because it meant that a properly constituted authority could, as a legal fiction, flexibly adapt to shifts in the actual balance of political forces in a state. This had happened in England, and Great Britain generally, in its transition from a monarchy to a parliamentary democracy: in some suitably indeterminate sense, "the king" (more accurately, "the king-in-Parliament") remained sovereign throughout this process. Once these beneficent features of sovereignty *qua* legal power were properly understood, McIlwain continued, then the objections of the pluralists to claims about the supremacy of the state were seen to rest on an exaggerated view of what sovereign power really was. The pluralists had "made too many concessions to their opponents" and "gone too far in admitting the claim of the Austinian sovereign to *Allmacht*, and in consequence [had] been compelled, in order to refute it, to deny *in toto* the possibility of any sovereignty whatsoever."[58]

Given the centrality of the function of the commissar in Schmitt's reconstruction of Bodin's theory of sovereignty and government, it is striking that McIlwain returned to Bodin with very different purposes in mind. McIlwain's Bodin blocked the path to a sharp split between sovereignty and government and in so doing prevented the identification of the general will of the people with the state that underpinned Schmitt's account of the sovereign dictator. "Bodin's sovereignty," wrote McIlwain, "is the sovereignty of a legally constituted organ, an organ created theoretically even if not historically by the whole state; but not identical with the whole state as Rousseau would have it."[59] As Dickinson saw it, Bodin's definition of sovereignty was in fact a solution to practical challenges of government as these had emerged from the fragmented medieval political order. The Bodinian sovereign was necessary for the delimitation of government competences. "The *legal* doctrine of sovereignty can therefore be summed up as fundamentally nothing but the demand for the unified organization of authority within the community in order to provide the necessary basis for a system of legal order." Sovereignty was "the answer to medieval conditions and medieval difficulties." Its purpose was to rationalize the overlapping jurisdictions and tangle of legal rules that dominated feudal Europe by providing "a single definite organ or organization within each territorial community." This organ would have "final authority to define and pronounce the law" within the territory and "likewise final authority to adjust rivalries and allot jurisdictions among all minor law-enforcement agencies." Such a function was "the core of Bodin's conception of sovereignty."[60]

It will be apparent that this conception of sovereignty, and its relations with constituted powers of government, is quite distant from Schmitt's notion—drawn from his own reading of Bodin—of a sharp distinction between the two. The juristic concept of sovereignty stressed its value as a means of settling questions of jurisdiction among the constituted orders of government. But it gave much less attention to the idea of sovereignty as a power that stands ready always to create or amend a constitution. The writers on this topic of the interwar years were not primarily interested in emphasizing the benefits of democratic or popular sovereignty and effective commissarial government. Looking at the Russia of 1917 and the Germany of 1933, they noted instead the revolutionary and potentially destructive tendencies of the constituent power.[61]

In a remarkable essay of 1930, the historian of Roman law Max Radin stated directly: "[T]he capital distinction between the sovereign and the government on which a great many publicists built so much does not seem to be of great value."[62] His reason for this view was that in a constitutional regime such as that of the United States the sovereign power to issue commands that overrode all other commands—constitutional commands as opposed to statutory ones—had been endlessly split up. Full popular sovereignty was ever present only in revolutionary conditions, when the people threw off one order or gave themselves a new one. But the amending power provided for in the US Constitution—in no less than three forms—was a much thinner version of popular sovereignty than this. Radin pointed out that, if the use of the amending power was an exercise of sovereignty, then "the sovereign of the United States is a series of persons beginning with those who constitute a two-thirds majority of Congress when the amendment is voted and ending with the majority of the legislature of the thirty-sixth state which ratified the amendment." Even if all the relevant people could be brought together in one assembly, "they would not be sovereign," which would occur only when "they acted successively in the sequence indicated and no other." In the United States, "the original [i.e., revolutionary] sovereign created, by the amending clause of the Constitution, a lesser sovereign almost coextensive with itself, and in the governmental organization of each state of the federal government still smaller sovereigns with considerably less extensive powers." In America, sovereignty "exhausts itself by the creation of minor or lesser sovereigns," with the result that sovereignty and government shade imperceptibly into one another.[63] For Radin, the democratic sovereign was not so much a sleeping power ready to be awakened at moments of constitutional amendment as a sputtering mechanism for issuing commands that had the power of overriding certain other commands. The only time full sovereignty was exercised was when government itself was being completely overthrown—which meant that there was no sense in conceiving of democratic sovereignty and commissioned government of whatever form working in parallel with one another.

I have dwelt on these claims about sovereignty and government in the interwar American literature in order to provide an explanation of why theorists like Friedrich, Watkins, and Rossiter were so unmoved by Schmitt's problem of sovereign dictatorship. I hope to have shown that there was ample motivation for such a view, even if this does prejudge the issue of whether Schmitt had the better of the argument. To round out this account of the context of the theory of constitutional dictatorship, it will suffice to observe that, for many of the theorists I have described, the major problem to be faced in public law and democratic theory was precisely the issue on which the theorists of constitutional dictatorship focused, namely, the problem of executive legislation. We have already seen that all three of these theorists trained their attention on the need for emergency legislation and examined the model of parliaments delegating powers to legislatures during the First World War and the Great Depression. If the undeniable need for temporary legislative dictatorship was the problem, then administrative law and the challenges it posed for constitutional government provided resources for the solution. Revealingly, many of those who wrote on dictatorship also addressed the problem of rule by executive ordinance and emergency decree. Dickinson, Radin, and Friedrich all wrote on the topic.[64] Much of Rossiter's and Watkins's studies of dictatorship also turned on this matter.

There was something close to unanimity among this group that the time had come to treat the regulations issued by administrative agencies as rules that should be treated by courts as possessing the force of statute or judicial decision. Or at least this should be so if the administrative decisions had been arrived at on the basis of procedures of adjudication appropriate to the tribunal or body given the power to regulate a given area of social or economic life. Radin and Dickinson, in particular, aimed to dispel the "fear of bureaucracy."[65] The active constitutional state that was needed in the modern world would simply have to rely more and more on administrative agencies in order to carry out its extended range of functions. Common law courts had a role in controlling this new leviathan, but their task was not to undermine it by subjecting it to doctrines that were destructive of administrative government. In his important textbook on this subject, *Administrative Justice and the Supremacy of Law*, published in 1927, Dickinson stated that the crux of the problem of administrative justice was understanding how legal rules might limit the discretion of administrative decision.[66] In a series of articles, he had shown that neither legal realism nor a tightly logical jurisprudence could cope with the overriding need to balance fact and legal judgment in administrative or executive ordinances.[67] He developed a pragmatic but normatively stringent theory of legal judgment in response and argued that this model could be extended across the whole range of judgments having the force of law in modern government, including the judgments of common law judges themselves. During the early years of the New Deal, he had an opportunity to put these views into practice as a senior figure in the Department of Commerce and the Justice Department.[68]

These contextual remarks are intended to provide evidence for my contention that the American theory of constitutional dictatorship was not a curio in the history of American legal and political thought. On the contrary, it fit well-established patterns of argument about executive discretion within the administrative state. These foundations for the constitutional theory of dictatorship were not naive instances of a pure, starry-eyed liberal legalism. They were principles born of hands-on experience with the complex structure of the democratic administrative state and with the limits of any clean account of sovereignty in explaining its operation. To be sure, uncabined sovereign dictatorship is not unknown in the modern world: the Committee on Public Safety is a case in point; so too, perhaps, is the Bolshevik regime in Russia. But these are instances of already-crumbling states succumbing yet further to what was, in effect, anarchy. It is unclear how such cases did or do speak to the experience of the American constitutional state. It is of course always wise to be on one's guard against the arrival of tyranny. But tyrannophobia, with the uncontrolled fear it brings, has its costs, too. The theorists of constitutional dictatorship were able to keep that fear in check and, thus, to offer a sober account of executive and legislative emergency powers. Their example is worth bearing in mind as we face the constitutional crises of our own time.

Notes

1. See, e.g., Eric A. Posner and Adrian Vermeule, *The Executive Unbound: After the Madisonian Republic* (Oxford: Oxford University Press, 2010), 4. See also the references in n. 3 below.

2. Carl Schmitt, *Political Theology: Four Chapters on the Concept of Sovereignty*, trans. George Schwab (Chicago: University of Chicago Press, 2005), 21.

3. John Ferejohn and Pasquale Pasquino, "Law of Exception: A Typology of Emergency Powers," *International Journal of Constitutional Law* 2 (2004): 210–39; Bruce Ackerman, "The Emergency Constitution," *Yale Law Journal* 113 (2004): 1029–91, and *Before the Next Attack: Preserving Civil Liberties in an Age of Terrorism* (New Haven, CT: Yale University Press, 2006); Oren Gross and Fionnuala Ní Aoláin, *Law in Times of Crisis: Emergency Powers in Theory and Practice* (Cambridge: Cambridge University Press, 2006); Richard A. Posner, *Not a Suicide Pact: The Constitution in a Time of National Emergency* (New York: Oxford University Press, 2006); Clement Fatovic, *Outside the Law: Emergency and Executive Power* (Baltimore: Johns Hopkins University Press, 2009).

4. David Dyzenhaus, *The Constitution of Law: Legality in a Time of Emergency* (Cambridge: Cambridge University Press, 2006).

5. Clement Fatovic, "The Political Theology of Prerogative: The Jurisprudential Miracle in Liberal Constitutional Thought," *Perspectives on Politics* 6 (2008): 487–501, "Settled Law in Unsettling Times: A Lockean View of the War on Terror," *The Good Society* 18 (2009): 14–19, and *Outside the Law*; Nomi Claire Lazar, *States of Emergency in Liberal Democracies (Cambridge: Cambridge University Press, 2009).*

6. See Carl Schmitt, *Dictatorship: From the Origin of the Modern Concept of Sovereignty to Proletarian Class Struggle*, trans. Michael Hoelz and Graham Ward (Cambridge: Polity, 2014). The major difference between the two editions was the inclusion in the second edition of a long appendix on Article 48 in the Weimer constitution.

7. I realize that *North American* is in many ways an infelicitous term for a group that includes an émigré like Carl Friedrich. But alternative formulations would be cumbersome, and I trust that the limits of my use of this shorthand to refer to the theorists of constitutional dictatorship will be clear.

8. As we shall see below, this is exactly the point made in Agamben's *State of Exception*.

9. A charge made first by Schmitt himself. See Schmitt, *Political Theology*, 21–26.

10. For the clearest statement of this overall line of development, see Schmitt, *Dictatorship*, xxxvii–xlv.

11. Max Radin, "The Intermittent Sovereign," *Yale Law Journal* 39 (1930): 514–31.

12. C. H. McIlwain, "Sovereignty Again," *Economica* 18 (1926): 253–68; John Dickinson, "A Working Theory of Sovereignty, I," *Political Science Quarterly* 42 (1927): 524–48, and "A Working Theory of Sovereignty, II," *Political Science Quarterly* 43 (1928): 32–63.

13. Clinton Rossiter, *Constitutional Dictatorship: Crisis Government in the Modern Democracies* (Princeton, NJ: Princeton University Press, 1948).

14. The most thorough recent survey is Gross and Ní Aoláin, *Law in Times of Crisis*.

15. Giorgio Agamben, *State of Exception*, trans. Kevin Attell (Chicago: University of Chicago Press, 2005); Frederick Mundell Watkins, "The Problem of Constitutional Dictatorship," in *Public Policy: A Yearbook of the Graduate School of Public Administration, Harvard University*, ed. Edward S. Mason and Carl J. Friedrich (Cambridge, MA: Harvard University Press, 1940), 324–79; Carl J. Friedrich, *Constitutional Government and Democracy: Theory and Practice in Europe and America* (Boston: Little, Brown, 1941).

16. See the references to Friedrich, Watkins, and Rossiter in Gross and Ní Aoláin, *Law in Times of Crisis*.

17. Rossiter, *Constitutional Dictatorship*, vii.

18. For the importance of Friedrich as a mentor to Watkins—despite marked differences in their methodological approach to political science—see Frederick Mundell Watkins, *The State as a Concept of Political Science* (New York: Harper & Bros., 1934), v and *passim*. Friedrich cites Watkins's essay in Friedrich, *Constitutional Government and Democracy*, 627, 629.

19. Watkins, "The Problem of Constitutional Dictatorship," 324.

20. Friedrich, *Constitutional Government and Democracy*, 236.

21. Rossiter, *Constitutional Dictatorship*, 3.

22. Friedrich, *Constitutional Government and Democracy*, 236–38.

23. Watkins, "The Problem of Constitutional Dictatorship," 342.

24. Watkins, "The Problem of Constitutional Dictatorship," 338–42.

25. Tellingly, Schmitt was dismissive of dictatorship as a viable model of specifically constitutional rule in the Roman republic. He claimed that the earliest dictators of the republic, in whom Friedrich and his colleagues found a paradigm of constitutional dictatorship, were "just commanders in chief in the event of war" and that this version of dictatorship was outmoded by the second century BCE. Schmitt, *Dictatorship*, 230–31 n. 2.

26. Friedrich, *Constitutional Government and Democracy*, 238–39.

27. Clinton L. Rossiter, "Constitutional Dictatorship in the Atomic Age," *Review of Politics* 11 (1949): 395–418, and "What of Congress in Atomic War?," *Western Political Quarterly* 3 (1950): 602–6.

28. Clinton L. Rossiter, "The Constitutional Significance of the Executive Office of the President," *American Political Science Review* 43 (1949): 1206–17, "The President and Labor Disputes," *Journal of Politics* 11 (1949): 93–120, "War, Depression, and the Presidency, 1933–1950," *Social Research* 17 (1950): 417–40, "The Impact of Mobilization on the Constitutional System," *Proceedings of the Academy of Political Science* 24 (1951): 61–69, and *The Supreme Court and the Commander in Chief* (Ithaca, NY: Cornell University Press, 1951).

29. Carl J. Friedrich, "Military Government as a Step toward Self-Rule," *Public Opinion Quarterly* 7 (1943): 527–41, and "Military Government and Dictatorship," *Annals of the American Academy of Political and Social Science* 267 (1950): 1–7.

30. Carl J. Friedrich and Douglas G. Haring, "Military Government for Japan," *Far Eastern Survey* 14 (1945): 37–40; Carl J. Friedrich et al., *American Experiences in Military Government in World War II* (New York: Rinehart, 1948); Carl J. Friedrich, "The Peace Settlement with Germany—Political and Military," *Annals of the American Academy of Political and Social Science* 257 (1948): 119–28, "The Peace Settlement with Germany—Economic and Social," *Annals of the American Academy of Political and Social Science* 257 (1948): 129–41, "Rebuilding the German Constitution, I," *American Political Science Review* 43 (1949): 461–82, and "Rebuilding the German Constitution, II," *American Political Science Review* 43 (1949):704–20.

31. See Ernst Fraenkel, *Military Occupation and the Rule of Law* (New York: Oxford University Press, 1944).

32. Carl J. Friedrich, *Constitutional Reason of State: The Survival of the Constitutional Order* (Providence, RI: Brown University Press, 1957).

33. Friedrich, *Constitutional Government and Democracy*, 19–23.

34. Frederick Mundell Watkins, *The Failure of Constitutional Emergency Powers under the German Republic* (Cambridge, MA: Harvard University Press, 1939).

35. Watkins, *The State as a Concept of Political Science*, 4.

36. Watkins, *The State as a Concept of Political Science*, 44.

37. Watkins, "The Problem of Constitutional Dictatorship," 330, 331.

38. Schmitt, *Dictatorship*, xliii, xlii, 9–10.

39. Schmitt, *Dictatorship*, 20–22, 25–32.

40. Richard Tuck, *The Sleeping Sovereign: The Invention of Modern Democracy* (Cambridge: Cambridge University Press, 2015).

41. Schmitt, *Dictatorship*, 18.
42. Schmitt, *Dictatorship*, 126.
43. Schmitt, *Dictatorship*, 127.
44. Schmitt, *Dictatorship*, 93–111, 121–31.
45. Friedrich, *Constitutional Government and Democracy*, 249.
46. Rossiter, *Constitutional Dictatorship*, 313.
47. Friedrich, *Constitutional Government and Democracy*, 239.
48. Rossiter, *Constitutional Dictatorship*, 153 (Rogers quote), 154.
49. Friedrich, *Constitutional Government and Democracy*, 241.
50. Watkins, "The Problem of Constitutional Dictatorship," 358.
51. Watkins, "The Problem of Constitutional Dictatorship," 360–61.
52. Watkins, "The Problem of Constitutional Dictatorship," 367.
53. Andrew J. Ziaja, "Hot Oil and Hot Air: The Development of the Nondelegation Doctrine through the New Deal, a History, 1813–1944," *Hastings Constitutional Law Quarterly* 35 (2007): 921–64.
54. Watkins, "The Problem of Constitutional Dictatorship," 378.
55. Westel W. Willoughby, *The Fundamental Concepts of Public Law* (New York: Macmillan, 1924), 12–13.
56. Westel W. Willoughby, "The Juristic Conception of the State," *American Political Science Review* 12, no. 2 (1918):192–208, 196–97, 194. See also Robert T. Crane, "The Juristic Conception of the State: Discussion," *American Political Science Review* 12 (1918): 209–14; and Westel W. Willoughby, "The Juristic Theories of Krabbe," *American Political Science Review* 20 (1926): 509–23.
57. McIlwain, "Sovereignty Again," 256.
58. McIlwain, "Sovereignty Again," 257–60.
59. McIlwain, "Sovereignty Again," 263.
60. Dickinson, "Working Theory of Sovereignty, I," 527–28.
61. Friedrich, *Constitutional Government and Democracy*, 131–53.
62. Radin, "Intermittent Sovereign," 525–26. On Radin's general theory of law and his professional career, see Max Radin, "Max Radin," in *My Philosophy of Law—Credos of Sixteen American Scholars* (Littleton, CO: F. B. Rothman, 1987), 287–306; William O. Douglas, "Max Radin," *California Law Review* 36 (1948): 163–68; and A. M. Kidd, "Max Radin," *California Law Review* 38 (1950): 795–98.
63. Radin, "Intermittent Sovereign," 522–23, 525.
64. The relevant writings of Dickinson and Radin will be cited below. See also James Hart, "The Emergency Ordinance: A Note on Executive Power," *Columbia Law Review* 23 (1923): 528–35; Maurice S. Culp, "Executive Power in Emergencies," *Michigan Law Review* 31 (1933): 1066–96; and Friedrich, *Constitutional Government and Democracy*, 90–91.
65. Max Radin, "The Courts and Administrative Agencies," *California Law Review* 23 (1935): 469–81; John Dickinson, "Administrative Law and the Fear of Bureaucracy, I," *American Bar Association Journal* 14 (1928): 513–16, and "Administrative Law and the Fear of Bureaucracy, II," *American Bar Association Journal* 14 (1928): 597–602.
66. John Dickinson, *Administrative Justice and the Supremacy of Law in the United States* (Cambridge, MA: Harvard University Press, 1927). For

background on Dickinson—an unwarrantedly neglected figure in the history of American political thought—see Dickinson's eponymous essay in *My Philosophy of Law*, 91–106; and George L. Haskins, "John Dickinson: 1894–1952," *University of Pennsylvania Law Review* 101 (1952): 1–25.

67. John Dickinson, "Legal Rules: Their Function in the Process of Decision," *University of Pennsylvania Law Review and American Law Register* 79 (1931): 833–68, "Legal Rules: Their Application and Elaboration," *University of Pennsylvania Law Review and American Law Register* 79 (1931): 1052–96, and "The Problem of the Unprovided Case," *University of Pennsylvania Law Review and American Law Register* 81 (1932): 115–29.

68. John Dickinson, "The Major Issues Presented by the Industrial Recovery Act," *Columbia Law Review* 33 (1933): 1095–1102, "Understanding and Misunderstanding the Recovery Program," *Annals of the American Academy of Political and Social Science* 172 (1934): 1–7, "Political Aspects of the New Deal," *American Political Science Review* 28 (1934): 197–209, "The Constitution and Progress," *Annals of the American Academy of Political and Social Science* 181 (1935): 11–18, *Hold Fast the Middle Way: An Outline of Economic Challenges and Alternatives* (Boston: Little, Brown, 1935), and "Problems of Recovery," *Journal of the American Statistical Association* 30 (1935): 155–58.

Part Three

Broadening the Exception

10

Frederick Douglass and Constitutional Emergency: An Homage to the Political Creativity of Abolitionist Activism

Mariah Zeisberg

What possibilities does the idea or experience of an emergency create politically? What identities, strategies, and resources do emergencies foster or suppress on the part of the state? And how do actors use the concept or event of emergency in service of their political goals? I am especially interested in these questions in the context of the antebellum struggle to transform the Constitution in the face of slavery.

For many, the idea of emergency suggests the exposure of roots, origins, political foundations. Giorgio Agamben has argued that the exceptional revealed in an emergency is an ordinary feature of life in modernity.[1] Others see in emergency a possible deepening of the resources of legal, deliberative, or consensus-seeking practices, asserting the primacy of those materials for ordinary times as well.[2] Bonnie Honig calls for reframing emergencies not as known political experiences calling for enhanced executive power but rather as moments in which an essential "paradox of politics" becomes visible.[3] And Carl Schmitt's idea of the "state of exception" suggests that all of politics—the very definition of politics—comes down not to a cultural code, a mobilization of popular power, a discursive practice, or a moral horizon but to a moment, exposed in emergency, when the sovereign's decision on the enemy creates a collective existential dimension for experiences of power.[4] From one viewpoint, if we want to explore emergency in the context of antislavery agitation, there could be no more promising starting point than Schmitt's understanding of politics itself as existential self-definition in a field of violence and of emergency as the revelation of this truth.

I myself doubt that any one window can expose the root of political structure. But moments of emergency may call on actors to reorient, reconceive, and rearrange structures of political authority, identity, and belonging, and these moments can tell us something about how an experience of crisis can shift actors' self-understandings, aims, and strategic relations. Frederick Douglass experienced emergency as an event in the Fugitive Slave Act of 1850. By exploring his abolitionism in 1851—an emergency moment within an activist community—from within a framework set by Carl Schmitt, on the one side, and a consent-based form of constitutional legalism, on the other, I hope to demonstrate how, for Douglass, the experience of emergency was linked to a profoundly creative form of constitutional activism.

Understanding Douglass's activism, in turn, reveals Schmitt to be, not a neutral expositor about the meaning of emergency, but instead a political contender—a theoretician with stakes, wooing us with a specific vision of what emergency can do. Schmitt argues that emergency entails a return to a sovereign actor behind the law who can suspend the law across the board. This is a reading of emergency likely drawn from Article 48 in the Weimar constitution, which allowed for legal suspensions by the executive power. Emergency, for Schmitt, entails a moment when political allies are challenged to define themselves as a fighting entity in combat with enemies. It means executive empowerment over and against the legislature. It means the suspension of legal categories as relevant restrictions on political life. Ultimately for Schmitt, emergency reveals that the moral content of constitutional categories (due process, equal protection, free speech) and the moral content of state policies are subject to abandonment when the survival of a polity is at stake. Accordingly, many have noticed how emergency functions opportunistically for him. It creates opportunities for sovereign leaders to set the terms of alliance and the terms of combat, which for Schmitt are the constitutive terms of political life.

Where Schmitt's project entailed executive empowerment, Douglass's entailed mobilizing a public toward a moral achievement. The first implicit argument of this chapter is that to use Schmitt's analytic categories is to further his political project, a project that I will show is very different from that of Frederick Douglass. A second aim of this chapter is to use the analytic leverage of Schmitt's perspective to demonstrate the depth and complexity of Douglass's activism. Some of their apparent similarities as well as their profound divergences allow Schmitt's theory of emergency to function as a backdrop against which the creativity of Douglass's constitutional approach can be brought into sharper focus.

To make this case, I will explore Douglass in relation to figures beyond Schmitt, most especially Lysander Spooner. Spooner's consent-based constitutional legalism gave Douglass the resources to articulate in 1851 a transformed understanding of the role of the Constitution in antislavery politics. In a moment of emergency, Spooner and Douglass together created a brilliant constitutional reworking whose principled terms could not have been further from those of Schmitt. Looking at their work together underscores both the radicalism and the conventionalism of antebellum activism that centered on resisting harm to black lives. Douglass and the abolitionists allied with him worked to reclaim the Constitution and its liberties rather than simply reject the document (the abolitionist William Lloyd Garrison publicly burned it) or suspend it (as Schmitt would do and as, arguably, the Emancipation Proclamation did). For Douglass and Spooner, emergency provoked creative constitutional adaptations rather than either suspension or destruction.

But Douglass and Spooner did not work in lockstep. And, where Douglass parted ways with Spooner, he did so on terms that again challenge Schmitt's conceptualization of the imperatives of emergency. It turns out that Schmitt's theory is not analytically robust enough to help us understand this moment in American political life, but, interestingly enough, his very lack of traction here actually highlights certain profound aspects of Douglass's constitutional project that otherwise remain obscured. Douglass's legacy calls on theorists to develop new categories of constitutional meaning and practice, and Schmitt's theory of emergency helps me make that case.

Antebellum Emergencies

What were the emergencies of life before the Civil War for abolitionist activists? Of course, this question can be answered very differently depending on how we approach the concept of emergency itself. The brutality that enslaved people and that free black people faced in this country during Douglass's lifetime was certainly an emergency in the sense that their situation "pose[d] an immediate risk to health, life, property, or environment" and required immediate action to save lives.[5] From the point of view of black people, the Constitution itself can be argued as an emergency: a governing blueprint that, both in its ratification and in its sustenance for slavery over time, consolidated structures that constituted a clear threat to the well-being of black lives. This is a historical point. Edmund Morgan has argued that the ideology, practice, and success of free citizenship for whites was ideologically, materially, politically, and economically linked to the rewards that whites accrued from enslaving others.[6] For Morgan, practices of racial slavery and the development of free white citizenship are endogenously linked. Research on racial capitalism and the role of slavery in the consolidation of early capitalist structures makes this point emphatically.[7] If *emergency* refers simply to a profound and gathering threat to human life, the very ratification of the Constitution would count as an emergency moment for black lives.

But the fact that the Constitution was a structure meant to last challenges the usefulness of treating that text as an emergency, which many people consider involves quick events. Also, insofar as sovereignty itself was identified with white supremacy, whatever challenge the Constitution posed to black lives was not a challenge to sovereignty but rather a consolidation of it. Agamben's categories are less temporally wedded and give traction here: in the antebellum United States, it is easy to understand both free and enslaved black people as living a state of exception in an otherwise ordinary, normative white state.

Beyond that conceptual point, there is also a very prosaic way of reading the 1840s and 1850s, specifically, as crisis days for the nation and for the Constitution itself. In these decades, there were just too many terrifying events. There was the Mexican War (1846–48) and the attendant expansion of slavery through military conquest. There was the Fugitive Slave Act, whose significance in creating a sense of dangerous urgency cannot be overstated. The amendment of the Kentucky Constitution of 1850 to guarantee a right of property in slaves (specifying that that right was "before and higher than any constitutional sanction")[8] and the Kansas-Nebraska Act (1854) signaled the ultimate failure of the Wilmot Proviso and the Compromise of 1850, which had been the foundation of elite hopes that the problem of slavery could be managed through constitutional means. Proslavery imperialism was on the rise in the 1850s, as were filibustering excursions by proslavery ex-military men.[9] Events like John Brown's Pottawatomie massacre (1856); the rise of spectacle lynching in the south; active defiance of the Fugitive Slave Act by some states and local governments; and the trials of abolitionists for treason heightened the sense of drama and crisis.[10] In the words of Matthew Karp: "In the 1850s the future of American slavery seemed bright."[11]

For abolitionists who were sensitive to politics abroad—and Douglass certainly was—there were also the European Revolutions of 1848, which he used at times as frames for understanding domestic upheaval.[12]

Within abolitionist activist circles, the 1840s and 1850s were also momentous. In 1837, Elijah Lovejoy was murdered by a proslavery mob. The year 1840 brought a dramatic schism between the Garrisonian American Anti-Slavery Society (AASS) and the Tappan-led American and Foreign Anti-Slavery Society (AFASS). This schism was creative in the sense that it proliferated the organizational resources available to antislavery activists, but it also consumed vast amounts of emotional, intellectual, and financial resources among abolitionists as they fought over aims, strategy, personal rivalries, moral failings, and everything in between. Also at this time, the formation of the Friends of Universal Reform and the Liberty Party (1840) further fractured abolitionist circles.

But the truly pitched emergency moment for abolitionism, the moment that arguably did the very most to transform activist identities, strategies, and notions of possibility, was the Fugitive Slave Act. Passed by bipartisan majorities in both houses, the act made officials who did not arrest alleged escapees personally liable for a fine of $1,000 and even more if an alleged fugitive managed to escape after detention. Marshals were required to arrest suspected escapees on no more than the allegations of a claimant, and core due process rights for accused fugitives were suspended. The act also expanded federal state capacity by creating the office of "commissioner," the holder of which exercised judicial authority and was paid $10.00 if an alleged fugitive was handed over to the claimant but only $5.00 if, after processing, the fugitive was allowed to go free. Those who interfered with the detention and rendition of alleged escapees were also subject to fines and imprisonment.

The Fugitive Slave Act radically transformed all antislavery activist identities. Enslaved and self-liberated people became more insecure than they ever had been. Free black people, already vulnerable to kidnapping, were rendered absolutely unsafe. White abolitionists saw the protection that their white identities could provide diminish as their resistance became criminalized. And the very fact that the act—this life-altering piece of legislation, this violation of the most basic elements of procedural justice—was one element of what had been required in the 1850 Compromise to hold the Union together demonstrated to many "the inability of American legal and political institutions to come to grips with slavery short of civil war."[13] Activism premised on the hopes of incremental progress toward emancipation was fundamentally called into question.[14] The act also revealed that the urgent need radical abolitionists articulated—emancipation *now*, which had always seemed unlikely—in fact lay completely outside any policy pathway conceivably available to any of the three major branches of government. This was an emergency for antislavery activism. It produced, for them, a profound organizational and intellectual creativity.

One result of these crisis days was, in the figure of Frederick Douglass, a productive, reworked, and pragmatic form of constitutional activism. Douglass's constitutionalism was reworked in that he chose to eschew traditional abolitionist thought about the Constitution as a proslavery document and instead advanced a radical project of rereading. His activism was productive in that his new theories advocated political action through representative institutions, which he and his allies used to great effect. And it was pragmatic in that it was centered, not in a web of abstract principle, but rather in a self-consciously transformative goal of shouting out the moral urgency of protecting black lives. The constitutionalism that Douglass and Spooner produced in this emergency moment was disruptive, but, contra Schmitt, its disruption was not centered on the executive branch. It forswore emergency powers. It intensified, rather than abandoned, its emphasis on the moral content of constitutional categories. And, rather than focusing on a single decisive actor or sovereign as a warrant of security, its ideological parameters can best be understood in terms of cooperation between institutions, responsiveness to moral imperatives, and intensely focused, coordinated goal-seeking behavior. This new constitutionalism helped create political conditions that supported Lincoln's rise. In none of these guises can Douglass's constitutional activism be treated in Schmittian terms without distortion or collapse.

Constitutional Strategies

Rooted in Quaker pacifism, Garrisonian perfectionism, and the white nationalism of the American Colonization Society, early white abolitionist activism's internal debates centered on the role of the church in slavery and then, over time, on the challenges that black abolitionists made to the idea of colonizing Liberia as any kind of acceptable abolitionist response. During the 1840s and 1850s, the ground changed. Moral exhortation economic boycott, and nonparticipation in voting and representational politics—what we can call *the strategy of moral appeal*—no longer seemed adequate to the moment. Garrison's vision of moral suasion—reflected in core abolitionist texts such as Angelina Grimké's "An Appeal to the Christian Women of the South" (1836), published by Garrison's AASS—had failed to convince the southern slavocracy to emancipate its slaves voluntarily. And the threat seemed to be rising. What now?

In the 1840s and 1850s, the failures of the moral appeal led abolitionist activism to center on a set of questions about constitutional strategy. Debate within antislavery circles came to focus on the question of how much to remain within a constitutional framework versus where, how, and when to step outside it. William Lloyd Garrison and the Quakers had been urging revolutionary *nonviolence* for some time, and black abolitionists had been urging black self-defense and uprising. After the Fugitive Slave Act, however, revolutionary violence became a more plausible strategy for both white and black abolitionists.[15] During this period, Lysander Spooner, William Lloyd Garrison, and Wendell Phillips fielded a debate about the relationship between slavery and the Constitution that, as I will show, tracked the question how a movement in crisis should navigate the Constitution. And, because of the relevance of gender itself as a constitutive constitutional category, this inside/outside dynamic was equally manifest in the challenge that women's rights posed for movement dynamics. (The splinter between the AASS and the AFASS was in part about whether abolitionism implied women's rights. Garrison's AASS had seen women's rights and antislavery as mutually implicated— and had benefited from women's energy in using their limited powers to launch slavery onto the national agenda—but the AFASS wanted to broaden the political appeal of antislavery activism by compromising on the message of gender equality.)

The question of the 1840s and 1850s was this: To what extent should activists work within a received legal order, and to what extent should they rebel against the terms of that order? In one way of looking at things, they faced a classic Schmittian moment: introduced to the necessity of politics by the series of emergencies of the 1840s and 1850s, they were pressed to define who or what is the "inside" and how the enemy ought to be defined. Ultimately, however, this Schmittian framing actually precludes an understanding of the unique alternative that Douglass developed from within the emergency he faced. To understand his unique contribution, let us begin by laying out the array of constitutional strategies that abolitionists offered at this moment.

First was *revolutionary nonviolence*. Garrisonian abolitionism had been the standard-bearer of the movement. William Garrison had been active in antislavery since the 1820s, founding *The Liberator* in 1831 and the AASS in 1832. Garrisonian abolitionism viewed the Constitution as a proslavery pact. If it was a "covenant with death and an agreement with

Hell,"[16] then to participate in its institutions in any way—to use the political powers of voting, running for office, or participating in the judicial system—was to implicate oneself in the greatest moral wrong. Garrisonian activism recommended the use of "moral powers" instead—direct moral appeals to slaveholders and churches, economic boycott of the products of slavery, petition to the legislature, and nonviolent confrontation—as a means of bringing about a new world of cooperation with God's destiny for humanity. The constitutional dimensions of this view were expressed by Wendell Phillips in *The Constitution: A Pro-Slavery Compact* and "Review of Lysander Spooner's Essay on the Unconstitutionality of Slavery."[17] Phillips read the Constitution through the intentions of the Framers as a decidedly proslavery text. His approach was positivist in its resistance to reading abstract legal categories through a morally saturated lens and historicist in how it articulated the Framers' specific intentions as core to the content of legal language. The proper ethical and strategic response for an abolitionist (for Garrisonians, the categories were one and the same) amounted to nonviolent revolution—withdrawal from corrupted political structures as they existed and active nonviolent work to create a new world.

But for political elites—and certainly within Congress—the dominant abolitionist strategy was obviously not nonparticipation. These actors instead favored *restrictionism*. From the early 1840s, Salmon P. Chase argued in his legal practice and from his position as a Liberty and Free Soil Party organizer and ultimately a senator that the Framers had intended a speedy abolition of slavery.[18] He articulated what would become the "restrictionist" point of view in abolitionist politics: while slavery was secure in the states, the duty of Congress was to restrict and cordon off the extension of slavery into the territories, abolish slavery in the nation's capital, and apply pressure to convince southern states to emancipate enslaved people through state action. This would become, in the 1850s, the basis of the Republican Party doctrine of free soil and nonextension and the goal Lincoln brought to office when he assumed the presidency. The constitutional basis of this vision was the "federal consensus"—the idea that the Constitution protected the power of states to entrench slavery but that Congress was free to act against it elsewhere.[19] This vision, too, is positivist in its willingness to read the legal meaning of the Constitution apart from moral necessity and historicist in its articulation of the meaning of constitutional categories through the Framers' specific intentions, although Chase read those intentions differently than Wendell Phillips or William Garrison did. The strategic implication of this view was that activists should assume power by capturing national institutions and then use those institutions to contain the spread of slavery while also maintaining moral and economic pressure on southern states to induce them to voluntarily abolish slavery.

A third form of abolitionism worked in tandem with restrictionism but targeted the courts. *Incrementalist antislavery legalism* focused on using white people's access to legal institutions to protect, in marginal ways, the rights of self-liberated people, free blacks in danger of kidnapping, and white abolitionists in trouble with the law. This group asked for jury trials for alleged fugitives, free speech rights for abolitionists, and the strict enforcement of due process. Incrementalist antislavery legalism could be extraordinarily savvy. For example, Justice Joseph Story, an antislavery Supreme Court judge, ruled in *Pennsylvania v. Prigg* (1842) that the states could not interfere in the capture of allegedly fugitive people in free states and that the apprehension of allegedly fugitive people was entirely a federal matter. Story made his decision in the context of poorly developed federal police capacity, suggesting in effect that the Constitution's goal of returning fugitives would be hampered by limited federal resources. But, despite its legal savvy, the core premise of incrementalist antislavery legalism—the idea that the goals of abolitionism could be achieved, slowly but surely, with dedicated time and effort—was profoundly disrupted, even destroyed, by the 1850 Fugitive Slave Act. With its nationalization of the guarantee of property in slaves and its extreme violations of due process, the act called into question the very sense of self for a generation of activists who had pursued incremental changes in the courts out of an idea that policy progress over time was possible.[20]

Black abolitionists offered yet a fourth antislavery response whose appeal intensified after 1850: *revolutionary violence*. Rooted in events and texts like the Vesey Rebellion (1822), David Walker's *Appeal, in Four Articles; Together with a Preamble, to the Coloured Citizens of the World* (1829), and Nat Turner's Rebellion (1831), a movement for revolutionary violence that was centered in African American communities had broadened and deepened in the 1840s and 1850s. Walker had instructed his readers: "[I]t is no more harm for you to kill a man who is trying to kill you, than it is for you to take a drink of water when thirsty."[21] Notable in this context was Henry Highland Garnet, a self-freed person who actively lectured in the 1840s for black self-help through the use of violence. A high point of this moment was Garnet's "Call to Rebellion" at the 1843 National Negro Convention in New York, which Douglass witnessed, challenged, and was ultimately inspired by.[22] Garnet joined the AFASA, formed in 1840 in a split from Garrison's organization, lectured for decades, and inspired an emerging group of white practitioners of revolutionary violence, including John Brown. The Fugitive Slave Act obviously enhanced the appeal of this strategy.[23]

Finally, and most important to Frederick Douglass, was *radical antislavery legalism*. In the 1840s, Lysander Spooner wrote *The Unconstitutionality of Slavery* (first edition 1845), a "methodologically rigorous, absolutist commitment to the position that slavery was unconstitutional."[24] This work was funded by Gerrit Smith, a wealthy abolitionist and rival in activism to William Garrison. Smith was committed to using political tools to fight the slave power; he urged voting and eventually participated in creating the Liberty Party, the first antislavery political party. Although Spooner himself was not a political person, his constitutional argument was funded by an emerging political movement that sorely needed it.

Spooner's theory has been variously characterized as being in the tradition of natural law, as anarchist, or looking to the "reason to the law" rather than to concrete intentions of historic individuals.[25] Robert Cover referred to Spooner and his adherents as "antislavery legalists" and "constitutional utopians."[26] Spooner started with a demanding, philosophically coherent, and classically rooted argument about legitimate rule: that government power must not be a matter simply of will or strength because "the numbers concerned do not alter the rule."[27] In the enlarged version of the essay, he argues that, as governments are legitimately founded in consent, "*in theory* 'all the people' *consent* to such government as the constitutions authorize." However, "this consent of 'the people' exists only in theory" and "has no existence in fact," a problem that is greatly amplified both by restrictions on the suffrage and by decision making through majorities (rather than through universal consensus).[28] To rectify this problem, the meaning of the law must be interpreted by reference "to the presumed object of all laws, justice."[29] For Spooner, justice meant natural rights. This consent-based schema gives a story about the meaning of the Bill of Rights and other rights protections in the Constitution; in this account, far from being historic contingencies that now bind us, these rights are critical warrants for whatever authority the Constitution possesses. His theory of consent also, according to Spooner, creates a rule for constructing vague language: "Where rights are infringed, where fundamental principles are overthrown, where the general system of the laws is departed from, the legislative intention must be expressed with irresistible clearness to induce a court of justice to suppose a design to effect such objects."[30] Essentially, Spooner used consent theory to instruct jurists that they should read the Constitution through natural law categories.

This orientation to the Constitution generated specific results when it came to controversies that radically challenged Spooner's contemporaries. In practice, Spooner's discipline of requiring "irresistible clearness" in the text in order to achieve proslavery legal outcomes signified a strategy of hyperliteral constitutional construction. His essay insisted that the Constitution made citizens of all people present in the colonies at its adoption who were not slaves, that "the State constitutions, then existing, authorized no slavery at all," and, ultimately, that, after ratification, it was "forever too late" for any state to reduce any person to slavery.[31] In other words, the founding moment entailed the citizenship of free blacks and many enslaved people, a reading that would directly repudiate the logic of *Dred Scott* (1857). Spooner went on to reimagine all the major constitutional controversies of the moment—the meaning of the importation and migration clause, the implications of the habeas corpus guarantee for enslaved people, the relationship of the federal government to the states, the meaning of *republicanism*, and more—to demonstrate the lack of any textual warrant for the enslavement of any people by the federal government *or* the states. This meant that, contra Chase's restrictionist position, constitutional legalists could attack slavery anywhere and everywhere. Antislavery judges need not resign their seats.[32] Because the Constitution never expressed a commitment to slavery with "irresistible clearness," it was in fact an antislavery document through and through.

Highly significant was the reading Spooner adopted of the fugitive persons clause: "No Person held to Service or Labour in one State, under the Laws thereof, escaping into another, shall, in Consequence of any Law or Regulation therein, be discharged from such Service or Labour, but shall be delivered up on Claim of the Party to whom Service or Labour may be due" (Art. 4, Sec. 2). This was the tip of the southern spear into the North. Spooner's hyperliteralism interpreted this language right out of its relationship to slavery. He argued that it "sanction[ed] nothing contrary to natural right" because, according to natural rights theory, the labor of an enslaved people can never be "due" to a master. Therefore, the referent of that language must be "the labor of an indentured servant." Enslaved people are not "held to service or labor," he argued, but are rather forms of property not necessarily accompanied by service or labor (in the case of enslaved people too sick, too young, or too old to labor). Furthermore, the laws of a state do not hold any enslaved people "to service or labor" but rather hold them in a property relation without creating or recognizing any obligation on the part of the enslaved person to labor. Hence: "[T]he words cannot, in this case, be strained beyond their necessary meaning, to make them sanction a wrong."[33] The result is that the Constitution gives no warrant for the forcible return of self-emancipated people.[34] What a surprise!

This argument created a new strategic pathway through which legalists could work through the law for radical transformation.[35] This work also enabled a form of political abolitionism and licensed state violence on behalf of emancipation. Abolitionists could, in good conscience, vote, run for office, and work through public institutions, secure in the knowledge that doing so did not implicate them in proslavery institutions. And the state, acting through this logic, could certainly use violence to end slavery, as the 1855 convention of the Radical Abolition Party proposed.[36] Nevertheless, Spooner's work, brilliant and creative, failed so completely to track public understandings of constitutional meaning that it was not actually taken up by legal actors.[37] In this sense his effort failed.

But, politically, Spooner's work undergirded a major transformation of one of the most important abolitionists, Frederick Douglass. It is worth it, then, to notice that Spooner's new theory of the US Constitution, deployed as a weapon in a political battle against the slave power, was decidedly anti-Schmittian. His discussion of the presidency emphasizes questions of legal eligibility, not emergency powers.[38] His discussion of prerogative centers on whether Parliament (not the executive) could ever have the power to abridge rights.[39] His discussion of war centers on slaves' right of rebellion and on the necessity of *not* reading the Constitution as a "war against the rights of man."[40] Throughout the text, Spooner inquires into questions like the meaning and power of voting, theories of representation and eligibility, and the moral obligation of oaths of office. This is a text focused on legal constraints, and on legislative and judicial powers. Its moral focus absolutely saturates its reading of legal language. And antislavery enters as a foundational commitment of politics rather than (as in the Emancipation Proclamation) a matter of emergency or necessity. In fact, central to Spooner's approach was the idea that no war would be required to compel all states of the Union to emancipate immediately. Emancipation was implied by the ordinary law of the moment. Institutions would have to work in coordinated ways to secure this ordinary law against slavery, and any government protecting slavery notwithstanding the ordinary law is for that reason a "fraud."[41]

Spooner's argument—principled as it was and resistant as it was to emergency powers in the presidency—was funded by Smith to undergird political abolition in an emergency moment. What kind of political action would be invited by this constitutional theory? Action centered on legislative and judicial powers, not, à la Schmitt, presidential emergency powers. Voters and politicians would demand legislation that accords with natural law theory, and such legislation would guarantee the liberties of freed people even if they lived in the southern states or territories. The president would use discretionary powers toward the same ends; the Court would use its powers of legal interpretation and judicial review actively to announce Dred Scott's citizenship and unapologetically issue his legal license to freedom. For the Court to act against the president and Congress, if need be, would create no problem of countermajoritarianism since, as Spooner argues, the simple power of the majority's numbers creates no right to rule. The correct response to this emergency was, for Spooner, Douglass, and their allies, that all people, all voters, all legislators, all jurists, in short all institutions and powers, would work cooperatively together toward advancing the natural rights of all people on all fronts.

The legal brilliance of Spooner's argument was matched only by the political value he rendered in creating a narrative of constitutional meaning that could justify the strategic judgment that many abolitionists made after 1850, namely, that nonviolent resistance was not enough, that political action was necessary, and that the categories of political belonging and the levers of political power in the Constitution could be ethically leveraged by abolitionists in service of their cause.

Douglass's New Constitutional Activism

In 1851, to great controversy and discord, Douglass publicly announced that he had converted from Garrisonian perfectionism to a belief in the antislavery nature of the US Constitution. Privately, he credited Spooner, as well as Gerrit Smith and William Goodell, for his transformation.[42] He was willing radically to challenge public understandings of the text. He was willing to read the three-fifths clause not as a structural advantage to the South but as a disadvantage to slave states.[43] And he now asked abolitionists to bend all their political power to antislavery agitation.

Because Douglass adopted the content of his new position on the Constitution from Spooner, his constitutional theory has been read by scholars through Spooner. Interlocutors have accepted Douglass's own characterization of himself as a strict textualist.[44] Robert Bernasconi presents Douglass as someone attached to the "plain meaning" of the

Constitution's text, taking at face value his assertion that, according to the "well-known rules of legal interpretation," the language of law must be construed "strictly in favor of liberty and justice."[45] (I will argue that this is Douglass's misrepresentation of his own practice.) Aileen Kraditor accepts his argument about the fugitive slave clause as an exercise in natural law reasoning, and she characterizes his and Spooner's approach as resting on an "extreme emphasis on theoretical principles."[46] In his book-length treatment of the constitutional thought of Douglass, one aimed at emphasizing Douglass's "claim to interpretive respect," Peter Myers reproduces his self-presentation as emphasizing the "plainly-written" aspect of constitutional meaning and as interpreting ambiguity according to natural law principles.[47] And Charles Mills has characterized his efforts as a form of "naïve textual formalism" meant to resist the "racial cryptography" of the Constitution.[48]

But, although these statements may be true as applied to Spooner, and although Douglass did appropriate Spooner's reading of the Constitution, in that appropriation Douglass also reimagined his own role as a constitutional interpreter. His contribution in the alliance he formed with Spooner was a new theory about the practice of interpretation itself, and it is a contribution that has gone remarkably untheorized. Douglass created a new and creative vision of constitutional activism, and his savvy development of that activism belies any characterization of him as naive.

The interpretive posture that Spooner was working from emphasized legal fidelity, impartiality, and natural law. Spooner was a dedicated adherent of natural law, a radical anarchist in sensibility, and uncompromisingly principled. Thus, in 1867 no less, in *No Treason* he opposed *northern* aggression in the Civil War on the grounds that the power to secede was entailed by consent theory.[49] His impartiality not only extended to his failure to align politically with other antislavery activists on the matter of the Civil War but also entailed serious activism on a matter that, in the context of the battle between slavery and antislavery, was trivial: the monopolistic practices of the post office. On the grounds that government monopolies on mail delivery corrupted a natural right to economic exchange, he argued in 1844, just a year before *The Unconstitutionality of Slavery*, for competition in mail delivery as an ethical matter of singular importance. He even started his own mail company and, at times, delivered mail for free.[50] Spooner was an activist. But his legacy does not suggest that he was an activist who sought allies in any conventional sense. He was an activist for natural law.

I read Spooner's life as a performance of principled anarchism and natural law theory: theoretically demanding, impartial, willing to shelter even political foes beneath the demanding implications of a radical theory of limited state power. His brilliance in reading the Constitution in a rigorously natural rights direction, thereby making it relevant for abolitionist political activism, was matched by a willingness to follow his natural rights conclusions even into the realm of the esoteric. Spooner was constitutionally principled and politically unfaithful. His activism offers a case study for Schmitt's belief that legal liberals cannot tell their friends from their enemies.

At the same time as he adopted Spooner's argument that the Constitution was antislavery, Douglass also developed a new conception of himself as an interpreter that ultimately resulted in a new constitutional pathway for abolitionist activism. Beyond the conventionally understood antislavery options listed above—revolutionary nonviolence, revolutionary violence, restrictionism, incrementalist legalism, and radical antislavery legalism—he received, I argue, and then deployed Spooner's constitutional arguments with a strategic intelligence that ultimately transformed their meaning. I call the new strategic category that he created *morally focused constitutional activism*. This contribution is submerged when Douglass is treated only as a principled theoretician of the law. I would like to explore it here.

Frederick Douglass was a self-liberated person whose rhetorical and intellectual powers as well as his fierce dedication to the cause made him a leading abolitionist within only a few years of his escape from slavery. He first aligned himself politically with Garrisonian abolitionists, joining their lecture circuit in the early 1840s to speak to his experiences as an enslaved person and a fugitive. He was, by all accounts, a fierce and powerful speaker, offering his own body as testimony to the cruelties of slavery, brilliantly skewering the hypocrisies of the slavocracy, leaving audiences, according to Elizabeth Cady Stanton, who saw him speak in 1842, "completely magnetized with his eloquence, laughing and crying by turns."[51] He performed to advance Garrisonian ideals of noncomplicity in US political institutions, nonviolent resistance, and northern secession from a corrupting Union. On the lecture circuit he was regularly attacked—having, for example, been "thrown off railcars" and had "bricks hurled at his head"—both for the content of his message and for his willingness to present himself in segregated spaces.[52] In true Garrisonian fashion, he would refuse to respond in kind to the assaults on his body. His pacifist responses—confrontational but nonviolent—served as yet more material for his lectures. Douglass was brilliant in intertwining his physical and rhetorical selves into an argument as to the brutality of slavery and the dignity of every person.

Douglass stayed true to the Garrisons through the first political fracture of that movement, that between the AASS and the AFASS. As a lecturer for the AASS, he was fully willing to denounce "the heresies of the 'new organization' men such as the Tappans, and the emerging political abolitionists in the Liberty Party." Hired as a full-time lecturer in early 1842, he toured the nation speaking "on virtually all the leading issues from proslavery churches to Northern racial prejudice, the virtues of moral suasion and the dangers of political parties, disunionism and nonresistance, and the psychological and physical character of slavery."[53]

But his own developing political judgment, his despair by 1850 at the position of antislavery, and his developing friendships with the political abolitionists Beriah Green and Gerrit Smith led Douglass in 1851 publicly to announce his conclusion that Garrisonian abolitionists were wrong to urge noncomplicity to the extent of not voting. His biographer David Blight dates the beginning of the transformation of his position on political violence to his attendance at the 1843 Colored Convention, a meeting of national black leaders at which he encountered Henry Highland Garnet, another self-liberated person who was urging violent resistance by blacks. He challenged Garnet in Garrisonian terms, arguing that "moral means" were preferable to revolutionary violence and that insurrection would leave blacks even more vulnerable than they were already. While his rejoinder to Garnet was powerful, Douglass was also deeply affected by Garnet's position, and, in a mob attack that he suffered the next day, he "forgot all about nonresistance, grabbed a club, and waded into the ground."[54] Over the years, other moments began to add up. Most notably, Douglass founded his own press, and his search for sponsors led to a friendship with the wealthy abolitionist Gerrit Smith, who began a decade-long persuasion campaign with Douglass on the strategic value of activism through representative institutions.

In 1851, Douglass announced that he had become a political abolitionist. He urged Americans to use not only the moral powers of direct appeal, petition, and assembly that Garrison had long sanctioned but also the political powers of voting and officeholding to resist slavery.[55] He was no longer concerned with the Constitution as an instrument of violence; he read it through Spooner's terms and wanted its powers exercised to advance the well-being of free and enslaved black people. This transformation was a pivotal, even momentous, moment in abolitionist politics. Garrisonian abolitionists charged Douglass with opportunism and roguery.[56]

Understanding Douglass's matured constitutional position requires understanding the details of this transformation. Douglass himself insisted that the core of his position had not changed. His firm commitment to abolitionism above all else was a hallmark of his thinking always about his "grand and commanding object."[57] What, then, made 1851 such a momentous year?

Douglass had come to believe that Americans would not support abolitionism if doing so meant rejecting the Constitution. Spooner's work had paved the way for an abolitionist to speak to the American people in the language of their text, so Douglass followed Spooner's lead in becoming an elaborator of the Constitution. But he also transformed his self-understanding as an elaborator of the Constitution, and here he broke original ground. He did not just announce that he had been swayed by Spooner's new reasoning. Rather, he also changed his orientation on a metatheoretical question about the practice of interpreting a text in politics. Douglass did not switch interpretive positions simply for instrumentalist reasons; the new position he adopted was self-consciously aware of and approving of the instrumental use of constitutional interpretation *for moral purposes like abolition*. The activist implications of his self-consciously instrumental use of constitutional interpretation have been neglected. Putting him in dialogue with both Spooner and Schmitt helps reveal this truly original element in his work.

What do I mean by this? In 1849, prior to his shift, Douglass had emphasized the complicity of the Constitution in supporting slavery. The fugitive slave clause, the power of the federal government to put down insurrections, and the power of slaveholders to move their slave property throughout the Union meant that the entire nation was complicit in the outrage of slavery.[58] He regarded the Constitution as a "foul curse" and desired to see it "shivered in a thousand fragments."[59] He may have adopted this reading for strategic purposes; in a few 1849 letters, he described his expectation that, the more strenuously southerners insisted on a proslavery reading of the Constitution, the sooner northerners would be "awakened" to their complicity.[60] But, whatever his expectations were, he did not describe his position itself in strategic terms. The language he used instead is familiar to those versed in the ideals of legalism. Douglass was sensitive to the idea that textual obligations could depart from the demands of justice and morality.[61] He indicated a respect for the requirements of faithful interpretation that he couched in the language of morality, asking whether it was "good morality to . . . put a meaning upon a legal instrument the very opposite of what we have good reason to believe was the intention of the men who framed it?"[62] The pretransformation Douglass responded to the political abolitionists that they could not "have a stronger wish to turn every *rightful* instrumentality against slavery, than we [the Garrisonian abolitionists] have": "[A]nd if the Constitution can be so turned . . . we shall readily, gladly and zealously turn our feeble energies in that direction." Notice the concern that abolitionists not make political use of instruments that were not rightfully theirs. This concern for the integrity of the constitutional text sits comfortably with the principled approach of the textualist. But, Douglass continued, given the Constitution's support for the practice of slaveholding, to adopt its ends as one's own would be "to become a guilty party to it, and in reply we say—No!"[63]

Although he was here following Garrison to reject the authority of the antebellum Constitution in particular, Douglass understood his insistence on respecting the Constitution's meaning as a general component of lawfulness. In this way, he was a constitutionalist well before he came to endorse the Constitution. He insisted: "The question is not . . . what a government ought to be, or to do, but what the government of the United States is *authorized to be, and to do, by the Constitution of the United States*. The two questions should be kept separate, that the simplest may understand, as blending them only leads to confusion." He hence resisted the political abolitionist Gerrit Smith's suggestion that, if the government has "a Constitution under which it cannot abolish slavery, then it must override the Constitution and abolish slavery." This doctrine he found "radically unsound," for a government acting outside its "very charter" would be "nothing better than a lawless mob, acting without any other or higher authority than its own convictions or impulses as to what is right or wrong."[64]

In resisting the Constitution's complicity with slavery, before 1851 Douglass had evoked what Robert Cover has termed *the language of helplessness*, where the interpreter, driven by the demands of formal reason, is compelled to arrive at certain legal conclusions no matter the consequences.[65] Consider the introduction to one of Douglass's most important pre-1851 addresses on slavery: "Of one thing, however, we can assure our readers, and that is, that we bring to the consideration of this subject no partisan feelings, nor the slightest wish to make ourselves consistent with the creed of either Anti-Slavery party, and that our only aim is to know what is truth and what is duty in respect to the matter in dispute, holding ourselves perfectly free to change our opinion in any direction, and at any time which may be indicated by our immediate apprehension of truth, unbiased by the smiles or frowns of any class or party of abolitionists."[66]

Douglass here rhetorically occupied the position of the textually faithful legal interpreter, bound by reason, but left free to judge the ends of the document according to his own moral lights. This metaposition on the practice of interpretation overlapped well with Spooner's extreme emphasis on legal coherence and impartiality, and, after 1851, Douglass could coherently have maintained that position while also adopting Spooner's new argument about what legal impartiality required in the context of this specific constitution. In short, he could have become a Spoonerian full stop.

However, in 1851, in a written defense of his new position, Douglass emphasized not the capacity of truth and reason to illuminate politically contentious questions but rather the interpretive "rights" of the people: "I [reject] the idea that the question of the constitutionality, or unconstitutionality of slavery, is not a question for the people. I hold that every American citizen has a right to form an opinion of the constitution, and to propagate that opinion, and to use all honorable means to make his opinion the prevailing one. Without this right, the liberty of an American citizen would be as insecure as that of a Frenchman."[67] Read literally, this passage attacks a confused target. Who among his interlocutors believed that the people did not enjoy the right to form an opinion of the constitutionality of slavery? Douglass had always considered himself entitled to form and advance such opinions. It is possible that he meant to assert his right to differ from those he admired so greatly, those Garrisonians who had been so vital to his growth.[68] But, in emphasizing the right to interpret the Constitution rather than the duty to interpret it according to truth and reason, he could also have been signaling a change in his conception of the proper relationship between citizen and Constitution. This passage is referring to a form of popular constitutionalism, but for Douglass the point was not to be popular but rather to protect the liberties of black people.

Certainly, Douglass had become willing to relate to sovereignty in a more pragmatic fashion. While Spooner's relationship to sovereignty entailed a highly demanding and philosophic legitimation test, Douglass had in 1847 expressed a more flexible relationship to sovereign power and a willingness to embrace even monarchical power on the basis not of abstract principle or natural right but of a specific social experience of respect:

> I went to England, monarchical England, to get rid of Democratic Slavery; and I must confess that at the very threshold I was satisfied that I had gone to the right place. Say what you will of England—of the degradation—of the poverty—and there is much of it there,—say what you will of the oppression and

suffering going on in England at this time, there is Liberty there, not only for the white man, but for the black man also. The instant that I stepped upon the shore, and looked into the faces of the crowd around me, I saw in every man a recognition of my manhood, and an absence, a perfect absence, of everything like that disgusting hate with which we are pursued in this country.[69]

In some ways, his 1851 transformation sprang from the same origins of pragmatic flexibility. Indeed, he told the AASS that he had arrived at the conviction that "the Constitution, construed in the light of well-established rules of legal interpretation, might be made consistent in its details with the noble purposes in its preamble." He insisted that the Constitution "be wielded in behalf of emancipation."[70] Rather than obsess about whether its ends could be his own, he now wished his audience to "wield" it—like a tool. His language emphasized not the revelation of constitutional meaning to the faithful interpreter but rather the interpreter's active management of that meaning. The Constitution was not revealed to be consistent with its own preamble; rather, it would be "made" to be so.

Douglass emphasized the political necessity of this switch as well as its integrity. In his editorial pages he emphasized: "Never . . . will the North be roused to intelligent and efficient action against slavery, until it shall become the settled conviction of the people, that slavery is anarchical, unconstitutional, and wholly incapable of legalization."[71] When Garrisonian abolitionists challenged his constitutional reading, he deflected their questions about the fugitive persons clause and insisted that he was focused on finding the best strategy for convincing America's citizens that the Constitution required them to commit the Union to abolishing slavery. Hence he chastised the Garrisonian abolitionists for their shortsightedness; they would give up "the firm basis of anti-slavery operation" that the Union provides while forsaking their responsibility to enslaved people.[72] And he emphasized that "[t]he slaveholder has the best of the argument the very moment the legality and constitutionality of slavery is conceded," for such a doctrine "drives conscientious abolitionists from the ballot-box, reduces the masses—who would be practical abolitionists into mere 'Free Soilers,' and arms the slaveholder with almost the only available power this side of *revolution* to defeat the anti-slavery movement."[73] These were not the terms within which Spooner argued.

When challenged by the Garrisonians as an inconsistent opportunist, Douglass articulated his understanding of the role of a reform movement: to work from the inside to bring the understanding of the vanguard position to the entire movement. He also emphasized that his consistency was of a higher order than that of the Garrisonians: "Anti-Slavery consistency itself, in our view, requires of the Anti-Slavery voter that disposition of his vote and his influence, which, in all the circumstances and likelihoods of the case tend most to the triumph of Free Principles in the Councils and Government of the nation. . . . Right Anti-Slavery Action is that which deals the severest deadliest blow upon Slavery that can be given at that particular time. Such action is always consistent, however different may be the forms through which it expresses itself."[74] Here, he justified his interpretive transformation by reference to the needs of abolitionism. Interpretation itself, or what Douglass now called *influence*, had become a political power that citizens had a responsibility to exercise on behalf of abolition. This is not Lysander Spooner's principled impartiality. Importantly, this is also not Schmitt's mobilization to empower a state's fighting posture or the existential thrill of political self-definition. This is highly focused political work to turn the Constitution and its state into a moral resource to protect people targeted by white supremacy. Douglass wove a specific pattern of principle and strategy that cannot be translated into either the language of consent-based legalism or the register of Schmittian opportunism.

This transformation conditions the meaning we should assign to Douglass's embrace of Spooner's hyperliteralism. Hyperliteralism was, for Spooner, entailed by a theoretical commitment to consent theory. In his hands, it amounted to an impartial legal strategy. But Douglass's referent for hyperliteralism was Portia in Shakespeare's *Merchant of Venice*—a false judge who uses a strategy of hyperliteralism in order to achieve her specific goals. She arrives at the trial dressed as a man, concealing her personal interest in the outcome of the proceedings, and manages to be accepted as a jurist. Once she is empowered, her strategy—"thy pound of flesh . . . but [not] One drop of Christian blood"[75]—represents a legalistic *subversion*, a way of defeating a contract from within so that she can marry the suitor she chooses while maintaining the legal prestige of a merchant city. This is not a character Spooner would have embraced. Yet Douglass exuberantly stepped into her role. In 1860, he said: "In all matters where laws are taught to be made the means of oppression, cruelty, and wickedness, I am for strict construction. I will concede nothing. It must be shown that it is so nominated in the bond. The pound of flesh, but not one drop of blood."[76] Later, criticizing Lincoln's inaugural address, he wrote: "He will have the pound of flesh, blood or no blood, be it more or less, a just pound or not. The Shylocks of the South, had they been after such game, might have exclaimed, in joy, and Abraham come to judgment!"[77]

Douglass's post-1851 position reconfigured the very notion of textual fidelity. His failure to address the distinction between legal and natural obligation (a theme that had greatly interested him before), his willingness to speak of the Constitution as a tool to be used for moral purposes, his emphatic arguments about the strategic value of constructing the Constitution in an abolitionist direction, and his explicit self-identification with Portia, legal imposter and subversive interpreter, all these make it appropriate to label his new position self-consciously strategic on behalf of a moral aim, the abolition of slavery.

Douglass was strategic on behalf of a moral end, and he justified his strategy in terms of what was needed to respond to an overwhelming evil of his time. It is hard, given the moral harm of slavery, to argue that he was wrong to take up the Constitution instrumentally in an effort to fight back the slave power. But instrumentalist constitutional interpretation absolutely challenges the theoretic posture of consent theory. Douglass was driven to find a reading of the Constitution that he could make work to suit his own aims. But, if we can interpret the Constitution as we wish in pursuit of our own aims, then on what terms would we reject it? And, if we can never reject the Constitution, can we be said to consent to it either? The theoretical plausibility of a moral posture of principled rejection is central to the activism of William Garrison and Wendell Phillips, central to the coherence of the intellectual edifice that Lysander Spooner constructed, and central to present-day natural law and consent-based theories of constitutional authority as well.[78] For that reason, perhaps, too few have seen what is emphatically *right* in Douglass's approach, and he has not received the kind of sophisticated theoretical treatment that another constitutional pragmatist, Lincoln himself, is customarily accorded.

Nowhere would the difference between Douglass and Spooner become clearer than in Douglass's buttressing of the Civil War effort. In *No Treason*, Spooner defended the consent principles of natural law, held that the Civil War was an unjust violation of natural law because it was fought on grounds of union, not antislavery, and ultimately argued that, in light of secession, the Constitution had no authority whatsoever. By contrast, in 1855, Douglass was already pressuring the northern states to prepare for war. He gathered with a convention of radical political abolitionists to declare "that the government which annihilates instead of protecting human rights, should be known, not as civil government, but only as a conspiracy, a usurpation," and announced:

> [W]e feel ourselves prepared for an aggressive—not a merely defensive—contest with the slave power. We take our position accordingly, and ask our fellow citizens to do the same. We sue for no needless amendments of the Constitution, requiring the concurrence of three fourths of the States. Properly construed, it already gives us all we need. We attempt no dissolution of the Union. The Constitution makes no provision for it, and nothing short of a revolution could effectuate it. We *consent* to no dissolution that would leave the slave in his chains. We demand the constitutional deliverance of the slave, and of the whole country, North and South—a deliverance by the peaceful ballot-box, and within the power of the non-slaveholders of the United States.[79]

During the Civil War, Douglass moved about wildly in his political alliances, searching for the right place to stand in a political space characterized by profound upheaval in order to support his ultimate aim of abolition. Sometimes working for the Liberty Party, sometimes for the Radical Abolition Party, and sometimes for the Republicans, producing mountains of essays and letters on matters of strategy, and ultimately arguing for the value (and constitutionality) of total war for emancipation, he fully participated in the effort to *turn* the meaning of the Civil War *toward* emancipation.[80] He was singularly *un*invested in questions of appropriate legal process. In early December 1860, he said that "all methods of proceeding against slavery," including both state-sanctioned war and the "John Brown way," should be used.[81]

Most of us know that emancipation did not occur on the constitutional grounds that Spooner and Douglass advocated in 1851. The constitutional theory of antislavery legalism helped mobilize antislavery voters to go to the polls and, thus, supported the rise of the Republican Party. But, when it came time to carry out emancipation as a project of the state, Lincoln kept emancipation in the domain of executive power and military necessity. This was arguably due to Lincoln's *conservatism*; from his point of view, to emancipate enslaved people on any grounds other than emergency necessity would be to deepen the radicalism of the Union war effort. Locating emancipation in conventional law was precisely the constitutional radicalism that Douglass and Spooner urged.[82] Notwithstanding Republican legislative achievements like the Compensation Acts and the abolishing of slavery in Washington, DC, and the territories, emancipation against the wishes of slaveholders during the war was a power carefully reserved for the executive and the executive alone.

Nothing in his previous work barred Douglass from approving Lincoln's work to come to emancipation through an entirely different route. He did not resist Lincoln's war powers, and he greeted the preliminary Emancipation Proclamation with a "shout for joy."[83] He wished only that the federal government would go further, faster, and deeper in destroying the slave power.[84] When radical Republicans in Congress worried about that body's power to emancipate slaves through law, he dismissed their "supposed constitutional objections"—"as if this were a time to talk of constitutional power!"[85] When he perceived that the Constitution had ceased to function to bind its public, he had even less patience with the claims of public officials that they were helpless in the face of constitutional constraint.

At the same time, his alliance with Lincoln was predicated on a strategic judgment as to where Douglass could best effectuate the abolition of slavery. He did not applaud Lincoln and the Union war effort simply on the theory that his enemy's enemy was his friend. Instead, he worked to pressure the North to entrench the aims of emancipation and, ultimately, civic equality for African American people in the heart of the war effort. His support for Lincoln did not mean that he was a partisan of Lincoln's or of the state's.

Lincoln's own constitutional theory—and the extent to which it can be understood in Schmittian categories—is contested and ultimately outside the scope of this chapter.[86] I have shown here that, unlike Spooner, Douglass did not hold himself captive to formalistic reasoning. But also, unlike Schmitt, he accepted the morally saturated meaning of the legal categories, activist appeals, and strategies that he invoked. He was strategically invested in the defining confrontation of his moment, but he was invested for a moral aim. More important than impartially interpreting the Constitution, and even more important than a Union victory, was the obligation to use the Constitution to *make* national politics, and then the Union war effort, liberating for African American people. By relentlessly advocating emancipation, working for black political rights like the vote and equal protection, recruiting troops, and ultimately supporting any antislavery move that Lincoln made even while fiercely pressuring the Republican Party to do more, Douglass made himself a part of a historic and monumental effort among African Americans to capture the energy of the Civil War and turn it toward black liberation.[87]

Was Douglass Subversive or Constitutionalist?

Is the pathway that Douglass created subversive, à la Schmitt? Is it not pure Schmitt to understand law as a tool wielded in political struggle? Does this transformation of Douglass's, wrought through emergency, his willingness to pick up and place down Spooner's principled legalism, and his willingness to support Lincoln's wartime measures toward emancipation, not speak precisely to the flexibility of legal language and the ultimate reduction of the meaning of that language into an alliance between friends against an existential confrontation with the enemy?

For some, Douglass's pragmatic instrumentalism does imply an unprincipled—indeed, an opportunistic—relationship to constitutional meaning. The tension between law as an impartial source of normative constraint and law as a field for instrumental manipulation is constitutive in the field of legal studies, and Schmitt falls clearly on the latter side. From within the terms of this tension, to demonstrate that someone's legal approach is *not* impartial necessarily implies a lack of principle.

Douglass, however, would never accept this characterization of himself. He was not wielding law as a tool to constitute an alliance among friends against an enemy. Rather, he was wielding law as a tool in a struggle to abolish the practice of enslaving black people. He was not committed to that struggle as a political one. He would have been happy for it to happen through social, economic, religious, or other means had his efforts on those fronts borne fruit earlier. He made it clear that he had no agenda other than abolition and helping black lives flourish. While it is true that abolitionism was a political struggle, both in the antebellum years and during the Civil War, confining its meaning there elides the moral imperatives that saturated Douglass's work and life both before and after 1851. Given how he identified emancipation as the "lodestar" of his entire life, misidentifying emancipation as a political project in Schmittian terms means misidentifying the terms of Douglass's life. How far from Schmitt was Douglass's famous line, "I would unite with anybody to do right; and with nobody to do wrong."[88] The priority that Douglass placed on what is right in the concrete and human dimension, beyond matters of theoretical commitment, makes it appropriate to call him principled even in his morally activist relationship to constitutional interpretation. While he may have been pragmatic, his activism was deeply principled as well.

On the other hand, some may read Douglass's embrace of Spooner's arguments as a turning toward constitutionalism in light of the chaos and urgency of American abolitionism and in light of his witness of the European Revolutions of 1848, the counterrevolution unfolding in the 1850s, and the emergence of the Second Empire in France in 1852. Certainly, his hope for liberties more secure than those of the French speak to an attitude to constitutional institutions informed by the European experience at hand. But this reading of Douglass—that his embrace of Spooner represented taking refuge in constitutionalism as a bulwark of liberties in an uncertain age—leaves out the transformation that he wrought in what it means to be constitutionally committed. Douglass was not just an expositor of Spooner. He appropriated Spooner's work for the end of helping black lives flourish. The extent to which abolishing slavery was for Douglass the measure against which all institutional, textual, and other constitutional appeals were judged, and his willingness to adopt goal-oriented constitutional reasoning to achieve that aim, together challenge certain notions about what constitutional commitment entails. Douglass, I argue, did not turn to a traditionally constitutionalist position because, unlike Spooner, Phillips, and Garrison, he was not willing to work through a view of constitutions as independently viable projects with independent moral and intellectual demands. Whether they rejected or embraced the Constitution, Spooner and Garrison shared in a formalist experience of constitutionalism. Rather, Douglass elevated the moral necessity of his time—abolishing slavery—over formalism of any kind.

The success of the Constitution, or of constitutionalism more generally, would be for Douglass a secondary question after that of the moral needs of African American people. But this does not mean that he eschewed constitutionalism. He used constitutional categories, and he did not participate in mob violence, shun political life, or seek escape through emigration. He came to accept the Constitution as a set of terms through which he would have to work to achieve his ends. In so doing, he also sought to reconfigure the terms of constitutionalism itself.

Constitutionalism could not, in my view, have survived through this time period had it been grounded in a Spoonerian insistence on uncompromising political consistency. Spooner's work, innovative though it was, needed Douglass's activist brilliance in order to do the work of salvaging a given constitutional order in crisis. Nor could constitutionalism do its work if it simply entailed a commitment to maintaining power through emergency by any means necessary. That disposition would compromise the moral work at the core of a commitment to constitutional politics. Douglass was conventional in his willingness to preserve and work within a given structure. He was radical in reconfiguring the meaning of that text and the terms of his alliance with it. And his work was morally saturated in the content of the vision he offered. Together, these offer us a plausible vision of what constitutional politics can be. Like Spooner, Douglass adapted the Constitution, but, unlike Spooner, he also adapted his own self-conception as a constitutional agent, and from these adaptations he created a strategic and ethical pathway whose contours differed profoundly from the pathways of those urging either the suspension, the destruction, or the maintenance of the Constitution as it stood.

At the heart of Douglass's story is his willingness to abandon the theoretical dilemmas constructed through faithful adherence to formal principle in constant pursuit of his single, overriding purpose, the redemption of black lives in the United States. The creative production during emergency of all the abolitionists, including Douglass, challenges the way in which Schmitt links emergency to a flattening of the terms of the political. And the moral content of their goal and the role that their work played in the Constitution's viability as an ongoing project challenge the limited vision that Schmitt gives us for maintaining a constitutional order through emergency.

Notes

1. Giorgio Agamben, *State of Exception*, trans. Kevin Attell (Chicago: Chicago University Press, 2005).
2. Bruce Ackerman, *Before the Next Attack: Preserving Civil Liberties in an Age of Terrorism* (New Haven, CT: Yale University Press, 2006); Elaine Scarry, *Thinking in an Emergency* (New York: Norton, 2011).
3. Bonnie Honig, *Emergency Politics: Paradox, Law, Democracy* (Princeton, NJ: Princeton University Press, 2011).
4. Carl Schmitt, *The Concept of the Political* (1932), trans. George Schwab (New Brunswick, NJ: Rutgers University Press, 1976).
5. Wiki, s.v. *Emergency*, https://en.wikipedia.org/wiki/Emergency.
6. Edmund S. Morgan, "Slavery and Freedom: The American Paradox," *Journal of American History* 59, no. 1 (1972): 5–29.
7. Cedric Robinson, *Black Marxism: The Making of the Black Radical Tradition* (1983; Chapel Hill: University of North Carolina Press, 2000); Eric Williams, *Capitalism and Slavery* (Chapel Hill: University of North Carolina Press, 1994); W. Johnson, *River of Dark Dreams: Slavery and Empire in the Cotton Kingdom* (Cambridge, MA: Belknap Press of Harvard University Press, 2013); Sven Beckert, *Empire of Cotton: A Global History* (New York: Knopf, 2014).
8. Kentucky Constitution, Art. 13, Sec. 3, cited in William M. Wiecek, *The Sources of Antislavery Constitutionalism in America, 1760–1848* (Ithaca, NY: Cornell University Press, 1977), 279. For a discussion of abolitionism in this era, see *ibid.*, 276–80.

9. Matthew Karp, *This Vast Southern Empire: Slaveholders at the Helm of American Foreign Policy* (Cambridge, MA: Harvard University Press, 2016).

10. On spectacle lynching, see Michael J. Pfeifer, *The Roots of Rough Justice: Origins of American Lynching* (Urbana: University of Illinois Press, 2011). See also the discussion of the Jerry rescue in Syracuse, New York, and of the Christiana massacre in Pennsylvania in Wiecek, *The Sources of Antislavery Constitutionalism*, 281.

11. Matthew Karp, "In the 1850s the Future of American Slavery Seemed Bright," *Aeon*, November 1, 2016, aeon.co/ideas/in-the-1850s-the-future-of-american-slavery-seemed-bright.

12. Frederick Douglass, "The Right to Criticize American Institutions" (1847), in *Frederick Douglass: Selected Speeches and Writings*, ed. Philip S. Foner and Yuval Taylor (Chicago: Lawrence Hill, 1999), 76–83. See also David W. Blight, *Frederick Douglass: Prophet of Freedom* (New York: Simon & Schuster, 2018), 197.

13. Steven Lubet, *Fugitive Justice: Runaways, Rescuers, and Slavery on Trial* (Cambridge, MA: Belknap Press of Harvard University Press, 2010).

14. Robert M. Cover, *Justice Accused: Antislavery and the Judicial Process* (New Haven, CT: Yale University Press, 1975).

15. Kellie Carter Jackson, *Force and Freedom: Black Abolitionists and the Politics of Violence* (Philadelphia, University of Pennsylvania Press, 2019).

16. On July 4, 1854, Garrison uttered this before burning the Constitution at a rally in Boston.

17. Wendell Phillips, *The Constitution: A Pro-Slavery Compact; or, Extracts from the Madison Papers, Etc. (1844)*, 3rd ed., enlarged (New York: American Anti-Slavery Society, 1856), archive.org/details/constitutionprosoolcphil/page/n1, and "Review of Lysander Spooner's Essay on the Unconstitutionality of Slavery: Reprinted from the 'Antislavery Standard,' with Additions" (Boston: Printed by Andrews & Prentiss, 1847), https://babel.hathitrust.org/cgi/pt?id=loc.ark:/13960/t2r49qtod;view=1up;seq=5.

18. Randy E. Barnett, "From Antislavery Lawyer to Chief Justice: The Remarkable but Forgotten Career of Salmon P. Chase," *Georgetown Public Law and Legal Theory Research Paper no. 12-122* (2013; rev. 2016), https://papers.ssrn.com/sol3/papers.cfm?abstract_id=2136974.

19. For a discussion of the role of the federal consensus in structuring antislavery constitutionalism, see Wiecek, *The Sources of Antislavery Constitutionalism*, 16.

20. See Cover, *Justice Accused*.

21. David Walker, *Walker's Appeal, in Four Articles; Together with a Preamble, to the Coloured Citizens of the World, but in Particular, and Very Expressly, to Those of the United States of America, Written in Boston, State of Massachusetts, September 28, 1829* (1829; rev. ed., Boston: David Walker, 1830), 30, Documenting the American South, docsouth.unc.edu/nc/walker/walker.html.

22. Blight, *Frederick Douglass*, 132–33.

23. Jackson, *Force and Freedom*.

24. Helen Knowles, "Securing the 'Blessings of Liberty' for All: Lysander Spooner's Originalism," *New York University Journal of Law and Liberty* 5

(2010): 34–62, 40. See also Lysander Spooner, *Essay on the Unconstitutionality of Slavery* (1860), Liberty Fund Online Library of Liberty, https://oll.libertyfund.org/titles/spooner-the-unconstitutionality-of-slavery-1860.

25. Letter from Lysander Spooner to George Bradburn, March 5, 1846, New York Historical Society, http://digitalcollections.nyhistory.org/islandora/object/islandora%3A142795.

26. Cover, *Justice Accused*, 154–58.

27. Spooner, *The Unconstitutionality of Slavery*, 12.

28. Lysander Spooner, *The Unconstitutionality of Slavery, enlarged ed.* (Boston: Bela Marsh, 1860), 153, https://babel.hathitrust.org/cgi/pt?id=loc.ark:/13960/t9n29zf53&view=1up&seq=9. See also Randy E. Barnett, "Was Slavery Unconstitutional Before the Thirteenth Amendment? Lysander Spooner's Theory of Interpretation," *Pacific Law Journal* 28 (1997): 977–1014.

29. Spooner, *The Unconstitutionality of Slavery (enlarged ed.)*, 172.

30. Spooner, *The Unconstitutionality of Slavery (original ed.)*, 155.

31. Spooner, *The Unconstitutionality of Slavery (original ed.)*, 56.

32. Spooner, *The Unconstitutionality of Slavery (enlarged ed.)*, 150.

33. Spooner, *The Unconstitutionality of Slavery (original ed.)*, 70.

34. Spooner, *The Unconstitutionality of Slavery (original ed.)*, 68–73. Wiecek also reports that in 1837 Elizur Wright wrote a report for the AASS claiming that to hold a person "to Service of Labour in One State, under the Laws thereof," would require a judicial proceeding conforming with the 5th Amendment, and that because slavery is "unknown" to the US Constitution, which announces only due process, any master would have to show a great deal. See Wiecek, *The Sources of Antislavery Constitutionalism*, 274 (and chap. 11 generally).

35. Cover, *Justice Accused*.

36. Blight, *Frederick Douglass*, 293.

37. Cover, *Justice Accused*, 177–78.

38. Spooner, *The Unconstitutionality of Slavery (original ed.)*, 99–100.

39. Spooner, *The Unconstitutionality of Slavery (original ed.)*, 24.

40. Spooner, *The Unconstitutionality of Slavery (original ed.)*, 102, 113.

41. Spooner, *The Unconstitutionality of Slavery (enlarged ed.)*, 143.

42. Peter C. Myers, *Frederick Douglass: Race and Rebirth of American Liberalism* (Lawrence: University Press of Kansas, 2008), 89.

43. Frederick Douglass, "The Constitution of the United States: Is It Pro-Slavery or AntiSlavery?," in Foner and Taylor, eds., *Frederick Douglass: Selected Speeches and Writings*, 379–89, 384.

44. Clarence Thomas, "Toward a 'Plain Reading' of the Constitution—the Declaration of Independence in Constitutional Interpretation," *Howard Law Journal* 30 (1987): 983–96; Sanford Levinson, *Constitutional Faith* (Princeton, NJ: Princeton University Press 1988), 38.

45. Robert Bernasconi, "The Constitution of the People: Frederick Douglass and the Dred Scott Decision," *Cardozo Law Review* 13 (1991–92): 1289–90.

46. Aileen S. Kraditor, *Means and Ends in American Abolitionism: Garrison and His Critics on Strategy and Tactics, 1834–1850* (New York: Pantheon, 1967), 194–95.

47. Myers, *Frederick Douglass*, 92.

48. Charles W. Mills, "Whose Fourth of July? Frederick Douglass and 'Original Intent,'" in *Frederick Douglass: A Critical Reader*, ed. Bill E. Lawson and Frank M. Kirkland (Oxford: Blackwell, 1999), 115.

49. Lysander Spooner, *No Treason: The Constitution of No Authority (Boston, 1867)*. Spooner issued three versions of *No Treason*. See https://en.wikisource.org/wiki/No_Treason.

50. Lysander Spooner, "American Post Office," *American and Commercial Daily Advertiser,* February 28, 1844. See also Lysander Spooner, *The Unconstitutionality of Laws of Congress Prohibiting Private Mails* (New York: Tribune, 1844).

51. Blight, *Frederick Douglass*, 114.

52. Blight, *Frederick Douglass*, 120 (see generally chap. 8).

53. Blight, *Frederick Douglass*, 106, 108.

54. Blight, *Frederick Douglass*, 134.

55. Frederick Douglass, "Change of Opinion Announced" (1851), in Foner and Taylor, eds., *Frederick Douglass: Selected Speeches and Writings*, 173.

56. James A. Colaiaco, *Frederick Douglass and the Fourth of July Oration* (New York: Palgrave Macmillan, 2006), 77.

57. Frederick Douglass, "The Address of Southern Delegates in Congress to Their Constituents; or, The Address of John C. Calhoun and Forty Other Thieves" (February 9, 1849), Teaching American History, https://teachingamericanhistory.org/library/document/the-address-of-southern-delegates-in-congress-to-their-constituents-or-the-address-of-john-c-calhoun-and-forty-other-thieves.

58. Frederick Douglass, "My Slave Experience in Maryland" (1845), in Foner and Taylor, eds., *Frederick Douglass: Selected Speeches and Writings*, 11–14, 13.

59. Douglass, "The Right to Criticize American Institutions," 77.

60. Philip Foner, ed., *The Life and Writings of Frederick Douglass, vol. 1, Early Years, 1817–1849* (New York: International, 1950), 355.

61. "I know well enough that slavery is an outrage, contrary to all ideas of justice, and therefore cannot be law according to Blackstone. But may it not be law according to American legal authority?," Frederick Douglass, "To Gerrit Smith, Esqr." (1851), in Foner and Taylor, eds., *Frederick Douglass: Selected Speeches and Writings*, 171.

62. Douglass, "To Gerrit Smith, Esqr.," 171.

63. Frederick Douglass, "The Constitution and Slavery" (1849), in Foner and Taylor, eds., *Frederick Douglass: Selected Speeches and Writings*, 129–33, 133 (emphasis added).

64. Frederick Douglass, "Comment on Gerrit Smith's Address," *The North Star,* March 30, 1849, Frederick Douglass Project Writings, https://rbscp.lib.rochester.edu/4383.

65. Cover, *Justice Accused*, 236–38.

66. Douglass, "The Constitution and Slavery," 129.

67. Frederick Douglass, "The Meaning of July Fourth for the Negro" (1852), in Foner and Taylor, eds., *Frederick Douglass: Selected Speeches and Writings*, 204.

68. John R. McKivigan, "The Frederick Douglass–Gerritt Smith Friendship and Political Abolitionism in the 1850s," in *Frederick Douglass: New Literary*

and Historical Essays, ed. Eric J. Sundquist (Cambridge: Cambridge University Press, 1990).

69. Douglass, "The Right to Criticize American Institutions."

70. Douglass, "Change of Opinion Announced," 173.

71. Frederick Douglass, "The True Ground upon Which to Meet Slavery" (1855), in Foner and Taylor, *Frederick Douglass: Selected Speeches and Writings*, 333–34, 333.

72. Frederick Douglass, "The Dred Scott Decision" (1857), in Foner and Taylor, eds., *Frederick Douglass: Selected Speeches and Writings*, 344–58.

73. Douglass, "The True Ground upon Which to Meet Slavery," 333–34.

74. Frederick Douglass, "Fremont and Dayton" (1856), in Foner and Taylor, eds., *Frederick Douglass: Selected Speeches and Writings*, 338–42, 339.

75. William Shakespeare, *The Merchant of Venice*, act 4, scene 1.

76. Douglass, "The Constitution of the United States," 386.

77. Frederick Douglass, "The Inaugural Address" (1861), in Foner and Taylor, eds., *Frederick Douglass: Selected Speeches and Writings*, 435.

78. Hadley Arkes, *Beyond the Constitution* (Princeton, NJ: Princeton University Press, 1990); Sotirios A. Barber, *On What the Constitution Means* (Baltimore: Johns Hopkins University Press, 1984); Ronald Dworkin, *Law's Empire* (Cambridge, MA: Harvard University Press, 1986).

79. "Proceedings of the Convention of Radical Political Abolitionists, Held at Syracuse, N.Y., June 26th, 27th, and 28th, 1855" (New York: Central Abolition Board, 1855), http://www.wvculture.org/history/jbexhibit/radical.html.

80. See Frederick Douglass, "Is It Right and Wise to Kill a Kidnapper?" (1854), in Foner and Taylor, eds., *Frederick Douglass: Selected Speeches and Writings*, 277, "The Final Struggle" (1855), in ibid., 335, "Peaceful Annihilation of Slavery Is Hopeless," in ibid., 344, and "Captain John Brown Not Insane" (1859), in ibid., 375; and Blight, *Frederick Douglass*, chaps. 16–20.

81. Blight, *Frederick Douglass*, 330 (citing Frederick Douglass, "Speech on John Brown" [Boston, December 3, 1860]).

82. On the relationship between Douglass and Lincoln, see James Oakes, *The Radical and the Republican: Frederick Douglass, Abraham Lincoln, and the Triumph of Antislavery Politics* (New York: Norton, 2007).

83. Blight, *Frederick Douglass*, 379.

84. Blight, *Frederick Douglass*, chap. 17.

85. *Douglass' Monthly*, September 1, 1861, 514.

86. See James Oakes, *Freedom National: The Destruction of Slavery in the United States, 1861–1865* (New York: Norton, 2013); and Mark E. Neely, *The Fate of Liberty: Abraham Lincoln and Civil Liberties* (New York: Oxford University Press, 1991).

87. Vincent Harding, *There Is a River: The Black Struggle for Freedom in America* (New York: Harcourt Brace Jovanovich, 1981); James M. McPherson, "Who Freed the Slaves?," *Proceedings of the American Philosophical Society* 139 (1995): 1–10.

88. Frederick Douglass, "Anti-Slavery Movement: A Lecture before the Rochester Ladies' Anti-Slavery Society" (1855), in Foner and Taylor, eds., *Frederick Douglass: Selected Speeches and Writings*.

11 Delegated Governance as a Structure of Exceptions

Elisabeth S. Clemens

The modern state may be delineated in many ways: at the boundaries of formal institutions, through flows of funds and services, or by the distribution of activities over which rights claims are recognized. These different ways of bounding the state do not, however, necessarily coincide. Publicly funded and mandated activities may be contracted to private corporations, resulting in situations where the employees of those contractors have fewer protections and rights than their equivalents recognized as government employees. Soldiers, sailors, and private contractors may fight side by side, but their standing in relation to the state will differ substantially.[1] Citizens may be committed to private prisons or care facilities, they may choose to attend publicly funded but privately owned and managed schools or join the millions whose relationship to the Internal Revenue Service is mediated by a privately held corporation providing widely used tax preparation software. In all these instances, responsibility for providing publicly funded or authorized services is delegated to private actors.

These administrative arrangements, typically clotted with the legal language of contracts and compliance, seem far afield from the drama of "the emergency" that has animated so much of the contemporary discussion concerning states of exception. But philosophical treatments of the temporally defined emergency have built on analyses of exception as an intrinsic feature of modes of governance, both ancient and modern, namely, the simultaneity of being both inside and outside a political order.[2] For the sovereign, this "inside and outside" speaks to the recognized power to suspend the legal order, initially closely tied to external threat or crisis. For individuals, the paradox lies in the divergence between membership in a society and inclusion or representation in the state.[3] The legislative, as a body that is both representative and lawmaking, aligns—albeit imperfectly and partially—with principles of popular sovereignty.[4] Consequently, the erosion of legislative authority through the expansion of executive powers exacerbates the mismatch between membership and representation. But, even in the context of crisis, citizens may secure protections from arbitrary acts of executive authority: principles of habeas corpus and due process, rights to demand transparency and accountability. Claims such as these inform the politics of resistance to expanded executive authority, as well as to the politics of emergency that can result in lasting restrictions on legislative authority.

In these formulations, there is an implicit zero-sum relationship between the legislative and the executive. The latter gains power and authority at the expense of the former. Writing in 1940, Frederick M. Watkins identified this possibility as an aspect of "dictatorship by delegation" in which "the private law relationship of principal and agent is simply invoked as an emergency measure to govern the relations between legislative and executive branches of government." Although the phenomenon of dictatorship by delegation was initially framed by a temporally bounded sense of emergency, Watkins also linked it to "the intensity of political cleavages" and the influence of special interests, both of which present obstacles to the achievement of "national unified action" in the legislative.[5]

In Watkins's analysis, these pressures generate a displacement of decision making from the legislature to the holder of executive office. As Sanford Levinson and Jack Balkin have argued: "[T]he key development in the modern state has been an expansion of *Congress's* power to regulate a wide range of social and economic questions, and to delegate the power to regulate these matters to others." Consequently: "[T]he reason the President became so powerful in the modern period is that Congress became powerful first."[6] Each new right won by individuals against the state power, each new claim for some form of protection or social provision, "always simultaneously prepared a tacit but increasing inscription of individuals' lives within the state order, thus offering a new and more dreadful foundation for the very state power from which they wanted to liberate themselves."[7] The magnitude of such delegation, however, depends on the scale of existing legislative powers. Just as legislative powers have migrated to the executive, the implications of exception blur into the organization of administrative and semigovernmental activities. Decision making may be pushed from the legislature to the executive, from the executive into administrative agencies, and from agencies to contractors. In the process, general mandates and appropriations are translated into effective action through a chain of delegation that erodes or obscures clear lines of accountability and control even as the delegation of power to the executive is dispersed and decentralized.[8] The risks in such a chain are signaled by the elaboration of law around delegation itself. If, in the classic state of exception, sovereign authority is handed to the executive, under conditions of dictatorship by delegation the legislative cedes control through its own inabilities to act, to implement those decisions that are made, or to exercise appropriate supervision and control of those to whom government functions have been delegated.[9] Because restrictions on delegation apply most forcefully to "inherently governmental" functions, opportunities are created to outsource or delegate other "not inherently governmental" functions to private actors with the requirement that public officials retain responsibility for analysis, decision, and oversight.[10]

This drift of authority from legislatures and the executive to agencies—and perhaps to contractors or other "unelected bureaucrats"—generates fear of a "big government" that is unresponsive to the people and potentially dangerous to political liberty.[11] The dystopian scenario of delegated governance is not the authoritarian dictator but rather the all-powerful yet unaccountable bureaucracy hand in glove with congressional committees courted by the lobbyists of private corporations.[12] When the implementation of government policy is outsourced to private organizations, whether firms or not-for-profit organizations, authority may escape the constraints—for transparency, equity, and accountability—that are imposed on explicitly public agencies. Some protections against the sovereign are lost when government action is indirect or when the violation of rights is the result of private action.[13] Thus, delegation—whether to the executive itself or to the agencies and agents of the executive—generates a mixed and murky architecture of governance, one that challenges expectations of equal protection and procedural justice.

Dictatorship by Delegation

Delegation has the potential to create a system in which exception is produced in multiple forms and in varying degrees. The defining feature of such arrangements is not the stark "lawlessness within the laws" associated with a temporally discrete emergency but rather a sometimes "lesser lawfulness" within the laws. Within such an architecture of indirect social provision and contracting out, governing activities are delegated to actors and organizations held to different standards of accountability, transparency, and public responsiveness. As with the "spaces of exception" in American history discussed by Gary Gerstle and Desmond King (chapter 12 in this volume), these are arrangements that may constrain or erode the full rights of citizenship as well as the exercise of democratic accountability that subjects the legislature to the will of the electorate. Such exceptions result not from the eventful impact of emergencies[14] but rather from the institutional relationships that are created by practices of delegated governance.

Take, for example, the procedures established under the Freedom of Information Act (FOIA) of 1966 and subsequently strengthened by the Privacy Act Amendments of 1974. Rooted in an effort to limit the ability of the executive branch to restrict access by declaring documents confidential, this line of legislation embodied "a general philosophy of full agency disclosure."[15] To promote the exercise of democratic accountability, citizens would be empowered to demand transparency with respect to the decisions of their representatives. Yet the scope and implementation of these statutes have been repeatedly contested and amended in the decades since, often prompted by moments of emergency and national security concerns. Over the same period, a second transformation in the implementation of these mechanisms for assuring the accountability of executive agencies has proceeded, less noticed because seemingly so mundane. Much of the work of preparing the responses to requests for information has been contracted out to private firms who may support the formulation of replies but not actually approve or deny such requests, decisions that are considered inherently governmental. As the policy director of the Sunlight Foundation observed: "If I was in charge of an agency and wanted to create an unaccountable FOIA process, the first thing I would do is put an outside contractor in charge of it because fewer of our accountability laws apply to them."[16] Here, the shift is not solely in the expanded reach of executive power at the expense of the legislature but also in the reorganization and reallocation of executive functions, moving them outside the scope of multiple provisions intended to strengthen accountability either to the legislative branch or to citizens at large.

This analysis moves from the temporally bounded suspension of law tied to emergency or tumult to a condition in which exception has become a durable and routine feature of the contemporary state, in which something inside (government authority or function) moves outside. But this movement does not always follow the same path. Giorgio Agamben's stylized narrative, for example, moves from the totalitarian regimes of World War II, through the height of the Cold War, and on to the massive expansion of the security state in the wake of 9/11 and the era of the global War on Terror.[17] Focused on geopolitical threat, this narrative suggests that the move from a temporally bounded state of exception as a response to a discrete emergency (the descendent of the "tumults" associated with the death of a Roman emperor)[18] to a durable transformation of democratic regimes is driven by the extension of a sense of emergency, sustained by either repeated crises or the cultural construction of a sustained sense of insecurity. In this account, the prime movers are the expansion of executive power and the erosion of the prerogatives of the legislative and the judiciary. This is the path of "sovereign dictatorship."

Yet, in his effort to locate the central elements of the state of exception, Agamben also directs his analysis in a different direction, toward the (dis)articulation of sovereignty, legislation, and administration.[19] The lawlessness within the law that is characteristic of the classic state of exception appears here in the multiplying fissures between law as legislated, law as promulgated, law as translated into regulations, regulations as enforced, and actions as carried out by those who may or may not be tightly bound by the principal-agent relations of public employment. As Watkins observed in a much earlier reflection on constitutional dictatorship, the tendency to shift responsibility for governance from the legislative to the executive may be driven not only by emergency but also by the incapacity and political bankruptcy of the legislative itself.

Under conditions of such dictatorship by delegation, the legislative in effect appoints the executive as its agent. Watkins identified the First World War as a moment of unprecedented expansion of such arrangements, but he argued that the New Deal's National Industrial Recovery Act operated on the same principles by "giving the president almost unlimited authority to issue regulations in the economic realm."[20] The key distinction between the two cases lay in the source of legislative incapacity. Whereas Britain's Defense of the Realm Act was a response to war and an existential threat to the nation, the New Deal measure reflected not only economic collapse but a "breakdown in the political" and the intensification of political cleavages. "In time of war common motives of patriotism can usually be relied upon to prevent individual selfishness from getting out of bounds," Watkins noted. At a moment of economic crisis, however, "each class of the community is strongly tempted to protect its own economic position by refusing to shoulder its share of the resulting sacrifices."[21] Under such conditions, a legislature may be tempted to authorize the executive to act in its stead, at least for the duration of the crisis. The resulting landscape of exceptions, in which civic rights and political voice are transformed, obstructed, and constrained by the organizational of governance, has generated distinctive dynamics of political development.

A Government Long "Out of Sight"

In the United States, just such a trajectory of political development has been driven by robust defenses of private property and personal liberty combined with preferences for decentralized government in a polity long marked by strong antistatist sentiments. Rather than being a product of the era of the Washington Consensus and its celebration of marketization or even of the postwar period more broadly, the neoliberal projects of the late twentieth century have built on a long history of antistatism and the reliance on what John C. Calhoun described as an "expansible state."[22] Consequently, governing has often taken the form of "a government out of sight" that relies on private actors as government agents rather than requiring the construction of a classically Weberian state with its offices inhabited by bureaucrats wielding stamps and official seals.[23] This pattern of legislative delegation—whether to the executive or to private entities—can be traced through a sequence of wartime mobilizations in the United States, from the Civil War through the particularly intense confrontation of wartime challenges with fierce antistatism in the aftermath of World War II and the Korean crisis. These moments of conflict between wartime mobilization and heightened defense of an ideologically constructed vision of free enterprise as the key to American power[24] add a key element to Watkins's analysis. In addition to political gridlock and crosscutting pressures from interest groups that might give rise to dictatorship by delegation, the growing landscape of delegated governance furthers the erosion of electoral responsibility and legislative accountability. This path leads not to the intensification and extension of concentrated executive power that is associated with the totalitarian threats of midcentury but rather to configurations of "infrastructural power" in which the state acts with and through the organizational capacity of civil society and the economy.[25]

As Brian Balogh has argued, this suggests that in the United States the federal government may not govern less so much as it governs differently. For those who equate stateness with the absolutist regimes of early modern Europe or the Weberian imagery of bureaucracy, the United States has long been both a mystery and something of a disappointment. The national capital was migratory for its first years, then underwhelming, muddy, and uncomfortable. The head count of employees of the "general government" remained small, with federal policy carried out by delegation to private individuals serving as its representatives.[26] Even the wrenching experience of a four-year civil war did not leave a legacy of greatly expanded and rationalized federal agencies.[27] President Lincoln's suspension of habeas corpus might have signaled the start of a robust and durable expansion of executive power, but, in the wake of the Civil War, the federal government did not retain a capacity to respond to such a crisis. Through the nineteenth century, opposition to a strong federal government and limited resources produced one configuration of expansible governance in which capacities were borrowed from private actors in time of crisis.[28] During the Civil War, for example, workers in war industries repeatedly called for the expansion of government armories and production facilities, but military procurement continued to rely heavily on private firms (and thus war workers remained private employees).[29]

Late nineteenth-century reformers struggled to expel patronage hiring from national administration and establish in its place a government in line with principles of national, meritocratic, civil service. But, even after these "expansions of national administrative capacities," the head count for the national government remained comparatively limited.[30] An expansion of federal jurisdiction without substantial increase in the bureaucratic staff could also be accomplished by the creation of new regulatory bodies (e.g., the Interstate Commerce Commission) that deployed new forms of expertise cultivated within the regulated industries or auxiliary areas such as the law[31] or by voluntarist arrangements in which the federal government borrowed capacity from private individuals and firms as in the extensive participation of "dollar-a-year" men in the mobilizations for the First and Second World Wars. At the federal as well as the state and local levels, the expansion of governing capacities often took the form of complex and fragmented alliances between public authorities and private associations or firms.[32] In contrast to Charles Tilly's summary claim that "states make war, war makes states," war making in the United States intensified the interpenetration of public and private organizations in the system of governance that had been a durable feature of governing arrangements.

The resulting underdevelopment of a centralized bureaucratic state was welcomed by many inasmuch as it provided a method for increasing the capacity of the national government in the face of an emergency without laying the foundations for a greatly expanded central state. This dynamic was particularly clear in the mobilization for the First World War, directed by a Democratic administration with many leading figures who had been boys in the South in the decade after the Civil War. Many had imbibed an antipathy to strong central government and sought a way to harness the full strength of the American economy to the war effort while preempting the expectation that wars would make states. As Frederic Paxson reflected after the conclusion of the First World War: "[I]n every military crisis war has been begun first and armies have been created after. . . . As a result, the standing agencies of government, including even the army and the navy, are never prepared for any emergency which has not been foreseen."[33] Even after a few years of watching Europe being ravaged by conflict, the United States entered the war with relatively little government capacity for guiding industrial and military mobilization.

As a consequence, the federal government borrowed as well as built new capacity. In 1916, Congress had created both the Council of National Defense and the US Shipping Board.[34] Advisory commissions had also been established for the navy and in the new field of aeronautics. Nevertheless: "[T]he breach with Germany, early in February, 1917, brought to full and abrupt realization the positive lack of agencies for national mobilization."[35] In each of these domains, the advisory apparatus was staffed with formerly private individuals who were charged with promoting cooperation and coordination among private firms and associations; in some cases, notably railroads, these arrangements would be superseded by direct government control.[36] Advocates of more centralized control despaired in the first year of the war: "The more committees, the more lack of coordination. . . . No one wants to give the power to one man."[37] By early 1918, critics were making public claims that the model for mobilization had failed. Yet the response was not a call for enhanced executive authority but rather for an even clearer delegation of authority over war mobilization to private citizens. The charge was led by members of the National Security League and, in particular, by Senator George Chamberlain of Oregon, who proposed a war cabinet composed of "three distinguished citizens" whose powers would include assignments of commissioned officers (in conflict with the president's role as commander-in-chief) and the authorization to hire a staff of indeterminate size at "just and reasonable compensation," a formulation that some read as a recipe for corruption.[38] In opposition to the Chamberlain bill, President Wilson encouraged support for a competing proposal that would vest the authority to reorganize federal agencies in the president, prompting "protests that Wilson was trying to destroy the republican form of government."[39]

In the face of these demands for greater government intervention and centralization, Secretary of War Newton Baker fiercely, and largely successfully, defended the war mobilization efforts from critiques of inefficiency and incompetence. Through an apparatus of collaborative committees, private corporations became allies of the national war effort without foreclosing the possibility of dismantling the wartime state once hostilities had ceased. And, as collaborators, they were also vulnerable to the exertion of state power when private management failed to overcome threats to the realization of war production. Coerced procurement and even the seizure of plants to settle labor disputes followed the entrance of the United States into the war early in 1917.[40] The arrangement of advisory councils also created a situation in which the borrowing of business capacity for supervision of the war spilled over into the borrowing of business capacity for industrial mobilization. As war contracts were awarded, "committeemen were forced to pass upon awards to their own companies," a practice that generated predictable condemnation and was soon followed by the Lever bill, which prohibited "the award of contracts by government officials to themselves."[41] Borrowings of capacity crisscrossed, becoming entangled with policies meant to avoid corruption and self-dealing by public authorities with control of public funds.

Just as moments of war foreground the possibility of exception, they also illuminate the politics of containing the expansion of executive power. The process of mobilization for and demobilization from the First World War represents a pattern that begins with insufficient state capacity to meet the threat. Mobilization then draws private firms as well as voluntary associations into the war-making project at the same time as government funds and authority flow to private actors. The experience of collaborative mobilization also strengthens and multiplies aversions to big government, which fuel, in turn, demands for rapid demobilization and transfer of government-funded industrial capacities into private hands. The growth of the federal government in other policy domains often hinged on similarly decentralized, collaborative, and arm's-length arrangements[42]—a combination that generated comparable surges of antistatism. Through new instruments of governance—federal matching grants to states and from states to local governments along with targeted deductions in the context of an expanding system of taxation—the capacity to govern through private entities became more powerful and sophisticated. This same matching-grant device was appropriated to navigate the constitutional challenges to the social insurance programs that formed the heart of the New Deal's social welfare legacy. That legacy was also organizational, generating the much-maligned "alphabet soup" of new agencies, and, by the end of the decade, prompting a presidential effort at executive reorganization.

But events came on more quickly than any reorganization could proceed. Consequently, when the conflicts that would become World War II intensified, government planners pulled organizational reports from World War I out of the files, following many of those suggestions to create yet another centralized but collaborative committee at the heart of the effort to harness the national economy to the war effort.[43] Once again, dollar-a-year men made their way to Washington, DC, and filled many of the important posts directing the wartime government. Embodying the height of logistic expertise in both conflicts, a representative of Sears, Roebuck was a prominent member of each wartime board. For all the expansion of its activities, the wartime state of the 1940s still rested on harnessing private organizational capacities to expand to meet the geopolitical challenges. But those private businessmen were now veterans of nearly a decade of New Deal policy implementation as well as memories of the incomplete demobilization after the First World War and, thus, came to this renewed collaboration with an intense awareness of its possible aftermath. Although the wartime expansion of industrial capacity was substantially financed by the federal government—through arrangements such as the government-owned, contractor-operated plant—business associations and private firms sponsored a sustained public relations effort to present the war as a triumph of private enterprise.[44]

As this quickly sketched history of administrative development suggests, the antistatist tradition in American political culture has left a profound mark on organization and methods of governing. Federal capacities and funding increased massively across the two world wars and the response to the Great Depression, but government expanded in ways that left a great deal of decision making and capacity—whether personnel or expertise—under the control of individuals who were not on the public payroll. Even in wartime, the flood of dollar-a-day men into Washington, DC, represented a surge of managerial expertise that—by virtue of its almost voluntary character—retained a sense of autonomy vis-à-vis central authority. In the face of repeated crises—military and natural, international and domestic—private firms and voluntary associations could be harnessed to national projects and then demobilized once the crisis had passed. This template for mobilization, captured in the concept of an expansible state,[45] substantially muted the developmental ratchet effect by which wars are presumed to make states. Yet, in the wake of World War II, the combination of sustained military mobilization and durable antistatism produced a significant inflection in the trajectory of state development, injecting private actors ever more deeply in the circuits of government action.

Postwar Involutions of the Expansible State

The language of national emergency took on new relevance in the years after World War II, creating the conditions under which one might expect a durable expansion of the power of the bureaucratic state. One important limit on administrative growth had been lifted during the war with the adoption of a national income tax. As soldiers began to be demobilized, it was at least imaginable that this funding stream might support a permanently expanded administrative state in Washington, DC. But, even as the troops began to return home, the sense of military threat did not ebb. The perceived threat of Soviet aggression replaced anti-Nazism as a motivation for military and intelligence efforts. But, in those initial struggles between the military eager to gain control of German weapons specialists and State Department officials worried about the diplomatic consequences of being seen to harbor Nazis, collaborations with private firms provided one means for relocating former enemy scientists so that they were partially insulated from oversight by other state agencies.[46] In the key domain of military technology, President Eisenhower would eventually tip the scales away from government-controlled production toward collaborations with private industry even as he eventually warned of the military-industrial complex.

Thus, the postwar years saw a continuation of the complex flows of federal funds to private industry, particularly in the domain of the military. Such arrangements allowed for the projection of national might while deflecting opposition to the continued expansion of the federal government, particularly in domestic policy domains. But this balancing act was soon challenged by President Truman's declaration in 1950 of a national emergency, prompted by the outbreak of conflict on the Korean Peninsula. Although that conflict infamously failed to be terminologically promoted from a *police action* to a *war*, the resulting declared emergency remained in force until it was explicitly terminated by the National Emergencies Act of 1976.[47] While Truman's declaration sits squarely on the main line of Agamben's narrative, one of the major legislative responses to that emergency declaration points toward that disarticulation of sovereignty, administration, and accountability as a different face of exception.

Faced with the rapid expansion of the defense establishment in response to the emergency, some members of Congress worked to disrupt the mechanisms by which wars make states. While supporting the military effort in Korea, they sought to prevent a greatly enlarged federal government. One vehicle for this effort was the strengthening in 1952 of the 1951 Whitten Amendment (sec. 1310)[48] to Public Law 253, the 1947 legislation enacted "to promote the national security by providing for a Secretary of Defense; for a National Military Establishment; for a Department of the Army, a Department of the Navy, a Department of the Air Force; and for the coordination of the activities of the National Military Establishment with other departments and agencies of the Government concerned with the national security" (July 26, 1947). The provisions of the Whitten Amendment sought to facilitate the transfer of federal personnel to defense activities while preventing nondefense agencies (however those were defined) from filling the resulting empty positions with permanent employees. A further check on the cost of the federal bureaucracy was created with a new rule that restricted any given employee to one promotion within fifty-two weeks. In this way, the Whitten Amendments promised to protect those jobs for employees who would presumably want to return to their nondefense positions after the termination of the emergency and prevented the expansion of the permanent federal workforce during the emergency. But, as critics immediately noted, the consequence would be an intensified hiring of temporary employees, "many of whom are unemployable except for menial work," that would eventually undercut any intended economies of the legislation through the decline in the efficiency of the workforce, particularly in the post office.[49]

By early 1953, a Senate report described the expected decline in "the number of permanent employees in the competitive service" (estimated to fall from 1.5 million in June 1950 to a projected 900,000 in June 1956) and cataloged the difficulties created by these provisions, including the additional costs imposed on both agencies and the Civil Service Commission. This report noted the "adverse effect on recruitment, especially in shortage occupations where the Government is in competition

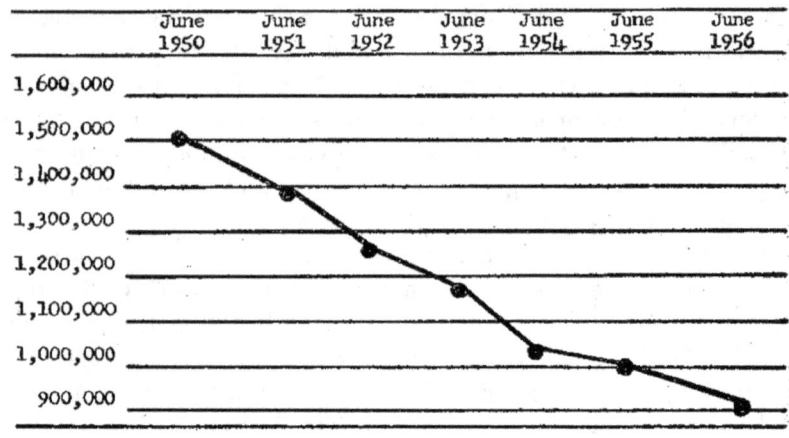

Source: "Analysis of the Whitten Amendment," Senate, 83rd Congress, 1st Session, Document No. 35 (Washington, DC: Government Printing Office, 1953.

with private industry for employees": "Potential employees are dissuaded from entering Federal Government because (with certain exceptions discussed above) their appointments are only temporary. This has an important psychological effect on the job security aspect."[50] It went on in considerable detail to describe the increased administrative efforts and sometimes elaborate work-arounds involved in managing the federal workforce under these constraints of overall size, rate of promotion, and accommodation of transfers from nondefense to defense activities. Alone or in combination with the national emergency, this long-standing commitment by some political factions to ensure that wars *not* make states produced an intensification and even transformation of familiar patterns of public-private state building.

The combination of the mass income tax and a surging postwar economy left the federal government with a robust capacity to raise revenues. As a percentage of GDP, federal revenue remained remarkably steady from the Second World War (when it just topped 20 percent), varying between 15 and 20 percent through the turn of the twenty-first century while both population and the absolute size of the economy grew substantially.[51] But, even with an enlarged population to govern and serve, this fiscal base supported an increasing range and penetration of government activity and regulation. A rough measure can be gained by counting the pages in the Federal Register, which grew from a new high point of just below twenty thousand pages during the Second World War to over eighty thousand pages by the first decade of the next century.[52] Yet, as revenue grew and regulations multiplied, the core of the Weberian state—the professional bureaucracy—grew comparatively little, constrained by legislation such as that advanced by Whitten.[53] In 1965, as Congress adopted an amendment to exclude the postal service from the employment cap, a report to the House of Representatives explained that, although the "Korean emergency has long since ended," the caps were in effect and effective: "Employment in the executive branch has shown no tendency to increase rapidly in recent years despite the general growth of the Nation in population and production, the advent of large-scale new Federal programs such as the space program, and the continued need for heavy defense efforts."[54]

Although there were occasional upward ticks, most notably during the late 1960s, when the combination of population growth, the Vietnam War, and the Great Society programs drove it higher, the federal workforce remained remarkably immune to the ongoing expansion in its resources or its responsibilities. As the *Wall Street Journal* observed in November 2014: "Not since July 1966 has the federal government's workforce been so small. (The spikes every decade are the hiring of several hundred thousand temporary workers to conduct the census.) Federal government hiring climbed in the 1960s, moved sideways in the 1970s, climbed to the highest level ever outside of a census in the 1980s, declined in the 1990s and then again held steady for most of the 2000s."[55]

In combination, the continued increase in revenues, expansion of regulations, and serious constraint on the size of the federal workforce drove a distinctive trajectory of state building that presented multiple challenges to principles of democratic accountability. In many policy domains, above all those touching on national security, the shadow state of government contracting surged. In new areas of government activity, including those centrally involved in the expansion of the growing security state, there were strong incentives to construct new government agencies in new ways: "Congress and the president established the Atomic Energy Commission in 1946, knowing that it would rely on private contractors for much of the work in harnessing the atom, and created the National Aeronautics and Space Administration in 1958 knowing full well that the agency would become a 'surge tank' filled with contractors. Better the jobs be in the private sector than in a bloated federal bureaucracy."[56] These arrangements, not entirely unlike those used to place German weapons experts just after the war, also provided opportunities to elude some of the strictures of federal hiring policy and allowed government to fund the comparative high salaries required by scientists and other technical experts who could easily be wooed away by private industry.

In this emerging template of state building, private efforts were no longer linked closely to those moments of expansibility in the face of war or domestic crisis. Instead, the concern to limit any increase in the permanent federal workforce consolidated a new approach to institutional design, a shift evident both in the design principles and in those enacting them. Consultants from McKinsey were contracted to map out the new agency, informed by their commitment to the principle that the country's "free enterprise society dictates that industry should be given as extensive a role as possible."[57] Their analysis was framed by the assumption that "NASA's problem . . . was not preventing excessive numbers of contractors from decreasing the agency's efficiency, but deciding how few internal experts NASA could employ to coordinate their efforts effectively."[58]

As the policy initiatives at the federal level expanded through the 1960s, this pattern of federal extension was replicated with ever-new variations. Medicare, for example, represented both a major new commitment of government funds and a policy that left key decision making in the hands of private hospitals, physicians, and insurers.[59] New federal initiatives, including the Community Mental Health Centers Act of 1963 and the community programs adopted as part of the Equal Opportunity Act of 1964, sent additional streams of federal funds into organizational populations that, hitherto, had been largely dependent on varying combinations of private and state or local funding. Thus, ongoing, as opposed to crisis-driven, commitments from government were designed to depend on an architecture supported by private organizations: "Faced with public pressure to expand social services, particularly for the poor, Congress enacted the 1967 Amendments to the Social Security Act (commonly called Title IV-A) which specifically encouraged states to enter into purchase-of-service agreements with private agencies."[60] And, whenever the increasing reliance on outside experts and organizational capacity threatened their control over policy, government administrators could respond by hiring outsiders of their own: "By the mid-1970s, management consulting firms were as likely as internal bureaucrats to conduct the special surveys and the routine reports for federal agencies like the Office of Technology Assessment, the Environmental Protection Agency, and the Department of Energy."[61]

The cumulative result was what public administration scholars came to describe in terms such as *the hollow state* or *the shadow state*.[62] Intensified by congressional efforts to reduce the size of government and introduce programs based on market models (e.g., school vouchers, public choice elements within Medicare), the result has been a kind of governing regime in which restrictions on the scale of the formal administrative apparatus produced a symbiotic arrangement between public institutions and private organizations (both for-profit and nonprofit) as well as the activities of individuals directed toward carrying out a wide range of federal mandates. As a result, political struggles came to be organized around the question of which kinds of private groups would be designated as the delegates responsible—and funded—for the implementation of federal policy: community action agencies versus mayors' offices in many of the Great Society programs, local and state government versus business coalitions in the oscillating employment-training initiatives represented by the Comprehensive Employment Training Act of 1973 (which was supplanted by the Job Partnership Training Act of 1982).[63]

Sustained by the fiscal power of the federal government, a number of these borrowed capacities were contracted on a regular basis, producing a system in which durable federal commitments were delivered through systems of delegation to both nonprofit and for-profit entities. Since at least the 1970s, however, efforts to contain or reduce the size of federal government have shifted the balance within these contracting relationships, leaving government agencies dependent on private funds for leverage. In the process, exchanges between citizens and their governments—of taxes, services, duties, obligations—are transformed into potential profit points, shifting the terms of government accountability and the incentives for political participation but also the configuration and autonomy of the executive.[64] In these ways, the capacity of the administrative state could expand by evading legislative limits in the form of caps on spending or the size of the federal workforce. As a consequence, the executive becomes entangled in ever more complex agency relationships with those charged with day-to-day responsibility for a dizzying array of activities authorized and/or funded by some government entity.[65]

Although this pattern of delegated governance was established in the United States long before the 1980 election of Ronald Reagan and the ascendance of modern conservatism, the legacies of the Great Society energized additional turns against big government, providing distinctive tactical advantages to those who sought to cut back programs of public provision without bearing the political costs. One of the characteristics of contracted or delegated governance is that it is less visible to voters; responsibility for cuts or declines in the quality of service are more difficult to attribute directly to elected officials and also often less potent with respect to mobilizing constituencies of those who will suffer from a loss of benefits. As a consequence, even when conservative officials have been unable—or unwilling—to cut the funding for government programs, they may attempt to restructure the organized provision of those services to increase deniability[66] and decrease the likelihood of an organized backlash in defense of public spending.[67]

Over the decades that followed, the discourse of antistatism increasingly focused on the introduction of market models and entrepreneurialism in public service, often under the banner of the "new public management."[68] In this context, even those who sought to expand government faltered when confronted by those with stakes in mixed and convoluted systems of public-private social provision. The Clinton health care initiative of 1993 (d. 1994) serves as one poster child for this dilemma.[69] The political clout of the defense industry (expanded to include contractors in national security and surveillance) would be another. Among the most striking developments has been the transformation of border enforcement. During the administration of President George W. Bush, the Secure Border Initiative was intended to engineer a shift from "simply buy[ing] an amalgam of high-tech equipment" that would help government agents patrol the borders to "a unitary technological system." As a consequence, expertise increasingly developed within private firms. This familiar set of major defense contractors also developed new abilities to shape and make key decisions about apprehension and the enforcement of the borders of sovereign territory. As Paul Verkuil observed of the then newly formed Department of Homeland Security, the core problem is that, while that agency "must have known that inherent government functions are involved in these assignments, . . . there has been no review of whether these duties have been properly delegated to contractors."[70] Little more than a decade later, it is evident that these complexities are not limited to relations with private defense contractors. As the politics of border enforcement intensifies under the Trump administration, not only private firms but also nonprofit organizations (at times closely entwined with for-profit providers) are charged with the care in confinement of migrants, both adults and children, sometimes together, often apart.[71]

In an effort to grasp the scale of these arrangements, Paul Light developed estimates from 1997 survey responses to the question, "How much time do you spend doing things in your work that are required by the federal government?"[72] The total came to 4.6 million full-time equivalents. Imagined as concentric circles, the resulting complex political dynamics are evident: a core of federal employees, bound by the rules of the civil service and, presumably, embedded in the strongest principal-agent relationships to elected officials, outnumbered more than two to one by employees of contractors with interests in the perpetuation, and indeed expansion, of federal spending, both encircled by almost five million full-time-equivalent employees carrying out unfunded mandates and, in many cases, presumably eager to have those lifted. Those full-time, career employees at the center of this arrangement have become targets for a particularly fierce resentment in right-wing politics, envied for their benefits and secure retirements guaranteed by pensions paid for by taxpayers unsure of how they themselves will manage in old age or whether Social Security will be there for them.[73] But those rising tax burdens are also supporting a complex, often submerged network of government-funded and authorized activity that is not easily recognized as "what the government does for you."

Delegated Governance as a Structure of Exceptions

While these developments in contracting and procurement are known to scholars of public administration, they pose a different kind of question to those interested in the lawful character of contemporary democratic governance. The reliance on delegated governance need not inject elements of lawlessness within the law as formulated in terms of the state of exception. This result follows only to the extent that those private entities or individuals charged with carrying out federally mandated and/or funded activities are subject to different and lesser requirements for accountability and transparency than public agents providing the same services to citizens would be. This is a space not simply of the attenuation of accountability or the loss of transparency but also of opportunity for the political mobilization of private interests via the institutional channels of the administrative state, evading what countervailing forces might still be mobilized in the formal arenas of democratic politics. Such erosion of democratic accountability is particularly dangerous when essentially government functions—analysis, evaluation, and decision making—slip from strictly government control.[74]

Just such a pattern of delegated governance by a financially strapped administrative state has transformed the democratic qualities of the contemporary American polity as well as of many other advanced industrial democracies. Adopting Michael Mann's concept of infrastructural power, Sidney Tarrow illuminates the structural transformations wrought by more than a decade of a global War on Terror conducted in large part through the deployment of complex technologies produced and often controlled by private firms.[75] Expansion of the formal capacities of state agencies and the executive are constrained, but the reach of government action expands. Yet those exercising delegated authority are not necessarily bound to the same expectations of equity and transparency that apply to public agencies and elected officials.

When state building is conceptualized as a make-or-buy decision,[76] big state versus small government arguments are replaced by an analysis of the trench warfare over whether public funds will be spent by public agencies or transformed into contracts to be allocated to private firms. In the same year that Britain saw one large firm shuddering toward bankruptcy and, with it, a vast range of services that it provided to government agencies, the United States saw policy reversals with respect to federal use of for-profit prisons and private bank participation in the federal student loan program. Erik Prince, the founder of what was once Blackwater, offered to take the Afghan conflict off federal hands by outsourcing responsibility for counterterrorism.[77] While the proponents of such plans may also demand lower taxes, what they are fundamentally calling for is not a small government but rather a government that has opted to buy rather than make public services and, thereby, contribute to the systematic opacity of agency relationships within a formally democratic regime.[78]

The resulting landscape of exceptions, in which civic rights and political voice are transformed, obstructed, and constrained by the organization of governance, generates distinctive dynamics of political development. Indirect forms of service provision—contracting out, voucher programs, and tax subsidies—depress the mobilization of constituent support for those services by making it ever more difficult for citizens to answer the question, "What are my tax dollars doing for me?"[79] As political support for explicitly public programs has ebbed and critiques of big government have been joined to programs of privatization, opportunities for the exercise of political voice and citizens' rights have been refigured in a polity that comprises both public and private domains. This link to electoral politics is only one slice of the complex interactions between governance and democratic politics that play out across the fragmented landscape of democratic politics, itself the focus of an increasingly rich historical analysis of delegated sovereignty and governance in American political development. The challenges of the present moment are the product of a long history of constructing hegemonic state power in a polity marked by persistent antistatism. Driven by crisis and repeated bouts of mobilization in the face of persistent antistatism, the path from delegated governance may lead not to classic forms of dictatorship but rather to new forms of lesser lawfulness within the law.

Notes

1. P. W. Singer, *Corporate Warriors: The Rise of the Privatized Military Industry* (Ithaca, NY: Cornell University Press, 2003); Paul R. Verkuil, *Outsourcing Sovereignty: Why Privatization of Government Functions Threatens Democracy and What We Can Do about It* (New York: Cambridge University Press, 2007), 26–28.
2. To trace this development, see Giorgio Agamben, *Homo Sacer: Sovereign Power and Bare Life,* trans. Daniel Heller-Roazen (1995; Stanford, CA: Stanford University Press, 1998), and *State of Exception,* trans. Kevin Attell (Chicago: University of Chicago Press, 2005).
3. Agamben, *Homo Sacer,* 15, 24–25, 37–38; Verkuil, *Outsourcing Sovereignty,* 14–15.
4. On the limits and internal tensions of popular sovereignty, see Agamben, *Homo Sacer,* 177. For a discussion of passive and active rights, see ibid., 130.
5. Frederick M. Watkins, "The Problem of Constitutional Dictatorship," *Public Policy* 1 (1940): 368–69, 371, 373.
6. Sanford Levinson and Jack M. Balkin, "Constitutional Dictatorship: Its Dangers and Design," *Minnesota Law Review* 94 (2010): 1836.
7. Agamben, *Homo Sacer,* 121.
8. As Watkins wrote of the then-recent history of the New Deal: "Prior to 1934 the doctrine that Congress might not delegate its legislative powers was supported by nothing more compelling than a series of judicial dicta. Although the validity of such an act of delegation had been repeatedly denied in theory, the fact remained that no single act of Congress had ever been rejected on these grounds. This circumstance encouraged Congress, in the crisis conditions which prevailed at the beginning of the present Roosevelt administration, to pass a number of acts vesting the executive with broad powers of emergency legislation." Watkins, "The Problem of Constitutional Dictatorship," 377–78.
9. As part of the Executive Reorganization Act of 1951, the Subdelegation Act allows for the executive to subdelegate powers delegated to it by the legislature, but with the restriction that such second-order delegations "can only be made to officers of the United States." Verkuil, *Outsourcing Sovereignty,* 122–24.
10. Verkuil, *Outsourcing Sovereignty,* 124–29. Watkins explicitly bracketed such concerns, observing: "[S]o long as the ban on redelegation is applied to the activity of legislatures, the forms of constitutional amendment are left as the only legitimate basis for the passage of enabling acts." Watkins, "The Problem of Constitutional Dictatorship," 378.
11. The principal of "Chevron deference" to administrative agencies in the interpretation of rules is the target of sustained challenge in a series of suits currently under review. See "Waiving *Chevron* Deference," *Harvard Law Review* 132 *(2019):* 1520, https://harvardlawreview.org/2019/03/waiving-chevron-deference.
12. On "iron triangles" and "issue networks," see Hugh Heclo, "Issue Networks and the Executive Establishment," in *The New American Political*

System, ed. Anthony King (Washington, DC: American Enterprise Institute, 1971), 87–124.

13. On the constitutional dilemmas created by civil rights protests for service from private firms, see Christopher W. Schmidt, *The Sit-Ins: Protest and Legal Change in the Civil Rights Era* (Chicago: University of Chicago Press, 2018).

14. As Craig Calhoun has written, "the emergency" has been "woven into a social imaginary" in which "international and global affairs have come to be constructed largely in terms of the opposition between more or less predictable systems of relationships and flows and the putatively unpredictable eruptions of emergencies." Craig Calhoun, "A World of Emergencies: Fear, Intervention, and the Limits of Cosmopolitan Order," *Canadian Review of Sociology* 41, no. 4 (2004): 374. For an earlier critique of this formulation, see the discussion of Walter Benjamin's response to Carl Schmitt in Agamben, *State of Exception*, 59.

15. "FOIA Legislative History," National Security Archive, http://nsarchive.gwu.edu/nsa/foialeghistory/legistfoia.htm.

16. John Wonderlich quoted in Danielle Ivory, "Transparency Outsourced as U.S. Hires Vendors for Disclosure Aid," Bloomberg, October 8, 2012, http://www.bloomberg.com/news/articles/2012-10-09/transparency-outsourced-as-u-s-hires-vendors-for-disclosure-aid.

17. Referencing works by Watkins, Friedrich, Rossiter, and Tingsten, Agamben notes: "[These books] record for the first time how the democratic regimes were transformed by the gradual expansion of the executive's powers during the two world wars and, more generally, by the state of exception that had accompanied and followed those wars." Agamben, *State of Exception*, 6.

18. Agamben, *State of Exception*, 67–69.

19. Agamben, *State of Exception*, 82–84.

20. Watkins, "The Problem of Constitutional Dictatorship," 369–70. Britain's Defense of the Realm Act was singled out as a particularly striking instance of such delegation.

21. Watkins, "The Problem of Constitutional Dictatorship," 371–72.

22. Ira Katznelson, "Flexible Capacity: The Military and Early American State-Building," in *Shaped by War and Trade: International Influences on American Political Development*, ed. Ira Katznelson and Martin Shefter (Princeton, NJ: Princeton University Press, 2002), 82–110. For an extended argument on this point, see Elisabeth S. Clemens, *Civic Gifts: Voluntarism and the Making of the American Nation-State* (Chicago: University of Chicago Press, 2020).

23. On the associational state, see Brian Balogh, *"A government out of sight": The Mystery of National Authority in Nineteenth-Century America* (New York: Cambridge University Press, 2009), and *The Associational State: American Governance in the Twentieth Century* (Philadelphia: University of Pennsylvania Press, 2015).

24. Mark R. Wilson, *Destructive Creation: American Business and the Winning of World War II* (Philadelphia: University of Pennsylvania Press, 2016), 92–138.

25. Michael Mann, "The Autonomous Power of the State: Its Origins, Mechanisms and Results," *European Journal of Sociology* 25, no. 2 (1984): 185–213;

Sidney Tarrow, "Mann, War, and Cyberspace: Dualities of Infrastructural Power in America," *Theory and Society* 47 (2018): 61–85. The political theorist Sheldon Wolin has termed such configurations an "inverted totalitarianism" that, "while exploiting the authority and resources of the state, gains its dynamic by combining with other forms of power, such as evangelical religions, and most notably by encouraging a symbiotic relationship between traditional government and the system of 'private' governance represented by the modern business corporation." Sheldon Wolin, *Democracy Inc.: Managed Democracy and the Specter of Inverted Totalitarianism* (Princeton, NJ: Princeton University Press, 2008), xxi.

26. Balogh, *"A government out of sight."*

27. Richard Bensel, *Yankee Leviathan: The Origins of Central State Authority in America, 1859–1877* (New York: Cambridge University Press, 1990).

28. Katznelson, "Flexible Capacity."

29. Mark R. Wilson, *The Business of Civil War: Military Mobilization and the State, 1861–1865* (Baltimore: Johns Hopkins University Press, 2006).

30. Stephen Skowronek, *Building a New American State: The Expansion of National Administrative Capacities, 1877–1920* (New York: Cambridge University Press, 1982). See also Daniel P. Carpenter, *The Forging of Bureaucratic Autonomy: Reputations, Networks, and Policy Innovation in Executive Agencies, 1862–1928* (Princeton, NJ: Princeton University Press, 2001).

31. For quite different perspectives on these developments, see Gabriel Kolko, *The Triumph of Conservatism: A Reinterpretation of American History, 1900–1916* (New York: Free Press, 1963); and Thomas K. McCraw, *Prophets of Regulation: Charles Francis Adams, Louis D. Brandeis, James M. Landis, Alfred E. Kahn* (Cambridge, MA: Harvard University Press, 1984).

32. William Novak, "The Myth of the 'Weak' American State," *American Historical Review* 113, no. 3 (2008): 752–72; Elisabeth S. Clemens, "Lineages of the Rube Goldberg State: Building and Blurring Public Programs, 1900–1940," in *The Art of the State: Rethinking Political Institutions*, ed. Ian Shapiro, Stephen Skowronek, and Daniel Galvin (New York: New York University Press, 2006), 187–215; Carol Nackenoff and Julie Novkov, eds., *Statebuilding from the Margins: Between Reconstruction and the New Deal* (Philadelphia: University of Pennsylvania Press, 2014).

33. Frederic L. Paxson, "The American War Government, 1917–1918," *American Historical Review* 26, no. 1 (1940): 56–57. For a close study of the local impact of these arrangements, see Adam J. Hodges, *World War I and Urban Order: The Local Class Politics of National Mobilization* (London: Palgrave Macmillan, 2016).

34. Paxson, "The American War Government," 57. For Agamben's treatment of this moment, see *State of Exception*, 21.

35. Paxson, "The American War Government," 57 (see also 61). On railroads, see Max Thelen, "Federal Control of Railroads in War Time," *Annals of the American Academy of Political and Social Science* 76 (1918): 14–24. See also James Miller Leake, "The Conflict over Coördination," *American Political Science Review* 12, no. 3 (1918): 365–80.

36. Margaret L. Coit, *Mr. Baruch* (Boston: Houghton Mifflin, 1957), 166.
37. Leake, "The Conflict over Coördination," 369, 372.
38. Robert D. Ward, "The Origins and Activities of the National Security League, 1914–1919," *Mississippi Valley Historical Review* 47, no. 1 (1960): 51–65. The bill's supporters were motivated by their concern that the Wilson administration had refused to do one very state-like thing: call for universal military training. Leake, "The Conflict over Coordination," 375.
39. James Startt, *Woodrow Wilson, the Great War, and the Fourth Estate* (Austin: Texas A&M University Press, 2017).
40. Wilson, *Destructive Creation*, 10–11.
41. Paxson, "The American War Government," 67.
42. Gerald Berk, *Louis D. Brandeis and the Making of Regulated Competition, 1900–1932* (New York: Cambridge University Press, 2009).
43. Coit, *Mr. Baruch*, 475.
44. Wilson, *Destructive Creation*, 59–76, 92–138.
45. Katznelson, "Flexible Capacity."
46. Brian E. Crim, *Our Germans: Project Paperclip and the National Security State* (Baltimore: Johns Hopkins University Press, 2018).
47. Public Law 94-412, September 14, 1976. See "Emergency Powers Statutes: Provisions of Federal Law Now in Effect Delegating to the Executive Extraordinary Authority in Time of National Emergency," Report of the Special Committee on the Termination of the National Emergency, Report No. 93-549, US Senate, 93rd Cong., 1st sess., November 19, 1973.
48. Paul C. Light, *The True Size of Government* (Washington, DC: Brookings Institution Press, 1999), 99–103.
49. As Leo George, the president of the National Federation of Post Office Clerks, argued: "The Whitten rider does not effect a saving in manpower, in dollars or in facilities required, and it results in lowered morale of all employees and a deteriorated service." Leo George, "The Foolish Whitten Rider," *American Federationist* 49, no. 4 (1952): 22–23.
50. "Analysis of the Whitten Amendment," Document No. 35, US Senate, 83rd Cong., 1st sess., March 18, 1953, 2–3 (see also 12–13). In 1965, the House recommended exempting the Postal Field Service from the limits imposed by sec. 1310. Report No. 220, US House of Representatives, 89th Cong., 1st sess., April 1, 1965.
51. "U.S. Federal Government Revenue (Current and Inflation Adjusted)," September 5, 2012, http://www.truthfulpolitics.com/http:/truthfulpolitics.com/comments/u-s-federal-government-revenue-current-and-inflation-adjusted/?utm_source=twitter&utm_medium=friendly%2Blinks&utm_campaign=twitter%2Bfl%2Bplugin.
52. "Plumbing Presidential Power: Pens, Phones, and Paperwork," Math of Politics, January 31, 2014, http://www.mathofpolitics.com/2014/01/31/plumbing-presidential-power-pens-phones-paperwork.
53. Jamie L. Whitten, it should be noted, served in the House of Representatives from 1941 to 1995, a career capped by a long spell (1979–92) as chair of the powerful House Appropriations Committee.

54. "Exemption of Postal Field Service from Section 1310 of Supplemental Appropriation Act, 1952 (Whitten Amendment)," House of Representatives, Report No. 220, 89th Cong., 1st sess., April 1, 1965. 1–2. See also "Pressure Groups Happy with 1965 Legislation," *Congressional Quarterly Almanac, 1965, 1440–49.*

55. Josh Zumbrun, "The Federal Government Now Employs the Fewest People since 1966," *Wall Street Journal,* November 7, 2014, http://blogs.wsj.com/economics/2014/11/07/the-federal-government-now-employs-the-fewest-people-since-1966.

56. Light, *The True Size of Government,* 101–3. See also Kimberly Morgan and Andrea Campbell, *The Delegated Welfare State: Medicare, Markets, and the Governance of Social Policy* (New York: Oxford University Press, 2011), 62.

57. Quoted in Christopher D. McKenna, *The World's Newest Profession: Management Consulting in the Twentieth Century* (New York: Cambridge University Press, 2006), 104.

58. McKenna, *The World's Newest Profession,* 105.

59. Morgan and Campbell, *The Delegated Welfare State.*

60. Steven Rathgeb Smith and Michael Lipsky, *Nonprofits for Hire: The Welfare State in the Age of Contracting* (Cambridge, MA: Harvard University Press, 1993), 54–55.

61. McKenna, *The World's Newest Profession,* 108.

62. H. Brinton Milward and Keith G. Provan, "Managing the Hollow State: Collaboration and Contracting," *Public Management Review* 5, no. 1 (2003): 1–18; Jennifer R. Wolch, *The Shadow State: Government and Voluntary Sector in Transition* (New York: Foundation Center, 1990).

63. Robert Guttman commented that, in a piece written "following the enactment of CETA," he wrote "that 'though all agreed on the need to decentralize not all agreed on who would control under decentralization.'" The Job Training Partnership Act established "a private industry council for each service delivery area": "The majority of the membership will be representative of the private sector, one of whom will be selected to be chairperson. The remaining members will be representatives of educational agencies, organized labor, rehabilitation agencies, community-based organizations, economic development agencies, and the Employment Service." Robert Guttman, "Job Training Partnership Act: New Help for the Unemployed," *Monthly Labor Review* 106 (March 1983): 3–10, 7. I am grateful to LiChung Cheng for introducing me to this episode of policy history.

64. See, e.g., Brian Gran and William Henry, "Holding Private Prisons Accountable: A Socio-Legal Analysis of 'Contracting Out' Prisons," *Social Justice* 34, nos. 3–4 (2007–8): 173–194.

65. Think Edward Snowden, to cite only the most obvious example.

66. Paul Pierson, *Dismantling the Welfare State? Reagan, Thatcher, and the Politics of Retrenchment* (New York: Cambridge University Press, 1994); Jacob S. Hacker and Paul Pierson, *Off Center: The Republican Revolution and the Erosion of American Democracy* (New Haven, CT: Yale University Press, 2005).

67. Andrea Louise Campbell, *How Policies Make Citizens: Senior Political Activism and the American Welfare State* (Princeton, NJ: Princeton University Press, 2003).

68. This was a transnational movement of government reform. See Ezra Suleiman, *Dismantling Democratic States* (Princeton, NJ: Princeton University Press, 2003).

69. Theda Skocpol, *Boomerang: Clinton's Health Security Effort and the Turn against Government in U.S. Politics* (New York: Norton, 1996); Paul Starr, *Remedy and Reaction: The Peculiar American Struggle over Health Care Reform* (New Haven, CT: Yale University Press, 2011).

70. Verkuil, *Outsourcing Sovereignty*, 34.

71. "He's Built an Empire, with Detained Migrant Children as the Bricks," *New York Times,* December 2, 2018.

72. Light, *The True Size of Government*, 19–36.

73. Katherine J. Cramer, *The Politics of Resentment: Rural Consciousness in Wisconsin and the Rise of Scot Walker* (Chicago: University of Chicago Press, 2016), 127–38.

74. Verkuil, *Outsourcing Sovereignty*, 124–32.

75. Tarrow, "Mann, War, and Cyberspace."

76. For the classic discussion, see Ronald Coase, "The Nature of the Firm," *Economica* 4, no. 16 (1937): 386–405.

77. Erik Prince, "Contractors, Not Troops, Will Save Afghanistan," *New York Times*, August 30, 2017, https://www.nytimes.com/2017/08/30/opinion/erik-prince-contractors-afghanistan.html.

78. On the dangers of conflating antigovernment and small government positions, see Cramer, *The Politics of Resentment*, 216.

79. Suzanne Mettler, *The Submerged State: How Invisible Government Policies Undermine American Democracy* (Chicago: University of Chicago Press, 2011).

12 Spaces of Exception in American History

Gary Gerstle and Desmond King

Virtually every modern state generates a Foucauldian force field of governmentality that envelops people encapsulated in its territory. Governmentality usually involves classification and, thus, the elaboration of hierarchies or systems of inclusion and exclusion meant to ensure a polity's smooth functioning.[1] These processes unfold even in states that are founded on liberal and democratic principles and dedicated to the proposition that all inhabitants ought to be judged by the same standards. Historically, subordination and exclusion have often been imposed on citizens or aspirant citizens or involuntary residents on grounds of national origins and ethnicity, race, and gender. In the case of the United States, the nature, timing, and duration of these impositions have attracted a great deal of scholarly attention.

In this chapter, we introduce a *spatial* dimension to this framework of state-sanctioned subordination, exclusion, and control. We problematize what we label *spaces of exception*—spaces inhabited by certain groups in which the full rights of citizenship do not apply. More often than not, these spaces have been sanctioned by law, so they are not illegal or extralegal. They do not require emergency decrees and are not part of a Schmittian state of exception characterized by the suspension of law and the assumption by the state of emergency powers. They are normal parts of the polity, authorized by law, designed to serve long-term political purposes.

In principle, there are numerous spatial zones. They include, for example, the home, where for centuries the father and husband exercised control over his wife and children, and prisons, where lawbreakers are stripped of their freedom and rights. Both spaces have been legal forms of power configurations. Prisons, for example, are evidently spaces where a sovereign state exercises extraordinary power and men and women have few rights. They can arise in the case of emergency or perceived emergency, as the case of Japanese American incarceration during World War II demonstrates. But in a liberal society they are not primarily about emergency. They are a normal part of the rule of law, which requires that lawbreakers be punished by confinement and by being stripped of their freedom. Liberal polities disagree on how thoroughly prison space ought to be marked as different from the free space in which the masses of law-abiding citizens reside. Some countries, for example, disenfranchise inmates, and some do not.[2]

Our space of exception is a distinct category. We define it as *a zone in a liberal democracy that the sovereign controls but where liberal-constitutional principles do not govern or govern only partially*. Such spaces are not formulated in response to emergency and, thus, are not, in the first instance, characterized in terms of exceptional measures temporarily imposed. They arise to provide solutions to particular sets of problems that a liberal polity has encountered. Because the problems addressed are dense and persistent, the spaces of exception assume a more permanent or durable form than might have been expected. The durability imperative usually results in spaces of exception not only existing for relatively long periods of time but also spawning robust governing structures. They tend to be thickly regulated, and they tend to have material spatial demarcation. They come to be seen as different but acceptable features of society. We discuss three instances in this chapter: the unincorporated territories of Puerto Rico and the Philippines in the half century after they became colonies of the United States, the fluid space occupied by immigrant aliens, and the ex-Confederate states during the era of Jim Crow.

We contend that across American history spaces of exception have occupied territory significant both in size and in terms of the numbers of people who lived or resided therein. Questions about these spaces abound: What purposes did they serve? How was their existence legitimated? How did their configuration change over time? That is, did they expand or contract in territory and population, and why? If some spaces shrank in significance, did others come to the fore? Can we construe these very different kinds of spaces as constituting a single genre of exception? And, if we can, what does the history of these spaces tell us about the liberalism of the society in which they arose?

To our knowledge, Giorgio Agamben was the first to deploy the phrase *space of exception*. Our use of the term is different from his, however. Agamben viewed the concentration camp—introduced at the turn of the twentieth century by the Spanish in Cuba, the British in South Africa, and the Americans in the Philippines and perfected by the Nazis in the 1930s and 1940s—as the emblem of political modernity. He regarded these spaces of exception as constituting something more permanent and sinister than the statist form of exception, which he saw as a temporary measure that could be overcome. Particular spaces could be dismantled—as the Nazi death camps were—but new ones were always opening up. For Agamben, the frequency with which regimes in the modern world resorted to roundups, detention centers, and mass forms of incarceration signaled that the exception was no longer exceptional but the rule.[3]

Agamben, to our way of thinking, gives the Nazis too much credit; not all detention centers should be understood through the lens of their death camps. A *space* of exception, as we explain in the pages that follow, is a form of governance distinct from a *state* of exception, the two serving different purposes. The former exists alongside the latter, sometimes intersecting, sometimes not. It needs to be understood on its own terms and not as a state of exception's highest and most permanent form.

This chapter examines three spaces of exception. The first is the *unincorporated territory*, defined as land that the United States ruled but in which the federal government had been authorized (by US courts) to withhold normal constitutional governance. In the late nineteenth-century United States, this phrase became the agreed-on term to denote America's formal colonies. The second is space occupied by immigrant aliens in the United States. From the late nineteenth century on, this space was conceived of as foreign space, its inhabitants not protected by the Constitution in ways in which citizens were. Small parts of it were real, fixed spaces, such as Ellis Island and Angel Island. But most of it was fluid. When immigrant aliens moved, this space of exception moved with them, always bracketing them, encasing them in an extraconstitutional bubble or parenthesis.

The third space was the Jim Crow system that structured the ex-Confederate states for the first half of the twentieth century. Unlike the system prevailing in the unincorporated territory, Jim Crow was implemented in space existing within the continental United States that long ago had been designated *incorporated*, meaning a space where the Constitution was meant to rule. But here, in important ways, it did not.

Each of the three spaces had a spillover effect informing the attitudes of those located outside them toward those located within them. This spillover was most severe with respect to Jim Crow since many of the de jure rules in the ex-Confederate spaces had complementary de facto counterparts in the other parts of the United States. Yet spaces of exception and nonexception are, to our way of thinking, analytically distinct entities. It is this difference that we propose to analyze.

All the spaces that we examine in this chapter will be familiar to readers. But rarely have they been looked at alongside each other or treated as analogous forms of spatial exception.[4] We analyze each in detail to determine their role in America's state-building history. They constitute a distinct configuration of spatial and rights exclusivity. We have plenty of accounts of the deprivation and restoration of rights in the history of American nation building but rather fewer about how the territorial specification of exclusion augmented this process.

Six general points inform our analysis of spaces of exception. First, identifying certain districts as exceptional spaces of constitutional governance does not mean that no laws governed them. To the contrary, these spaces were thickly governed, generating important questions about illiberal practices within a nominally liberal state.

Second, we should resist the urge (marked among historians of postbellum and early twentieth-century America) to assume that the existence of these spaces demonstrates that the US federal state was becoming ever more powerful and unconstrained in its activities. The first two types of spaces—the unincorporated territory and the space occupied by aliens—fit this "strong state" paradigm since they can be interpreted as demonstrations of expanding federal power at a moment when America was seeking international repute.[5] But the third space, Jim Crow space, was something else: a demonstration of the inability of the federal government to control a space over which it might have exercised full jurisdiction. This last space of exception was a demonstration less of federal power than of its absence and helps throw some light on how federalism—itself a spatial grid governing the distribution of power within America's governing system—held back constitutional rights building.[6]

Third, the delineation of these spaces was often bound up with racial anxiety and racial threat, specifically the fear that the inhabitants of these spaces—racially suspect African Americans, Puerto Ricans, East and South

Asians (including Filipinos), and eastern and southern Europeans—could not handle the responsibilities of American citizenship.

Fourth, the existence of these spaces was always in some manner contested, the charge being that they were spaces over which constitutional protections and mechanisms of self-government ought to have had more sway. The struggles that erupted did make a difference: the use of the unincorporated territory mechanism declined over time, immigrant aliens gained expanded constitutional protections between the 1970s and the 1990s, and the civil rights movement conquered and transformed the space of Jim Crow. This level of contestation makes spaces of exception crucial to accounts of state building and exposes how they can become sources of state instability even as most are designed to buttress state authority.

Fifth, spaces of exception vary widely in duration, character, and permeability. Some are meant to be temporary: holding lawbreakers until they serve their sentences or holding immigrants on Ellis Island until they are processed. Others are meant to be long-term: the position of African Americans in the South during the age of Jim Crow or of residents of the Philippines under US control from the 1890s to the 1940s. And then there is the status of Puerto Ricans and Filipinos (until the 1930s), who inhabited a space of exception as long as they stayed at home but could become full citizens of the United States if they migrated to the mainland, as they were free to do. One has to reckon as well with the uncertain status of African Americans who fled the Jim Crow space of exception (which they were legally permitted to do) for northern city spaces characterized by a de facto but not a de jure system of inequality.

The variability in how these spaces of exception were constituted—some of them for the short term, others for the long term, some offering an easy mode of escape, others not—points to their significance in state building. Each was meant to solve a nettlesome problem of rule in a liberal-constitutional republic. Some spaces worked as intended; others did not. Those that did work sometimes incubated within their borders political sentiments and movements that would lead to their subsequent dissolution. Thus, even as they solved some problems for state builders, they were laying the foundations for new ones. To take the example of exclusion by spatial design: Jim Crow in the South removed the issue of post-Reconstruction racial equality from the federal center of the polity but stored up forces that would erupt and rupture the very same federal state decades later.

Finally, we cannot understand the history of spaces of exception and state building simply in terms of the linear advance of constitutional space and rights, a process that might allow us to declare with evident satisfaction that the era of spaces of exception is in some real sense now over. We should take care to avoid such an agreeable linearity and the teleological temptation that is linearity's handmaiden. The history of American democracy contains within it liberal and illiberal tendencies, the latter always capable of gaining the upper hand. Thus, for example, the alien immigrant space of exception that contracted during the presidencies of Nixon, Carter, and Reagan expanded under those of Clinton and Obama and metastasized under Trump. Meanwhile, new spaces of exception have arisen as the significance of older spaces faded. This is the argument that Michelle Alexander has made in identifying America's late twentieth-century archipelago of prisons as the "New Jim Crow."[7] And it may also be the case that America's worldwide system of military bases, themselves spaces of exception, has replaced the unincorporated territory as the key spatial device for projecting American power abroad. The impermanent and contested nature of particular spaces of exception does not, then, necessarily challenge the principle of exceptional space itself. The dissolution of one can simply lead to the creation of another. Such sequences imply that spaces of exception are a recurring dynamic in a state-building process located in a "liberty and coercion" miasma.

Space of Exception 1: Unincorporated Territories

In the decades after the Civil War, the US government strove to expand areas where it could exercise its power in ways that were exempt from strict constitutional review. This initiative is especially apparent in the central government's success in enlarging its freedom of action in administering land formally designated as territories. The central government had, on the one hand, always enjoyed broad latitude of action in its territories. On the other hand, precedents laid down in the original territorial legislation, the Northwest Ordinance of 1787, circumscribed that latitude for a century. The 1787 ordinance, passed initially by the Confederation Congress and reaffirmed by the first US Congress, prohibited slavery and guaranteed freedom of religion in the designated territories. It also defined land in the Northwest Territory as *incorporated territory*—a legal status granting the settlers who lived in it the right to petition the central government for a rapid transition to statehood. The 1803 treaty with France through which the United States purchased the Louisiana Territory contained a similar incorporating provision, as did most land-acquiring treaties that the United States ratified with foreign nations across the nineteenth century, a practice ending only with the Treaty of Paris signed with Spain in 1898.[8]

Under the incorporated territory provision, every new state was to receive the same broad authority that the Constitution had conferred on every existing state. Territorial incorporation also put the people living in these lands—sometimes all of them, other times only the white majority among them—on the road to American citizenship. This commitment to endowing new states with the same powers as the old ones ensured that the expansion of the United States would not make America an empire in the traditional British mold, with those residing in the core enjoying rights and privileges denied to those living on the periphery. Designating territory as incorporated ensured that this land would not become exceptional space in the Republic, subject to arbitrary exercise of power from the national metropole.[9]

The transformation of territories into states is a story thoroughly familiar to American historians: it is the spatial-political form that western expansion took. But that familiarity should not be allowed to dull an appreciation for the remarkably innovative character of this mode of expansion: implanting on land that varied greatly in size, topography, and population political-administrative systems that were virtually identical with each other and to those of the original thirteen states.

This mode of expansion began to weaken, however, during the Civil War era with respect to three territories that the United States had organized out of land taken from Mexico during the Mexican-American War (1846–48). Two of those territories—Arizona and New Mexico—contained large numbers of Indians and Mexicans, peoples whom many white Americans thought could not handle the responsibilities of republican statehood and citizenship. A third territory, Utah, contained a Mormon majority that wanted to write its polygamous practices into its state constitution. Each of these territories eventually gained statehood, but not before the process had stalled for decades (and not before Mormons in Utah formally relinquished the right to practice polygamy).[10] The lengthy period of time in which these territories were kept in limbo encouraged the courts to invent a new form of rule—the *unincorporated territory*—that, for the first time, explicitly freed the central government from the obligation to put newly acquired land on the road to statehood. This new legal category gave the US government the power to establish colonies—polities that it could rule indefinitely and without having to worry about representation, rights, due process, and other liberal/democratic imperatives imposed on it by the Constitution. Arizona, New

Mexico, and Utah escaped this unincorporated designation, but much of the land that America acquired as a result of the Spanish-American War—notably, Puerto Rico, Guam, and the Philippines—did not. By the early twentieth century, the US central government had acquired what it had not hitherto possessed: a *legal* mechanism for pursuing formal empire. In this respect, the federal government had secured a permanent zone or space of exception. It was defined as territory external to the continental United States and over which America would assert sovereignty without granting its people the full complement of rights and duties set forth in the Constitution and bestowed on previous territory designated as incorporated and placed on the road to statehood.[11]

A new membership category, the *national*, was invented to define the rights of the inhabitants of these newly defined unincorporated territories. Nationals occupied a status similar to that held by a monarchy's subjects: they were individuals who owed allegiance to the United States and were, in return, entitled to its protection. To Americans who saw themselves as believers in equality, the word *national* seemed preferable to *subject*, which connoted subservience. But little distinguished the status of one from the other. As was the case with kings and their subjects, the US government could choose to extend rights and privileges to its nationals but was under no obligation to do so. Indeed, the category *national* was inscribed into law alongside that of *citizen* precisely to define a subordinate status of belonging. It described a colonial status in fact, if not in name.[12]

This designation aroused considerable controversy from the start, especially in the case of Puerto Rico. Many in Congress seemed to have been prepared to extend citizenship to Puerto Ricans as an appreciative gesture for the latter's apparent embrace of the "liberating" US troops who came ashore in 1898. Many congressmen also seemed to believe that a majority of Puerto Ricans were Spanish and, therefore, white and capable of assimilating to republican practices. The United States retreated from its intention to confer citizenship not so much because of anything Puerto Ricans did after 1898 but because of what Filipinos were doing: engaging the United States in a fierce war to secure their independence. The Philippines were America's nightmare colonial possession. If the United States extended citizenship to Puerto Ricans, paving the way perhaps for the inclusion of their territory as a state, would it not have to do something similar for the feared Filipinos? To close off that possibility, Congress was determined to set the appropriate precedent, denying people in every unincorporated territory the rights of citizenship. The status of *national* was thus imposed on Puerto Ricans and

Filipinos, an imposition that the Supreme Court ratified with its ruling in the 1901 Insular Cases.[13]

These decisions hardly settled the matter as the apparent differences between the compliant Puerto Ricans and the defiant Filipinos remained stark. Moreover, the notion of America holding colonial possessions in the European mold continued to arouse domestic controversy. The United States took steps in 1916 to solve the Philippines problem by promising to put the nation on the road to independence; this commitment, in turn, allowed it to reward Puerto Ricans for their good behavior by extending to them US citizenship, which Congress did in 1917.[14] But granting citizenship to Puerto Ricans turned out to be a modest concession. Congress had persuaded itself that a grant of citizenship to people living in an unincorporated territory could be done without issuing them a package of rights and privileges similar to that given to citizens of the forty-eight states (and promised to the denizens of Alaska and Hawaii, which had achieved incorporated territory status). It had no intention in 1917 of putting Puerto Rico on even the slow Alaskan-Hawaiian path to statehood. To the contrary, the legislation conferring citizenship on Puerto Ricans—the Jones Act—seemed to put off the question of statehood indefinitely. The act affirmed Puerto Rico's status as an unincorporated territory, thereby solidifying its subordination.[15]

The Puerto Rican case demonstrated the free hand that Congress enjoyed in any territory defined as unincorporated, a power that made the island's continuing status as a space of exception appealing. When the Supreme Court reviewed the Jones Act in 1922, it constrained congressional power over Puerto Ricans in one way: citizenship, it ruled, conferred on Puerto Ricans an inalienable right "to move into the continental United States and become residents of any State there to enjoy every right of any other citizen of the United States, civil, social, and political."[16] In other words, Puerto Ricans could gain full US citizenship by individually relocating from unincorporated to incorporated territory, a move permissible at any time. But, within their home island, they enjoyed only those citizenship rights that Congress chose to bestow on them. And those rights did not include the right to be free and self-governing, starkly distinguishing them from the peoples who inhabited the forty-eight states.[17]

Filipinos in the early twentieth century fared even worse than Puerto Ricans at the hands of Congress. Lawmakers on Capitol Hill did not contemplate giving Filipinos a blanket grant of citizenship. Filipinos were simply too troublesome, not just in the Philippines, where a colonial war had lasted more than a decade, but, increasingly, in the continental

United States as well. As American nationals, they, like Puerto Ricans, gained unrestricted travel rights to the United States. By the 1920s, they were coming in large numbers, especially to Hawaii and the West Coast, where they constituted an important segment of the agricultural labor force. On the West Coast, they were quickly resented by American workers, for the same reasons that Chinese migrants had been two generations before: they allegedly lowered wages and working conditions for native-born workers.[18] Additionally, migrating Filipinos, heavily dominated by men, were seen as a threat to white womanhood. More and more reports of male Filipino–female white American liaisons began to circulate on the West Coast and then across the country via the press. The Filipino "invasion" had to be stopped. It was a key motive for the Tydings-McDuffie Act of 1934, which declared that the United States would grant the Philippines its independence ten years after a new (and US-sanctioned) constitution for this island nation was approved. The price of promised independence was the immediate revocation of the Filipino status of national. The 1934 law remade Filipinos into immigrant aliens, subject to the harsh provisions of the 1924 Immigration Restriction Act, which barred much of the world—and virtually all of Asia—from entering the United States. They lost the right to enter the United States at will; from 1934 on, only fifty Filipinos per year were permitted to "immigrate" to the continental United States.[19]

The 1934 law expressed fierce anti-Filipino sentiment of course. But it also constituted an admission by the United States that the unincorporated territory designation was not serving the country well as a mechanism of imperial control. The benefits expected from this newly invented space of exception did not outweigh the liabilities incurred.[20]

Space of Exception 2: Immigrant Alienage

As the federal government was engaged in its unincorporated territory experiment, it was also increasing its power to regulate immigration. Prior to the Civil War, it had shared control of immigration with the states. In the postbellum years, it alone had control. The Supreme Court made immigration regulation a plenary power, meaning that it was exempted from strict constitutional scrutiny. The Court justified this exemption by arguing that the regulation of immigration was an element of foreign policy, an area of governance in which the courts had long given the central state a free hand.[21] In 1892, it declared: "[I]t is an accepted maxim of international law, that every sovereign nation has the power, as inherent as sovereignty, and essential to self-preservation, to forbid the entrance of foreigners within its dominions, or to admit them only in such cases and upon such conditions as it may see fit to prescribe."[22] This exemption rendered immigration a vital instrument of executive branch engagements in state building.

Prior to the 1880s, the federal government had adhered to an open immigration policy. America possessed a rapidly expanding economy that was chronically short of labor. As a result, almost anyone from any part of the world was allowed to enter the United States and stay for as long as he or she wished. In the forty-year period from the 1880s to 1920s, however, Congress and the executive branch replaced this open borders policy with a closed border one. Approximately one million immigrants were entering the United States annually in the early years of the twentieth century. By the 1920s, the US government had shrunk this total by 80 percent, to less than 200,000 a year. It had the authority to do so.[23]

The government also possessed the authority to achieve such reductions through racial exclusions. Congress banned the immigration of Chinese laborers in 1882, and President Theodore Roosevelt ended the immigration of Japanese laborers in 1907. Congress prohibited all immigration from East and South Asia in 1917, and, in 1921 and 1924, it extended that ban to most of the world, for the first time striking at Europe and, in particular, groups from southern and eastern Europe that were also thought to be racially inferior and, hence, damaging to America's "Anglo-Saxon" or "Nordic" stock.[24]

Frankly racist justifications underlay such discriminatory practices: Chinese and Japanese were so different from Americans of European origin and so primitive, restrictionists argued, that they could never be civilized or acculturated. Here is how multiple legislators in the House of Representatives described eastern and southern European immigrants in 1924. "There is little or no similarity," declared Congressman Fred S. Purnell of Indiana, "between the clear-thinking, self-governing stocks that sired the American people and this stream of irresponsible and broken wreckage that is pouring into the lifeblood of America the social and political diseases of the Old World."[25]

The legislation excluding East and South Asians, eastern and southern Europeans, and, by the 1920s, virtually all Africans and West Asians was not vulnerable to court challenges. Because the right to control immigration was a plenary power, the actions of the central state were not held to the nondiscrimination standards laid out in the Fourteenth Amendment. If the United States wanted to bar specific groups from entering the country on the basis of race, nationality, sexuality, ideology, or poverty, it was free to do so.[26] In a critical Chinese Exclusion Case of

1889, Associate Justice Stephen Field had written that the judiciary had no authority over actions that Congress had taken with regard to an immigrant group determined to be unassimilable and dangerous to American "peace and security."[27]

Naturalization policy likewise lay beyond the reach of constitutional rights protection. The 1790 naturalization law had created a racial test for citizenship. An immigrant had to be free and white in order to qualify for membership in the American nation. While it was revised during Reconstruction to exempt immigrants of African descent from its exclusions, the law itself remained on the books for another eighty plus years, preventing virtually all immigrants from East and South Asia from becoming citizens of the United States. Once again, few of these individuals could find a remedy in the federal courts.[28] Immigrant aliens occupied a space both outside and inside the United States where the normal rights provisions of the Constitution did not rule.

The most vivid demonstration of this was Ellis Island itself, land owned by the federal government since 1808 and used for most of the nineteenth century as a fort or a storage site for munitions. In 1892, it became the central portal through which millions of immigrants coming to the United States by boat would have to pass in order to enter the country legally. Ellis Island itself was a space of exception: immigrants who disembarked there had set foot on American territory, but that landing had conferred no rights on the arrivals, not even a right of entry. The US government held exclusive jurisdiction (previously the island had been part of New York State). In legal terms, Ellis Island was known as a *federal enclave*, which meant space appropriated by the federal government from an existing state. Most commonly, enclaves were spaces taken for forts, military bases, prisons, and federal civilian buildings. Once a space of this sort passed from a state to the federal government, it lost its status as incorporated territory. An enclave was an unincorporated space *avant la lettre*, meaning that the federal government possessed not only exclusive jurisdiction over it and all its inhabitants but also the ability to rule it as it saw fit.

The immigration reception center on Ellis Island had originated in part as a humanitarian gesture. Prior to its opening, immigrants usually had to remain on crowded and unsanitary boats while they were waiting for admission interviews in Castle Garden, the previous immigration reception center in Lower Manhattan. Now they could put their feet on dry land, use decent toilet facilities and be held in accommodations superior to those made available on the boats on which they had arrived. But immigration agents with unlimited power were the ones whose decision it was to extend these comfort measures. They could remove these privileges at will. Immigration officers on Ellis Island had the right to detain people indefinitely, to quarantine them if they were diseased or otherwise unfit, and to turn them away. Prospective immigrants who disembarked on Ellis Island had stepped onto American territory but had access to no rights other than those that rulers of the space might bestow on them.[29]

In a literal sense, Ellis Island (and its West Coast counterpart, Angel Island) was a space of exception: space that was fully controlled by a sovereign nation but in which the normal rules of citizenship did not apply. That this space was an island vividly illustrated its function. It was in sight of the mainland but separated from it; it was a part of the United States but had no land connection to it. Visually, it looked like a space over which a sovereign could easily establish and maintain his or her power.[30] That it occupied a space that was but a stone's throw from the Statue of Liberty, situated on the appropriately renamed Liberty Island, illustrated the close cohabitation of liberty and coercion in America's republican and constitutional order.[31]

Alien immigrant space also operated in a less literal and more metaphoric sense. It followed and encased aliens wherever they went if they successfully transited from Ellis Island to the US mainland. Aliens were accorded some due process rights; states, for example, were prevented from engaging in "invidious discrimination" against them.[32] But other due process rights that were routinely extended to citizens were denied immigrant aliens. Thus, excludable aliens could not demand a judicial hearing at which the government would have to present evidence to justify deportation. Congress and the attorney general could grant such hearings if they so chose but were not obligated by the federal courts to do so. The Palmer Raids illustrate this point well. In the most famous of those raids, on January 2, 1920, the Department of Justice broke into the homes of more than four thousand suspected radicals in thirty-three cities spread across twenty-three states. Those arrested were jailed for weeks and in some cases months without being charged with a crime. Many of them were sent to Ellis Island, which in World War I had become a prison for enemy aliens and a staging area for deportation. Of the thousands arrested in the raids, nearly six hundred would be deported by spring 1920.[33]

Virtually all those detained as a result of the January 2 arrests were immigrant aliens. Once the wartime state of emergency ended in 1919, the Bureau of Investigation possessed clear authority to arrest and deport only foreign-born radicals. The nineteenth-century jurisprudential decision to make immigration a plenary power was the source of this expansive authority. The Bureau of Investigation did not possess this power with respect to American citizens, whether native born or naturalized. J. Edgar Hoover, a rising star in the bureau whose involvement in the Palmer Raids helped establish his reputation, desperately wanted to pursue native-born radicals on his subversives list, which, by this time, was 450,000 names long. Yet he could not. So he pursued only those radicals who were vulnerable to his jailing and deportation authority: immigrant aliens. The ground on which immigrant aliens stood offered fewer due process protections than that occupied by citizens.[34] Immigrant aliens lived in a rolling space of exception.

Congress and state legislatures possessed the power to limit alien immigrant access to substantive rights as well. Thus, immigrant aliens customarily had no voting rights. Some immigrant alien groups, especially East and South Asians in the West, were barred by states from owning land. From the 1930s on, many were barred from substantive benefits that governments had begun to provide: employment on public works, unemployment insurance and other welfare benefits, and even scholarships and professional licenses.[35] They were encased in a constitutional parenthesis.

Space of Exception 3: Jim Crow

Officially, the Jim Crow states were not spaces of exception. They were polities long ago designated as incorporated, their white population deemed citizens of the United States, their state governments endowed with the full complement of US republican institutions: two elected legislative bodies, elected governors, and a mixture of court-appointed and popularly elected judges charged with superintending the law. That the Supreme Court had blessed Jim Crow in its 1896 *Plessy v. Ferguson* ruling was interpreted by many to mean that these southern states were fully in compliance with the federal Constitution and with the Fourteenth Amendment in particular. But it is equally true that, with regard to their black citizens, these states did not feel constitutionally obligated to honor individual rights that were supposedly guaranteed by the federal Bill of Rights—freedom of speech, freedom of assembly, and due process of the law (including protection from arbitrary search and seizure and from cruel and unusual punishment). Violence often greeted rights seekers.

Federal courts honored this disposition for two reasons: first, for nearly a century, judges had been interpreting the language of the Bill of

Rights literally. The First Amendment declared: "*Congress* shall make no law abridging freedom of speech" (emphasis added). And, indeed, Congress could pass no law abridging freedom of speech, the press, or religion (except in circumstances of emergency). But the First Amendment said nothing about what state legislatures could and could not do in this respect. A state wanting to abridge freedom of the press or assembly could do so, subject only to the restrictions that its own laws or constitution imposed. Second, justices across the nineteenth century interpreted the tenth and last of the Bill of Rights amendments as endowing state governments with extraordinary power. This amendment reserved to the states powers not expressly given to the federal government. Legal scholars have long referred to this power as *residual power*. But there was nothing at all residual about it; rather, it was understood to be expansive, protean, and versatile. It permitted states to act for the "people's welfare" across a broad front. The residual power inhering in the Tenth Amendment, in combination with judicial decisions exempting states from an obligation to adhere to the first eight amendments, effectively freed the states from multiple constitutional limitations that applied to the exercise of federal power.[36]

State constitutional conventions could, of course, insert a mini–bill of rights into the foundational documents of self-rule that they had been assembled to craft. Some of the strongest of these bills appeared in the constitutions of states emerging from the Northwest Territories in the late eighteenth century and the early nineteenth. The federal government had required these states to outlaw slavery and guarantee freedom of religion. Initially, it imposed no parallel requirements on the states emerging from the Louisiana Territory, though that would change with the Missouri Compromise of 1820. Even then, would-be states south of the 36°30′ parallel remained free to write slavery into their constitutions. A similar settlement was derived for states emerging from the Mexican cession, ratified in the Compromise of 1850. The states that emerged from these territories had broad authority in other areas as well to exempt their actions from federal Bill of Rights scrutiny.[37] The ability to so exempt themselves is what constituted these states as partial spaces of exception.

The constitutional changes emerging from the Civil War and Reconstruction were meant to narrow, even eliminate, these state spaces of exception. Indeed, the Fourteenth Amendment seemed to give the federal government the authority to compel states to honor the expansive conception of individual rights and limits on the exercise of any government's power laid out in the Bill of Rights. But the counterrevolution that ended Reconstruction restored to the states much of the power that they had enjoyed prior to the Civil War.³⁸ This restoration of states' rights, more than the separate but equal doctrine announced by the Supreme Court in *Plessy*, is what gave Jim Crow its power. Release from the obligation to honor the Bill of Rights bestowed on the southern states the authority to use a great variety of techniques, including that of terror, to enforce a harsh regime of racial segregation and black subservience.

Given this exemption from the Bill of Rights, it seems plausible to treat the Jim Crow states as a partial space of exception—as places where the Constitution, or vital parts of it, did not rule. Interestingly, in this regard, twentieth-century lawyers and judges who wanted to close this southern space of exception began talking about their work in these terms. Specifically, they spoke of the need to "incorporate" the ex-Confederate states under the Bill of Rights, thereby implying that these spaces had been in some meaningful way "unincorporated." Invoking this phrase, of course, connected the condition of the southern states to that of the unincorporated territories of Puerto Rico and the Philippines. These were all places where the inhabitants did not have full access to the rights set forth in the Constitution. The meaning of *unincorporation* was not precisely the same in the two cases. In Puerto Rico and the Philippines, the federal government unilaterally decided what institutions of self-rule these territories should possess and how much power they should have. Each southern state, by contrast, had a full complement of state-level republican institutions that were created and sustained by the (white) people of each state themselves. In the case of the southern states, it was specifically the Bill of Rights that did not apply. Still, that both these sections of the United States were deemed by jurists to be unincorporated linked them as similar in being spaces of exception.³⁹

White residents of Virginia, South Carolina, Alabama, and other ex-Confederate states in the early twentieth century would have flinched at the thought of being designated residents of unincorporated polities. White Virginians, in particular, would likely have been outraged. Their forebears, they would have argued, had done more than any other group to make America a constitutionally governed republic. One of those ancestors, Thomas Jefferson, had authored the Declaration of Independence. Another, James Madison, had been the Constitution's principal architect. A third, George Washington, had become the Republic's first president, resisting all efforts to render him a monarch. Through the cession of their western lands to the nation, moreover, Virginians helped set the terms under which new territories would gain status as incorporated entities and the ability to enter the Union as full, rights-bearing states.

Finally, many Virginians regarded their state Bill of Rights as a model for the federal Bill of Rights and Jefferson's treatise on freedom of religion as a precursor to the religious toleration clause of the First Amendment. Was not Virginia the largest, most prestigious, and most constitutionally precocious state in the early republic? How, then, could this space be regarded in constitutional terms as a space of exception? And yet it was if we measure exception in terms of exemption from the federal Bill of Rights. Madison himself grasped this possibility, which is why, when representing Virginia in the First Congress, he had proposed adding an eleventh amendment to the Bill of Rights to ensure the imposition of the other ten amendments on Virginia and all the other states. But this Madisonian proposal, in contrast to so many others, did not prevail.[40]

Northern and western states likewise had the capacity to exempt themselves from adherence to the federal Bill of Rights. But no northern or western state had anything resembling Jim Crow. The latter's existence in the South rendered the southern states by far the most unincorporated space in the continental United States. The legal foundation of Jim Crow rested on the exemption of these states from the federal Bill of Rights. Had the Fourteenth Amendment been applied vigorously and consistently to state governments after its ratification—this, we would argue, was the intention of the amendment's framers—a system of Jim Crow would have been far more difficult both to erect and to sustain. That the people of the southern states were barred from access to the federal Bill of Rights gave southern state governments the opportunity to constitute their dominions as spaces of exception.

These spaces arose not as a result of a federal executive or a federal court suspending the Constitution in the southern states, as had occurred during Reconstruction. No martial law or emergency power was invoked. Rather, this space was made possible by a series of federal court decisions determining that the southern states were not bound by the Bill of Rights. Federal courts sanctioned the Jim Crow space of exception by enforcing the Constitution, not by suspending it. They drew on a well-established doctrine in American law that the states operated under a different, less liberal theory of government than did the federal state itself. American federalism, we might say, offered a fully constitutional mechanism for experimenting with spaces of exception.

Antebellum conceptions of federalism might have perished as a result of the Civil War and Reconstruction; the constitutional status of the southern states might have been enduringly reconfigured. This future is what the Fourteenth Amendment seemed to augur. But this is not what happened. Rather, in the postbellum years, the courts resuscitated older understandings of the powers that inhered in state governments, powers that the federal government itself did not have. Thus, the road toward incorporating the southern states under the Bill of Rights was long and winding, with fierce resistance erupting at every step of the way. The repercussions arising from the most intense moment of incorporation— the 1960s, under the aegis of the Warren Court—convulse American politics to this very day.[41]

Struggles to Shrink Spaces of Exception

What the white South experienced as coercion in the 1960s the black South experienced as liberation, a freedom that was achieved in the first instance not through the decisions of the Warren Court but rather through decades of struggle known to us as the civil rights movement. The history of that movement and of the pressures it placed on the federal government to act legislatively and jurisprudentially to remedy racial discrimination have been ably chronicled. From our point of view, we might say that the civil rights movement impelled the federal government to extinguish one very important space of exception. Ironically, the federal government that did this work was the same that for decades previously had tolerated unequal rights of citizenship.

Less familiar is the movement allied to the civil rights movement to expand the rights of immigrant aliens. Making the federal Bill of Rights the law of the entire land, arguably the signal achievement of the civil rights movement, made it possible to rethink the rights of aliens. The Bill of Rights referred several times to actions that the federal government could not take against any "persons." So did the Fourteenth Amendment. Deploying such language in the Constitution suggested that the status of personhood was not to be considered inferior to that of the citizen. If that were true, was it not possible to imagine that immigrant aliens, whose personhood was visible for all to see, might avail themselves of Bill of Rights and Fourteenth Amendment protections? The Supreme Court had first established the personhood principle as the basis for rights in *Yick Wo v. Hopkins* (1886), only to allow it to languish for a century. But, as the struggle for black equality in the 1960s compelled the courts to rethink matters of individual rights yet again, some groups of attorneys began to argue successfully for the expansion of alien rights. In one signal case, *Graham v. Richardson* (1971), the Supreme Court extended to immigrant aliens substantive welfare and employment rights long denied them, including access to public welfare programs, scholarships, civil service employment, and professional licenses.[42] In another case of equal significance, *Plyler v. Doe* (1982), the Court ruled that states were compelled to provide free public education to undocumented alien immigrant children. These decisions reversed long-standing precedents that alien immigrants, because they inhabited a space of exception, could not claim substantive rights. In *Plyler v. Doe*, the Court ruled that even those who had entered the country illegally were entitled to the protection of the country's laws, thus breaking the bond between space of exception and rights denial.[43] Meanwhile, Congress's passage of refugee legislation at about this same time created a new category of immigrant—that of the asylum seeker—whose plea to remain in the US would have to be heard by an administrative court in accordance with procedures originating outside the Executive Branch of government. Refugee legislation thus further eroded the exceptional space that had long encased the immigrant alien.[44]

So, too, of course, did the principle of birthright citizenship, at least among those immigrant aliens who gave birth to children on the soil of the United States. Birthright citizenship originated with the Fourteenth Amendment, which declared: "All persons born or naturalized in the United States and subject to the jurisdiction thereof, are citizens of the United States." The immediate purpose of this clause had been to offer African Americans an ironclad citizenship guarantee. It was designed to, and in fact did, deny future courts or any state within the Union the ability to do what the Taney Court had done in *Dred Scott*: strip native-born people of African descent of their citizenship.[45]

From the start, however, the supporters of this constitutional amendment made known their belief that the protections of the birthright citizenship clause extended to other groups whose color and/or culture had rendered them suspect populations in the United States. Chief among these groups in the 1860s were the Chinese who, since the San Francisco gold rush, had begun coming to California in large numbers. Senator Lyman Trumbull of Illinois, a Fourteenth Amendment architect, declared on the floor of Congress in 1866 that, under the proposed amendment's terms, "the child of an Asiatic is just as much a citizen as the child of a European."[46]

The manifest intent of Trumbull and his allies to construe birthright citizenship broadly became particularly important a few years later when Congress declined to repeal the 1790 law barring nonwhite immigrants from becoming citizens. In 1870, Congress had exempted black immigrants from this law but not other nonwhites. Thus, East and South Asian immigrants continued to be regarded as ineligible for citizenship and as living, therefore, in a space of exception. But not entirely.

In *United States v. Wong Kim Ark* (1898), the Supreme Court ruled that the Fourteenth Amendment automatically conferred US citizenship on children born on American soil to immigrant parents who, for reasons of race, had been barred from citizenship. The clear language of the birthright citizenship clause in combination with the clear intent of its framers had compelled the Court to arrive at this rather stunning (and racially illogical) conclusion.[47]

In delivering its *Wong Kim Art* judgment, the Court effectively created a mechanism for transforming part of the exceptional space occupied by lifelong immigrant aliens into the space of citizens. That space, of course, was the household, where alien parents and citizen children cohabited. Birthright citizenship made it possible for aliens to populate their space with citizens and thereby shrink the exceptional character of that space over time and across generations. Arguably, it prevented the transformation of East and South Asian populations into an American version of the untouchables—hereditary castes sealed off spatially and sociologically from the polity's mainstream space across generations. It may well be that forestalling the creation of such a permanent untouchable space helped facilitate the rather rapid transformation of Asian Americans from despised to model minority in the several decades after World War II.[48]

Nothing as dramatic as Jim Crow's fall or the shrinking of immigrant alien space happened with regard to the third space of exception—that of the unincorporated territory. This category of space has not disappeared: the territorial status of Puerto Rico, Samoa, Guam, the US Virgin Islands and the Northern Mariana Islands remains defined by this space of exception. But the category also has not expanded in size or significance across the twentieth century. With Filipino independence in 1946, its physical size shrank. One might say that the expectations of the unincorporated territory's early twentieth-century architects—that it would serve as a major mechanism of overseas US expansion—have been only partially fulfilled.

It is possible to discern in each of the three spaces of exception discussed in this chapter a form of liberal progress, manifest in the shrinking rather than the expanding over time of extraconstitutional space. Much of the shrinkage occurred in the forty-year period between the mid-1940s and the mid-1980s. This timing hints that the contraction was bound up with the civil rights and anticolonial revolutions of the postwar decades and with the parallel human rights movement emerging from a reckoning with the totalitarian horrors of World War II.[49]

But part of the analytic robustness of our notion of spaces of exception arises from the fact that it presumes no path of liberal linearity connecting past and present. First, equal rights for African Americans once again lie challenged. Michelle Alexander has argued that mass incarceration has replaced Jim Crow, generating, in the process, a massive new space of exception in which large numbers of African Americans are confined, their freedom and rights impaired. The sociologist Loïc Wacquant similarly has described a new ghetto stage prevailing over an older commitment to liberal integration.[50]

Second, the United States seems to have supplanted its troublesome unincorporated territorial space with a globe-spanning constellation of military bases. It does not literally own the land on which it has built most of these bases, having chosen (or been compelled) to lease it over the long term from the foreign states on whose territory these bases reside. But it is the sovereign power on these bases, its authority insulated from both the US Constitution and the lessor nation's legal regime. The appeal of Guantanamo to US policy makers during the War on Terror lay precisely in its functional equivalence to that of the unincorporated territory: a space where the American flag flew but the US Constitution did not hold sway. As US Army general Barry McCaffrey bluntly noted in 2006: "The great value of the platform of Guantanamo was that it was a military space in which no Federal District Court had primary jurisdiction."[51]

Finally, with regard to immigrant aliens, the United States has not invented a new space of exception to handle these troublesome subjects, but the shrinking of the space of exception enveloping them that occurred across the Nixon-Ford-Carter-Reagan years was halted in the 1990s and is now being reversed.[52] Under the Trump administration, the alien space of exception has widened dramatically. The vigorous work of Immigration and Customs Enforcement (ICE) under both the Obama and the Trump administrations has thrust undocumented migrants back into the kind of no-man's-land that had been their lot decades ago. The task of avoiding an ICE confrontation has created quasi-invisible, out-of-sight spaces of exception, again defined by marginality. Undocumented migrants increasingly occupy a space in which they have no access to rights: picked up by ICE, taken to holding spaces for indefinite periods, parents separated from children, and then summarily deported with no recourse to legal support and often unable even to contact family.[53]

Spaces of exception arise in response to an emergency (e.g., a wartime circumstance) or as a solution to a political or social problem of unanticipated scale or seriousness. Spaces that endure become reinterpreted as something other than emergency and temporary measures. They are accepted as necessary parts of the polity. Systems of rule take root in these places to ensure their smooth functioning and stability.

These exceptional spaces and their systems of rule contradict the idea of liberalism on which democratic states are constructed. The norms that govern these spaces cannot be permitted to be seen as the norms that govern the entire society. The very point of confining illiberal features of society to particular spaces is to underscore that these spaces are not the norm and that they do not unduly impinge on mainstream political space, where liberal and constitutional principles are thought to prevail.

The border between exceptional and normal space must thus be carefully patrolled. The exceptional must not be allowed to penetrate the normal too much. Of course, penetration is always, to some extent, occurring, rendering the border unstable and susceptible to the charge that it cannot hold or, worse, that it is an illusion. Border instability and confusion have, in liberal polities, given rise to movements to shrink or eliminate spaces of exception. The movement to end Jim Crow and narrow alien immigrant space can be understood in these terms. These movements have succeeded in important ways, or they succeeded for a time, but they have not succeeded altogether. Mass incarceration arguably reconfigures and sustains key features of Jim Crow, and military bases have supplanted unincorporated territory. Meanwhile, the third space of exception—that inhabited by immigrant aliens—has been expanding once again after several decades of shrinkage.

The recurrence of these spaces suggests how difficult it has been and will continue to be to create a polity that is uniformly liberal across all the territory in which it is sovereign. It appears that spaces of exception are not only a useful category of analysis but also a recurring and, arguably, necessary feature of the liberal polity.

: : :

We were grateful for the opportunity to present this chapter at Columbia University (March 2017), the University of Chicago (May 2018), New York University (September 2018), University College London (October 2018), and the University of Cambridge (June 2019). We have benefited from the comments and suggestions made by many participants in those seminars.

Notes

1. For a discussion of Foucault's governmentality, see Michel Foucault, *Security, Territory, Population: Lectures at the College de France, 1977–78* (London: Palgrave Macmillan, 2009); and Graham Burchell, Colin Gordon, and

Peter Miller, eds., *The Foucault Effect: Studies in Governmentality* (Chicago: University of Chicago Press, 1991). On the US case, see Desmond King and Marc Stears, "How the US State Works: A Theory of Standardization," *Perspectives on Politics* 9 (September 2011): 505–18; and Matthew G. Hannah, *Governmentality and the Mastery of Territory in Nineteenth-Century America* (New York: Cambridge University Press, 2000). See also James Scott, *Seeing Like a State: How Certain Schemes to Improve the Human Condition Have Failed* (New Haven, CT: Yale University Press, 1998).

2. On different national approaches to incarceration, see Nicola Lacey, David Soskice, and David Hope, "Understanding the Determinants of Penal Policy: Crime, Culture and Comparative Political Economy," *Annual Review of Criminology* 1 (2018): 195–217. For an overview of the most recent literature on incarceration in the United States, see Robert T. Chase, *We Are Not Slaves: State Violence, Coerced Labor, and Prisoners' Rights in Postwar America* (Chapel Hill: University of North Carolina Press, 2020), introduction. On how prisons function in liberal societies, see Michel Foucault, *Discipline and Punish: The Birth of the Prison* (New York: Vintage, 1991).

3. Giorgio Agamben, *Homo Sacer: Sovereign Power and Bare Life*, trans. Daniel Heller-Roazen (1995; Stanford, CA: Stanford University Press, 1998), 168–75.

4. In addition to the home and prisons, Indian reservations might qualify as spaces of exception. But, before placing Indian lands under this heading, one must grapple with the concept of tribal sovereignty and its relationship to US sovereignty and with the legal and political implications of designating Indian lands as *domestic dependent nations*. We hope to explore these matters in future work.

5. For the now-classic statement of the strong state paradigm, see William J. Novak, "The Myth of the 'Weak' American State," *American Historical Review* 113 (June 2008): 752–72; and the roundtable in response that appeared two years later: John Fabian Witt, "Law and War in American History," Gary Gerstle, "A State Both Strong and Weak," Julia Adams, "The Puzzle of the American State . . . and Its Historians," and William J. Novak, "Long Live the Myth of the Weak State? A Response to Adams, Gerstle, and Witt," *American Historical Review* 115 (June 2010): 768–78, 779–85, 786–91, and 792–800.

6. On the centrality of federalism to conceptions of American state building, see Gary Gerstle, *Liberty and Coercion: The Paradox of American Government from the Founding to the Present* (Princeton, NJ: Princeton University Press, 2015).

7. Michelle Alexander, *The New Jim Crow: Mass Incarceration in the Age of Colorblindness* (New York: New Press, 2010).

8. José A. Cabranes, *Citizenship and the American Empire: Notes on the Legislative History of the United States Citizenship of Puerto Ricans* (New Haven, CT: Yale University Press, 1979), 20–21 n. 63.

9. Gerstle, *Liberty and Coercion*, chap. 1.

10. Oklahoma was another territory whose statehood was long delayed, in this case because the region's large Indian population was (like the Mexican and Indian populations of New Mexico and Arizona) thought to lack the attributes necessary for good citizenship. See David A. Chang, *The Color of the Land:*

Race, Nation, and the Politics of Land Ownership in Oklahoma, 1832–1929 (Chapel Hill: University of North Carolina Press, 2010).

11. Gary Lawson and Guy Seidman, *The Constitution of Empire: Territorial Expansion and American Legal History* (New Haven, CT: Yale University Press, 2004); Linda C. Noel, *Debating American Identity: Southwestern Statehood and Mexican Immigration* (Tucson: University of Arizona Press, 2014); Robert W. Larson, *New Mexico's Quest for Statehood, 1846–1912* (Albuquerque: University of New Mexico Press, 1968); Howard R. Lamar, *The Far Southwest: A Territorial History, 1846–1912* (Albuquerque: University of New Mexico Press, 2000); George H. Alden, "The Evolution of the American System of Forming and Admitting New States into the Union," *Annals of the American Academy of Political and Social Science* 18 (November 1901): 79–89; Sarah Barringer Gordon, *The Mormon Question: Polygamy and Constitutional Conflict in Nineteenth-Century America* (Chapel Hill: University of North Carolina Press, 2002); Nancy F. Cott, *Public Vows: A History of Marriage and the Nation* (Cambridge, MA: Harvard University Press, 2000); Steven Hahn, *A Nation without Borders: The United States and Its World in an Age of Civil Wars, 1830–1910* (New York: Penguin, 2017).

12. G. Hackworth, *Digest of International Law* 3 (1942): 1–7; J. Pratt, *America's Colonial Experiment* (New York: Prentice-Hall, 1950); Abbott Lawrence Lowell, "The Status of Our New Possessions—a Third View," *Harvard Law Review* 13 (1899): 155–76; Alexander Aleinikoff, *Semblances of Sovereignty: The Constitution, the State, and American Citizenship* (Cambridge, MA: Harvard University Press, 2002); Christina Duffy Burnett and Burke Marshall, eds., *Foreign in a Domestic Sense: Puerto Rico, American Expansion, and the Constitution* (Durham, NC: Duke University Press, 2000); Lawson and Seidman, *The Constitution of Empire*; Sanford Levinson and Bartholomew Sparrow, eds., *The Louisiana Purchase and American Expansion* (Lanham, MD: Rowman & Littlefield, 2005); Paul A. Kramer, *The Blood of Government: Race, Empire, the United States, and the Philippines* (Chapel Hill, NC: University of North Carolina Press, 2006); Mae M. Ngai, *Impossible Subjects: Illegal Aliens and the Making of Modern America* (Princeton, NJ: Princeton University Press, 2004); A. G. Hopkins, *American Empire: A Global History* (Princeton, NJ: Princeton University Press, 2018), 337–436; Alfred W. McCoy and Francisco A. Scarano, eds., *Colonial Crucible: Empire in the Making of the Modern American State* (Madison: University of Wisconsin Press, 2009); Daniel Immerwahr, *How to Hide an Empire: A History of the Greater United States* (New York: Farrar, Strauss, & Giroux, 2019).

13. The main Insular Cases are *De Lima v. Bidwell*, 182 U.S. 1 (1901); *Goetze v. United States*, 182 U.S. 221 (1901); *Cooley v. United States*, 182 U.S. 222 (1901); *Armstrong v. United States*, 182 U.S. 243 (1901); *Downes v. Bidwell*, 182 U.S. 244 (1901); and *Huus v. New York and Porto Rico Steamship Co.*, 182 U.S. 392 (1901). See also Robert C. McGreevey, *Borderline Citizens: The United States, Puerto Rico, and the Politics of Colonial Migration* (Ithaca, NY: Cornell University Press, 2018); and Bartholomew Sparrow, *The Insular Cases and the Emergence of American Empire* (Lawrence: University Press of Kansas, 2006).

14. Similar awarding of citizenship would be extended to the peoples of other territories in subsequent years: the Virgin Islands in 1927, Guam in 1950, and

the Northern Mariana Islands in 1976. Cabranes, *Citizenship and the American Empire*, 95.

15. Cabranes, *Citizenship and the American Empire*, passim; Sam Erman, "Citizens of Empire: Puerto Rico, Status, and Constitutional Change," *California Law Review* 102 (October 2014): 1181ff., and *Almost Citizens: Puerto Rico, the U.S. Constitution, and American Empire* (New York: Cambridge University Press, 2019). On Hawaii's road to statehood, see Sarah Miller-Davenport, *The Gateway State: Hawai'i and the Global Origins of Modern Racial Liberalism* (Princeton, NJ: Princeton University Press, 2019).

16. *Balzac v. Porto Rico*, 258 U.S. 298, 308 (1922); Frederic R. Coudert, "The Evolution of the Doctrine of Territorial Incorporation," *Columbia Law Review* 26 (1926): 823–50; Peter H. Shuck, "The Transformation of Immigration Law," *Columbia Law Review* 84 (1984): 11–12.

17. That contrast remains stark, as evidenced in the federal government's inferior treatment of Puerto Rican victims of Hurricane Maria relative to its treatment of the Texan victims of Hurricane Harvey. Both hurricanes struck in 2017.

18. Ngai, *Impossible Subjects*, 96–126; Barbara S. Posadas, *The Filipino Americans* (Westport, CT: Greenwood, 1999). On the Chinese, see Erika Lee, *At America's Gates: Chinese Immigration during the Exclusion Era, 1882–1943* (Chapel Hill: University of North Carolina Press, 2003); Lucy E. Salyer, *Laws as Harsh as Tigers: Chinese Immigrants and the Shaping of Modern Immigration Law* (Chapel Hill: University of North Carolina Press, 1995); and Andrew Gyory, *Closing the Gate: Race, Politics, and the Chinese Exclusion Act* (Chapel Hill: University of North Carolina Press, 1998).

19. Kramer, *The Blood of Government*; Ngai, *Impossible Subjects*, 96–126; Hopkins, *American Empire*, 441–688; and Nayan Shah, *Stranger Intimacy: Contesting Race, Sexuality, and the Law in the North American West* (Los Angeles: University of California Press, 2011).

20. Though it had reaped some: the erection of a large naval base in the Philippines and the ability of the United States to project its power from there across East Asia. But the projection of power through military bases entailed moving from the unincorporated territory to the leased military base as the basis for the space of exception, a turn that will be discussed later in this chapter.

21. Gerald L. Neuman, *Strangers to the Constitution: Immigrants, Borders, and Fundamental Law* (Princeton, NJ: Princeton University Press, 1996); Aristide Zolberg, *A Nation by Design: Immigration Policy and the Fashioning of a Nation* (New York: Russell Sage Foundation, 2006); Aleinikoff, *Semblances of Sovereignty*, chaps. 2 and 7; Kunal Parker, "Citizenship and Immigration Law, 1800–1924: Resolutions of Membership and Territory," in *The Cambridge History of Law in America*, vol. 2, *The Long Nineteenth Century (1789–1920)*, ed. Michael Grossberg and Christopher Tomlins (New York: Cambridge University Press, 2008), 168–203.

22. *Nishimura Ekiu v. United States*, 142 US 651, 659 (1892).

23. Gary Gerstle, *American Crucible: Race and Nation in the Twentieth Century* (Princeton, NJ: Princeton University Press, 2017), chap. 3; Katherine Benton-Cohen, *Inventing the Immigration Problem: The Dillingham Commission and Its Legacy* (Cambridge, MA: Harvard University Press, 2018).

24. Gary Gerstle, "Inclusion, Exclusion, and American Nationality," in *Handbook on American Immigration and Ethnicity*, ed. Ronald Bayor (New York: Oxford University Press, 2015), 144–65; Salyer, *Laws as Harsh as Tigers*; Rogers M. Smith, *Civic Ideals: Conflicting Visions of Citizenship in U.S. History* (New Haven, CT: Yale University Press, 1997); Desmond King, *Making Americans: Immigration, Race, and the Origins of the Diverse Democracy* (Cambridge, MA: Harvard University Press, 2000); Benton-Cohen, *Inventing the Immigration Problem*.

25. Quoted in *Congressional Record*, 68th Cong., 1st sess., 65 (March 17, 1924): 4839.

26. Aleinikoff, *Semblances of Sovereignty*, chap. 7.

27. *Chinese Exclusion Case*, 130 U.S. 581 (1889).

28. The few who did usually had to find a judge willing to certify that they possessed certain key attributes, cultural or physical, of whiteness. The Supreme Court closed that loophole with its *Ozawa* and *Thind* decisions of 1922 and 1923, respectively. See Ian F. Haney Lopez, *White by Law: The Legal Construction of Race* (New York: New York University Press, 1991); *Ozawa v. United States*, 260 U.S. 178 (1922); and *United States v. Thind*, 261 U.S. 204 (1923). See also James H. Kettner, *The Development of American Citizenship, 1608–1870* (Chapel Hill: University of North Carolina Press, 1978); Matthew Jacobson, *Whiteness of a Different Color: European Immigrants and the Alchemy of Race* (Cambridge, MA: Harvard University Press, 1998); Ngai, *Impossible Subjects*; Lee, *At America's Gates*; and Salyer, *Laws as Harsh as Tigers*.

29. Thomas Pitkin, *Keepers of the Gate: A History of Ellis Island* (New York: New York University Press, 1975); Vincent J. Cannato, *American Passage: The History of Ellis Island* (New York: HarperCollins, 2009); Barry Moreno, ed., *Encyclopedia of Ellis Island* (Westport, CT: Greenwood, 2004). See also Erika Lee and Judy Wang, *Angel Island: Immigrant Gateway to America* (New York: Oxford University Press, 2010).

30. On the role of islands more generally in representing and defining sovereignty, see Lauren Benton, *A Search for Sovereignty: Law and Geography in European Empires, 1400–1900* (New York: Cambridge University Press, 2009); Alison Bashford, *Imperial Hygiene: A Critical History of Colonialism, Nationalism and Public Health* (London: Palgrave Macmillan, 2004); and Sujit Sivasundaram, *Islanded: Sri Lanka, Britain, and the Bounds of an Indian Ocean Colony* (Chicago: University of Chicago Press, 2013).

31. On Angel Island, see Lee and Wang, *Angel Island*; and Adam McKeown, "Ritualization and Regulation: The Enforcement of Chinese Exclusion in the United States and China," *American Historical Review* 108 (April 2003): 377–403.

32. Shuck, "The Transformation of Immigration Law," 12.

33. Thomas M. Pitkin, *Keepers of the Gate* (New York: New York University Press, 1975), 121–28; Gary Gerstle, "The Immigrant as Threat to American National Security: A Historical Perspective," in *From Arrival to Incorporation: Migrants to the U.S. in a Global Era*, ed. Elliott R. Barkan, Hasia Diner, and Alan M. Kraut (New York: New York University Press, 2008), 217–45.

34. Gerstle, *Liberty and Coercion*, chap. 4.

35. Christian Joppke, *Immigration and the Nation State: The United States, Germany and Great Britain* (New York: Oxford University Press, 1999).
36. Gerstle, *Liberty and Coercion*, chap. 2.
37. Gerstle, *Liberty and Coercion*, chap. 2.
38. Gerstle, *Liberty and Coercion*, chap. 2; Gary Gerstle, "The Civil War and Statebuilding: A Reconsideration," *Journal of the Civil War Era* (March 2017), http://journalofthecivilwarera.org/forum-the-future-of-reconstruction-studies/the-civil-war-and-state-building.
39. Some legal scholars have argued that there was no linkage between the two uses of incorporation, seeing the simultaneous use of both as coincidental and running entirely in parallel, without points of intersection. See, e.g., Neuman, *Strangers to the Constitution*, 89 and passim. See also Gerald L. Neuman, "Whose Constitution?," *Yale Law Journal* 100 (1991): 910–91. But we side with Christina Duffy Burnett (now Christina Duffy Ponsa) as seeing the two as profoundly interconnected, both terms referring to spaces in which the Constitution did not fully apply. See Christina Duffy Burnett, "A Convenient Constitution? Extraterritoriality After Boumediene," *Columbia Law Review* 109 (June 2009): 973–1046, esp. 982 n. 22. See also Carlos R. Soltero, "The Supreme Court Should Overrule the Territorial Incorporation Doctrine and End One Hundred Years of Judicially Condoned Colonialism," *Chicano-Latino Law Review* 1 (2001): 19–34; and Roszell Dulany Hunter IV, "The Extraterritoriality Application of the Constitution—Unalienable Rights?," *Virginia Law Review* 72 (1986): 649–76.
40. Gerstle, *Liberty and Coercion*, chap. 1.
41. Gerstle, *Liberty and Coercion*, chap. 9.
42. Joppke, *Immigration and the Nation State*.
43. Sarah Coleman, *The Walls Within: American Immigration since 1964* (Princeton, NJ: Princeton University Press, forthcoming).
44. On the evolution of refugee legislation, see Carl Bon Tempo, *Americans at the Gate: The United States and Refugees during the Cold War* (Princeton, NJ: Princeton University Press, 2008).
45. US Constitution, Amendments 11–27, http://www.archives.gov/exhibits/charters/constitution_amendments_11-27.html; Eric Foner, *Reconstruction: America's Unfinished Revolution, 1863–1877* (New York: Harper & Row, 1988), and *The Story of American Freedom* (New York: Norton, 1988); Garrett Epps, "The Citizenship Clause: A Legislative History," *American University Law Review* 60 (December 2010): 331–91; Neuman, *Strangers to the Constitution*. See also Martha Jones, *Birthright Citizenship: A History of Race and Rights in Antebellum America* (New York: Cambridge University Press, 2018).
46. Quoted in *Congressional Globe*, 39th Cong., 1st sess., 1866, 39, pt. 4:498.
47. *United States v. Wong Kim Ark*, 169 U.S. 649 (1898).
48. Ellen D. Wu, *The Color of Success: Asian Americans and the Making of the Model Minority* (Princeton, NJ: Princeton University Press, 2014); Madeline Y. Hsu, *The Good Immigrants: How the Yellow Peril Became the Model Minority* (Princeton, NJ: Princeton University Press, 2015).
49. On the impact of human rights discourse, see Samuel Moyn, *The Last Utopia: Human Rights in History* (Cambridge, MA: Harvard University Press, 2010).

50. Alexander, *The New Jim Crow*; Loïc Wacquant "Deadly Symbiosis: When Ghetto and Prison Meet and Mesh," *Punishment and Society* 3 (2001): 95–133, and *Punishing the Poor: The Neoliberal Government of Social Insecurity* (Durham, NC: Duke University Press, 2009). See also Naomi Murakawa, *The First Civil Right: How Liberals Built Prison America* (New York: Oxford University Press, 2014); Elizabeth Hinton, *From the War on Poverty to the War on Crime: The Making of Mass Incarceration in America* (Cambridge, MA: Harvard University Press, 2016); Julilly Kohler-Hausmann, *Getting Tough: Welfare and Imprisonment in 1970s America* (Princeton, NJ: Princeton University Press, 2017); and Heather Ann Thompson, *Blood in the Water: The Attica Prison Uprising of 1971 and Its Legacy* (New York: Pantheon Books, 2016).

51. Quoted in Jonathan M. Hansen, *Guantanamo: An American History* (New York: Hill & Wang, 2011), 352–53. See also Michael J. Strauss, *The Leasing of Guantanamo Bay* (Westport, CT: Praeger Security International, 2009). Guantanamo's apparent imperviousness to the Constitution was dealt a blow in 2008, when in *Boumediene v. Bush* the Supreme Court decided that the habeas corpus provision applied to a naturalized US citizen indefinitely detained there. See *Boumediene v. Bush* 553 U.S. 723 (2008); and Burnett, "A Convenient Constitution?" For a historical probe of the application of American law to foreign territories, see Daniel S. Margolies, *Spaces of Law in American Foreign Relations: Extradition and Extraterritoriality in the Borderlands and Beyond, 1877–1898* (Athens: University of Georgia Press, 2011).

52. Juliet Stumpf, "The 'Crimmigation Crisis': Immigrants, Crime and Sovereign Power," *American University Law Review* 56 (2006): 367–419; Yolanda Vazquez, "Perpetuating the Marginalization of Latinos: A Collateral Consequence of the Incorporation of Immigration Law into the Criminal Justice System," *Howard Law Review* 54 (2011): 639–74.

53. Franklin Foer, "How ICE Went Rogue: Inside America's Unfolding Immigration Crisis," *The Atlantic*, September 2018, 56–70.

Afterword

Gary Gerstle and Joel Isaac

All liberal democracies at some point must grapple with states of exception. There are inevitably times, typically sparked by war, natural disaster, or economic depression, when the normal constitutional processes of even the sturdiest republic do not work, when the messy, deliberative, give-and-take politics of a national legislature must temporarily be pushed aside, and when the rule of law itself must be suspended. One can hope that such moments will be rare and brief. But one cannot pretend that they will never occur.

Nor can one pretend that decisions on the exception will be clear-cut. Although his views have come under heavy criticism in this volume, Carl Schmitt was surely right to point out that the decision on the exception is necessarily a political act—and that, as such, it may be decried by the opponents of those who hold the reins of power. Many a critic stood ready to assail Lincoln's suspension of habeas corpus during the Civil War, or Wilson's assumption of sweeping powers during the First World War, or any number of FDR's executive orders and proclamations a generation later. The National Emergencies Act of 1976 was designed to take the politics out of the use of presidential emergency powers, but as recently as 2019 the act has been invoked to justify an emergency declaration at the southern border of the United States that is widely seen as a political action on the part of the president and his advisers.[1] Not only, then, do emergencies put great pressure on the legal resources of a state. They also raise the specter of serious political conflict.

We write these words in May 2020, at a time when American society and the world in general are struggling to cope with the staggering impact of the coronavirus pandemic. This pandemic is a true emergency, with hundreds of millions of Americans told to shelter in place and governments at every level ordering so many activities to cease that the very engines of the American economy have ground to a halt. It will be months, and perhaps even years, before we will be able to declare that this emergency has passed and that emergency powers can be safely retired.

This state of affairs makes the subject matter of this book—how America, as a liberal democratic polity, has in the past managed its emergencies—all the more relevant. Some of the admiration for Lincoln—arguably the greatest liberal figure in American history—rests on the conviction that he handled his state of exception well. During the Civil War, he suspended habeas corpus, declared martial law and substituted military commissions for civilian courts, and, by the stroke of a pen, outlawed slavery in all the Confederate states even though the Constitution had made clear that slavery was legal. And he did all this without waiting for Congress to ratify his decisions or for the American people to change the Constitution via amendment. Lincoln's actions as president, either individually or collectively, might have undermined the American republic. Instead, they are perceived as having strengthened the liberal-democratic foundation of the nation and as having given the country and its people a new birth of freedom.

Nevertheless, suspending fundamental elements of a republic in order to save it is an inherently perilous enterprise and, in Schmitt's eyes, a hypocritical one. Schmitt argued that only a sovereign dictator, freed from all liberal norms and constitutional rules, was capable of handling mortal challenges to a liberal polity's existence. But the very actions of a sovereign dictator, in their nature so deeply illiberal, would destroy the liberal foundations of the regime that he ostensibly set out to save. In Schmitt's mind, Lincoln became the exception, not the rule. Liberal polities were doomed. The Weimars of the world would, of necessity, give way before Hitler-like strongmen.

Schmitt's prose swaggers; his accurate prediction that Weimar would collapse into dictatorship has given him a stature usually reserved for

Old Testament prophets. Especially since September 11, 2001, when America turned to torture, indefinite detention of suspected enemies, and widespread spying on its own citizenry to combat terrorists pledged to its destruction, Schmitt's thunderings about the lawlessness that must accompany war emergency have made him the most cited and quoted theorist of liberal-democratic failure. Under George W. Bush in particular, liberal democracy in America seemed to be morphing into a polity dark in its intent and ruthless—and Schmittian—in its instruments of rule. Many theorists of democracy as well as ordinary citizens view the Trump presidency as confirmation that sinister forces released during the Bush years have now thoroughly eviscerated the democratic foundations of the American polity.

The contributors to this volume insist, however, that we measure democracy in America not simply by what has transpired in the last twenty years. Our aim here has been instead to take the longer view. We have inquired into other moments in American history when states of exception have been declared, and we have recovered the voices of theorists of political emergency who, for a long time, have been ignored. John Locke himself, in his seventeenth-century treatises on liberalism, identified the need for a sovereign to be given a prerogative power that could be used to supplant the will of the people as expressed by Parliament. A contemporary of his, Algernon Sidney, wrote in 1680 that a "virtuous man" would sometimes be called on to assume dictatorial powers, "limited in time, circumscribed by law, and kept perpetually under the supreme authority of the people."[2] The architects of the US Constitution were themselves preoccupied with the question of what to do in circumstances of emergency, fearing that an antagonistic European empire or an Indian confederation (or angry settlers marching on statehouses with pitchforks) would strike hard at their new young republic, seeking to destroy it. The Civil War crisis gave rise to an elaborate code of war designed by the Prussian immigrant and Lincoln consigliere Francis Lieber, a code that both legitimated the concept of emergency powers and fenced those powers with liberal and humanist borders. Nearly a century later, political scientists such as Frederick Watkins, Carl Friedrich, and Clinton Rossiter wrote extensively and thoughtfully about what America ought to do in circumstances of total war—what principles of liberal democracy ought to be suspended and what measures ought to be taken to ensure that the violation of liberal-democratic norms would be temporary, less rather than more injurious to liberal aspirations.

Recovering these discourses—which constitutes one of this book's principal achievements—has enabled us to comprehend that, when addressing questions of emergency, influential theorists and policy makers have refused Schmitt's deal with the devil, namely, that to declare a state of exception is to undermine the basis of liberal rule. It is worth identifying the two principal arguments that these theorists and policy makers have made regarding how liberal principles of rule can be preserved in circumstances of emergency. One of these is grounded in temporality, the other in political culture.

The temporal argument derives from the experience of the Roman republic, which appointed more than seventy dictators across its three-hundred-year existence. A dictator so appointed was called on to resolve a foreign or domestic crisis. His appointment could be for no more than six months, during which he was expected to set the republic's house in order. Then he would step down. These stipulations were set forth in Roman law, making the man appointed a "constitutional dictator," fully in keeping with the rule of law. That this device was used so frequently without destroying the republic persuaded subsequent theorists, such as Sidney and Rossiter, that it had worked. The prescription of a six-month tenure, Rossiter observed, might not hold under circumstances of modern warfare, but the principle of a temporary resort to such measures still could. Rossiter gave this idea its most extensive modern treatment in *Constitutional Dictatorship*, as the chapters by Joel Isaac and Ewa Atanassow and Ira Katznelson show. Writing in the post–World War II period, Rossiter believed that the Roman mechanism had broad applicability to the United States and other liberal democracies of the twentieth century. Both the Civil War and World War I had demonstrated to him how well this mechanism could work in the United States.[3]

The chapters by Nomi Claire Lazar, David Dyzenhaus, and John Fabian Witt, by contrast, argue that the temporal checks on dictatorial powers have mattered less and political culture constraints more. Lincoln is their star witness. Lazar emphasizes that, even as Lincoln assumed dictatorial powers, he was guided by a "rule-of-law" vision dedicated to preserving, as he told Congress in 1861, "a government of the people by the same people."[4] His vision was not simply aspirational, Lazar reminds us, but rooted in a rich rule-of-law culture that had been thickening since the republic's creation in the late eighteenth century. As a result, Lincoln's emergency decrees were "surrounded with normative constraint both formal and informal and countervailing sources of power." Subsequent presidents, too, who declared states of emergency would find themselves "influenced by, structured by, and in some cases constrained by a mass of experience, informal and formal legal and moral norms, advice, protocol, preordained bureaucratic procedure, and, notably, the banked legitimacy of decision makers."

Witnessing politics in Trump's America helps us see that a thick rule-of-law culture can, indeed, constrain a norm buster and a would-be sovereign dictator, at least for a time. Its continued vitality requires, Lazar tells us, a citizenry itself committed to a rule-of-law project and willing to enforce democratic norms on its leaders. As long as said citizenry is vigilant, a Schmittian state of exception will have trouble emerging. Dyzenhaus concurs, identifying a "virtuous cycle of legality" similar to Lazar's rule-of-law culture; so does Witt, who writes that, even during the years of Lincoln's war presidency, America's democratic system remained saturated by norms and principles drawn "from the constitutive commitments of the republic—commitments whose basic character defines the scope of what is reasonably necessary under even the most difficult of circumstances."

This emphasis on the constraining work done by a rich legal culture begs the question, of course, of how new democratic polities that lack such cultures can survive a state of exception. It would seem that, unlike mature democracies, young ones would be at great risk of failure once a state of exception is declared. This is what the example of Weimar appears to demonstrate. Future work on states of exception in new democracies ought to address this question directly.

And countries with a rich rule-of-law culture, such as the United States and Great Britain, would themselves be wise not to become complacent about their own ability to survive states of exception with their democratic institutions and values intact. Chapters by James T. Sparrow and Stephen W. Sawyer reveal that two distinguished liberal American thinkers—John Dewey and Charles Merriam—labored mightily to show that democracies could balance emergency powers with democratic norms. Dewey is particularly interesting in this regard, because, as Sawyer shows, his concept of "a public" was meant to offer democracies an alternative to Schmitt's sovereign dictator path. In "normal" times, Dewey's notion of a public making known the people's will worked pretty well, but one wonders whether this notion was as reliable an instrument of democratic rule during emergencies. How could the public interest express itself when a crisis constricted the time frame of decision to days or even hours?

Atanassow and Katznelson remind us, meanwhile, that the argument for managing crises with temporary constitutional dictatorships became obsolete almost as soon as Rossiter had proposed it. The invention of nuclear weapons and the concomitant turn to a cold war—a war without a formal beginning and seemingly without end—meant that it would be hard to impose term limits on sovereign dictators. A nuclear age seemed to require that the executive be endowed indefinitely with extraordinary powers. A country's preparedness to counter a nuclear strike by—or launch a preemptive one on—an adversary required nothing less. A state of exception declared during a nuclear age might offer no exit. Elisabeth S. Clemens offers us a sobering view of the implications of such a never-ending state of war governance. Her chapter traces the dramatic growth in the size and reach of the federal government during the Cold War and the transfer of more and more of its work to private contractors who were allowed to conduct their operations out of the public eye, well insulated from mechanisms of democratic accountability.

And then we have the fascinating but deeply troubling case of Reconstruction, the subject of Gregory P. Downs's essay. After the North won the Civil War, its armies remained in the South to ensure that freed people would be included in the new colorblind democracy that the Thirteenth and Fourteenth Amendments had mandated. White southerners understood that their legislatures had to ratify those amendments in order to be readmitted to the Union. As these conditions were satisfied, they demanded that martial law in their territory end, that northern armies be sent away, and that the peoples of the ex-Confederate states become free and self-governing once again. Yet everyone—white and black, southerners and northerners—understood that the withdrawal of northern troops in the 1860s or 1870s would likely be accompanied by the resurgence of white political power and by white vigilantism, both aiming to return freed people to conditions of subordination and subservience. The only guarantee that a liberal democracy would prevail in the South—one man, one vote; equal rights for all; individual justice before the law—was to maintain northern troop presence for twenty or thirty years or even longer. In other words, the integrity of a liberal democratic regime and the deepening of a Lazar-like rule-of-law project required the maintenance of a warlike state of exception in ex-Confederate territories. How long could this state of affairs continue before Dyzenhaus's virtuous cycle of legality turned into its opposite? There was no easy answer to this question, which is one reason why Reconstruction ended before its work—establishing a colorblind democracy in the southern states—was done.

The conundrum of Reconstruction also points to American democracy's deeply troubled relationship to race, a problem that was orthogonal to that posed by the problem of martial law. From the beginning of the Republic, many whites made known their belief that people of color were ill suited to democratic practices and habits. Somehow, people of color had to be cordoned off from full participation in democratic politics. This could not be done through a politics of emergency—a politics understood to involve extreme measures *temporarily* imposed. What was required, Gerstle and King write in their chapter, was not a state of exception but a *space* of exception—territory where the Constitution ruled but its full provisions did not apply. Gerstle and King consider three such spaces: "unincorporated territories," chiefly land acquired outside the continental United States in 1898 such as Puerto Rico and the Philippines, colonies in fact if not in name; the Jim Crow states of the South, in which from the 1890s through the 1950s blacks were formally denied the full rights of citizenship; and ground occupied by immigrant aliens, many of them—Chinese, Japanese, eastern and southern Europeans—thought to be members of inferior races. These spaces were built to last. They were large and consequential—but not so large as to expose the norm of liberal democracy as a sham. A space of exception had to retain its character as an exception to the norm or else lose its raison d'être.

Lazar points to the inevitability of these spaces, which she calls *zones of exception*. "In every legal system," she writes, "there are of necessity places and times where the law functions differently." But, in insisting on the routine nature of such zones, she may well underestimate how much they were used to ratify something that cannot be accepted as routine, namely, the disfiguring of liberal democracy through racial discrimination. Gerstle and King suggest that spaces of exception, heretofore ignored as mechanisms of rule, have posed as great a challenge to liberal democracy as have their better-known counterpart, states of exception.

Rescuing states of emergency from a Schmittian line of analysis does not, it turns out, solve all democracy's problems. Since 1776, Americans have never been able to avert their gaze from their democratic mountaintop; that summit, where the flags "all men are created equal" and "we, the people" still fly, has never lost its capacity to inspire. But Americans know all too well how often their efforts to scale it have fallen short. They will likely never be able to look down on states of exception or spaces of exception as depths from which they have permanently ascended and to which they will never return. Still, they can demand—indeed, they should demand—that exceptions, temporal and spatial, be kept within bounds and that democratic norms be vigilantly cultivated in the nation's institutions and culture.

Our historical examination has also shown how important popular forces of democratic renewal have been in preserving and improving the

American republic. The case of Frederick Douglass is paradigmatic in this regard, as Mariah Zeisberg's chapter reveals. The dogged insistence by Douglass and his supporters that the American Constitution could be turned against slavery was essential to its preservation and to the difficult struggle to forge a republic that would no longer discriminate on the basis of race. A belief in the possibility of democratic renewal also informs William J. Novak's excavation of the pragmatist tradition in American law, a tradition that valued innovation and adjustment more than adherence to the formalism that, Schmitt always insisted, must lie at the heart of all liberal constitutional regimes. Indeed, across American history, democratic movements have matched emergencies as sources of political dynamism and creativity; they have been indispensable to the maintenance and reinvigoration of what Lazar has identified as America's rich rule-of-law culture. The future of America as a liberal republic will likely depend as much on the quality of democratic mobilization as on the mechanisms it devises to allow safe transit through its states of exception. Such democratic mobilizations seem to be all the more crucial now, a moment in which those mechanisms, on their own, appear to be unequal to the task of reinvigorating the American republic and the principles for which it stands.

Notes

1. "Presidential Proclamation on Declaring a National Emergency concerning the Southern Border of the United States," February 15, 2019, https://www.whitehouse.gov/presidential-actions/presidential-proclamation-declaring-national-emergency-concerning-southern-border-united-states.

2. Algernon Sidney, *Discourses concerning Government* (Indianapolis: Liberty Fund, 1996), 158.

3. See Clinton Rossiter, *Constitutional Dictatorship: Crisis Government in the Modern Democracies* (New York: Harcourt, Brace, 1963).

4. Abraham Lincoln, "Special Session Message," July 4, 1861, *The American Presidency Project*, ed. John Wolley and Gerhard Peters, https://www.presidency.ucsb.edu/documents/special-session-message-5.

Contributors

EWA ATANASSOW is Junior Professor of Political Thought at Bard College Berlin. Her work focuses on the history of democracy and liberalism in Europe and the United States, with an emphasis on Tocqueville. She is the coeditor of *Tocqueville and the Frontiers of Democracy* (2013) and of *Liberal Moments: Reading Liberal Texts* (2017) and the author of articles that have appeared in the *American Political Science Review*, *Global Policy*, *Perspectives on Political Science*, and the *Tocqueville Review*, among others. Her new book, *Liberal Dilemmas: Tocqueville on the Crisis of Democracy in the Twenty-First Century*, is forthcoming from Princeton University Press.

ELISABETH S. CLEMENS is William Rainey Harper Distinguished Service Professor of Sociology at the University of Chicago. Exploring organizational and institutional change in the context of American political development, she has published *The People's Lobby: Organizational Innovation and the Rise of Interest Group Politics in the United States, 1890–1925* (1997) and *Civic Gifts: Voluntarism and the Making of the American Nation-State* (forthcoming). She has also edited a number of volumes, most recently *Remaking Modernity: Sociology, History and Politics* (2005) and *Politics and Partnerships: Voluntary Associations in America's Political Past and Present* (2010).

GREGORY P. DOWNS is Professor of History at the University of California, Davis. He is the author of two books of history and a book of short stories. His latest work is *The Second American Revolution: The Civil War–Era Struggle over Cuba and the Rebirth of the American Republic* (2019). With Kate Masur, he wrote the National Park Service's first-ever Theme Study on Reconstruction, helped edit the Park Service's first-ever handbook on Reconstruction, and helped lead historians' lobbying for the creation of the first National Park Site devoted to Reconstruction, created by proclamation of President Obama in January 2017.

DAVID DYZENHAUS is University Professor of Law and Philosophy at the University of Toronto and a Fellow of the Royal Society of Canada. He is the author of *Hard Cases in Wicked Legal Systems: South African Law in the Perspective of Legal Philosophy* (1991) (now in its second edition), *The Constitution of Law: Legality in a Time of Emergency* (2006), *Legality and Legitimacy: Carl Schmitt, Hans Kelsen, and Hermann Heller in Weimar* (1999), and *Judging the Judges, Judging Ourselves: Truth, Reconciliation and the Apartheid Legal Order* (1998).

GARY GERSTLE is Paul Mellon Professor of American History and Fellow of Sidney Sussex College at the University of Cambridge, where he has taught since 2014. His books include two prize winners: *Liberty and Coercion: The Paradox of American Government from the Founding to the Present* (2015) and *American Crucible: Race and Nation in the Twentieth Century* (2017). He is currently writing *The Rise and Fall of America's Neoliberal Order, 1970–2020*, a sequel to his 1989 coedited book *The Rise and Fall of the New Deal Order, 1930–1980* (1989).

JOEL ISAAC is Associate Professor in the John U. Nef Committee on Social Thought at the University of Chicago. He is the author of *Working Knowledge: Making the Human Sciences from Parsons to Kuhn* (2012) and the coeditor of *The Worlds of American Intellectual History* (2017).

IRA KATZNELSON is Ruggles Professor of Political Science and History at Columbia University. His *Fear Itself: The New Deal and the Origins of Our Time* (2013) was awarded the Bancroft Prize in History and the Woodrow Wilson Foundation Award in Political Science. Other books include the recently published *Southern Nation: Congress and White Supremacy After Reconstruction* (2018) (coauthored with David Bateman and John Lapinski).

DESMOND KING is Andrew W. Mellon Professor of American Government at the University of Oxford and a Fellow of the American Academy of Arts and Sciences and the British Academy. His books include *Separate and Unequal: African Americans and the US Federal Government* (2007), *Still a House Divided: Race and Politics in Obama's America* (2013) (with Rogers M Smith), and *Fed Power: How Finance Wins* (2016) (with Larry Jacobs).

NOMI CLAIRE LAZAR is Associate Professor of Politics and Associate Dean of Faculty at Yale-NUS College in Singapore. She is the author of *States of Emergency in Liberal Democracies* (2009, 2012) and *Out of Joint: Power, Crisis and the Rhetoric of Time* (2019).

WILLIAM J. NOVAK is Charles F. and Edith J. Clyne Professor of Law at the University of Michigan Law School. He is the author of *The People's Welfare: Law and Regulation in Nineteenth-Century America* (1996), which won the American Historical Association's Littleton-Griswold Prize for Best Book in the History of Law and Society. He has also coedited *The Democratic Experiment*, *The Boundaries of the State in U.S. History* (2015) and *Corporations and American Democracy* (2017).

STEPHEN W. SAWYER is Professor of History and Director of the Center for Critical Democracy Studies at the American University of Paris. He has coedited numerous volumes, including *Boundaries of the State in US History* (2015) (with James T. Sparrow and William J. Novak) and is the author of *Demos Assembled: Democracy and the International Origins of the Modern State, 1840–1880* (2018) as well as *Adolphe Thiers: La contingence et le pouvoir* (2018).

JAMES T. SPARROW is Associate Professor of History and Master of the Social Sciences Collegiate Division at the University of Chicago. He is a political historian of the twentieth-century United States who is interested in problems at the intersection of state formation, democratic power, and conceptual or cultural conflict. He is the author of *Warfare State: World War II Americans and the Age of Big Government* (2011) and the coeditor (with William J. Novak and Stephen W. Sawyer) of *Boundaries of the State in U.S. History* (2015). His chapter in this volume is drawn from his current book project, *Atomic Liberty: Rethinking the Democratic State for the American Century*.

JOHN FABIAN WITT is Allen H. Duffy Class of 1960 Professor of Law, Professor of History, and Head of Davenport College at Yale University, where he teaches and writes in the field of legal history. His book *Lincoln's Code: The Laws of War in American History* (2012) was awarded the 2013 Bancroft Prize and the American Bar Association's Silver Gavel Award and was a finalist for the Pulitzer Prize in history. His edition of a lost nineteenth-century manuscript on martial law is *To Save the Country: A Lost Manuscript of the Civil War Constitution* (2019).

MARIAH ZEISBERG is Associate Professor in Law, Courts and Politics at the University of Michigan, Ann Arbor. Her book *War Powers: The Politics of Constitutional Authority* (2013) won the American Political Science Association's 2014 Neustadt Prize for best book on the presidency.

Index

abolitionist movement, 259–62; differences within, 261, 263–69, 272, 276–77; importance of Fugitive Slave Act to, 258, 260, 261–62, 263, 265. *See also* Douglass, Frederick; Garrisonian abolitionists
Abu Ghraib prison, 28, 29–30
Ackerman, Bruce, 59, 96
Adams, John Quincy, 125–26, 128, 129, 132; on emergency powers, 125, 128, 131, 132, 141
Agamben, Giorgio, 5, 18, 28, 229, 260, 292; influence of, 5, 28, 35–36; pessimism of, 10, 18, 26, 28, 58, 315; and Schmitt's writing, 9–10, 24, 26, 58, 101–2; on sovereignty, 19, 26, 27, 30; on spaces of exception, 315; on state of exception, 9–10, 58, 59, 257; on zone of distinction, 9–10
Albright, Charles, 168
Alexander, Michelle, 318, 333

Andrews, Charles, 104–5
Angel Island, 315, 325
antistatism, 293, 297–98, 304, 305–6
Aristotle, 100
Articles of Confederation, 95, 96, 97
Atanassow, Ewa, 7, 31, 344, 345; chapter coauthored by, 39–63
Atkin, Lord (James Richard Atkin), 79, 80–81
Atomic Energy Commission, 54, 221, 301
Austin, John, 208
Awlaki, Anwar al-, 58

Baker, Newton, 296
Balkin, Jack, 289–90
Balogh, Brian, 294
Barker, Ernest, 181
Bayard, Thomas, Sr., 170
Beck, James, 167
Bendersky, Joseph, 71
Benjamin, Walter, 26
Berlin Conference of 1884, 205
Bernasconi, Robert, 269–70

Bill of Rights, 266, 327; and Jim Crow South, 326–30; and police power, 111
bin Laden, Osama, 57
Binney, Horace, 130–32, 137
birthright citizenship, 331–32
Black, Jeremiah S., 140
Blackstone, William, 99, 109, 126–27, 137
Blaine, James G., 155, 157, 172
Blight, David, 272
Block, Maurice, 105
Bobbitt, Philip, 143
Bodin, Jean, 205, 234–35, 244, 246
Bonaparte, Napoléon, 124, 128, 129, 214, 234
Boumediene v. Bush (2008), 340n51
Bourne, Randolph, 192–93, 194
Britain. *See* Great Britain
Brown, John, 260, 266, 279
Bryan, William Jennings, 202
Bryce, James, 244, 245
Bullert, Gary, 191
Burgess, John W., 203
Burnham, James, 215
Burrows, Julius Caesar, 167
Burton, Michael, 62
Bush, George W., 33, 56, 66n55; administration of, and post-9/11 policies, 56–58, 68, 74, 304, 342–43
Butler, Samuel, 211

Calhoun, Craig, 308n14
Calhoun, John C., 135, 206, 293
Canada, 34, 82
Carpenter, Matthew, 163
Carter administration, 318, 333
Chamberlain, George, 295–96
Charles X (king of France), 241
Chase, Salmon P., 111, 114, 137, 264, 267
Chicago Times, 160
Chilcot, John, 61–62
Cicero, 91n53
civic virtue, 18–19, 30, 35, 41, 89n30
Civil Rights Act of 1866, 157
Civil Rights Act of 1875, 168

civil rights movement, 48, 317, 330
Civil War, 3, 40, 116, 294, 295; martial law in, 130, 132, 160, 342; military commissions in, 124, 134, 135, 139, 140, 160, 342
 as case study for theorists of emergency, 6, 123; and the Liebers' theory of emergency powers, 86, 123–25, 128, 130–33, 134, 136–40, 141–45
 suspension of habeas corpus in, 21, 123, 124, 159–60, 206, 294, 342; controversy over, 130, 160, 341; Francis Lieber's defense of, 124, 130, 206; Lincoln's justification for, 21–22, 133
Clark, J. Reuben, Jr., 116–17
Clausewitz, Carl von, 129, 140
Clemens, Elisabeth S., 10–11, 345–46; chapter by, 288–306
Clinton, Bill, 304, 318
Coburn, John, 166–67
Coke, Edward, 109
Cold War, 4, 7, 54, 231, 345
Cole, G. D. H., 182
colonialism, 138, 205, 206–7, 320–21
Colored Convention of 1843, 272
commissarial dictatorship, 63, 235; American theorists of emergency on, 51, 59, 227, 230, 237; Schmitt on, 6, 25, 26, 49–51, 76, 227, 237
Committee on Public Safety, 237, 249. *See also* French Revolution
common law, 126–27, 248; and martial law, 126–27, 135–36, 148n19, 230; and police power, 98, 103, 108–9, 110–11, 113, 115
Commonwealth v. Alger (1851), 104
Communications Assistance for Law Enforcement Act (1994), 55–56
Community Mental Health Centers Act of 1963, 302
Constitution, US: adoption of, 95–97; and police power, 111, 114–15; and slavery, 125–32, 259–83. *See also* Supreme Court

INDEX   355

amendments to. *See* Bill of Rights;
   Fifteenth Amendment; Fourteenth Amendment; Thirteenth
   Amendment
   and emergency powers, 2–3, 11,
   19, 131, 144; Founders on, 39,
   46, 61; Lincoln and, 47, 160
   and spaces of exception, 313–
   18, 332–34. *See also* immigrant
   aliens; Jim Crow South; unincorporated territories
constitutional dictatorship, theory
   of, 50–51, 52, 71, 78–79, 228–33,
   248–49; and concept of sovereignty,
   243–47; Friedrich on, 9, 50–51, 71,
   229–30, 231–32, 233, 238, 239–
   40; and legislative dictatorship, 231,
   233, 239–43; model of, in Roman
   republic, 9, 41–42, 50, 52, 227,
   230, 231, 237, 344; Rossiter on,
   41–43, 47, 53, 63n8, 228–31, 239,
   248; and Schmitt's theories, 227,
   228, 233–37, 238, 243, 247; Watkins on, 9, 50–51, 229–30, 232–33,
   239, 240–44, 248
Cooley, Thomas, 97, 110
Corwin, Edwin, 85, 86, 99
Cover, Robert, 103, 266, 274
Cromwell, Oliver, 49, 206
Curley, Tyles, 52
Cushing, Caleb, 157, 170
Cushman, Robert E., 114–15
cycles of legality: empty, 76, 78; virtuous, 76, 78–83, 344, 346

Dahl, Robert, 63n11
Dane, Nathan, 96
Davis, David, 140, 141, 144
Davis, Jefferson, 127, 138
Dawes, Henry, 171–72
Dean, Mitchell, 106
decisionism, 181, 192, 194, 216;
   Merriam on, 214–15; Schmitt on,
   180, 183, 216–17
Defence of the Realm Consolidation
   Act of 1914 (DORA), 79, 80, 239,
   292

Delamare, Nicolas, 106
delegated governance, 10–11, 288–
   90; and antistatism, 293, 297–98,
   304, 305–6; post–World War II,
   299–306; as a structure of exceptions, 305–6; and wartime mobilization, 292, 293, 294–99; and weakened accountability, 291–93, 303–4
Denny, Collins, 105
Dewey, John, 178; on concept of legal
   personality, 184–85; on emergency
   powers, 8, 180, 192–95, 345; ideas
   of, compared with those of Schmitt,
   179–81, 184–91, 195–96; on nature of law, 102, 190–91; on pluralism, 181, 184–89, 191, 195; and
   pragmatism, 179–80, 184, 191–93,
   194; on the public, 185–86, 187,
   190, 195, 345; on sovereignty, 8,
   179–80, 189, 194; and World War I,
   191–96
Dicey, Albert Venn, 100–101, 179,
   244
Dickinson, John, 244, 246, 248
dictatorship by delegation, 241–43,
   289, 290, 291–93
Douglas, William O., 105
Douglass, Frederick, 10, 258–59,
   261, 265, 347; changing views of,
   on the Constitution, 262, 269–78,
   281–83; and Civil War, 278–80;
   and Garrisonian abolitionists, 269,
   271–72, 273–74, 275, 276–77, 278,
   282; light shed by, on Schmitt's theories, 258–59, 262, 269, 277, 280,
   281, 283
   and Spooner, 259, 268, 269–70,
   272, 279, 281–82; differences
   between, 259, 271, 273, 275–
   76, 277–79, 280, 283
Downs, Gregory P., 8, 9, 346; chapter
   by, 154–74
Drake, Charles, 162
Dred Scott case (1857), 267, 331
Dubber, Markus, 106, 107
Duncan v. Khanamoku (1946), 23
Dunmore, Lord (John Murray), 125

Dyzenhaus, David, 7, 20, 143, 182, 226, 344, 346; chapter by, 68–87

Ebola outbreak of 2014, 31, 34
Edmunds, George, 162
Eisenhower, Dwight D., 53–54, 298
Ellis Island, 315, 317, 324–25
Emancipation Proclamation, 47, 48, 132, 135, 160, 161, 268, 280; and emergency constitutionalism, 123, 125, 141, 159; the Liebers' justification for, 124, 131–32; opposition to, 127, 132
emergency constitutionalism, 123, 143–44; Binney and, 130–31; debate over, before Civil War, 124–27; the Liebers and, 123–24
Emerson, Ralph Waldo, 95
Emmons, Delos, 22
enabling laws, 242, 243
enclaves, 324
English Civil War, 206
Equal Opportunity Act of 1964, 302
European Court of Human Rights, 81
Executive Reorganization Act of 1951, 307n9
Ex Parte McCardle (1868), 163
Ex Parte Milligan (1866), 127, 134, 135, 140, 144; the Liebers' critique of, 136, 137–38
Eyre, Edward Jonathan, 136

Fatovic, Clement, 30, 73, 75, 76
Federalist Papers, 46–47
Federal Trade Commission, 242, 243
Feldman, Leonard C., 88–89n14
Field, Stephen, 323–24
Fifteenth Amendment, 155, 157, 162, 164
Finlason, William F., 135, 136, 138, 140, 143
Food and Fuel Control Act of 1917 (Lever Act), 52, 116, 296
Foreign Intelligence Surveillance Act of 1978 (FISA), 55, 56

formalism. *See* legal formalism
Founders, American, 3, 30, 45–46, 96–97
Fourteenth Amendment, 155, 157, 173, 328–32, 346; court interpretations of, 172, 323, 326, 329–32; passage and ratification of, 161–62, 346
Frankfurter, Felix, 100
Frankfurt School, 72
Freedmen's Bureau, 161
Freedom of Information Act (FOIA, 1966), 291
French Revolution, 49, 203, 228, 234, 237, 249
Freund, Ernst, 112–13, 115; on police power, 108, 112–14
Friedrich, Carl J., 40–41, 58, 233, 248; background of, 39–40, 227; defense of liberal democracy by, 40–41, 84, 86–87, 343; and theory of constitutional dictatorship, 9, 71, 227, 229–32, 238, 239–40
Fugitive Slave Act (1850), 260, 261–62; and abolition movement, 258, 260, 261–62, 263, 265, 266; citing of, in Reconstruction debates, 155, 157, 161
fugitive slave clause (of US Constitution), 270, 273
Fuller, Lon, 107

Gandhi, Mahatma, 212
Garfield, James, 171
Garland, Augustus, 154–55
Garnet, Henry Highland, 265–66, 272
Garrison, William Lloyd, 263, 266, 272, 278; on the Constitution, 259, 264, 282. *See also* Garrisonian abolitionists
Garrisonian abolitionists, 261, 262–64; Douglass and, 269, 271–72, 273–74, 275, 276–77, 278, 282
general will, 201–2
Geneva Convention, 29

INDEX

Gerstle, Gary, 10, 11, 158, 159, 291, 346–47; chapters by, or coauthored by, 1–2, 313–34, 341–48
Gierke, Otto von, 204
Gilded Age, 200, 204
Goebel, Julius, 99–100
Goldsmith, Jack, 59, 74–75, 76, 77, 84, 88n14
Goodell, William, 269
Graham v. Richardson (1971), 330
Grant, Ulysses S., 160, 164, 165, 168
Grayson, William, 96–97
Great Britain, 61–62, 81–82, 109, 135–36, 170, 245, 306; habeas corpus in, 130, 131; Schmitt on, 183; during the two world wars, 1, 79–81, 239, 292. *See also* common law
Great Depression, 9, 297. *See also* New Deal
Great Society programs, 301, 303
Great Strike of 1877, 169
Green, Beriah, 272
Grimké, Angelina, 262–63
Groves, Leslie, 220
Guam, 319–20, 332
Guantánamo detention center, 10, 28–29, 333, 340n51
Guttman, Robert, 311n63

habeas corpus, 29, 56, 129, 340n51; in the Constitution, 19, 22, 130–31 suspension of, 23; in Great Britain, 130, 131; in Reconstruction, 156, 158, 163, 164–65, 166, 167, 168. *See also under* Civil War
Habermas, Jurgen, 178–79
Hale, Matthew, 126, 127, 137–38
Hamburger, Philip, 101
Hamdan v. Rumsfeld (2004), 29
Hamdi v. Rumsfeld (2004), 29
Hamilton, Alexander, 39, 45–46, 75
Hawaii, 321, 322; martial law in, during World War II, 22–23, 28, 29–30
Hayek, Friedrich, 101, 107

Hayes, Rutherford B., 158, 168, 169, 172
Hays, Samuel P., 112
Heller, Herman, 72
Hewitt, Abram, 169–70
Hickox, Kaci, 31, 34
Hitler, Adolf, 1, 196n9, 209, 212, 214
Hobbes, Thomas, 194; Merriam on, 201, 205, 206, 208; Schmitt on, 235, 236
Hochheimer, Lewis, 105
Holmes, Oliver Wendell, 99, 102, 110
Holmes, Stephen, 58, 59
Honig, Bonnie, 72, 257
Hughes, Charles Evans, 114
Hurricane Katrina, 33, 34
Hurst, Willard, 103
Huxley, Aldous, 211

immigrant aliens, 322–26, 333; courts and, 322–24, 330–32; efforts to expand rights of, 330–32, 334; Filipinos as, 321–22; in Great Britain, 81; racial distinctions among, 321–22, 323–24, 331–32, 347; and spaces of exception, 11, 314, 315, 324, 325, 326
Immigration and Customs Enforcement (ICE), 333
Immigration Restriction Act of 1924, 322
Intelligence and Security Committee (ISC), 61, 62
Internal Security Act of 1950, 54–55
International Emergency Economic Powers Act (1977), 19
Interstate Commerce Commission, 242, 243, 294
Investigatory Powers Tribunal (IPT), 62
Isaac, Joel, 9, 71, 158, 159, 344; chapters by, or coauthored by, 1–12, 225–49, 341–48
Issacharoff, Samuel, 57

Jackson, Andrew, 3
Jackson, Robert, 144–45
Jamaica, 135, 136
James, William, 182
Japanese American internment camps, 4, 141, 144, 314
Jay, John, 46
Jefferson, Thomas, 45, 58, 61, 75, 328, 329
Jellinek, Georg, 206, 244
Jim Crow South, 4, 37n28; civil rights movement and, 317, 330; and end of Reconstruction, 172, 174, 317, 326–30; as space of exception, 11, 314, 315–16, 317, 326–30, 346–47
Johnson, Andrew, 64n23, 134, 156, 161
Johnson, Reverdy, 160
Jones Act (1917), 321

Kalyvas, Andreas, 72
Kansas-Nebraska Act (1854), 260
Kant, Immanuel, 182, 202
Karp, Matthew, 260
Katyal, Neal, 96
Katznelson, Ira, 7, 31, 344, 345; chapter coauthored by, 39–63
Kelsen, Hans, 69; differences of, with Schmitt, 69, 70, 72, 73, 77–78
Kent, James, 99, 109–10
King, Desmond, 291, 346–47; chapter coauthored by, 313–34
Kleinerman, Benjamin A., 73–74, 75, 76
Knott, James P., 170
Korean War, 55, 298–99, 301
Kraditor, Aileen, 270
Ku Klux Klan, 162, 164, 165
Kuhn, Thomas, 98

Lasker, Eduard, 106–07
Laski, Harold, 43, 182
Lasswell, Harold, 53, 63–64n11
law of necessity, 137–38, 142. *See also* overruling necessity
Lazar, Nomi Claire, 6–7, 143, 226, 344, 347, 348; chapter by, 17–36

Lee, Henry, 97
Lee, Richard Henry, 96, 97
Lee, Robert E., 160
legal formalism, 70, 78, 84–85, 103, 200, 282, 347
legal liberalism, 69, 86, 103; Carl Schmitt's critique of, 6, 69–70, 72, 84
legal personality, 184–85, 190, 244
legislative dictatorship, theory of, 231, 233, 239–43
legitimacy, 18–19, 31–36, 69
Lenin, Vladimir, 212
Lever Act (Food and Fuel Control Act of 1917), 52, 116, 296
Levinson, Sanford, 289–90
liberal tradition of emergency powers, 44, 48–52, 55; importance to, of rule-of-law culture, 22–23, 28–30, 31, 86, 99, 100–101, 344–45; Roman republic as inspiration for, 9, 41–42, 50, 52, 227, 230, 231, 237, 344

   in American political thought: Adams and, 125, 128, 131, 132, 141; Dewey and, 8, 180, 192–95, 345; Douglass on, 279–80, 282–83; Founders and, 3, 7, 30; the Liebers and, 8–9, 60, 86, 123–25, 136–40, 141–44, 145; Merriam and, 207, 211, 212, 215, 218–19, 221, 222; Spooner on, 259, 268–69; Watkins and, 9, 50–51, 229–30, 232–33, 239, 240–44, 248. *See also* Friedrich, Carl J.; Rossiter, Clinton

   in Great Britain: Locke and, 7, 27, 39, 45–46, 49, 51–52; Sidney and, 42, 43, 44, 49, 50, 51, 52, 59, 63; in wartime, 79–81

   in the US: in Civil War, 21–22, 28, 47–48, 133–34, 144–45, 342, 344–45; in World War I, 52, 239–40, 241–42; Cold War, 4, 7, 54, 231, 345; nuclear weapons, 7, 231, 345; responses to 9/11 attacks, 4, 56–58, 68–70, 226, 231, 342, 345

Liberty Party, 261, 266, 272, 279
Lieber, Francis, 8–9, 112, 128–33, 134, 137, 140, 206, 343; background of, 124–28; unexpected death of, 123, 136
  in Lincoln administration, 60, 123; 1863 code of war formulated by, 124, 132, 136, 139, 141, 142
  manuscript on emergency powers by (with G. Norman Lieber), 8–9, 60, 86, 123–25, 136–40, 141–44, 145; contrast of, to writings of Schmitt, 124
Lieber, G. Norman, 124, 136; manuscript cowritten by, on emergency powers (*see under* Lieber, Francis)
Light, Paul, 304–5
Lincoln, Abraham, 6, 7, 60, 116, 130, 160, 164, 241; commitment of, to rule of law, 21–22, 28, 344–45; Douglass and, 277–78, 280, 281; and emancipation, 132, 160, 279, 280 (*see also* Emancipation Proclamation); emergency powers claimed by, 47–48, 133–34, 144–45, 159–60, 342; Francis Lieber and, 60, 123, 131, 132, 144, 343; Rossiter on, 47, 48, 64n21, 123; Schmitt on, 6, 342
Lippmann, Walter, 215, 218–19
Liversidge v. Anderson (1941), 79, 80–81
Livingston, James, 194
Llewellyn, Karl, 102–3
Locke, John, 45, 73; on emergency powers, 39, 45–46, 73; in liberal tradition, 7, 27, 49, 51–52; on prerogative power, 74, 88–89n14, 143, 226, 343
Logan, John, 166
Lovejoy, Elijah, 261
Lowe, William, 171
Luce, Clare Booth, 54
Ludendorff, Erich, 215

Mably, Gabriel Bonnot de, 236
Machiavelli, Niccolò, 31, 49
Madison, James, 45, 46, 58, 96, 97, 328, 329
Manhattan Project, 22
Manin, Bernard, 52
Mann, Michael, 305
Marshall, John, 108, 111, 114
martial law, 125–27, 135–36, 231; in Civil War, 130, 132, 160, 342; common law and, 126–27, 135–36, 148n19, 230; in Hawaii during World War II, 22–23, 28, 29–30; the Liebers on, 8–9, 124, 128–29, 130, 136–38, 142, 160; in Reconstruction, 158, 161–62; and rule-of-law culture, 23–24, 28; Supreme Court on, 23, 134, 137–38, 140. *See also* military commissions
Marx, Karl, 178, 216
Marxism, 71, 72, 169n9, 212
mass incarceration, 333, 334
Maugham, Frederick, 81
McCaffrey, Barry, 333
McCardle case (*Ex Parte McCardle*, 1868), 163
McCloy, John J., 144–45
McCoid, Moses, 171
McIlwain, Charles, 244–46
McKenna, Joseph, 105
McKinsey corporation, 32
Medicare, 302–3
Merriam, Charles E., 8, 200–201, 207–9, 219–22; on authority, 201, 202, 209–11; embrace of democracy by, 213–19, 345; on emergency, 207, 211, 212, 215, 218–19, 221, 222; on Hobbes, 201, 205, 206, 208; and pragmatism, 208, 213; role of, in New Deal planning, 200–201, 220, 221; on Rousseau, 201, 205, 206; on sovereignty, 8, 200, 201–7, 208, 210, 215, 217, 219–20, 221; on totalitarianism, 212, 213–14, 215, 219
Mexican-American War (1846–1848), 40, 260, 319
military bases, 318, 333, 334, 337n20; as spaces of exception, 318, 333

military commissions, 173; in Civil War, 124, 134, 135, 139, 140, 160, 342; debates over, in Reconstruction, 134–35, 161, 162–63, 167; the Liebers on, 124, 129, 138; Supreme Court on, 23, 127, 134, 139, 140. *See also* martial law
military tribunals. *See* military commissions
Mill, John Stuart, 216
Milligan, Lambdin, 134. See also *Ex Parte Milligan*
Milliken, C. W., 167
Millikin, Eugene, 54
Mills, Charles, 270
Milton, John, 95
Mohl, Robert von, 105–6
Moore, Michael, 21
Morgan, Edmund S., 260
Mouse's Case (1608), 109
Murray, John (Lord Dunmore), 125
Myers, Peter, 270

National Aeronautics and Space Administration (NASA), 301
National Emergencies Act of 1976, 19, 55, 298–99, 341–42
National Industrial Recovery Act (1933), 243, 292–93
National Security Act of 1947, 54
National Security Administration (NSA), 57
National Security League, 295
Nat Turner's Rebellion (1831), 265
Nazis, 207, 215, 298, 315; seizure of power by, 180, 207, 212, 216; in World War II, 1, 2, 53
Neumann, Franz, 216
New Deal, 48, 220, 221, 297; and delegated authority, 242, 292–93, 307n8; Merriam's role in, 200–201, 220, 221; Supreme Court and, 115, 243
New York Times, 68, 130, 131
Nicholas, Samuel Smith ("Kentuckian"), 126–28, 132, 135, 144

9/11 attacks, 4; government's response to, 56–58, 68–69, 226, 342; and growing interest in Schmitt's writing, 58, 68–70, 342
Nixon administration, 318, 333
Northern Mariana Islands, 332
Northwest Ordinance of 1787, 318
Novak, William J., 7–8, 85, 86, 347; chapter by, 95–118
nuclear weapons, 231, 345

Oakes, James, 125
Obama, Barack, 56, 58, 318, 333
overruling necessity, 98, 102; and police power, 98, 105, 106, 108, 110, 117, 118

Packer, Herbert, 107
Paine, Thomas, 99
Palmer Raids, 325–26
Pasquino, Pasquale, 106, 140
Paxson, Frederic, 295
Pennsylvania v. Prigg (1842), 265
People v. Budd (1889), 104–5
performance, 18–19, 32–36
Philippines, 317; migration from, 321–22; as unincorporated territory, 11, 314, 320–22, 328, 346; US war in, 139, 315
Phillips, Wendell, 263, 264, 278, 282
Plessy v. Ferguson (1896), 326, 328
pluralism, 180, 211, 232, 244, 245; Dewey on, 181, 184–89, 191, 195; Schmitt on, 77–78, 180–84, 185, 188, 189, 195
Plyler v. Doe (1982), 331
Poindexter, Joseph, 22
police power, 3, 98, 103–11, 157, 226; attempts to define, 104–7; and common law, 98, 103, 108–9, 110–11, 113, 115; nationalization of, 111–17; and overruling necessity, 98, 105, 106, 108, 110, 117, 118; in Revolutionary era and early republic, 3, 7–8, 104, 117–18; and rule of law, 106–9; and *salus populi*, 98, 109–11, 112, 115

Poole, Thomas, 143
populist tyranny, 19, 31–32, 34, 35, 36
Posner, Eric, 144
Posner, Richard, 3, 56, 61
posse comitatus, 156, 157, 170; 1878 legislation on (Posse Comitatus Act), 127, 170–71
Posse Comitatus Act of 1878, 127, 170–71
Potter, Platt, 108–9
pragmatism, 85, 103, 178, 199–200, 213, 278; Dewey and, 179–80, 184, 191–93; Merriam and, 199, 208, 213; Schmitt on, 181, 182, 183–84, 195
Prentice, W. P., 108, 110, 111
prerogative power, 19, 27, 45–46, 74, 143, 226; Goldsmith on, 74, 84; Lincoln's use of, 22, 27; Locke on, 39, 45–46, 74, 88–89n14, 143, 226, 343
Preuss, Hugo, 202, 204
Prince, Erik, 306
prisons, 28, 314, 318. *See also* mass incarceration
Privacy Act Amendments of 1974, 291
Progressive era, 113–14
progressives, 114, 199–200, 208, 213. *See also* Dewey, John; Merriam, Charles E.
Public Health Service Act (1944), 19
Puerto Rico, 316–17, 320–21; as unincorporated territory, 11, 314, 320–21, 328, 332, 346
Purnell, Fred S., 323

Quakers, 262, 263

racial discrimination, 316–17, 346–47; in immigration policy, 321–22, 323–24, 331–32, 347. *See also* Jim Crow South
Radical Abolition Party, 268, 279
Radin, Max, 228, 246–47, 248

Raeff, Marc, 105
raison d'etat, 143, 232
Reagan, Ronald, 303, 318
reasonable person standard, 60, 142–43, 160
Reconstruction, 324, 327, 346; and blurred boundary between wartime and peacetime, 9, 155–56, 158, 165, 167, 171–73; and emergency powers, 141, 154–74; ending of, 327–28, 329–30, 346; and *Milligan* case, 134, 135; violent resistance to, 162, 164, 165–66, 168. *See also* Jim Crow South
Rogers, Lindsay, 41, 52, 53, 239
Roman republic, 31
  temporary dictators in, 25, 41, 91n53, 235, 237; as inspiration for liberal theories of emergency powers, 9, 41–42, 50, 52, 227, 230, 231, 237, 343–44; limited terms of, 41, 42, 43, 54, 344; Schmitt on, 25, 49, 251n25
Roosevelt, Franklin D., 1–2, 11–12, 53, 115
Roosevelt, Theodore, 323
Rorty, Richard, 178, 179
Rosanvallon, Pierre, 186–87
Rose, Nikolas, 106
Rossiter, Clinton, 12, 53, 343; countering of Schmitt by, 50, 59, 240, 247; and liberal tradition, 44
  and theory of constitutional dictatorship, 41–43, 51, 52, 53, 228–30, 231, 233, 237, 345; and delegated powers, 243, 248; and example of Roman republic, 41, 50, 230, 344; Lincoln as paragon of, 47, 48, 64n21, 123; and World War I, 116, 239
Rousseau, Jean-Jacques, 201, 205, 206, 236–37, 246
rule-of-law culture, 28–30, 99, 348; importance of, to liberal tradition of emergency powers, 22–23, 28–30, 31, 86, 99, 100–101, 344–45;

rule-of-law culture (*cont.*)
  Lincoln and, 21–22, 28, 344–45; threats to, 36, 82; in World War II, 23, 28. *See also* cycles of legality: virtuous
rule-of-law project. *See* rule-of-law culture
rule-of-law tradition. *See* rule-of-law culture
Runciman, David, 180

salus populi, 24, 96–97, 98; in ancient Rome, 91n53; and police power, 98, 109–11, 112, 115
Samoa, 332
Sawyer, Stephen W., 7, 8, 345; chapter by, 178–96
Scalia, Antonin, 100
Schmitt, Carl, 5–6; on American government, 6, 100–101, 181–82, 342; on commissarial dictatorship; 6, 25, 26, 49–51, 76, 227, 237; on decisionism, 180, 183, 216–17; importance of, to discussions of emergency powers, 5–7, 24–25, 40, 72–73; on legal liberalism, 6, 69–70, 72, 84; on pluralism, 77–78, 180–84, 185, 188, 189, 195; on pragmatism, 181, 182, 183–84, 195; on Roman republic, 25, 49, 251n25; on Third Reich, 40, 49, 196n9; on Weimar Republic, 49, 71, 72, 258, 342
  American reception of, 6–7, 8, 70–73, 83, 84; growing interest in, after 9/11, 4–5, 58, 68–70, 342. *See also* Friedrich, Carl J.; Rossiter, Clinton; Watkins, Frederick Mundell
  critique of liberal democracy by, 5–6, 24–26, 49–50, 101–2, 124, 226; countervailing viewpoint on (*see* liberal tradition of emergency powers)
  ideas of, compared to: Agamben, 9–10, 24–26, 58, 101–2; American theorists of constitutional dictatorship, 50, 59, 227, 228, 233–37, 238, 240, 243, 247; Dewey, 179–81, 184–91, 195–96; Douglass, 258–59, 262, 269, 277, 280, 281, 283; Kelsen, 69, 70, 72, 73, 77–78; the Liebers, 8–9, 86, 124, 138, 140, 142, 143
  sovereign dictatorship theory of, 25–26, 76, 128, 233–37, 238, 246, 292, 342; contrast of, to liberal theories of emergency powers, 142, 227, 228, 237–38, 243, 246, 247, 345; defined, 49, 128
  on sovereignty, 6, 26, 83, 179, 180–84, 186, 189, 191, 226–28, 235
  on state of exception, 6–7, 24–26, 101–2, 227–28, 257–58; as allegedly insoluble problem for liberal regimes, 5–6, 49–50, 124, 342–43; and sovereignty, 25–26, 75, 76, 124, 142, 343 (*see also* sovereign dictatorship)
Schurz, Carl, 166
Schwab, George, 71
Scott, Winfield, 159–60
Second War Powers Act (1942), 53
September 11, 2001, attacks, 4; government's response to, 56–58, 68–69, 226, 342; and growing interest in Schmitt's writing, 58, 68–70, 342
Shaw, Lemuel, 104, 108
Shays Rebellion, 40
Sheridan, Philip, 165, 166
Sherman, John, 166
Sherman, William T., 160–61
Short, Walter, 22
Sidney, Algernon, 42
  on emergency powers: conditions stipulated by, 42, 43, 49, 50, 51, 52, 59, 63; in liberal tradition regarding, 42, 44, 50, 51
Sieyès, Abbé, 234, 236–37
Smith, Gerrit, 266, 268–69, 272, 274
Smith, Melancton, 96–97

sovereign dictatorship, Schmitt's theory of, 25–26, 76, 128, 233–37, 238, 246, 292, 342; contrast of, to liberal theories of emergency powers, 142, 227, 228, 237–38, 243, 246, 247, 345; defined, 49, 128

sovereignty, 45, 199, 235, 244–47; Agamben on, 10, 26, 40; American theorists on, 244–47; Dewey on, 8, 179–80, 189, 194; Merriam on, 8, 200, 201–7, 208, 210, 215, 217, 219–20, 221; Schmitt on, 6, 26, 83, 179, 180–84, 186, 189, 191, 226–28, 235, 238; Watkins on, 232–33, 243–44

spaces of exception, 11, 156, 291, 313–34; in Great Britain, 81; immigrant aliens and, 11, 314, 315, 324, 325, 326; Jim Crow South as, 11, 314, 315–16, 317, 326–30, 346–47; unincorporated territories as, 11, 314, 315–16, 317, 318–22, 328, 346

Sparrow, James T., 7, 8, 345; chapter by, 199–222

Special Immigration Appeals Commission (SIAC), 81–82

Spooner, Lysander, 263, 266–69, 270–71, 277, 278; and Civil War, 278; on emergency powers, 259, 268–69; and natural law, 266–67, 269, 270–71, 278

and Douglass, 259, 268, 269–70, 272, 279, 281–82; differences between, 259, 271, 273, 275–76, 277–79, 280, 283

Stanbery, Henry, 134–35
Stanton, Elizabeth Cady, 271
state of siege, 230–31, 237, 239
states of exception, 6, 18, 19, 25–26, 30, 290; Agamben on, 26, 28, 58, 101, 260, 292, 308n17; defined, 17–18, 24, 341; different meanings of, 6, 17–18, 24; growing body of scholarship on, 17, 24; limited applicability of, to US, 18, 26–30, 36, 344; and performance legitimacy, 35–36; and police power, 106; rhetoric of, 19, 35–36; and rule-of-law culture, 9, 20–24, 28, 344–45. *See also* spaces of exception; zones of exception

Schmitt on, 6–7, 24–26, 101–2, 227–28, 257–58; as allegedly insoluble problem for liberal regimes, 5–6, 49–50, 124, 342–43; and sovereignty, 25–26, 75, 76, 124, 142, 343 (*see also* sovereign dictatorship)

Story, Joseph, 265
Straumann, Benjamin, 143n53
Sturm, Albert, 54
Sumner, Charles, 132, 165
Sunlight Foundation, 291
Supreme Court, 243, 265, 320–21; and immigration, 322–23, 330–31, 332; and Jim Crow, 326, 328; on military jurisdiction, 23–24, 127, 134, 137–38, 140, 160; and New Deal, 115, 243; on police power, 105, 108, 111, 114, 115; on post-9/11 measures, 29, 340n51

Taney, Roger, 130, 133, 160, 331
Tarrow, Sidney, 305–6
Telos, 71, 72
Tennessee Valley Authority (TVA), 216, 220, 221
Terminiello v. City of Chicago (1949), 144
Thirteenth Amendment, 48, 135, 155, 157, 346; ratification of, 64n23, 161
Thompson, Leonard, 112
Tilden, Samuel, 168, 169
Tilly, Charles, 294–95
Tomlins, Christopher, 106–7
torture, 21, 61, 139; the Liebers on, 139–40, 142–43; post-9/11, 28, 56, 342
totalitarianism, 50, 213, 215, 332; Merriam on, 212, 213–14, 215, 219
Treaty of Versailles (1919), 24
Trudeau, Pierre, 34
Truman, Harry S., 54, 55, 288–89, 299

INDEX

Trumbull, Lyman, 165, 331
Trump, Donald, 56, 344; and claims of presidential power, 56, 68–69; and immigration, 304, 318, 333
Tuck, Richard, 235
Tushnet, Mark, 88n14
Tydings-McDuffie Act of 1934, 322

unincorporated territories, 11, 317, 318; defined, 315, 333; as spaces of exception, 11, 314, 315–16, 318–22, 328, 332
United Kingdom. *See* Great Britain
United Nations, 201, 220
United States v. Dewitt (1870), 111
United States v. Wong Kim Ark (1898), 332
US Virgin Islands, 332

Vallandigham, Clement, 160
Valverde, Mariana, 106
Verkuil, Paul, 304
Vermeule, Adrian, 144
Vesey Rebellion (1822), 265
Vietnam War, 17, 55, 301

Wacquant, Loïc, 333
Walker, David, 265
Wall Street Journal, 301
Wallas, Graham, 200
Walzer, Michael, 21
War of 1812, 3, 40
War on Terror, 7, 74, 173, 292, 305, 333
Washington, George, 96, 328
Watkins, Frederick Mundell, 9, 41, 232, 343; on delegated powers, 10–11, 241–43, 289, 292–93, 307n8; and Friedrich, 41, 229, 232; on sovereignty, 232–33, 243–44; and theory of constitutional dictatorship, 9, 50–51, 229–30, 232–33, 237–39, 240–44, 248
Webster, Daniel, 206
Weimar Republic, 49, 87; collapse of, 31, 40, 50, 342; Schmitt on, 49, 71, 72, 342;

constitution of, 49, 72; Article 48 of, 71, 77, 116, 207, 212, 232, 258
Wellington, Duke of, 137
Wells, H. G., 211
Westbrook, Richard, 192, 193, 194
White, Leonard D., 112
White v. Steer (1946), 23
Whitten Amendment (1952), 299–300, 301, 310n49, 310n53
Wickersham, George, 108
Willard, George, 167
Willoughby, Westel W., 244
Wilmot Proviso, 260
Wilson, Henry, 165
Wilson, Woodrow, 52, 116–17, 191–94, 239, 296
Witt, John Fabian, 8–9, 86, 112, 159, 344–45; chapter by, 123–45
Wolin, Sheldon, 309n25
Wood, Fernando, 171
Woodworth, John, 105, 108
World War I: Dewey and, 191–96; Great Britain during, 79, 239, 292; lessons drawn from, by theorists of emergency powers, 40, 49, 50, 239–40, 241–42, 248, 292; US during, 52, 116–17, 191–92, 195–96, 295–96, 297, 325, 341
World War II, 1–2, 3, 52–53, 239; delegation of power in, 295–97; Great Britain during, 79–81, 239; Japanese internment during, 4, 141, 144, 314; martial law in Hawaii during, 22–23, 28, 29–30
Wynehamer v. People (1856), 110

Yeaman, George, 132
Yick Wo v. Hopkins (1886), 330
Yoo, John, 57–58

Zeisberg, Mariah, 10, 347; chapter by, 257–83
zone of distinction, 9–10
zones of exception, 28–29, 44, 54–58, 347

www.ingramcontent.com/pod-product-compliance
Lightning Source LLC
Chambersburg PA
CBHW051348290426
44108CB00015B/1929